The Young People's

History
of the
United States

The Young People's

HISTORY
OF THE
UNITED STATES

JAMES CIMENT, PH.D.

B&N BOOKS

NEW YORK

Created in association with Media Projects Incorporated

C. Carter Smith, *Executive Editor*
Carter Smith III, *Project Editor*
Bernard Schleifer, *Art Director*
Arlene Goldberg, *Cartographer*
Christina Hamme, *Production Editor*
Marilyn Flaig, *Indexer*

1998 Barnes & Noble Books

ISBN 0-7607-0639-5
Printed and bound in the United States of America
98 99 00 01 02 M 9 8 7 6 5 4 3 2 1

Contents

Introduction   7

I. Old World, New World   8

II. Making a Nation   36

III. A Nation Grows,
    A Nation Grows Apart   64

IV. Divided and Reunited   84

V. A Nation Transformed   112

VI. A New World Power 136

VII. Between the Wars 160

VIII. World War II 188

IX. Times of Turmoil 216

X. Toward a New Century 246

The Fifty States 274

Presidents of the United States 278

Index 284

INTRODUCTION

"History is more or less bunk. It's tradition. We don't want tradition. We want to live in the present and the only history that is worth a tinker's damn is the history we make today." —HENRY FORD, 1918

Thus spoke Henry Ford, the famous American car maker, back in 1918. Ford's feelings about history sum up a feeling shared by many Americans. Ever since our days as European colonies, we have been a people with our eyes on the future. We have rarely cared to look back at the past.

Although Ford knew a lot about making cars cheaply and quickly, he didn't know much about history. Understanding history is not about memorizing long lists of names, dates, and events, any more than knowing how to drive is about knowing the names of all the nuts and bolts that hold the car together. The real engine that drives history is the story of the people who made it, from the famous like George Washington or Eleanor Roosevelt, to infamous, like Benedict Arnold or Lee Harvey Oswald.

Even more important are those whose names are not usually contained in our school textbooks. Perhaps that person is a Cherokee Indian child forced to journey westward to Oklahoma in the 1830s, or an elderly Jewish woman arriving on Ellis Island in 1900. Maybe that person is Henry "Box" Brown, an African-American slave who shipped himself to freedom in Philadelphia inside of a wooden crate. Or Ryan White, a young boy with AIDS who bravely helped teach Americans of the 1980s that his deadly disease could strike people from all walks of life. American history might be the story of your great-grandparents, grandparents, or parents and how each of them, in their own way, has contributed to the larger story of America. Finally it might be the story of you, and of the path that you are choosing to build, both today and on into the 21st century.

Taken together, all of these stories, whether from the last decade or from three centuries ago, teach us about ourselves. Where do we come from? How did we get to be the way we are? What do we believe in, and how well have our actions kept faith with those beliefs? These questions are the real stuff of history.

As you read this book, you'll find that for most Americans, two goals—freedom and justice—have been especially important. The framers of the Constitution worked hard to construct a government that guaranteed freedom in many forms—such as to express one's opinion, to choose one's own religion, and to peacefully assemble. They also worked to guarantee justice, by providing the right to register a complaint with the government, and to receive a speedy and fair trial, for example.

Too often however, freedom for some has denied justice to others. The Constitution itself denied women the right to vote, a right not granted until early in this century. And in order to draft a Constitution that balanced the need for a federal government with the demand that states operate as freely as possible, the Constitution's framers gave legal protection to a slave system that denied millions of African-Americans the right to simply be treated as human beings instead of property. Not until the nation fought the bloodiest war in its history did slavery become illegal in this country.

Not all of the issues that have faced Americans are as easy to decide about today as slavery. In most cases, deciding what was right was—and still is—a matter of opinion. No one group has ever had all the right answers. As you read the stories in this book, try to put yourself in the shoes of the people involved. What would you have done?

As the United States enters the next century, its people will keep debating how best to balance goals that sometimes contradict each other. As one of those people, you will be called upon to make your voice heard in the debate. How the people in this book made their decisions just might help you make yours.

I. OLD WORLD, NEW WORLD

Above: Native Americans watch Henry Hudson's boats sail up the river that would one day be named for him. Natives traded beaver and otter skin to Hudson in exchange for beads, knives, and hatchets.

AMERICAN HISTORY began before there was an America. It began before natives saw their first white men, and before Europeans dreamed that a land of such riches existed. Until Columbus set sail in 1492, Europe and the Americas had charted completely separate paths.

By the 15th century, Europe began to seek out new lands. While Columbus's discovery had happened by accident, it encouraged other Europeans to follow in his wake. For almost 200 years, explorers and colonists from Spain, England, France, Holland, and other nations came to begin a new life. Some came for money and fame. Others came for freedom of religion. For whatever reason they came, they risked great danger and showed great bravery in staying.

For millions of natives, this new way of life for Europeans spelled disaster. For millions of Africans bound in chains and forced to live as slaves, life in America also meant a loss of hope. Gradually, regardless of race or circumstance, the course of events turned all people living there into Americans.

The First Americans

In the southwestern deserts of the United States live a people called the Apache. Like people all over the world, the Apache have a story to explain where they come from. Their story goes like this:

In the beginning, the sky was dark and the earth was covered in water. There were no animals or people. There were only four spirits called the Hactcin. Then, long ago, the Hactcin created four great mountains—one each to the north, south, east, and west.

The Hactcin then built a ladder, made from the rays of the sun. They placed it on top of the tallest mountain so that it could reach a hole in the sky. From out of the hole climbed the first man and woman.

To the Apache, the meaning of this story is clear. They believe that they are the children of the Sky-Father and the Earth-Mother who climbed down the ladder so long ago. The mountains of Colorado and New Mexico where the Apache live today are those on which their first people were born.

Nomads from Asia

Archaeologists, or scientists who study ancient peoples, tell another story. They say the Apache and other Native Americans came from Asia between 10,000 and 50,000 years ago during a time called the Ice Age.

During the Ice Age, the world was so cold that icepacks at the poles of the earth grew larger. The oceans froze and the sea-level dropped. Toward the end of the Ice Age, a land bridge formed between Siberia in Asia and Alaska in North America.

Archaeologists say nomads, or people who travel continuously instead of living in one place, used this bridge to cross into North America. Within several thousand years, these nomads had journeyed all the way to the tip of South America. Many settled in lands along the way. These people have come to be called Native Americans.

No one is sure how many people lived in North and South America before European explorers and settlers arrived. Many believe there were about 100 million. Of those, about 10 million lived in what is now the United States.

Although Native Americans may have a single origin, they speak many different languages. Some Native American languages are as different from each other as English is from Japanese. They also have different ways of life, different kinds of government, and different religions. Some hunt, fish, and gather wild plants. Others farm.

Early Native Societies

In the Eastern forests and Mississippi Valley, rich soil supported farming. Archaeologists believe that the Algonquian people started farming these lands about 2,000 years ago.

In dry desert lands of the West, however, farming was more difficult. Some, like the Pueblo of New Mexico, learned to save water with irrigation systems. They grew crops like corn and beans that do not need much rain.

Most natives lived in small villages or wandering bands. They were ruled by chiefs chosen by older members, or elders, of the community. Most chiefs were men, but a few were women. The Iroquois of modern-day New York were known for their powerful women leaders.

Usually, native bands and villages were part of larger groups known as tribes. The tribes usually included villages and bands that spoke the same language. Some of the tribes formed even larger groups. About 500 years ago, the Cayuga, Mohawk, Oneida, Onondaga, and Seneca tribes formed the Iroquois Confederation. Each of these tribes controlled its own affairs, but they united in self-defense

"And this is what our Creator decided. There will be plants growing on earth and each will grow and mature according to its own season. They will come from the earth and mature and will be available as medicines for the people who move about the earth."

—MOHAWK
THANKSGIVING
PRAYER

This carved necklace stone was made by Native Americans from what is now southeastern Tennessee.

Above: The skill of Algonquian mound builders can be seen in these carved pipes, found in an Ohio mound. Many other treasures, however, have probably been broken into pieces by farmers plowing their fields.

Right: This stone Olmec head was found in Mexico. Many historians have noticed African facial features in the sculpture. Such heads are as big as nine feet high and can weigh as much as two hundred tons.

and trade. Benjamin Franklin, one of the writers of the U.S. Constitution, would borrow many ideas from the Iroquois Confederation.

Most Native Americans lived peacefully and traded with each other. In the Pacific Northwest, Native Americans held great fairs each year. Tribes from the coast brought shells and seal skins. Tribes from farther inland brought buffalo hides and baskets. On New York's Long Island, the Shinnecock gathered special shells. These shells, known as wampum, were used as money all over the Northeast. Even early English colonists would later use them.

Native Americans didn't always live in peace. Sometimes, natural disasters or overpopulation would lead to wars between tribes. If rains stopped falling or too many people lived on the land, a tribe would move, sometimes onto another tribe's land. The tribes would go to war.

Most of these wars were short, however, and not very bloody.

Religion was very important to Native Americans. Most Native Americans believed that everything on earth—people, animals, plants, even rocks—had souls. People were created to protect the Earth, not to rule over it. They wrote these beliefs into many of their laws. For example, the Great Law of the Iroquois Confederacy states: "In our every thought, we must consider the impact of our decisions on the next seven generations."

Native Americans did not leave their environment completely untouched. The people of the eastern woodlands set fires to burn away undergrowth. This created meadows that attracted animals and made them easier to hunt.

Not all Native Americans lived in small villages and bands. The Anasazi of the Southwest built towns in the faces of cliffs

AMERICA'S FIRST VISITORS

Although Vikings saw America almost five centuries before Columbus, others may have visited even earlier. A 5th-Century Chinese priest named Hwui Shan wrote about crossing the Pacific to Mexico. He said that he lived in Fusang, which may be near Acapulco. "That region has many Fusang trees and these give it its name," he wrote. "The people . . . spin thread from its bark . . . The wood is used to build houses." This tree may be the century plant, which was also used this way.

Historians have also found Buddhist ideas in Mayan religion. Some think these ideas came from Hwui Shan. But is Hwui Shan's story true? The Chinese did have sailboats 2,000 years ago. Some probably were blown off course and landed in America.

If Asians landed here, did they

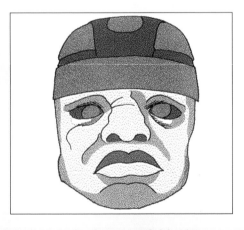

teach people they met? Maybe. Archaeologists have found pottery in Ecuador just like pottery from Japan at the same time. Also, both the Olmecs and the Chinese placed jade in the mouths of the dead so that the spirits of their loved ones would live forever.

Africans might also have crossed the Atlantic. West African myths tell about sailing west on rafts. The Olmecs carved huge stone heads that look African. Were the Olmecs from West Africa? Until there is more proof, we can't say for sure.

for protection from their enemies. In the Mississippi Valley about 1,000 years ago, small cities also began to form. Cahokia was an enormous city located near the mouth of the Missouri River. It covered five square miles and included more than 30,000 people.

In Georgia, Mississippi, and Ohio, archaeologists have uncovered great mounds of earth, some in the shape of snakes and other animals. Others are pyramid-shaped. Some archaeologists say these earth mounds were foundations for temples. Others argue they were burial sites. One thing is clear; they were huge. One mound covered more than seven acres.

About 600 years ago, these cities were abandoned. Nobody knows for sure why. It may have been because of war, or because the people farmed the surrounding land too heavily, causing the soil to lose its nutrients.

While archaeologists do not know what ended these civilizations, they think they understand how they started. In the buried ruins of these cities, archaeologists have found arts and crafts that came from peoples who lived far to the south. It may be that the mound-builders learned their building skills from the great civilizations of Central America.

The Maya and the Aztecs

The land that is now Mexico is the birthplace of Native American civilization. Beginning 3,000 years ago, the Olmec people carved great stone heads over six feet in diameter. About 1,000 years ago, the Mayan people developed the most accurate calendar of its time.

Around modern-day Mexico City lie the ruins of two of the greatest ancient cities in history. In Tenochtitlán and Teotihuacán, ancient tribes carved pyramids rivaling those of ancient Egypt.

By about 1300 A.D., both cities were controlled by a fierce tribe of warriors known as the Aztecs. At its height, Teotihuacán housed 100,000 people. "When we arrived at the great marketplace," one of the first Spanish explorers

to visit Teotihuacán in the 1500s would write, "we were astounded at the number of people and the quantity of merchandise . . . for we had never seen such a thing before." As impressive as Teotihuacán was to arriving explorers, it was Tenochtitlán that became the Aztec capital. It was from there that the Aztecs launched attacks on their neighbors, quickly becoming the most powerful tribe in central America.

Farther south, in Peru, the Incan people built the city of Cuzco. Like the Aztecs, the Incas were also warriors. They conquered weaker neighbors and forced them to learn their language and worship their gods.

Both the Aztecs and the Incas were feared, and sometimes hated, by the people that they had conquered. The day would come, however, when both the Aztecs and the Incas would face an enemy unlike any they had known before. And when it came, the tribes that they had conquered would help the new invaders destroy them.

Above: During the 12th century, the Anasazi people built these homes in canyon walls in what is now New Mexico.

"Here no one fears to die in war . . . Keep this in mind, oh, princes!"
— AZTEC SCRIBE

"Everything that is most rare and valuable in the world finds its way to this city. This is particularly true for rich goods from India, such as precious gems, pearls, and spices. From other parts of Cathay [China] itself, at least 1,000 carriages and pack-horses loaded with raw silk enter the city each day."
— MARCO POLO, describing the Chinese city of Khanbalik

Below: This 14th century map shows the voyage of the Italian merchant and adventurer Marco Polo along the Silk Road to China.

New Horizons for Europe

By the mid-15th century, European Christians and the Muslims of Africa and the Mideast had been fighting for over 700 years. Since the year 1000, Muslims had controlled the Middle East, North Africa, Spain, and much of India. Most of Europe, on the other hand, was controlled by Christians, and starting in about 1100, thousands of them left home to invade the Middle East. These wars were called the Crusades.

Muslims and Christians didn't just go to war over their religions. They also fought over trade. For centuries, the Europeans had traded with China and India by way of the Silk Road of Asia. The Muslims finally closed this route, making it impossible for Europeans to get the spices and silks they wanted from Asia.

Other great changes had been taking place in Europe as well. Until about the year 1300, most Europeans had stayed close to home. Most were peasants, growing food on land owned by rich and powerful local rulers called lords. Lords had their own small armies of knights. Kings had little power to control the lords. This arrangement was called the feudal system.

By about 1300, the feudal system had begun to break down. One cause was a great plague, called the Black Death. The Black Death killed one third of Europe's population, leaving much of the land empty. This meant peasants could easily find land of their own to work.

Another reason for the collapse of the feudal system had to do with the Crusades. Excited by stories of new, far-off lands told by returning soldiers, peasants began leaving farms for villages, and villages for cities. Local lords began to lose their power.

As cities grew, a new group, called merchants, became powerful. Merchants ran a growing number of banks and other businesses in the cities. They asked kings to provide them with protection against lords. In response, kings began collecting taxes to pay for bigger armies. The kings' armies soon became strong enough not only to defeat local lords, but also to find riches in foreign lands.

The Age of Exploration

With this interest in new lands came an interest in new ideas. Scientific theories and studies of the stars suggested that the Earth was round, not flat, and that it revolved around the Sun. These theories

made the idea of travel less frightening. While almost everybody still believed in God, some also began to believe God gave people the ability to explore the world, invent new creations, and get rich in the process.

In 1418, Prince Henry of Portugal decided to search for a sea route to Asia to replace the old land route. To his castle on the Portuguese coast, he brought astronomers to chart the skies, and geographers to chart the land. With their help, each of Henry's ships sailed farther than the one before. Soon, new and bigger ships were built, and navigation instruments like the compass were borrowed from the Arabs.

Christopher Columbus

By the late 15th century, other Europeans had ideas about sailing to Asia. One of them was Cristoforo Columbo, who we know now as Christopher Columbus. As a boy, Columbus had loved to read. One of his favorite books was *The Travels of Marco Polo*, about a merchant from Venice, a powerful Italian port city. Polo had traveled thoughout Asia as far as China in the 13th century and had written about his experiences.

As an adult, Columbus was both religious and scientific. He wanted to spread Christianity and discover a new route to Asia. He also hoped to become rich and famous. Like most educated Europeans, Columbus knew the world was round, not flat. But he believed it was smaller than it really is. He thought he could sail west 3,000 miles and reach China.

In the 1480s, Columbus asked Portugal to pay for his voyage west. The Portuguese king was dead set on an eastern route to Asia and turned him down. Columbus then went to the government of Spain.

For seven centuries, the Spanish Christians had been fighting a Muslim people from North Africa called the Moors. The Moors had conquered most of Spain in 714. In 1474, Ferdinand, the king of Castile, and Isabella, the queen of Aragon, united their lands to form Spain. By 1492, Ferdinand and Isabella

Above: King Ferdinand and Queen Isabella of Spain financed Christopher Columbus's voyage after Portugal turned him down.

had defeated the last Moorish kingdom in their new nation. Now, they wanted to grow more powerful. They offered Columbus money "to discover and acquire islands and mainland in the ocean sea."

On August 3, 1492, Columbus set sail with three tiny ships from the port of Palos. He was sure he would soon land in Asia. His crew was not. They almost forced Columbus to turn around. Then, on the morning of October 12, a sailor spied land.

Columbus landed on the island of San Salvador in the Bahamas. The local Carib and Arawak people called it Guanahani. Over the next several weeks, Columbus and his men sailed the Caribbean. "I found very many islands," he wrote, "peopled with inhabitants beyond number. And, of them all, I have taken possession for the King and Queen of Spain."

Even as he explored the Caribbean, Columbus thought he had reached the Indies, islands off the coast of China. Because of this, he called the people he found Indians. Although he would make three more trips back to the

Above: Ferdinand and Isabella are depicted waving farewell to Columbus's three ships, the Niña, *the* Pinta, *and the* Santa Maria.

"Sir, forasmuch as I know that you will take pleasure in the great triumph with which Our Lord has crowned my voyage, I write to you, from which you will learn how, in twenty days I reached the Indies . . . And there I found very many islands filled with people without number, and of them, I have taken possession for their Highnesses . . . and nobody objected."

—CHRISTOPHER COLUMBUS, *in a letter written during his voyage home.*

Columbus's voyage actually took 33 days, not 20.

Caribbean, when he died in 1506, he still believed he had reached Asia.

In 1499, an Italian sailor Amerigo Vespucci became the first European to land on the continent of South America. Ten years later, after it became clear that these lands were not the Indies, a German mapmaker named the new world "America" after Vespucci.

The Spanish Conquistadors

While Vespucci gave his name to the New World, it was a native Spaniard who found the gold. Hernando Cortéz was a conquistador, or conqueror, who sailed to America at age 18. In 1519, he was sent to build a settlement at Veracruz, in Mexico. Cortéz, however, had bigger plans. After arriving in Mexico, he burned his ships so his men couldn't retreat. Then he headed for Tenochtitlán, the Aztec capital. Within two years, Cortéz's army had defeated the Aztecs and killed their leader Montezuma. Cortéz then renamed the city Mexico City, and made it capital of New Spain, the name given to all land in the Americas that Spain controlled.

Soon, other conquistadors launched expeditions. In 1539, Hernando de Soto landed in Florida. He became the first European to explore the Mississippi River. Also in 1539, the Spanish governor of Mexico sent an African slave named Estevan Dorantes to find out if a legend telling of seven cities built entirely of gold was true. Because he couldn't write, Estevan carried crosses of different sizes with him. He sent bigger and bigger crosses back to the governor to say that he was getting nearer to the cities. Then the crosses stopped coming. Some believe Dorantes was killed by Indians. Others say he joined them.

The next year, Francisco Coronado

CHRISTOPHER COLUMBUS: HERO OR VILLAIN?

Above: Christopher Columbus (1451-1506)

Christopher Columbus is best remembered for his courage. By setting off across unexplored oceans, he opened the way to the New World. Not everything he did was worth praise, however. After landing in the New World, he became greedy for wealth and power. In direct disobedience of Queen Isabella, he forced many of the Taino into slavery. Columbus then forced those Indians that he did not sell into slavery to pay heavy taxes. If Indians refused to pay, he cut off their hands. When the Taino fought back, Columbus ordered his men to use guns and dogs to crush them.

When news of the way Columbus was treating the natives reached Spain, the Queen was very angry. She ordered him bound in chains and returned home. Although he was eventually freed, he was never allowed to return to the New World. He died in disgrace, still believing that he had sailed to the Indies islands off the coast of Asia.

headed north, also in search of the Seven Cities of Gold. He found the cities of the Pueblo Indians, but no gold.

In 1530, Francisco Pizarro landed on the coast of Peru. The next year, he marched on the Incan capital of Cuzco, high in the Andes mountains. When the emperor, Atahuallpa, refused to become a Christian, Pizarro held him hostage. Pizarro demanded enough gold to fill a large room. The Incas brought the gold, but Pizarro killed Atahuallpa anyway.

Gold, silver, and Aztec and Incan treasures made Spain rich. Soon, other European countries would send expeditions in search of their own riches and sea routes to Asia.

In 1498, an Italian mariner named John Cabot sailed to the New World from England. Despite Cabot's voyage, the English were not very interested in exploration. Instead, they became pirates. English captains and crews, including many runaway Spanish slaves, robbed Spanish ships carrying gold and silver from the Americas to Spain. In the 1570s, England's most famous pirate, Francis Drake, attacked and looted Spanish settlements along the Pacific Coast. He escaped by sailing around the world. As a reward, England's Queen Elizabeth I made him a knight.

In 1588, the Spanish decided to teach the English a lesson. They sent a great navy (an armada) to attack England. Most of the Spanish ships were destroyed by storms. The rest were defeated by faster English ships. The sinking of the Spanish Armada opened up the Atlantic to safe passage for ships of the rest of Europe. Spain's power in America and Europe would never be the same.

France began exploring America in the early 1500s. Jacques Cartier explored Canada's St. Lawrence River in the 1530s, also looking for a sea passage to Asia. At the same time, Henry Hudson, an Englishman working for Holland, sailed up the river that would be named for him.

Above: Wearing armor and carrying lances, Francisco Coronado and his men march across the desert in search of the fabled Seven Cities of Gold.

Below: Sir Francis Drake, English Pirate (1540-1596)

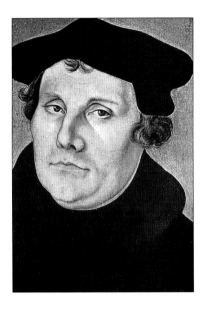

Above: Martin Luther (1483-1546), founder of Protestantism, led protests against the Catholic Church. The Catholic kings of Spain poured the money that their explorers found in New World riches into battling Protestants in Europe. This made it easier for England, France, and other European nations to found their own American colonies.

Right: Natives met by the first English colonists in Virginia used several methods of fishing, including scoop nets in dugout canoes, reed traps, and spears. All three of these methods are shown in this painting by John White, governor of the doomed Roanoke colony founded in 1587.

The First European Settlers

Sixty years after Columbus first reached America, the king of Spain arranged a debate. The subject was Spanish treatment of the Indians. The debaters were Juan Gines de Sepulveda, the king's historian, and Bartolomeo de las Casas, a priest from South America.

"Before the arrival of the Christians, the Indians had the nature, customs, religion, and practice of evil sacrifice," de Sepulveda argued. "Now, on receiving our writing, laws, morality, and religion . . . they are as different . . . as men from beasts."

De las Casas disagreed. "The Indians are not ignorant, inhuman, or animal-like," he argued. "Long before they heard the word Spaniard, they had properly organized states, wisely ordered by excellent laws, religion, and custom . . . I call the Spaniards who rob that unhappy people torturers." De las Casas asked the king to spare the Indians by allowing slaves to be imported from Africa instead. The king agreed.

Slavery Begins in America

Life was not easy for the Indians under the Spanish. Spaniards stole Indian farms and turned them into ranches or sugar plantations. They also turned natives into slaves. The Spanish crown allowed Indian slavery through a plan called the encomienda system. As long as colonists agreed to convert Indians to Christianity, they would be allowed to keep the Indians as slaves.

The encomienda system made just staying alive almost impossible for the Indians. At one silver mine in South America, Indians who went into the mine on Monday afternoon weren't allowed out until Saturday night. In Mexico, the Indian population fell from 20 million to 3 million in just 120 years. About one million Indians had lived on the island of Hispaniola when Columbus arrived

A Cannow.

there in 1492. One hundred years later, there were less than a thousand.

Before long, the Spanish needed new workers. For a while, they used white and black slaves from Spain, but soon they turned to Africa. They built forts for use in the slave trade along the African coast. Millions of captured African slaves died from overcrowded slave ships, disease and overwork. Even so, by 1540, over 100,000 African slaves were working the Spanish sugar fields of the Caribbean.

For over three hundred years, the Spanish would rule Mexico and much of North America. In 1547, they founded Santa Fe, New Mexico, the first European settlement in today's United States. In 1565, they built a fort at St. Augustine, in Florida. The reason for the fort was simple—to keep other Europeans out.

Even as the Spanish were expanding their empire in America, trouble was brewing back home. In 1517, a German monk named Martin Luther had nailed to a church door a letter listing his complaints about corruption in the Catholic Church. This simple act began a revolt against the Catholic Church called the Reformation. Those people protesting the Church were called Protestants.

Of all European rulers, the kings of Spain were the most loyal to the Catholic Church. During the Reformation, Spain used much of the wealth found by conquistadors in America to fight Protestants in Europe. For over a hundred years, the Protestants and Catholics fought many wars. While these wars weakened Spain, they gave France, England, and Holland the chance to start their own colonies.

Other European Colonies

In 1562, French colonists founded Port Royal, in South Carolina. Three years later, another group built Fort Caroline, in Florida. Both ended in disaster and the half-starved colonists sailed back to Europe.

France's colonies in Canada were more successful. In 1608, Samuel de Champlain founded Quebec, and later,

Montreal. The French were also active in the Mississippi and Ohio River Valleys. In 1681, René de la Salle sailed down the Mississippi River to the Gulf of Mexico. At the mouth of the river, the French founded the city of New Orleans. France built forts at Detroit, Pittsburgh, and St. Louis. Overall, however, the French were great explorers, but not very good settlers. By 1700, only 15,000 French colonists lived in North America. Most were soldiers, missionaries, and merchants who traded for Indian-trapped furs.

Holland was interested in trade with the Indians and also began founding settlements in America. In 1624, Peter Minuet established New Amsterdam (today's New York) as the capital of its New Netherlands colony. A trading village was later built at Albany.

The English also hoped to colonize. Inspired by maps made Richard Hakluyt and Richard Hakluyt Jr., Sir Walter Raleigh explored the coast between Florida and North Carolina in 1584. He named the land Virginia in honor of England's unmarried queen. Two years later, Raleigh founded England's first colony at Roanoke Island, North Carolina.

The Roanoke settlement was a total failure. The 112 colonists disappeared without a trace. When a rescue expedition arrived three years later, all they found was the word "croatoan," the name of the local Indian leader, carved on a gate.

The Jamestown Settlement

The English did not launch another settlement until 1607. England's first permanent colony in America was

OFFERING MOST Excellent fruites by Planting in VIRGINIA.

Exciting all such as be well affected to further the same.

LONDON
Printed for SAMVEL MACHAM, and are to be sold at his Shop in Pauls Church-yard, at the Signe of the Bul-head.

Above: This 1609 book was published to encourage settlers to come to Virginia.

Jamestown, in what is now Virginia. Unlike Spanish colonies, Jamestown was not paid for by the government. Instead, it operated as a private company, called the Virginia Company. Investors bought stock in the company, which helped pay for the colony. In return, investors hoped the colonists would find gold and make them rich.

The Jamestown colonists didn't find any gold, even though the first colonists were so busy looking for it they refused to farm. Before long, they began to die of starvation and malaria. For a while, the local natives helped to feed them. Soon, the colonists decided to attack the Indians and steal their food. John Smith, the leader of the colony, was captured by the local Indian chief Powhatan. Smith, who had tried to make peace with the Indians, was saved at the last minute by Powhatan's daughter Pocahontas.

For ten years, Jamestown struggled. Then the settlers began experimenting with tobacco, a plant that only grew in the New World. Although King James I would call tobacco "harmful to the brain and dangerous to the lungs," his opinion didn't seem to matter. Before long, Europeans were hooked on smoking. Jamestown's tobacco planters grew rich.

As the people of Jamestown grew more successful, they began to resent the rules made for them by the Virginia Company. In 1619, they created their own government. It was called the House of Burgesses.

The very next year, another group of English colonists left England for America. Unlike the Jamestown settlers, they did not come to get rich. Instead, they came looking for religious freedom.

During the 1530s, King Henry VIII had banished the Catholic Church from England. He had replaced it with the Church of England. The only real difference between the old church and the new one was that King Henry was in charge instead of the pope. Some in England, known as separatists, wanted more change. They didn't want any church officials. The church and the king had them put in prison for this.

The Pilgrims

In 1620, 100 separatists, or Pilgrims, sailed for America to escape persecution. Before they landed, they wrote a constitution. They named it after their ship. They called it "The Mayflower Compact."

The Pilgrims landed at a place that had been named Plymouth on a map made by Jamestown's former leader, John Smith. Plymouth is on the coast of

Below: Pocahontas, dressed in English clothing on a visit to London, is shown here shortly before her death at age 21.

Ætatis suæ 21 A°.1616.

POCAHONTAS (C.1595–1617)

When the colonists arrived in Virginia, they weren't ready for the difficult struggle that awaited them. During the first winter, many froze or starved to death. Still more died from disease in the Jamestown swamps. Chief Powhatan, leader of a confederacy of local Native American tribes, worked to set up a system of trade with the newcomers. But it was his daughter, Pocahontas, who made the most lasting impression on the colonists. "She, under God, was the instrument to preserve this colony from death, famine, and utter confusion," wrote Captain John Smith.

Pocahontas visited the colonists often. She brought them corn and other supplies. She even stopped her father from executing John Smith. When she turned 18, she married English colonist John Rolfe. Their marriage established peace between her tribe and the colonists.

Sadly, Pocahontas did not live long enough to see peace and prosperity come to Jamestown. At age 21, she died of smallpox on a trip to London.

Massachusetts. When the Pilgrims first arrived, they were cold and hungry. A local Indian named Squanto taught them to grow corn and other crops. The Pilgrims were grateful and invited the local Indians to their first Thanksgiving feast. The Pilgrims were a peaceful people and got along well with their Indian neighbors.

The Puritans

Meanwhile, back in England, struggles over religion continued. Those who disagreed with the Church of England were now being called Puritans by their enemies because they wanted to "purify" the church of its Catholic traditions. King Charles I, as both king and head of England's church, did not like seeing his power challenged.

Under their leader John Winthrop, the Puritans decided that if they couldn't change the Church of England, they would create a new community. In 1629, the government granted the Massachusetts Bay Colony permission to build a colony in New England.

John Winthrop was made governor of the new colony. He was a very religious man, who had strong ideas about what kind of colony the Puritans should create. During the voyage to New England, Winthrop said the community would be "a City Upon a Hill," and that God "has sifted a whole nation that He might send choice grain over into this wilderness." Thousands of Puritans heard his call and followed him to America.

The Puritans were very strict. They did not celebrate Christmas or play sports on Sunday. All life in the Massachusetts Bay Colony centered around the Puritan church. The church made all the laws. Education was very important, and laws were passed that required that everyone know how to read. The Puritans felt reading the Bible was most important of all. In 1636, Harvard College was founded to teach ministers how to explain Puritan teachings.

Some Puritans started colonies outside of Massachusetts. In 1636, Thomas

King Powhatan comands C: Smith to be slain daughter Pokahontas beggs his life his than

Hooker and his congregation moved to the Connecticut Valley. Together, they wrote the Fundamental Orders of Connecticut. These were the laws that would govern the new colony.

Although the Pequot Indians already lived in Connecticut, the Puritans felt they could take it anyway. As John Winthrop put it, "If we leave them enough for their own use, we may lawfully take the rest." In 1637, Puritan soldiers, helped by Indians from other tribes, surrounded the Pequot fort at Mystic River. During the night, they set fire to it. Almost 500 Pequot men, women, and children died. The survivors were sold into slavery and sent to work on sugar plantations in the Caribbean where the English had also settled.

Above: An engraving from John Smith's **Generall Historie of Virginia** *shows Pocahontas pleading with Powhatan to spare Smith's life.*

Below: John Winthrop (1588-1649), first governor of the Massachusetts Bay Colony.

New Colonies in a New World

Anne Hutchinson, a Puritan colonist, was a busy mother of fifteen and wife of a Boston merchant. She worked as a midwife, helping women give birth. But it was her role as spiritual advisor that got her into trouble.

Hutchinson knew her Bible well. Up to 60 women attended weekly prayer meetings at her house. Hutchinson taught that salvation came from God, not from the good deeds of the believer. The Bible and prayer, she said, were the only ways to learn what God wanted. But she took her faith one step further. The believer, she argued, could learn God's will without the help of ministers.

This message upset the leaders of Puritan society. They put Hutchinson on trial. During the trial, she said her teachings were by "immediate revelation," or direct communication from God. That was heresy, or false teaching, the ministers decided.

Hutchinson's beliefs were not the only thing that got her into trouble. So did her sex. According to John Winthrop, since she was not a man, she should have "attended her household affairs, and such things as belong to woman."

Rhode Island Settled

Other colonists also angered Puritan leaders. Two years earlier, a minister named Roger Williams said that the king of England had no right to give away Indian land. Then he made Puritan leaders madder by saying that no government had the right to tell their people how to practice religion. Banished from Massachusetts in 1635, Williams purchased land from the Narraganset Indians and founded the colony of Rhode Island.

Rhode Island became a home for people of all faiths. Williams's group introduced the first Baptist congregation to America. Quakers, a group that had branched off from the Puritans in England during the 1650s, settled in Rhode Island. And America's first Jewish congregation was established in Newport, Rhode Island, in 1677.

Maryland and Virginia

Meanwhile, others founded colonies to the south. In 1632, the English government gave Lord Baltimore a huge land grant on the Chesapeake Bay, north of Virginia. Lord Baltimore called his colony Maryland, and helped Catholics settle there. To attract settlers, he allowed others to settle in Maryland as well. Soon there were more Puritans in Maryland than Catholics.

Almost from the start, Virginia had been England's most important colony. Tobacco plantations soon spread along the many rivers of the Virginia tidewater, or coastal plain. Unlike the Spanish, how-

Below: By the late 17th century, the English, French, and Spanish held colonial territories in North America. The map below shows where each of the three nations held land.

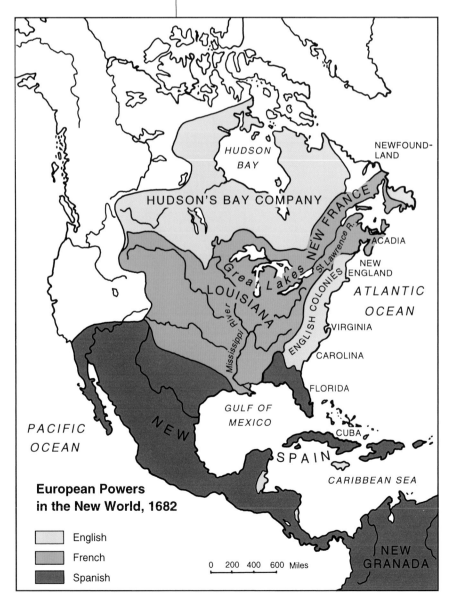

European Powers in the New World, 1682

English
French
Spanish

HUDSON BAY

HUDSON'S BAY COMPANY

NEWFOUND-LAND

NEW FRANCE

St. Lawrence R.

ACADIA

NEW ENGLAND

Great Lakes

LOUISIANA

Mississippi River

ENGLISH COLONIES

VIRGINIA

ATLANTIC OCEAN

CAROLINA

FLORIDA

PACIFIC OCEAN

NEW

GULF OF MEXICO

CUBA

SPAIN

CARIBBEAN SEA

NEW GRANADA

0 200 400 600 Miles

Above: The first coin made in New England was called the Pine Tree Shilling. It was minted between 1651 and 1683 by the Bay Colony.

Left: Peter Stuyvesant (1592-1672), the Dutch governor-general of New Netherlands, angrily reacts to his colony's surrender to invading English forces.

ever, the English could not get Indians to work for them. Instead, the planters brought in indentured servants from England. Indentured servants had traded seven years of work for their passage to Virginia.

Gradually, many former servants started their own farms. These farmers, or yeomanry, lived on the frontier and fought with Indians. Planters in the House of Burgesses taxed the yeomanry but offered no protection. In 1676, the yeomanry, led by Nathaniel Bacon, rebelled. Only the arrival of an English warship saved the planters.

The wealthy planters needed workers they could control. After 1676, they began importing African slaves by the thousands.

In the mid-1600s, trouble arose between England and New Netherlands, which the Dutch had established in 1624. New Netherlands lay right between New England and Maryland.

The Dutch Found New Netherlands

Following Henry Hudson's exploration, the Dutch West India Company founded New Netherlands in the Hudson Valley and on Long Island. The company offered land to rich men called patroons. If patroons could attract settlers, the government would give them the land. But patroons had trouble getting people to settle on their lands. Holland was small and prosperous. Few wanted to risk their lives in the colonies.

England did not want the Dutch trading with its colonists. During the mid-1650s, the English government passed a series of Navigation Acts. The laws were meant to keep Dutch traders out of the colonies. Soon there were also controls on manufacturing that forced colonists to buy only English products.

The colonists hated these laws. Southerners wanted to trade with all countries to get the highest price for their crops. Northerners also wanted local control over trade. Everybody hated paying more for English products.

In the 1660s, England and Holland went to war. In 1664, Netherlands surrendered. The king of England gave their land to his brother, the Duke of York. New Netherlands became New York. Its largest city, New Amsterdam, became New York City.

The Duke of York gave part of his new land to friends. Lord Berkeley and Sir John Carteret promised settlers religious freedom, and a colonial government to represent the people.

William Penn and Pennsylvania

In 1681, the king of England owed a man named William Penn money. To pay

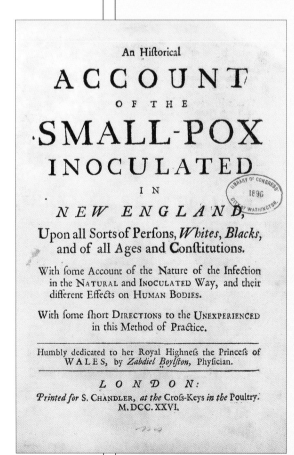

An Hiſtorical
ACCOUNT
OF THE
SMALL-POX
INOCULATED
IN
NEW ENGLAND,
Upon all Sorts of Perſons, *Whites, Blacks,* and of all Ages and Conſtitutions.

With ſome Account of the Nature of the Infection in the NATURAL and INOCULATED Way, and their different Effects on HUMAN BODIES.

With ſome ſhort DIRECTIONS to the UNEXPERIENCED in this Method of Practice.

Humbly dedicated to her Royal Highneſs the Princeſs of WALES, by *Zabdiel Boylſton*, Phyſician.

LONDON:
Printed for S. CHANDLER, *at the* Croſs-Keys *in the* Poultry. M.DCC.XXVI.

COTTON MATHER, PURITAN MINISTER AND HEALER

Doctors did not know as much about disease in the 18th century as they do now. Even so, some breakthroughs did take place. One happened during a 1721 smallpox epidemic.

Cotton Mather, the famous Boston minister, had heard that doctors in Turkey had found a way to prevent the disease. When healthy people had pus from smallpox victims applied to small cuts in their arms, they only got slightly sick.

Mather convinced a doctor named Zabdiel Boylston to try this cure on Bostonians. Many Bostonians were angry. One person even threw a bomb into Mather's home.

Yet, 287 Bostonians volunteered for the experiment. Eventually, half of Boston's population got smallpox. Fifteen percent died. Of those that tried the cure, only 2 percent died.

The cure had worked. Cotton Mather had started the first successful immunization program in Western medicine.

him back, he gave the territory between New York and Maryland to Penn's son. The younger William Penn named the new colony Pennsylvania.

The younger Penn was a Quaker. He believed in equality between Europeans and Indians. Instead of just taking land, Penn paid for it. He also preached religious freedom. Before long, Philadelphia was the largest city in the colonies. Later, Penn bought more land. This land became Delaware.

Georgia and the Carolinas

The lands south of Virginia took longer to settle. In 1663, King Charles I gave the territory to eight rich landowners. They named it Carolina. In 1729, the English government split it into North Carolina and South Carolina.

Carolina's first landowners wanted huge estates worked by servants. The servants had other ideas. There was so much open land in America that they felt they should be working their own land. Other poor farmers moved to Carolina from Virginia.

Settlers came to the Carolinas from Barbados, a sugar island in the Caribbean. These settlers preferred African slaves to English servants.

The islands along South Carolina's coast were perfect for growing rice. Although Englishmen did not know how to grow rice, Africans did. They built a system of canals needed to grow rice. Slavery made the planters rich.

Georgia was the last colony to be settled. In the 1730s, James Oglethorpe asked King George II for land south of the Carolinas. Oglethorpe wanted to create a haven for England's poor. The king liked the idea. The settlers would provide defense against the Spanish in Florida. Many poor people settled in Georgia. But so did wealthy riceplanters from South Carolina. They brought their slaves with them.

Above: James Oglethorpe (1696-1785), founder of the Georgia colony, as a young man. Oglethorpe was known for his kind treatment of the poor and his fair dealings with the Native Americans he found in Georgia.

Below: William Penn the Younger (1644-1718), founder of Pennsylvania, negotiates a treaty with the Delaware Indians.

*"Whereas Hugh
Gwyn . . . hath
brought back from
Maryland three ser-
vants formerly run
away . . . the court
doth therefore order
that the three ser-
vants shall receive the
punishment of whip-
ping and to have
thirty stripes (lashes
on the back) apiece.
One called Victor,
a Dutchman, the
other a Scotchman
called James Gregory,
shall . . . serve out
their indentures . . .
And the third being
a Negro named John
Punch shall serve
his said master . . .
for the time of his
natural life here or
elsewhere."*

—from a Virginia
court decision, 1640

Daily Life in the Colonies

One was French and the other was German. One lived in New York, the other in Pennsylvania. One came to the colonies as a soldier and the other as a servant. Michael Crevecoeur liked what he saw. Gottlieb Mittelburger did not.

America, Crevecoeur wrote, is "the best poor man's country" on Earth. "It is not composed, as in Europe, of great lords who possess everything, and a herd of people who have nothing."

Mittelburger disagreed. He warned of the hard life facing people in America. He talked of servant families broken up and sold to the far corners of the colonies. "It often happens that such parents and children, after leaving the ship, do not see each other again for many years, perhaps no more in all their lives."

Different Colonies, Different Lives

The colonies were growing and becoming more diverse. With its long winters and rocky soil, New England turned to the sea. Great fishing and trading towns sprouted along the coast. New England merchants grew rich trading sugar, grain, and African slaves. The economic link between Africa, the Caribbean, and North America was called the "triangle trade."

Trade was also important in Pennsylvania, New York, Delaware, and New Jersey. These colonies produced wheat and corn. Some was sold to Europe. Some fed slaves in the Caribbean. Merchants supported craftsmen who made luxury goods, and built ships to move products around the world.

The South was almost completely rural. Small farmers worked land in the backcountry. Plantations with slaves on the coast grew tobacco, rice, and a blue dye called indigo. The planters exported almost everything they grew.

Each colony was maturing in its own way. In New England, religion had remained the center of people's lives. Puritan ministers like Cotton Mather guided churches and everyday lives. Punishment

for violating laws was swift and harsh.

As New England grew, things began to fall apart. While some grew rich, others feared that money was turning God away from their communities.

In Salem, Massachusetts, the fear got out of hand. In 1692, many poor members of the community accused richer families of witchcraft. Most of the accused were widows or unmarried women. Trials were held, with Cotton Mather and other ministers as judges. In the end, 175 women and men were arrested. Twenty-two were executed.

The witch trials shocked New England. More and more people had begun to look beyond superstition for scientific explanations of the world around them. Benjamin Franklin, born in Boston in 1706, was typical of this kind of person. His experiments with his kite to find lightning's cause were aimed at understanding the world.

By the time he was 20 years old, Franklin had left Boston for Pennsylvania. By the 1720s, the middle colonies were home to people from many countries and many religions. Between 1700 and 1776, the middle colonies grew from 50,000 people in 1700 to almost half a million in 1776.

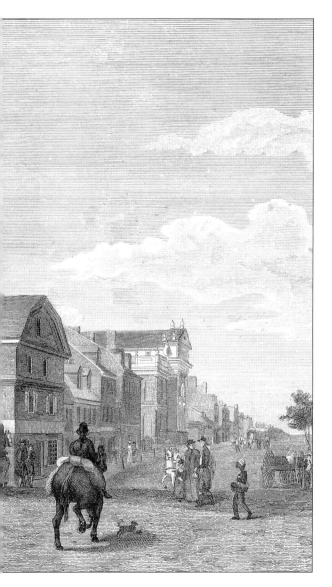

Above: The College of William and Mary in Williamsburg, Virginia, was founded in 1693. Its central building is one of the oldest academic buildings in the United States.

Left: Eighteenth century Philadelphia, showing the corner of Second and Market Streets.

Above: Until Ben Franklin came up with a new way to organize mail delivery in 1775, getting mail from one place to another was very expensive and took a long time. In this 1734 woodcut, a postrider blows a horn to announce his arrival in a colonial town.

Below: This portrait of Franklin shows a lightning-filled sky in honor of his experiments with electricity.

Most new immigrants were from Britain and Germany. Some, like Gottlieb Mittelburger, came as indentured servants. A majority lived out the seven years of their indenture. Some rented their land. Others bought it. Pennsylvania's Quaker founders were especially successful. Quaker merchants usually did business with each other. The Pennsylvania government was largely in their hands.

Many newer immigrants grew angry over the control that Quakers had over Pennsylvania. These immigrants had settled on the frontier where they fought with Indians. The Quakers believed in peace with Indians and offered no help. Finally, the different ethnic and religious groups tried to unite to take over the government, but they failed.

In New York, life for small farmers was even harder. Under the Dutch and English, huge estates had been given to aristocrats. Few immigrants wanted to work on someone else's land. As lands filled up in the rest of the colony, however, they had little choice. By 1765, Renssalaerswyck, one of the largest estates, had 700 tenants.

Colonial cities of the middle colonies had a culture and society of their own. By today's standards, they were very small. Philadelphia, the largest city in the 13 colonies, had only 25,000 people in 1776. Even so, the cities were very important. They were a mix of wealthy merchants, prosperous craftsmen, poor working people, and slaves, and were also centers of the arts, education, business, and government.

Life in the South was much different. The South had no cities, except for

BENJAMIN FRANKLIN (1706-1790)

From his simple beginnings as a Boston candle-maker's son, Benjamin Franklin rose to become one of the most influential men of his time. His father, unable to afford his son a proper education, sent him to work as a printer's apprentice when Ben was only 12. Franklin was a fast learner. In no time he had established his own printing shop in Philadelphia. There, he became famous for writing about politics and society, and for his many inventions and experiments. During the Revolution, he was asked to help write the Declaration of Independence. He also served as colonial diplomat in the courts of Britain and France. After the war was won, he helped draft the Constitution.

Despite his fame, Franklin was a simple man. He traveled around Europe wearing a coonskin cap. His honesty helped persuade France to lend the colonies money and arms to aid them in their revolution. When he died, he was mourned around the world.

Charleston, South Carolina. Differences between rich and poor were greater, too. Land along the coast and rivers was controlled by wealthy planters. By the 1770s, slaves did most of the work on these plantations.

Thousands of German and British immigrants settled on the Southern frontier. Like Nathaniel Bacon almost 100 years earlier, they did not like paying taxes to a government controlled by the rich. In the 1760s, a rebellion broke out in the Carolinas. The rebels called themselves "regulators" because they wanted to change the tax regulations, or laws.

The Great Awakening

Differences between rich and poor colonists were not just about money. By the 18th century, religious differences were growing as well. Unlike the rich planters who were mainly Anglicans, many small farmers were Presbyterians and Baptists. These churches preached that all people who believe in God were equal.

Ministers like George Whitfield and Jonathan Edwards were among the first to preach this new message. While they came from universities, many of the new preachers did not. They were regular folk who believed God had called them to preach. To them, religion wasn't just

about how to behave. It was about feelings that come from inside each person, whether that person is rich or poor.

Before long, this new spirit had swept through the colonies. Called the Great Awakening, it brought people together. Some began reaching out to Indians and blacks. Jonathan Edwards spent six years helping Indians at his frontier church in Stockbridge, Massachusetts.

The Great Awakening also led people to believe that government should be separate from religion. Within just a few decades, this idea would help lead to the revolution that would separate the colonies from Britain.

Above: During the 1760s, the British government began to impose heavy new taxes on colonial merchants. Some colonial merchants, like these meeting on the New York City waterfront, turned to piracy to avoid the new laws.

Left: Jonathan Edwards (1703-1758) was one of the leading ministers of the Great Awakening.

JOIN, or DIE.

Above: During the French and Indian War, representatives from seven colonies met in Albany, New York, with several Indian leaders to discuss their war against the French. The colonists proposed that a grand council meet every year to control a colonial army, pass laws for the general good, and levy taxes to pay for defense. Ben Franklin drew this cartoon to encourage the colonies to join together. The plan never passed.

Below: During the Battle of Quebec, British general James Wolfe fought with his troops right on the front line. Although Britain won the battle, Wolfe was shot in the chest and killed.

The Battle for Empire

Quebec, France's oldest and largest city in North America, stood upon a great rock overlooking the St. Lawrence River. The French commander, the Marquis de Montcalm, said it could never be taken by an enemy.

British Prime Minister William Pitt disagreed. He sent troops northward from New York to distract the French and their Indian allies. Then he sent 50 warships and 8,500 troops up the St. Lawrence.

Under the leadership of James Wolfe, the British studied Quebec's defenses. Late on a September night in 1759, Wolfe's troops scaled the 200-foot cliffs rising from the river behind the city. Wolfe was killed in the battle, but Quebec fell the next day. Although the peace treaty ending the French and Indian War would not be signed until 1763, the fall of Quebec had all but sealed France's fate.

The French and Indian War was the final episode in a 75-year struggle between Britain and France for North America. France and Britain fought four wars between 1689 and 1763. Sometimes the wars started in Europe, sometimes in America. In America, the wars usually involved the Indians.

Most Indians saw the British as a more dangerous threat than the French. For one thing, there were more of them. And they were taking Indian land. The French usually just traded with the Indians and left them alone.

A Series of Small Wars

The first struggle between English colonists and Indians, however, did not include the French. By 1675, New England had grown from a few hundred settlers to 55,000. Meanwhile, the Indian population had shrunk from about 120,000 in 1600 to about 12,000 in 1670. The Wampanoag Indian leader Metacom, whom the English called King Philip, feared for his people's future.

After being arrested and released for the murder of a colonist, Metacom decided to act. Together with warriors from the Narraganset and Nipmuck tribes, he attacked settlements across New England. Colonists fled to coastal towns. Then they sent out soldiers. After

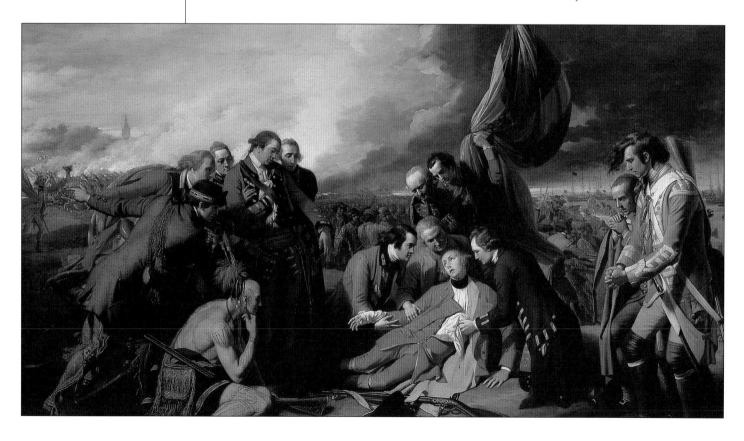

months of bloody fighting, Metacom and hundreds of his followers were dead.

In 1689, King William's War broke out in Europe. The war quickly spread to the colonies, but neither France nor England sent royal troops to America. Colonists and Indians did the fighting for them. The French sent their Indian allies to destroy English settlements in Maine. English colonists captured Nova Scotia. A peace treaty in 1697 returned things to the way they were before the war.

Five years later, the two sides were at it again. Queen Anne's War saw the English colonists recapture Nova Scotia, the Hudson Bay, and the Canadian Maritimes for good.

Just 35 years later, in 1748, King George's War broke out. Under a merchant named William Pepperell, New England colonists captured Louisburg, Quebec.

During these three wars, the French and Indians defended themselves against Britain and its colonists, but the odds were against the French. The English colonists wanted land in the west. Two forces stood in their way—powerful Indian nations and French forts.

In New York, the Iroquois Confederation controlled the rich Mohawk valley, west of Albany. Sir William Johnson, the British government's Indian agent, convinced the Iroquois to trade their land for manufactured goods. In the South, however, things did not go as peacefully.

The French and Indian War

Virginia planters wanted control of the Ohio Valley. The French had built Fort Duquesne, now known as Pittsburgh, at the source of the river. In 1754, the Virginia governor, who claimed 300,000 acres of this land, sent a young colonel named George Washington to survey it. The angry French attacked Washington and his men and the war began.

The British sent more soldiers to Ohio the next year but they, too, were defeated by a combined French and Indian force. The French and Indian War soon spread around the world. Eventually,

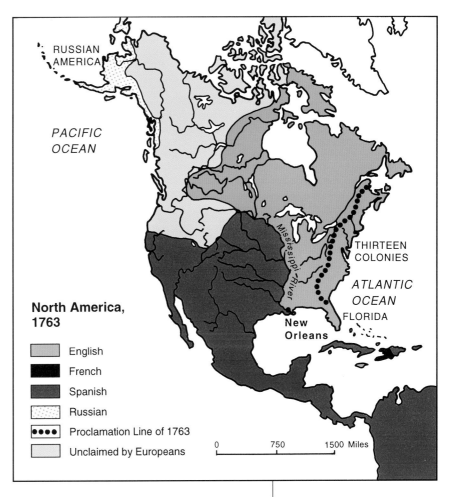

North America, 1763

- English
- French
- Spanish
- Russian
- ●●●● Proclamation Line of 1763
- Unclaimed by Europeans

RUSSIAN AMERICA

PACIFIC OCEAN

Mississippi River

THIRTEEN COLONIES

ATLANTIC OCEAN

New Orleans

FLORIDA

0   750   1500 Miles

the British used their powerful navy to defeat the French. In the 1763 Treaty of Paris, Britain gained control of Canada.

The Indians were more difficult to defeat. In the last year of the war, an Ottawa Indian leader named Pontiac sided with France. He also formed a great alliance of Indian nations in the Ohio Valley. Pontiac and his followers were angry with the British for trying to take their lands. They attacked British forts from Niagara to Detroit.

Eventually, the British signed a peace treaty with Pontiac. The Proclamation of 1763 gave the Indians control of all land west of the Appalachian Mountains. This meant that colonists were forbidden by law to settle on the land they thought they had fought for and won from the French. The law made the colonists furious with England. But the Proclamation of 1763, was only the beginning. New laws would soon be imposed on the colonists. Revolution would soon be in the air.

Above: This map shows the results of the French and Indian War. Following the war, Britain gained control of all lands east of the Mississippi, other than Florida, which were controlled by Spain.

AMERICAN TIMELINE

Above: A Florida Indian in about 1500

50,000-10,000 B.C. Nomads come across land bridges from Asia to the Americas.

1,000 Norsemen under the command of Leif Ericsson sail west from Greenland and establish a colony in Vinland, a land some believe to be present-day Newfoundland.

1492 Sponsored by Queen Isabella and King Ferdinand of Spain, Christopher Columbus takes command of three ships, the *Niña, Pinta,* and *Santa Maria,* and sets sail for the west in the hopes of opening new trade routes to Asia. Instead, he reaches the Bahama Islands. Thinking he is in the Indies, he calls the native people "Indians."

1494 Pope Alexander VI issues the Treaty of Tordesillas that divides the New World between Spain and Portugal.

1499 Italian navigator Amerigo Vespucci lands in the New World. A letter of his travels is printed throughout Europe. Eight years later, German mapmaker Martin Waldseemuller labels the discovered country: America.

1514 Despite Spain's Law of Burgos, which was designed to protect Native Americans from cruel treatment, a second law is passed that requires all natives to convert to Christianity or else face slavery or death.

WORLD TIMELINE

300-900 Mayan civilization flourishes in the Yucatán peninsula and parts of Guatemala.

1271 At only 17 years of age, Marco Polo sets off to explore China. He returns with tales of riches that spur a rush to establish trade with the Orient.

1492 Ferdinand and Isabella of Spain defeat the last of the Muslim forces at Granada.

1498 Portuguese explorer Vasco da Gama reaches India.

1517 Martin Luther's public protest against the Church's sale

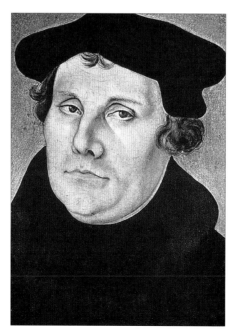

Above: Martin Luther

of pardons for punishment in purgatory marks the beginning of the Protestant Reformation.
■ Coffee is introduced in Europe.

1519 Sponsored by Spain, Ferdinand Magellan and his fleet leave Europe to sail around the world. Only one of their original five ships will make it home four years later.

1520 Sulayman I "The Magnificent" becomes sultan of the expanded Turkish empire, including Arabia.

1518 The first African slaves are sent to the New World.

1525 Employed by France, Italian explorer Giovanni de Verrazano reaches the North American coast. He sails north from the Carolinas and discovers New York Harbor and the Hudson River that is later named for the English explorer Henry Hudson.

1535 French explorer Jacques Cartier discovers the mouth of the St. Lawrence River in northern Canada and claims the surrounding lands for France.

1539 Hernando de Soto explores Florida. He heads northwest and becomes the first European to see the mighty Mississippi River.

■ California is claimed for Spain.

1540 A large expedition led by Francisco Coronado travels through the southwest and finds the Grand Canyon. The lands of present-day Kansas, New Mexico, Oklahoma, and Texas are claimed for Spain.

1562 After a failed first attempt, France sends out a colonizing expedition commanded by René de Laudonnière to settle in Florida.

1565 Angry that the French have laid claims to land they consider their own, the Spanish send out a force under Pedro Menéndez de Avilés to destroy Laudonnière's colony. Almost all of the French settlers are killed in the attack.

■ Spain establishes what is to become the oldest permanent settlement in the United States at St. Augustine, Florida.

1570 Led by Deganawida and Hiawatha, the Mohawk, Oneida, Onondaga, Cayuga, and Seneca tribes of northeastern America form an Iroquois peacemaking council called the League of the Five Nations.

1579 Sir Francis Drake lands near San Francisco Bay, California, and claims the surrounding area for England.

1584 Sir Walter Raleigh explores Atlantic coast from Florida to North Carolina and names it for England's unmarried queen.

1534 The Parliament's passage of the Act of Supremacy sparks the English Reformation and the beginning of Catholic-Protestant clashes across Europe.

1547 Ivan IV "The Terrible" is crowned czar of Russia.

1553 After the Incas introduce him to the potato, Sir Walter Raleigh brings the plant to Ireland. The potato thrives in European soil and soon becomes a staple of their diet.

1554 Mary, Catholic daughter of Henry VIII and Catherine of Aragon, is crowned Queen of England. She orders the execution of hundreds of Protestants, earning herself the name of "Bloody Mary."

1555 *Centuries* is published by French astronomer Nostradamus, prophesizing world history and events for the next 500 years.

1576 Forty-thousand African men, women, and children are kidnapped from their homelands and sold into slavery.

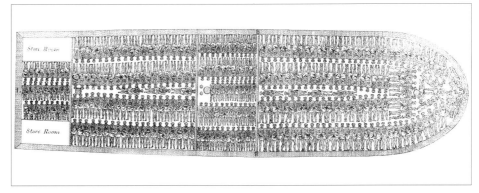

Above: Thousands of Africans died in slave ships such as this one.

AMERICAN TIMELINE

1585 An attempt is made to establish an English colony on Roanoke Island off modern-day North Carolina. Few colonists survive the brutal winter and the survivors return to England.

1586 Sir Richard Grenville arrives in Roanoke with supplies and men to bring relief to the settlers. Finding the site abandoned, he leaves fifteen colonists behind and returns to England.

1587 Led by John White, one hundred settlers arrive in Roanoke to find Grenville's fifteen settlers have disappeared. All that is left of them are a few bones and the word "croatoan" carved into the bark of a tree.
■ Virginia Dare is born. She is the first child born of English parents in America.

1602 Returning to England after exploring Cape Cod and Martha's Vineyard, Bartholomew Goswold brings large quantities of fur and lumber with him. His cargo convinces many Europeans that America is a land of wealth and opportunity.

1607 Granted a charter by King James I, the Virginia Company of London sends an expedition led by Goswold, John Smith, and Christopher Newport to the colonies. They found Jamestown, the first permanent English colony in the Americas.
■ John Smith is captured by Powhatan, chief of a local Indian confederacy. Powhatan's daughter, Pocahontas, saves the Englishman's life by begging her father for mercy.

1608 Samuel de Champlain, a French explorer, establishes an alliance with the Huron Indians by supporting them in their fight against the Iroquois. In return, the Hurons leave Champlain's settlement at Quebec alone.

1611 Bad weather, lack of preparation, and constant fighting among the settlers almost spells doom for the Jamestown colony.

1612 John Rolfe of Virginia discovers a method of curing the tobacco leaf and the plant takes off as a cash crop.

1613 Jamestown colonists launch an attack on French settlements in Maine and Canada, marking the beginning of a 150-year feud between the two nations as they struggle for control of the Americas.

WORLD TIMELINE

1588 In an attempt to capture England, the Spanish Armada crosses the English Channel.

1598 After 36 years of bitter fighting between French Protestants and Catholics, the Edict of Nantes is proclaimed, giving members of both religions equal protection under the law.

1603 A severe famine strikes Russia. Bands of starving peasants roam the countryside stealing grain from merchants and landowners.

Above: The Spanish Armada was destroyed by the English navy in 1588.

1616 An epidemic of chicken pox, relatively harmless to the settlers, proves fatal to the Native Americans. Thousands of New England Indians are wiped out.

1619 The first elected legislature in the colonies, the Virginia House of Burgesses, meets for the first time in Jamestown.

1620 The *Mayflower,* carrying Pilgrims seeking freedom of worship, lands on Cape Cod. The colonists head inland to Plymouth, where they make peace with the Wampanoag Indians who help them to survive the winter.

1622 The tribes of the Powhatan Confederacy attack the Jamestown settlement and kill 357 people in what later became known as the Jamestown Massacre.

Above: Pilgrims on the way to church

1624 Peter Minuet founds New Amsterdam at the southern tip of present-day Manhattan.

1637 In a series of bloody skirmishes with Massachusetts and Connecticut colonists, the Pequot Indians are wiped out.

1651 England passes the first of a series of Navigation Acts designed to control colonial trade. The law forces the colonists to sell their products only to the English and to ship only on English merchant vessels.

1606 En route to the Philippines, a Portuguese expedition under Luis Vaez de Torres discovers a new continent. He names it La Australia del Espiritu Santo, or Australia.

1618 The Thirty Years War breaks out between Protestants and Catholics in Germany. Soon, all of Europe has joined in the war.

1632 After the death of his beloved wife Mumtaz Mahal, the Emperor of India begins construction of the Taj Mahal in her memory.

Above: King Charles I of England was put on trial by the English Parliament.

1633 Fearing the growing influence of foreigners, the Japanese Shogun issues the Exclusion Decree, forbidding anyone to leave the country and threatening to put to death anyone living abroad should they return.

1642 Conflicts between King Charles I and the English Parliament erupt into civil war. Many Catholics and supporters of the king emigrate to America.

1648 The Treaty of Westphalia puts an end to the Thirty Years War. Germany grants Protestants and Catholics equal rights.

AMERICAN TIMELINE

Above: Peter Stuyvesant, governor-general of New Netherlands

1652 Maine is captured by the Massachusetts Bay Company, which declares itself independent of the English Parliament.

1664 Peter Stuyvesant, leader of the Dutch forces, is forced to surrender New Amsterdam to the commander of the English navy, Richard Nicolls, who renames the territory New York.

1675 King Philip, or Metacom, of the Wampanoag tribe is outraged by the execution of three of his tribesmen and launches a full-scale attack on the colonists. Although he manages to ally himself with several neighboring tribes, the armies of the settlers overwhelm him and the war is over within the year.

1682 Reaching the mouth of the Mississippi, Robert Cavalier, Sieur de la Salle, claims all the land along its banks for France. He names this territory Louisiana after his king.

1692 Twenty-two men and women in Salem, Massachusetts, are accused of witchcraft and put to death.

1697 William Penn, founder of Pennsylvania, reacts to colonial anger at the second Navigation Act with a proposal for the formation of a colonial congress.

1702 England declares war on France and Spain, sparking bitter fighting in the colonies. New England frontier towns are frequently raided by the French and their Indian allies, while the English army attempts to capture French and Spanish outposts.

WORLD TIMELINE

1666 A small fire starts in a baking house in London's Pudding Lane. Before it is put out, 400 acres are burned with 87 churches and 13,000 houses destroyed.

1668 A French army of 70,000 men seizes the Spanish Netherlands. England, Holland, and Sweden form the Triple Alliance to oppose the seizure.

1671 As the rule of Manchu emperor Kang-hsi spreads over China, Ming loyalists are forced to wear their hair in Manchu style, with shaven heads except for a long pigtail at the base of the neck.

1689 England's Declaration of Rights is passed, limiting the power of the king and prohibiting Catholic rule.

1698 Experimenting with a new blend of grapes, Dom Pierre Perignon creates a new style of wine. He calls it champagne.

1707 England and Scotland are united as Great Britain.

1718 Spain seizes Sicily and Sardinia. Angry at this aggression, England declares war. France follows them in their declaration a year later.

1722 On Easter day, Dutch navigator Jacob Roggeveen discovers a Pacific island inhabited by sun worshippers. He names it Easter Island.

1730 Russia and China sign trade agreements and a treaty of friendship.

1733 Riots break out in Tokyo as mobs swarm a rice store in protest against the high prices of food.

1740 Frederick II "The Great" becomes king of Prussia.

1712 Slavery is banned in Pennsylvania.

1713 The Treaty of Utrecht divides Canada by granting Britain Acadia, Hudson Bay, and Newfoundland, and France Cape Breton, and the St. Lawrence River islands.

1714 Tea is introduced in the colonies.

1718 New Orleans is founded at the mouth of the Mississippi by French colonists under Governor Sieur de Bienville. The city later becomes the capital of Louisiana territory.

1722 After fights with Virginia settlers, the leaders of the Iroquois Confederation sign a treaty agreeing not to cross the Potomac River or to move west of the Blue Ridge Mountains.

1729 French and Natchez Indian forces clash in the wilds of the Louisiana Territory, sparking a ten-year war.

1732 James Oglethorpe founds the colony of Georgia as a home for debtors and as a defense against the Spanish in northern Florida.

1740 Tensions rising between the British and Spanish colonists in the South, Oglethorpe invades Florida. His forces are finally turned back at St. Augustine.

1747 Virginia and Pennsylvania settlers move west into Ohio territory. The French, fearing hostilities from their neighbors and competition in the fur trade, build a line of forts in western Pennsylvania.

1754 The first shots of the French and Indian War are fired at Great Meadows in Pennsylvania, when French and British troops clash over land rights in the Ohio River Valley.

1758 Englishman Richard Shuckburgh composes the song "Yankee Doodle" which becomes popular during the Revolutionary War.

1763 The French and Indian War ends with the Treaty of Paris.
■ Charles Mason and Jeremiah Dixon set the boundary between Pennsylvania and Maryland that is termed the Mason-Dixon line.

1742 Juan Santos leads a rebel force of Indian slaves across central Peru to fight their Spanish masters. They manage to capture several towns and prepare to destroy the capital of Lima.

1748 The city of Pompeii is discovered near Naples, perfectly preserved under volcanic ash for nearly 2,000 years.

1750 Composer Johann Sebastian Bach, ill and blind despite two operations, dies in Germany at the age of 65.

1756 Frederick the Great learns of a secret alliance between the

Above: Frederick the Great, ruler of Prussia

European powers who plan to attack Prussia from all sides and divide his lands between them. He attacks Austria, gaining the support of Britain and beginning the Seven Years War.

1762 Czarina Catherine the Great seizes the Russian throne from her husband to the wild cheers of soldiers.

1763 The Treaty of Paris ends the Seven Years War.

II. MAKING A NATION

Above: Virginia's George Washington presides as representatives of each of the 13 states prepare to sign the U.S. Constitution. Benjamin Franklin of Pennsylvania is seen sitting, front and center.

WINNING THE REVOLUTION, John Adams said, was like trying to make 13 clocks strike at once. To get people in 13 colonies to fight together against the world's strongest army seemed impossible. From shipping merchants in Boston to tobacco plantation owners in South Carolina, America's people had little history of agreeing on anything,

Miraculously, the rebellious colonists did win. With victory, however, came an even tougher challenge. At war's end, each former colony considered itself a new, independent nation, with power to impose taxes, build an army, and make war and peace. The last thing these new states wanted was to give power away.

Even so, during the eight years following the war, the 13 states inched from a loose confederation of independent governments toward a nation in which each state government shared power with a federal government.

The choice of George Washington, the hero of the Revolution, as the nation's first president united the nation further. In time, another war with Britain would stir national pride. The nation would become more democratic, as more people were allowed to vote. Politicians were becoming answerable to the people. The ideas of the nation's founders were becoming reality.

The Road to Revolution

George Hewes, the twelfth child of a poor leatherworker, was born in Boston in 1742. When he was still a boy, his father died and Hewes was apprenticed to a shoemaker.

Hewes worked hard and obeyed the rules of society. On New Year's Day 1762, he visited a rich merchant named John Hancock. Hancock wanted to thank him for a pair of shoes he made. "I went with my hat in hand and my heart in mouth," said Hewes. "I made a right cute bow, ticked glasses [toasted]. . . and was out."

Hewes accepted that people like Hancock were born to a better class than him. It was only natural, he thought, that they made the decisions for everyone else.

Although Hewes was poor and Hancock rich, they found themselves together again 11 years later. They were on a ship dumping tea into Boston harbor. "I wasn't carrying as many coins in my pocket as Hancock," he said, "but we were equals in the fight nonetheless."

This episode taught Hewes an important lesson. The stories about the leaders of the Revolution, he said, "were fine. But the Revolution was more than that," he said. "The likes of me, we made the Revolution. And in making it, we were changed. A man could be poor but he was a citizen nonetheless. That's what made the Revolution matter."

The American Revolution did not happen overnight, and it did not begin violently. The Revolution started with ideas. True, the ways of life in New England, the Middle Colonies, and the South differed. But more and more, citizens in each of the colonies believed that they should control their government, and not the other way around. This also meant that they should be free to criticize the government when they disagreed with it.

The Zenger Case

As early as 1734, these beliefs had been put to the test. The royal governor of New York jailed John Peter Zenger, an immigrant publisher, for criticizing him. Under British law, this was a crime.

Zenger sat in jail for a year while his wife continued to publish. Finally, he got his day in court. His lawyer argued that Zenger had written the truth. The government's lawyer argued that the law said it didn't matter if what he wrote was true. The colonial jury ignored British law and set Zenger free.

Despite this willingness to ignore British law, few colonists in the first half of the 18th century even thought about seeking actual independence. Americans knew their frontiers were lined by French and Indian troops ready to fight for control of North America. The colonists knew that Britain could protect them.

The British weren't very worried about their colonists being loyal either. Even after France surrendered in 1763, ending the French and Indian War, there were other problems to worry about. With the war with France over, the British wanted peace with Indians, too. Pontiac's Rebellion made them afraid of another Indian war. In response, they sent 10,000 troops to North America. Then, in 1763, they issued a proclamation. It said that

Below: Members of the Sons of Liberty toss British tea into Boston harbor.

Below: George Washington as he looked during the French and Indian War. Washington was about 30 years old when this portrait was painted.

no colonists could settle west of the Appalachian Mountains on Indians' lands. This made colonists furious.

No Taxation without Representation

The British had another problem. At the end of the French and Indian War, the government found itself deeply in debt. To solve the problem, it decided to raise taxes on the colonists. British Prime Minister George Grenville argued that since war had ended the French threat in the colonies, it was only fair that colonists pay the government back. Besides, he said, the colonists paid far less in taxes than did Englishmen.

One of Grenville's first taxes was the Sugar Act, issued in 1764. The act put a three pence tax on French molasses. The colonists objected to being taxed when they had no representation in Parliament. Their cry was: "No taxation without representation."

The tax on molasses only hurt merchants, but the Stamp Act of 1765 hit every colonist. Almost all printed material — from newspapers to playing cards — needed a stamp sold by the government.

The British knew there would be protests, but they got more than they bargained for. Colonial leaders asked people to boycott, or stop buying, British goods. In Virginia's Assembly, Patrick Henry denounced the Stamp Act. A group of colonists, led by Boston patriot Samuel Adams and calling themselves the Sons of Liberty, began organizing working people.

That summer, anger turned to violence. Crowds attacked the house of Massachusetts Lieutenant Governor Thomas Hutchinson. Riots soon spread to other colonies.

In October 1765, representatives from nine colonies met in New York at the Stamp Act Congress to demand an end to the tax. It was the first time the colonies had worked together.

The boycott had begun to hurt merchants back in England and King George was getting nervous. He fired Prime Minister Grenville and appointed a new prime minister who repealed the Stamp Act. The colonists had won, but not for long.

GEORGE WASHINGTON (1732-1799)

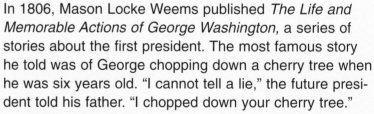

In 1806, Mason Locke Weems published *The Life and Memorable Actions of George Washington,* a series of stories about the first president. The most famous story he told was of George chopping down a cherry tree when he was six years old. "I cannot tell a lie," the future president told his father. "I chopped down your cherry tree."

Many similar tales illustrating Washington's honesty and goodness sprang up after his death. In one, an observer asked him why he raised his hat to a servant. "Why should I be less polite than my servant?" was the reply. And polite he was.

When he was still just a young boy, George Washington carefully copied a list of 110 rules for proper behavior. "Spit not in the fire . . ." he wrote. "Sleep not when others speak . . . In the presence of others sing not to yourself with a humming noise, nor drum with your fingers or feet . . ."

Washington's sense of diplomacy helped him to lead the young country in its war for independence and as its first president. As Thomas Jefferson once remarked: "His mind was great and powerful . . . His integrity was most pure, his justice the most inflexible I have ever known . . ."

In 1767, Britain's new finance minister, Charles Townshend, came up with new taxes on paper, paint, glass, and tea. Colonial leaders called for a new boycott. Women were asked to weave homespun cloth instead of buying British-made goods.

British soldiers were not well-paid, so when they were off-duty, they often took local jobs in the colonies. This deprived the poorer colonists of work. In March 1770, a group of Boston workingmen began throwing rocks at some British soldiers. The troops fired back, killing five people. Crispus Attucks, a black American sailor, was among the first to die. Colonists referred to the shootings as the Boston Massacre. Colonists were especially angry that none of the soldiers was punished. Even so, the Townshend Acts were repealed. The colonists were learning that they could change British laws by action.

Three years later, the British tried a new plan to raise money. A monopoly on tea sales in the colonies was given to the British East India Tea Company. A monopoly is when one company has total control of trade.

The Sons of Liberty called for a tea boycott. In port after port, British tea ships were turned away. One cold night in March, the Sons of Liberty boarded a ship loaded with tea in Boston harbor. Several dozen men, including John Hancock and George Hewes, dressed up as Indians and dumped the tea into the harbor.

King George decided enough was enough. "Concessions," he said, "have only made matters worse. The time has come for compulsion [force]." The Parliament passed laws that colonists called the "Intolerable Acts." Under these laws, no ships could enter Boston Harbor until the tea was paid for. The colonial government of Massachusetts was shut down. Thousands of British troops were sent to Boston. Bostonians were forced to put them up in their homes.

The First Continental Congress

Everyone knew that some response must be made to the Intolerable Acts. In the fall of 1774, Colonial leaders met in Philadelphia. Among those present at the First Continental Congress were Sam and John Adams, George Washington, and Patrick Henry. The delegates debated what to do about Parliament's high-handed actions, and some even argued for a complete break with Britain. They threatened to cut off all trade with England unless it repealed the Intolerable Acts. Finally, in the Declaration of Rights and Grievances, they stated their right to govern their own affairs. Still most delegates hoped for a peaceful resolution of the conflict.

When the British refused their demands, a boycott of British goods spread north and south, and from city to countryside. In Massachusetts, farmers closed down the courts. Then they began to collect guns and form militias in the town of Concord. The farmers called themselves "Minutemen" because they "would stand at a minute's warning in case of alarm." In New England, people were preparing for war.

The Battle of Concord and Lexington

On the night of April 18, 1775, the royal governor sent 3,500 troops to seize the weapons. Bostonians Paul Revere and William Dawes rode out to warn the Minutemen. On April 19, the troops arrived in Lexington, a town near Concord.

Historians do not know who fired the "shot heard around the world," but they know who won the day. The British were forced to retreat to Boston. By the end of the day, 73 British soldiers and 52 minutemen lay dead. The American Revolution had begun.

Above: After covering him in sticky tar and feathers, colonists pour tea down the throat of a British tax collector.

*Below: When angry
Bostonians began throwing
rocks at British troops one
day in March 1770, the
soldiers fired back, killing
five people. Patriot Samuel
Adams was the first to
name the shootings "the
Boston Massacre."*

Declaring Independence

Looking back more than 200 years, it seems natural that the colonists would declare their independence. But that's not the way it appeared at the time. The odds were stacked against them.

Britain was the superpower of its day. It had defeated its only remaining rival, France, in a great world war. It had 11 million people compared to the colonies' two and a half million. Its army included 50,000 well-trained troops. Together, the colonies had less than half that many, and most were poorly trained and equipped.

Britain was also the first industrial country. It was rich and could hire more troops from other countries. It had factories to build weapons, and its navy was the largest in the world.

On top of that, the people in the colonies were not united. Twenty percent of those living in the colonies were African slaves, whose masters would not permit them to fight. The colonies were also surrounded by great Indian nations who mostly supported the British. The Indians feared an independent America would take their land.

Even the white population was divided. John Adams estimated that only one third of the population wanted independence. Another third were against it and a third were undecided.

Perhaps most importantly, just the idea of independence was something entirely new. No colony had ever fought for its independence from Europe before. Colonial leaders knew the price of rebellion was high. If they lost the war, they would be hanged.

The Second Continental Congress

The Second Continental Congress began meeting on May 10, 1775, just as the news of Concord and Lexington was reaching the rest of the colonies. Most of the delegates were not prepared for war, but the colonial militias were already fighting the British. In May, patriot forces, led by Ethan Allen and Benedict Arnold, captured Fort Ticonderoga on Lake Champlain in upstate New York.

Events were forcing the Continental Congress to act. The first battles encouraged some colonists but scared others. Some delegates were for an all-out fight for independence. Others thought there was still time to settle the dispute with Britain. The Congress tried both ways. While it asked the king to grant the colonists their rights, it also began raising money for the Continental Army and appointed George Washington the commander.

The delegates at the Second Continental Congress passed a resolution called "the Declaration of the Causes and Necessities of Taking up Arms." It said that no one wanted war but the colonists were "resolved to die Freemen rather than to live [as] slaves."

The colonies had always been ruled by the British Parliament and king. Now that the colonists were fighting the crown, they had no government. The Continental Congress was to be the government of the colonies throughout the Revolutionary War, and for the eight years following it as well.

The Battle of Bunker Hill

On June 17, the British sent 3,000 troops to remove the Americans from Bunker and Breed's Hills near Boston. The British suffered heavy losses, but they now controlled the city.

The rebellion was also spreading southward. In June 1775, the royal governor of Virginia fled to a British warship in Chesapeake Bay. He promised indentured servants and slaves that if they fought for the British, they would be set free. In response, the planters organized their own troops and threatened any slave or servant who ran away with death.

In the Carolinas, colonists also took up arms. At the Battle of Moore's Creek, North Carolina, patriots captured more than 800 British troops. In Charleston, South Carolina, local workingmen defeated an attack launched from British warships.

Military action in the South was followed by patriot attacks on Canada to the North. In December 1775, American forces took Montreal but failed to capture Quebec.

Military moves were followed by economic actions. Patriot merchants decided to expand their boycott to all British goods. Parliament answered with the "Prohibitory Act." It outlawed all trade with the rebel colonies.

Together, the American boycott and invasion of Canada were too much for the British to stand. In early 1776, King George decided that Britain would use its huge military to crush the rebellion.

Radical Ideas

Boycotts and military campaigns were only part of the story. The first year of the Revolution proved the truth of the old saying: "The pen is mightier than the sword." As much as any battle, Thomas Paine's pamphlet "Common Sense" helped launch the American Revolution.

Paine emigrated from Britain to Philadelphia in 1774 and lived among the working people of that city. There, he met a lot of angry citizens. In street demonstrations, they shouted against the king. In "Common Sense," Paine captured the spirit of the times. He wrote in language regular folk could understand. "Monarchy," he wrote, "[has] laid the world in blood and ashes."

He ended with a cry for revolution. "A government of our own is our natural right . . . TIS TIME TO PART." "Common Sense" was the most popular pamphlet of its day. It could be found in hundreds of thousands of patriot homes.

Paine's words also inspired patriot assemblies that were meeting up and down the colonies. At the Virginia Convention, Richard Henry Lee introduced a proclamation that read, "These United Colonies are, and ought to be, free and independent states." The delegates at the Second Continental Congress still meeting in Philadelphia asked a young Virginia planter named Thomas Jefferson to write up a Declaration of Independence.

"I do not know what course others may take; but as for me, give me liberty or give me death!"

—PATRICK HENRY,
in a speech to the Virginia House of Burgesses, 1775

Left: Patrick Henry was one of the first colonial leaders to call for independence from Britain.

Below: Thomas Paine, author of the pamphlet "Common Sense," inspired patriotic Americans with the idea that the time had come to unite against Britain.

COMMON SENSE;

ADDRESSED TO THE

INHABITANTS

OF

AMERICA,

On the following interesting

SUBJECTS.

I. Of the Origin and Design of Government in general, with concise Remarks on the English Constitution.

II. Of Monarchy and Hereditary Succession.

III. Thoughts on the present State of American Affairs.

IV. Of the present Ability of America, with some miscellaneous Reflections.

Man knows no Master save creating HEAVEN,
Or those whom choice and common good ordain.
THOMSON.

PHILADELPHIA;
Printed, and Sold, by R. BELL, in Third-Street.
MDCCLXXVI.

The Declaration of Independence

The colonists wanted to justify their actions. The Declaration stated that they had a God-given right to revolt and that they were compelled to do so. Jefferson wrote, "Whenever any Form of Government becomes destructive (of these ends), it is the Right of the People to alter or to abolish it, and to institute new Government."

Jefferson did two things in the Declaration. He made a list of complaints against the king. "He has plundered our seas, ravaged our coasts, burned our towns, and destroyed the lives of our people," he wrote. "A [king], whose character is . . . marked by every act which may define a tyrant is unfit to be the ruler of a free people."

The Declaration of Independence is better known, however, for its statements about human rights and freedom. "We hold these Truths to be self-evident," Jefferson wrote, "that all Men are created equal, that they are endowed by their Creator with certain unalienable Rights, that among these are Life, Liberty, and the Pursuit of Happiness."

Below: Thomas Jefferson, the writer of the Declaration of Independence, owned slaves his entire life.

THOMAS JEFFERSON: FATHER OF FREEDOM, MASTER OF SLAVES

Thomas Jefferson has long been considered the greatest mind of the American Revolution. Not only did he write the Declaration of Independence, but he also served as governor of Virginia, ambassador to France, secretary of state, and the third president of the nation. He was also a farmer, and an architect who designed not only his estate Monticello, but also the grounds of the University of Virginia in Charlottesville.

Jefferson was also a slave owner. Despite criticizing slavery in the first draft of the Declaration of Independence, and banning the legal importation of slaves from Africa while he was president, he never freed his own slaves.

Some have argued that it is unfair to judge Jefferson according to how people behave in the late 20th century. As a plantation owner of the 18th century, it is only natural that he owned slaves, they say. Others argue that since Jefferson had himself argued against slavery, he had no right to keep slaves himself. Which argument is right? Perhaps a bit of both. Whatever the answer, the question of Jefferson and slavery has only made the study of this Founding Father even more fascinating.

ATION OF INDEPENDENCE

In Congress 4th July, 1776.

[The final draft of the Declaration of Independence is reproduced here in Thomas Jefferson's handwritten facsimile, followed by the signatures of the delegates including Th. Jefferson, John Adams, Benjamin Franklin, John Hancock, Roger Sherman, Samuel Adams, Elbridge Gerry, Robert Treat Paine, and others.]

> "There, I guess King George will be able to read that."

—JOHN HANCOCK, *talking about his large signature that he had just signed on the Declaration of Independence*

Left: The final draft of the Declaration of Independence

Although he himself owned slaves, Jefferson wrote that the king had forced slavery on the colonists. Fellow slave-owners made him take this out. The southerners did not want the war for independence to cause the end of slavery. The slave holders wanted their own freedom from England, but they would not give the same freedom to their slaves. This contradiction between independence for the white colonists but enslavement for blacks would be a stain on the nation's history.

On July 4, the delegates made the Declaration public. Patriots throughout the colonies celebrated the declaration by burning effigies [paper statues] of the king. In New York, they toppled his statue. In Boston, working people in rough cloth mixed with gentlefolk in silks in front of the state house to hear the news from Philadelphia.

"Great attention was given to every word," wrote Abigail Adams. "As soon as [the announcement] ended, the cry from the balcony was 'God save our American states,' and then three cheers." Adams was especially proud. Her husband John had gone to Philadelphia to help pass the Declaration of Independence.

"After dinner," she continued, "the King's Arms were taken down from the State House and . . . burnt in King Street. Thus ends royal authority in this State."

Thomas Jefferson's words in the Declaration of Independence were powerful and dangerous. Now came the hard part. The colonists would have to fight for five years to make them come true.

*Below: In a daring
Christmas Day attack in
1776 , George Washington
led his troops across the icy
Delaware River, where they
then defeated a surprised
enemy army.*

The Revolutionary War

"I am sick, discontented, and out of humor. Poor food, hard lodging, cold weather, fatigue, nasty clothes, nasty cookery . . . the devil's in it. I can't endure it."

The writer, an army doctor, was describing the conditions at Valley Forge, Pennsylvania where George Washington and his Continental Army camped here during the winter of 1777-1778.

The doctor was also angry. "Why are we sent here to freeze?" he wondered. "People who live at home in luxury and ease . . . have but a very faint idea of the unpleasing sensations . . . the man endures who is in a camp. . . . These same people are willing we should suffer everything for their benefit . . . and yet are the first to condemn us for not doing more!!"

Things were not going well for the patriots in the first years of the war.

British General William Howe had 32,000 troops along with 30 warships and 10,000 sailors. While patriots issued their Declaration in Philadelphia, Howe moved a massive force to Long Island, New York. On August 27, 1776, he attacked Washington and his 19,000 troops. The patriots were forced to retreat to Manhattan and then to New Jersey. By December, Howe had pushed them across the Delaware River into Pennsylvania.

The British army was not Washington's only problem. The spirit of American troops was low. Many soldiers were farmers and workers who had joined the army to earn land. By signing up, they would receive 100 acres and $20. Most had little training, and many fled at the first sound of gunfire. Washington knew he could not defeat the British in battle. "On our side," he told Congress, "the war should be defensive."

Washington needed to lift his sol-

diers' spirits. He knew that Britain's German mercenaries (hired soldiers) stationed at Trenton, New Jersey, would be celebrating Christmas. Crossing the icy Delaware River Christmas night 1776, he caught them off-guard. The victory kept the American army going.

Howe had three separate armies in the field. The largest force, led by Howe himself, defeated Washington at Brandy-wine Creek, Pennsylvania, and then marched into Philadelphia on September 26, 1777. Washington retreated into the hills of Pennsylvania.

A small force of Iroquois warriors and British officers fought the colonists at Oriskany, New York, in the bloodiest battle of the war. A larger force retook Fort Ticonderoga on Lake Champlain from the patriots. Then this army started marching south toward New York City. As the British troops moved slowly, the patriots had time to prepare.

The Battle of Saratoga

At Saratoga, New York, the patriots attacked. An English army doctor wrote that colonial troops "swarmed around the army like birds of prey." On October 17, 1777, the British general was forced to surrender. Patriots had captured 5,000 British troops and seized tons of weapons and supplies.

Saratoga was the most important American victory of the war. With this battle the British had lost New England to the colonists, and withdrew their forces. Even more importantly, Saratoga won the Americans a powerful friend.

The French were eager to take revenge on their former enemy. Their defeat by England in the French and Indian War, however, had made them nervous about helping the American colonists, whose cause seemed hopeless. The victory at Saratoga showed the French that the colonists could win. In February 1778, they agreed to ship weapons to patriot armies. Even more important, French money helped the American government pay its own soldiers, and two years later French troops arrived on American soil.

The British decided after Saratoga that New England was lost. Instead, they would attack the South and recruit the

During the Revolution, thousands of slaves ran away from plantations to seek freedom with the British. In 1787, Britain sent many of them back to Africa to start a new colony called Sierra Leone. It was the first effort to return blacks to Africa.

Overview of the Revolutionary War

As this map shows, the Revolutionary War was fought in two phases. Battles in the first half of the war took place in the North, and in the second half, the South.

slaves who made up over a third of the population.

At first, the new strategy worked. Planters kept their sons and servants at home to prevent the slaves from running away, so the colonies lacked soldiers. By spring 1780, the British controlled Georgia. They captured 5,000 American troops at Charleston, South Carolina. It was the largest surrender of patriots in the war.

War at Sea

Problems for Britain, however, were brewing on the Atlantic. The Americans had no real navy, but it did have privateers, or captains of privately-owned ships, who attacked the British, and kept what they captured.

In 1779, an American, John Paul Jones, asked the French for a ship. He renamed it the *Bonhomme Richard*, and used it to attack British ships. On September 23, 1779, he attacked a much larger British ship called the *Serapis*. When the British captain demanded his surrender, Jones replied "I have not yet begun to fight." After an American grenade blew up the *Serapis'* ammunition room, the British captain surrendered.

The Spanish and Dutch, who had also declared war on Britain, used their ships to attack the British in the Caribbean.

The Southern Battles

Washington appointed Nathaniel Greene as his general in the South.

MARY (MOLLY) HAYES (1754–1832)

When her husband John enlisted in the Continental Army, Molly Hayes went with him. Although she was not allowed to fight, she was determined to help him in the revolutionary cause. At the army camp, she took care of kitchen and laundry chores, as well as nursing sick soldiers back to health. Her bravery and kindness in the face of enemy fire earned her the affectionate nickname "Molly Pitcher," as she carried a pitcher of water to and from the thirsty soldiers during battle.

On June 28, 1778, at the Battle of Monmouth, she was performing this duty when her husband was shot. Quickly, she took his place at the battery and loaded the cannon. Despite the heat and the intense fighting, she remained at her post, loading and reloading the weapon, until the battle was won.

It was not until 44 years later that the legislature of Pennsylvania voted to recognize Molly Pitcher's wartime service. They awarded her $40 a year for the rest of her life, thus making her the first woman to receive a military pension in the United States.

Below: With her husband lying wounded at her feet, Molly Hayes takes his place loading the cannon at the Battle of Monmouth in 1778.

Greene faced large and well-armed British forces, but he refused to back down. "We fight, get beaten, and fight again," he said. Greene's determination eventually stopped Britain's southern offensive in North Carolina.

Surrender at Yorktown

General Lord Cornwallis, the British commander in the South, decided on one last plan. He would use all his troops in one giant attack on Virginia. He sailed up Chesapeake Bay and landed at Yorktown, but Washington and the French were ready. The Americans surrounded the British on land and the French navy trapped them by sea. On October 19, 1781, Lord Cornwallis was forced to surrender his 9,500 troops. As they piled their arms in front of Washington, the patriot band played the song "The World Turned Upside Down."

Many people in Britain were growing tired of the war. Some believed the patriots had a just cause. Others didn't like the higher war taxes. King George wanted to keep fighting, but many in Parliament did not, and it was Parliament that paid the bills.

In April 1782, Parliament and the former colonies began talks in Paris. In the Treaty of Paris, signed on September 3, 1783, the British gave America all the land east of the Mississippi River.

The British also offered their African-American soldiers freedom as they promised. On the other hand, the British ignored their Indian allies. The treaty said nothing about their rights to western lands.

Above: Shown here is the British surrender at Yorktown in October 1781. The French fleet that came to the aid of the patriot army can be seen off the coast.

47

Below: James Madison of Virginia, one of the authors of the U.S. Constitution. Madison later became the nation's fourth president.

The Birth of a Nation

Having begun a war with Britain, the colonists had to replace the British government appointed by the king with one of their own. In the midst of the Revolution, the Continental Congress told the 13 colonies to write out constitutions for themselves. What should these new governments be like? The Declaration said that governments should get "their just powers from the consent of the governed (people)." But which people?

From the very beginning, most Americans were not included. Few colonial leaders believed African-Americans, slave or free, should be able to vote. Indians were left out, too.

Women were not included, even though they helped win the Revolution. Many had kept farms and shops going while their men were off fighting. They helped organize boycotts and made things to replace British goods. On the battlefield, they brought food and drink to the fighting men and nursed the wounded.

The people, then, meant white men. Even here, however, there were differences. At the time, only men who owned property could vote. Some constitutions, like Pennsylvania's, got rid of the old property rules. Every white male could vote.

Other constitutions were not so open. A delegate to the New Hampshire convention said, "Government originates from the people . . . [but] the people [must] be taught . . . that they are not able to govern themselves." In South Carolina, the Constitution limited voting to men with $12,500 of property, which was a fortune in those days.

In general, the new legislatures were more democratic than the old colonial ones. An observer of the new Virginia assembly wrote that the members were "men not quite so well dressed, nor so politely educated, nor so highly born."

The Articles of Confederation

The greater difficulty was replacing the rule of the king with a single new government for all the colonies. This task fell to the Second Continental Congress. A Virginia delegate to the national convention said the new government should only "adjust disputes between the Colonies, regulate the affairs of trade, war, peace, alliances, etc. . . ." He also added that it "should by no means have authority to interfere with internal police or domestic concerns of any Colony."

While the war was still being fought, the Continental Congress came up with the Articles of Confederation. This first national constitution was passed on November 15, 1777. It took another four years until all the colonies ratified, or approved, it.

The Articles achieved some important things. They allowed the federal government to sign the treaty with France in 1778. Nine years later, in 1787, the new government would also pass the Northwest Ordinance, one of the most important laws in American history. The ordinance provided for new states to be carved out of the western frontier. When a territory had 5,000 settlers, it could form a legislature. When it had 60,000 residents, it could ask Congress for statehood.

Even with the Articles of Confederation, however, the national government was very weak. It had no president and only one house of Congress. Each state, no matter how big or small, had one vote. Important laws had to get a majority of nine delegates to pass. This made passing national taxes very difficult. If the government tried to pass taxes on trade, merchants from the northern states voted no. If it tried to pass land taxes, southern planters voted no.

Even before the Revolution was over, the country began going broke. The new government could not even pay the soldiers fighting for its independence. When troops marched on Philadelphia for their back pay, the delegates started moving from town to town to avoid them. For a while, even the Spanish ambassador had trouble finding the American government when he went looking for it in New Jersey.

The end of the war did not bring an end to the money problems. Times were hard for small farmers, shopkeepers, and workers. The new states passed taxes that hurt the poor and middle class. Many went into debt and were taken to court. Many lost their property. Some went to jail.

War veterans were especially angry. They had been given land in the west instead of pay. Because they needed money to feed their families, many sold their land to rich men for far less than it was worth.

Shays' Rebellion

In western Massachusetts, a group of farmers decided that they had had enough. Led by Daniel Shays, they organized meetings and protested higher taxes. "I have labored hard all my days," said one farmer, "and been loaded with class-rates [taxes], town-rates, province-rates, continental-rates, and all rates . . . [I] have been pulled and hauled by sheriffs, constables [police], collectors, and had my cattle sold for less than they were worth."

This farmer and others took up arms. They closed local courts and let people out of jail. Still, the state government in Boston, controlled by rich merchants, refused to hear their complaints.

The farmers decided to march on Boston. Frightened government leaders made the farmers' meetings illegal and asked the national government for 1,300 soldiers to defend Boston. In the end, the army was not needed. Shays' Rebellion collapsed by itself.

Even so, Shays' Rebellion worried national leaders. What if the farmers had taken over the state government? Would they have passed laws taxing the rich?

The weakness of the Articles of Confederation worried national leaders who had loaned money to the government to pay for the war. If the government could not raise taxes, it could not pay them back. Debts were also owed to the British. Under the Treaty of Paris, the

THE UNITED STATES
After the Treaty of 1783
Showing the claims of the older States to the Western Lands.
The Territory of the Thirteen Original States after claims had been ceded is tinted.
The Claims to the Western Lands are shown in border tint of the same color as the claiming State.
States having no claims are colored thus:

new American government agreed to pay the old bills of the colonies. Without taxes, the debts went unpaid. As a result, the British refused to leave their forts in the West. Americans worried that the British would arm the Indians.

The Constitutional Convention

In 1787, a Massachusetts farmer named Jonathan Smith addressed the president of his state's convention. The convention had been called to ratify, or approve, the new American Constitution.

"Dear Mr. President," he began, "I am a plain man, and get my living by the plow. I am not used to speak[ing] in public.

"I have lived in a part of the country where I have known [bad government]," he said. "When I saw this Constitution, I found that it was a cure for these diseases . . . I don't think the worse of the Constitution because lawyers . . . and

Above: This map shows the original 13 states in 1783, as well as the Western territories.

moneyed men are fond of it. [They] are all embarked in the same cause with us, and we must all swim or sink together . . . If we don't do it now, I am afraid we never shall have another opportunity."

In 1787, Congress called a new convention to change the Articles. When the delegates met in Philadelphia, however, they decided to throw the Articles out and start fresh.

The delegates faced many tough issues. The most difficult was sharing power among the states. Smaller states wanted all the states to have equal representation in the Federal government. Big states like Virginia thought they should have more power, since more people lived in Virginia. Out of the debate came the Great Compromise. The government would have two houses of Congress. In the Senate, all the states would be equal with each other. In the House of Representatives, the number of Representatives for each state would be based on the size of its population.

Slavery was a very serious problem for the draftees of the Constitution, who finally had made a compromise between the North and the South. Southerners wanted slaves to be counted in the population, because this would give southern states more representatives in Congress. Northerners did not want slaves counted at all since they could not vote, and representation was for voters. However, the southern slaveholders refused to join the new union of states if slaves were not counted. "The true question at present," said a South Carolina delegate, "is whether the southern states shall be parties to the Union." After another long debate, the North agreed to a compromise to get the South to join. Each slave would be counted as three fifths of a person. It was America's first, but not its last, compromise over slavery.

The Division of Powers

The Constitution divided the government into three parts: the president (the executive branch), the Congress (the

BENJAMIN BANNEKER (1731-1806)

Below: Benjamin Banneker

The son of a slave father and free mother, Benjamin Banneker was a brilliant mathematician, astronomer, and surveyor. He was a self-educated man, gaining most of his learning from the books of a Quaker neighbor. At an early age he won great fame for building the first wooden clock made in America, which ran for years and kept remarkably accurate time.

Banneker's intelligence and mechanical abilities drew him to the attention of Thomas Jefferson, who asked him to assist Pierre L'Enfant in the laying out of Washington, D.C. Unfortunately, L'Enfant was difficult to work with, and when Congress fired him, he stormed out of the city with his plans under his arm. Although some feared this would mean the city would have to be entirely redesigned, Banneker was able to reconstruct the plans from memory, and the layout of . the nation's capital was completed.

During this time, Banneker also published his first almanac of astronomical observations, which was widely distributed and received national recognition. He sent this almanac to his friend Jefferson, arguing that the publication was proof that African-Americans were just as smart as whites. For years after his death, opponents of slavery used Banneker's almanac and his letter to Jefferson as an argument to end slavery.

legislative branch), and the courts (the judicial branch). The president would control the nation's army and its foreign policy, and also enforce the laws made by Congress. A court system was set up as well. The Supreme Court would decide cases that involved laws passed by the Congress and enforced by the president. In short, each branch had power over the others. This was called the system of checks and balances. The Constitution, said Benjamin Franklin, was not a "perfect production." Yet it was amazing that the delegates had found a system "approaching so near to perfection as it does."

When the convention broke up in September, the Constitution still had to be ratified by at least nine states. The delegates went home to try to convince their states to ratify it. They called themselves "Federalists." Their job was not easy.

The Bill of Rights

Americans who feared a strong central government were called "anti-Federalists." Anti-Federalists demanded that the Constitution include protections against a powerful central government. To get the Constitution ratified, ten amendments called the "Bill of Rights" were added to it. They include rights like a free press, free speech, freedom of assembly, and freedom of religion. They also protect people against illegal searches and unfair punishment.

By the end of June 1788, although nine states had ratified the Constitution, New York, the biggest state in the North, had not.

Federalists James Madison, John Jay, and Alexander Hamilton wrote a series of newspaper articles to convince New Yorkers to ratify. The Federalist Papers said that America would be great only if it had a powerful central government. The argument worked and New York ratified the Constitution in July. The last state to ratify, Rhode Island, followed two years later.

The framers of the Constitution did not want the president to be chosen directly by voters, since they felt they would be unable to judge the qualifications of leaders from far away states properly. Instead they created the Electoral College, made up of prominent men that knew the candidates. Each state would have as many electors as it had senators and representatives. Initially, each elector voted for two candidates, with the candidate receiving the most "electoral" votes (as long as it was a majority) becoming president. The candidate with the second most votes would become vice president.

The Federalists swept the first national elections in 1788 and met in New York City, the temporary home of the government. One of their first acts was to unanimously approve George Washington as the nation's first president. On August 30, 1789, he was sworn into office.

Congress argued over what to call the new leader. Massachusetts's John Adams, who became vice president, suggested "His highness the President of the United States and Protector of their Liberties." Others said this made Washington sound too much like a king. Congress settled on "George Washington, President of the United States."

Above: Shays' Rebellion frightened many Americans, and convinced them that a strong central government was needed, at least to keep the peace.

The Early Presidents

Alexander Hamilton, the first secretary of the treasury, had big plans for America. The United States, he argued, should become an industrial country. On President Washington's orders, he wrote up a "Report on Manufactures."

In this report, he called for more business and a more "extensive use of machinery." He hoped to see American cities grow and more factories built. This, he said, would make America rich and powerful, like England.

Thomas Jefferson, the secretary of state, disagreed. "Those who labor in the earth are the chosen people of God," he wrote. Jefferson wanted the new republic to be a country of small, self-sufficient farmers. "While we have land to labour then, let us never wish to see our citizens occupied at a workbench . . . let our workshops remain in Europe."

The debate between Hamilton and Jefferson was the most important one facing the new nation. It was also about democracy, as well as work.

Hamilton said the rich should govern since they knew what was best for America. If common people governed, they would attack the rich who could make America wealthy.

Jefferson had more faith in average Americans, especially independent farmer-citizens. People who were their own masters could not be controlled by powerful rich men. Independent farmers could think for themselves and were the best citizens of a democracy. If people had to work for others, they would become servants, and democracy would die before it was born.

In 1792, Hamilton con-vinced Con-gress to pass a tax on whiskey. Western farmers who grew the grain needed to make the whiskey became angry. Before modern transportation, it was very expensive to transport grain east to the cities. It was cheaper to make it into whiskey and then ship it. But the tax would make even whiskey more expensive to ship. Thousands of Kentucky farmers picked up their guns and refused to pay the tax. President Washington decided he had to stop this challenge. He personally led a 15,000-man army to Kentucky to put down the Whiskey Rebellion.

Both Hamilton and Jefferson looked to Europe for models of what America should be. Hamilton respected Great Britain, an industrial country with great cities. It also had the kind of democracy he liked. England was ruled by a powerful king and its Parliament only included wealthy and well-educated men.

Jefferson preferred France. In 1789, France, in its own revolution, had overthrown the king and cut off his head. French nobles were driven from power and every man was allowed to vote for the new democratic government. The slogan of the French Revolution was "Liberty, Equality, and Brotherhood."

The Proclamation of Neutrality

Within several years, the French Revolution fell into chaos, with leadership of the country changing from month to month. How could the United States maintain an alliance with France when it was unclear who was running that country? Yet in return for help in the Revolution, the former colonies had promised to aid France if its colonies in the West Indies were attacked. When war broke out between France and England in 1793, President Washington quickly issued the Proclamation of Neutrality, which stated that although the United States would remain allied with France, it would not choose sides in this war.

During the war, France sent a diplomat, Edmund Genet, to the United States to enlist Americans to serve on French

Below: When Washington traveled to New York City on April 30, 1789 for the country's first presidential inauguration, parties were held all along his route. He is shown here arriving at a celebration in Trenton, New Jersey.

Above: The Bank of the United States

> "Hamilton was . . . honest in all private transactions, amiable in society, and duly valuing virtue in private life, yet so bewitched and perverted by the British example as to be under thorough conviction that corruption was essential to the government."
>
> —THOMAS JEFFERSON, on Alexander Hamilton

warships, and to convince the government to allow France to use U.S. naval bases in the war. Angry Federalists argued that Genet's visit broke the Proclamation of Neutrality. Americans rallied to President Washington's support when Genet attacked U.S. neutrality, and his efforts to win support badly failed. When the French finally called Genet home, even their ally Jefferson was glad to see him go.

Despite Genet's blunder, some American merchants found there was money to be made selling military supplies to France. To stop these sales, the British soon blockaded the French coast and declared that only ships carrying non-military supplies could get through. To avoid the blockade, France opened its colonies in the West Indies to U.S. ships. In response, Britain began seizing American ships. Although anti-Federalists in the government wanted to retaliate, President Washington knew that America was in no position to fight a war. He sent John Jay to make peace with the British. Although the British agreed to finally remove the rest of their troops from America's western frontier in return for payment of all old unpaid colonial debts, Jay's Treaty contained no assurances that the British would stop attacking American ships. Although anti-Federalists were furious, Federalists controlled government and the treaty passed the Senate.

John Adams's Administration

The anti-Federalists led by Thomas Jefferson and the Federalists led by Alexander Hamilton had such different philosophies of government that their supporters finally formed two opposing political parties. Hamilton's supporters formed the Federalist Party, while Jefferson's became known as "Democratic-Republicans" (today's Democratic Party). Despite public anger over Jay's Treaty, Federalist John Adams won the presidential election of 1796. Democratic-Republican Jefferson received the second highest number of votes and became vice president.

France was also angry over Jay's

Above: Alexander Hamilton

Below: Aaron Burr

Treaty, and shortly after the election, started attacking American ships. Then, when American diplomats arrived in Paris to work out a settlement, the French foreign minister refused to meet them. Instead, he sent three agents to tell the Americans that unless they paid the French foreign minister a $250,000 bribe, there would be no negotiations. The names of the diplomats were not released, so people called them X, Y, and Z. President Adams said the XYZ Affair insulted American honor and tore up the 1778 alliance with France.

In 1798, the Federalist government passed the Alien and Sedition Acts, which made it illegal to publish criticism of the president or Congress. Democratic-Republicans claimed this was an attack on the Bill of Rights. Jefferson warned that the Federalists were destroying American democracy. Adams, on the other hand, charged that Jefferson would lead the United States into another war with Britain.

Although anti-Federalist Jefferson won the election, it was several months before he took office. Adams used this time to name a strong Federalist, John Marshall, as chief justice of the Supreme Court. In the 1803 case of Marbury v. Madison, Marshall, who believed in a strong court, overturned a law passed by Congress. This was the first time the Supreme Court had used the power of judicial review.

As president, Jefferson did some things people expected and some things they did not. He pulled America away from England, but he didn't side with France. In 1807, he passed the Embargo and Non-Intercourse Acts, which stopped all American trade with Europe. Although it hurt merchants badly, it kept America out of war. Jefferson wasn't against all war. When pirates attacked American ships from the Barbary Coast in North Africa, Jefferson sent in the Marines.

THE BURR-HAMILTON DUEL

Twenty years of competition and political rivalry between Alexander Hamilton and Aaron Burr ended in disaster on July 12, 1804. The trouble began when they were still young soldiers in the Continental Army under George Washington. Although Hamilton and Burr were both promoted, Washington

disliked Burr and sent him away to fight under General Putnam. Hamilton, on the other hand, was asked to serve as Washington's aide-de-camp, or his "right-hand-man."

In 1800, Burr ran for president. He and Thomas Jefferson received the same number of votes, so the election had to be decided by the House of Representatives. Hamilton's strong opposition to Burr caused the vote to swing in favor of Jefferson, and Burr was elected vice president.

Four years later, Burr was nominated for governor of New York, and Hamilton again worked to defeat him. Burr flew into a rage and demanded a duel. They met at dawn in Weehawken, New Jersey. Burr shot Hamilton, and he died the next day. Alexander Hamilton is remembered as one of the most important figures in American history. Aaron Burr, who lived until he was 80, has become one of the most stigmatized men in our history.

Above: Aaron Burr fatally wounds Alexander Hamilton.

Right: Hamilton's dueling pistols

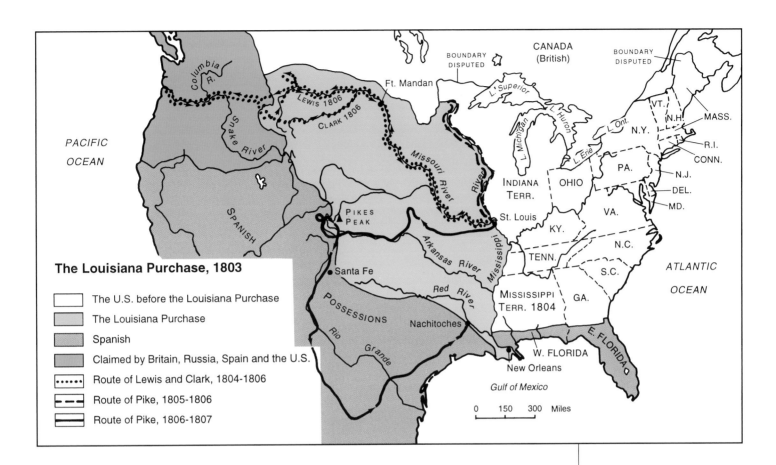

The Louisiana Purchase, 1803

- The U.S. before the Louisiana Purchase
- The Louisiana Purchase
- Spanish
- Claimed by Britain, Russia, Spain and the U.S.
- •••••• Route of Lewis and Clark, 1804-1806
- – – – Route of Pike, 1805-1806
- ——— Route of Pike, 1806-1807

Jefferson, as he had promised, made government smaller. He cut the debt and lowered expenses. On the other hand, he used the power of the central government to double the size of the country.

The Louisiana Purchase

In 1803, Jefferson sent two diplomats to meet with the new French emperor, Napoleon. France still controlled a huge territory in North America, but Napoleon was busy fighting wars in Europe and needed money more than faraway lands. For $15 million, he sold America the Louisiana Territory, which included all the land between the Mississippi River and the Rocky Mountains.

On July 5, 1803, he launched an expedition to cross the Louisiana Territory to its western border. His personal secretary, Meriwether Lewis, and an army officer, William Clark, headed the expedition. Jefferson was eager to learn about this territory. He also wanted to lay American claims to the West beyond the Louisiana Territory, and an unwritten international law said

that territory belonged to the country that first explored it. The two men and their assistants traveled up the Missouri River and across the Continental Divide, which was the border of the territory, then down the Columbia River to the Pacific Ocean. To guide them through unknown lands, the expedition hired a French interpreter and his Shoshoni wife, Sacajawea.

After more than two years, Lewis and Clark returned to the new capital of Washington with maps, journals, drawings, and tales of bison herds, schools of salmon, and Native American nations. They also reported that the mountains of the West were much higher and wider than people had thought.

Upon their return, an expedition under another army officer, Zebulon Pike, explored the southern Plains and Rockies. Like Lewis and Clark, Pike went beyond the Louisiana Territory to Spanish lands in the Southwest. His description of the Great Plains as a "great American desert" kept people from settling the Plains for many decades.

Above: This map shows the lands acquired by the United States in the Louisiana Purchase, as well as the exploration routes taken by explorers Lewis and Clark, and Zebulon Pike.

The War of 1812 and The Era of Good Feelings

From the very first days of independence, the new nation had been at war with the Indians of the Ohio Valley. In 1790 and 1791, a group of Indian nations, under Little Turtle, had defeated the American army. Four years later, a larger force under General "Mad Anthony" Wayne defeated Little Turtle at the Battle of Falling Timbers.

In 1795, the Indians signed the Treaty of Greenville, Ohio and gave up the Territory of Ohio, and half of Michigan. They also agreed to live "under the protection of the United States." White settlers quickly swarmed into the territory. In 1803, with over 100,000 white citizens, Ohio became the 16th state.

The new white settlers wanted to take more Indian land in what is now Indiana and Illinois. Indian leaders became alarmed. In the early 1800s, two Shawnee, a prophet named Tenskwatawa and his brother, Chief Tecumseh, traveled among the tribes of the region. Tenskwatawa spoke of Indian spirits and pride. Tecumseh organized a new confederation of tribes, and bought weapons from the British army in Canada.

In 1811, Tecumseh's warriors fought General William Henry Harrison's troops on the Tippecanoe Creek in Indiana. "It was fully believed among the Indians that we should defeat General Harrison," Chief Shabbona of the Potawatomi later recalled. "Our young men said: We are ten to their one. If they stay upon the other side, we will let them alone. If they cross the Wabash [river, in Indiana], we will take their scalps or drive them into the river."

The Indian warriors laughed at

Below: Dolley Madison, wife of President James Madison, rescued many of the White House's most valuable treasures when it was burned by the British in 1814.

the American army, said Shabbona. "These white soldiers are not warriors. One half of them are calico peddlers [clothes salesmen]. The other half can only shoot squirrels."

Sure of their victory, the Indians were not prepared for the awesome firepower of the Americans. In 1811, on the shores of the Tippecanoe Creek in Indiana, they were handily defeated. "Our women and children were in the town only a mile from the battlefield . . ." Shabbona said. "They wanted white prisoners . . . Oh how these women were disappointed! Instead of slaves and spoils of the white men coming into town with the rising sun, their town was in flames, and women and children were hunted like wolves or driven into the river and

Left: General Andrew Jackson at the Battle of New Orleans, in 1814

swamps to hide." With his victory, Harrison became a national hero and Indian resistance in the Great Lakes territory crumbled.

The War of 1812

Many Democratic-Republican leaders were not happy with the British for selling weapons to Tecumseh. But it was British actions on the high seas that really made them angry. Britain claimed that their sailors were deserting the navy to work on American merchant ships. The British began to stop these ships and capture those sailors they suspected of desertion. When the American government demanded that the British navy stop, it refused.

In June 1812, President James Madison and Congress declared war on Britain. Those who voted for war were called the "war hawks." Along with stopping Britain, they also wanted to defeat Indians in the West, and to take the British-controlled territories of Florida and Canada. The war hawks believed victory would be easy. After all, Britain had its hands full fighting France in Europe.

The war hawks would be sadly disappointed, but not at first. American privateers captured many British navy ships in the Atlantic. On the Great Lakes, the American navy, under William Perry, defeated the British in the Battle of Lake Erie. At Detroit, William Henry Harrison defeated a British and Indian force. The British forces defending Canada had been crushed by these two victories.

"The land is ours. No one has a right to remove us, because we were the first owners. The Great Spirit above has appointed this place for us, on which to light our fires, and here we will remain. As to boundaries, the Great Spirit knows no boundaries, nor will His red children acknowledge any."

— TECUMSEH,
chief of the Shawnees, to a messenger sent by President Madison, 1810

The Americans invaded Canada and won the Battle of Thames, Ontario. One of the dead was Tecumseh, who had joined the British. Then the Americans captured Toronto, the capital of western Canada, and burned it to the ground. When the British counterattacked, the Americans fled south of the border.

The tide quickly turned against the Americans. By 1813, the British controlled the Atlantic again. In 1814, a force sailed up the Potomac River to Washington, and burned down government buildings in revenge for the destruction of Toronto. First Lady Dolley Madison saved many precious items from the White House before she fled.

After burning Washington, the British surrounded Fort McHenry in Baltimore. Despite a night of bombardment, the American flag still flew over the fort in the morning. An American prisoner of war named Francis Scott Key watched from a British ship and wrote a song called the "Star Spangled Banner" that later became the national anthem.

The War of 1812 divided the country. Federalist merchants in New England who did not support it because it hurt trade met in 1814 in Hartford, Connecticut. Many wanted New England to secede from the Union. While the majority voted to stay with the Union, the Hartford Convention angered so many other Americans that the Federalist Party was never again elected to power.

By 1814, people on both sides of the Atlantic wanted peace. In December 1814, British and American diplomats met in Ghent, Belgium, to sign a treaty that left things as they had been before the war. The War of 1812 was a draw.

However, in those days, news traveled slowly. Before the news reached North America, there would be one more great battle. In early 1815, the British landed thousands of soldiers near New Orleans. They were met by an American force

TECUMSEH (1768?–1813)

Above: Tecumseh

As white settlers moved westward, Native Americans found themselves with less and less land. They were no longer able to live off the land, and were forced to rely on the white government for food and clothing. Tecumseh and his brother, the Prophet Tenskwatawa, were angered by what was happening to their people. Together, they traveled across the Midwest, urging the tribes to give up the ways of the white man and to unite as one nation. "Will we let ourselves be destroyed in our turn without making an effort worthy of our race?" cried Tecumseh. Soon, he and Tenskwatawa had a great following of people who saw power and truth in their words.

When the War of 1812 broke out, Tecumseh fought alongside the British in hope that they would help him form a new Indian nation. He was a great general, who frequently made up for the mistakes of the other generals with his bravery and shrewd leadership. On October 5, 1813, at the Battle of Thames, he was killed. After Tecumseh's death, Tenskwatawa crumpled in despair, and the unity of the midwestern tribes melted away. The dream of a unified nation of Indian tribes was lost.

under the command of a Tennessee general named Andrew Jackson. Jackson had already defeated the Creek Indians in a series of battles in 1813 and 1814. On January 8, Jackson's soldiers crushed the British army. News of the victory and the treaty arrived in the east at the same time. A headline in New York proclaimed: "Almost an Incredible Victory!!"

Peace in North America was followed by peace in Europe. From 1815 to 1819, the American economy grew rapidly. In 1818, four Quaker merchants started the Black Ball Line shipping company, the first regular shipping service across the Atlantic.

The Era of Good Feelings

Peace and prosperity quieted American politics. The Federalist Party was gone; only the Democratic-Republicans remained. In 1820, James Monroe was nearly unanimously reelected to the presidency by the Electoral College. Only one delegate voted against Monroe, because he wanted to make sure that George Washington would remain the only president elected by all the delegates. Historians call this period the "Era of Good Feelings."

In fact, the era was not always full of good feelings. Many Federalists had joined the Democratic-Republicans because there was no other party, but they still disagreed with Democratic-Republicans on many issues like taxes and trade. Eventually, these former Federalists would form a new party called the Whigs.

However, the biggest division facing America in 1820 was slavery. Despite the Constitutional Convention's decision to count a slave as three fifths of a person when determining how many representatives each state would get in the federal government, maintaining a balance between slave and free states remained a critical issue, especially as new states joined the Union. In 1819, settlers in Missouri wanted it to join the Union as a slave state. Northerners said this would give the South one more state than the North.

After a year of debate, Congress voted for a compromise. Missouri would come in as a slave state and Maine would come in as a free one. An imaginary line was drawn from the southern border of Missouri to the Pacific Ocean. Slavery would be allowed south of that line, but not north of it. Congress thought it had settled the problem for good. Thomas Jefferson, now retired on his slave plantation in Virginia, disagreed. Missouri he said was like "a tocsin [fire alarm] in the night."

Two years later, he was proven right. In July 1822, a free black carpenter in Charleston, South Carolina, named Denmark Vesey tried to organize a slave revolt. He got African blacksmiths to make swords and bayonets in secret. A few days before the revolt, however, a slave confessed. By August, Vesey and 30 other blacks had been hanged. It was not the first slave revolt in American history and it would not be the last.

Above: James Monroe, the fifth president of the United States

AMERICAN TIMELINE

1765 Riots erupt in New York City and Boston in protest against the Stamp Act that requires taxes to be paid on printed matter, legal documents, and other items such as dice and playing cards.

1766 In Philadelphia, Benjamin Franklin invents the first bifocal spectacles.

1767 Daniel Boone leaves North Carolina in early autumn in search of a pass across the Appalachian Mountains. Caught in a snowstorm, he and his companions are forced to spend the winter in the wilds.

1773 In furious protest of the Tea Act, patriots dressed as Indians storm British ships anchored in Boston harbor and throw their cargo of tea overboard. John Adams calls the act "bold and daring" and an "epoch in history."

1774 Delegates to the First Continental Congress meet in Philadelphia to draft a list of complaints for King George III. They declare their right to "life, liberty and property."

1775 Silversmith Paul Revere rides across Massachusetts to warn patriotic militiamen that the British are coming to ambush them. He makes it almost all the way to Concord before he is overtaken by two British soldiers.

Above: Paul Revere's ride

WORLD TIMELINE

1764 Stanislas Poniatowski, friend of Empress Catherine of Russia, becomes king of Poland.

1767 After a two-year siege, the capital of Thailand falls to the Burmese.

1768 Twenty-thousand Catholics and Jews are massacred in Poland in a Russian crackdown on Polish political and religious freedom.

1772 Austria, Prussia, and Russia seize Polish lands and divide the territory among themselves.

1775 Bread shortages and a poor harvest cause riots in parts of France.

1776 Tukulor chiefs led by Suleiman Bal seize power in Senegal, Africa.

1777 Captain James Cook discovers the Sandwich Islands, later known as Hawaii.

1778 Spain and France declare war on Britain.

1780 France abolishes the use of torture to force criminals to confess.

■ Catherine II of Russia appeals to European countries to support the American Revolution against Britain, in the League of Armed Neutrality.

1781 The Boers defeat the Khosian and Xhosa people in the South African Suurveld War.

1782 Irish Parliament is made independent of Great Britain.

1783 Spain, Sweden, and Denmark recognize the independence of the United States.

1776 Thomas Jefferson presents the Declaration of Independence to the Second Continental Congress. Some delegates fear that such a declaration will unite Britain against them and end in their ultimate destruction.

1777 Congress authorizes the flag of the United States with 13 stars, 13 stripes, and three colors: white to signify purity, red to signify valor, and blue to signify perseverance and justice.

1778 After a rough winter at Valley Forge, General George Washington writes Congress to say that unless they receive new clothing and supplies of food immediately, his soldiers will either freeze or starve to death.

1780 Two days after American general Benedict Arnold gives military secrets to the British, his deed is discovered, and he is forced to flee to the British side.

1781 Veterans of the Pennsylvania and New Jersey regiments raise up in rebellion over lack of pay and low rations. Although they demand a hearing, they also make it clear that they will continue to fight the British, regardless of their mutiny.
■ A bitter Cornwallis surrenders to Washington at Yorktown. Ashamed of his defeat, he cannot face Washington and instead sends his general to accept the terms of surrender.

1783 Treaty of Paris is signed, formally ending the Revolutionary War.

1784 Stating that the eagle is a bird of "bad moral character," Benjamin Franklin suggests the turkey as the national bird.

■ African-American poet Phyllis Wheatley dies.

1787 John Fitch demonstrates his invention, the steamboat, which travels a remarkable three miles an hour in either windy or calm weather.

1788 The U.S. Constitution is ratified by nine of the thirteen states and goes into effect.
■ A fire started by a candle decimates the entire city of New Orleans. Eight hundred and fifty-six buildings are destroyed, including the cathedral.

1789 George Washington is unanimously elected President of the United States.

1790 The ship *Columbia* returns from a three-year journey around the world. She is the first American vessel to make the trip.

1785 French chemist Antoine Laurent Lavoisier develops a machine to turn gas into water. He declares that water is actually not just a single substance, but rather a mixture of gases.

1787 Many slaves who supported the British in the Revolutionary War are freed and establish Granville Town in Sierra Leone, West Africa.

1789 A French mob storms the Bastille prison in protest against the king's rule.

Right: The storming of the Bastille, Paris, in 1789

AMERICAN TIMELINE

1791 Ten amendments to the Constitution, known as the Bill of Rights, are passed.
■ Vermont is admitted to the Union as the 14th state.

1793 Eli Whitney invents the cotton gin, which removes seeds quickly from the plant. This enables rapid production and transforms the southern economy, turning cotton into a major cash crop.
■ Over 4,000 residents of Philadelphia die in an outbreak of yellow fever. Doctors are baffled as to the source of the disease.

1794 General "Mad Anthony" Wayne defeats an Indian force at Fallen Timbers, effectively ending the threat of Indian attack in the Northwest Territory.

1797 Johnny Appleseed, born John Chapman, passes through

Pennsylvania planting young apple trees and spreading the word of his religion, Swedenborgianism. Although the trees take root, his religion does not.

1800 The United States government moves from Philadelphia to its new capital of Washington. Some officials complain that the district is little more than a swamp.

1802 The U.S. Military Academy is established by Congress in West Point, New York, on the Hudson River.
■ All states north of the Mason-Dixon line with the exception of New Jersey have passed emancipation laws. The South is plagued by slave uprisings, but has made no move toward abolition.

1803 The United States doubles its size, purchasing the Louisiana Territory for $15 million.

■ Captains Meriwether Lewis and William Clark set off to explore the unknown West on a government expedition.

1804 Alexander Hamilton works to defeat rival Aaron Burr's candidacy for governor of New York. Furious, Burr challenges Hamilton to a duel. Hamilton accepts, and Burr kills him.

1805 After 18 months of journey, Lewis and Clark finally reach the Pacific.

1809 Shawnee Chief Tecumseh launches a campaign to unite the Indians west of the Mississippi River in opposition to American expansion.

1811 General William Henry Harrison defeats a large Shawnee force at Tippecanoe in Indiana territory.

WORLD TIMELINE

1791 After attempting to flee, the French royal family is arrested at Varennes and brought back to Paris for a trial.

■ Rebel slaves in Santo Domingo throw plantation owners off their land and capture much of the island.

1792 Mutineers face a court marshall for stealing the H.M.S. *Bounty* and setting their captain adrift in a small lifeboat.

1793 Louis XVI, king of France, is beheaded by the revolutionaries.

1796 Englishman Edward Jenner devises a life-saving vaccine for smallpox.

1797 Leading the French army, Napoleon Bonaparte forces Austria to surrender.

Left: The French royal family is arrested, 1791.

Above: Meriwether Lewis
Below: William Clark

1812 The United States declares war on Britain. The U.S. frigate *Constitution* scores a major victory over the 38-gun *Guerriere* in a battle on the St. Lawrence River.
■ Louisiana becomes the 18th state.

1814 The British set fire to Washington, D.C. Before the city is consumed by flames, Dolley Madison rescues the original Declaration of Independence and Gilbert Stuart's portrait of George Washington and carries them to safety in Virginia. Four months later, the Treaty of Ghent is signed, ending war.

1816 A bizarre cold spell hits the United States. Snow falls intermittently all summer long in Vermont, and across the land crops are dying. Some farmers call this "The Starvation Year."

1817 Work begins on the 500-mile-long Erie Canal. It will open the West to settlement and trade.
■ Thomas Hopkins Gallaudet establishes the first school for the deaf in Hartford, Connecticut.

1818 Britain and the United States set the 49th parallel as the boundary between the United States and Canada. They agree on joint occupation of the Oregon territory.

1820 Henry Clay proposes the Missouri Compromise in an effort to stem the tide of hostilities over the slavery issue; Maine is to enter the Union as a free state and Missouri as a slave state.

1821 Sequoyah, a Cherokee Indian, creates the first alphabet for an Indian language.
■ Despite a total lack of schooling, Davy Crockett is elected to the legislature of Tennessee.

1823 In response to a threat of foreign intervention in Latin America, President James Monroe announces his doctrine stating that the United States will not tolerate European interference in American affairs.

Above: Jane Austen

1798 Fearing an invasion from France, the Irish rise up against the British occupation.
■ Bonaparte captures Egypt.

1805 In a great sea battle, the British defeat the French at Cape Trafalgar.
■ Jean-Jacques Dessalines, president of Haiti, dies.

1811 King George III of England sinks further into madness, and his son takes the throne.

1813 English author Jane Austen publishes *Pride and Prejudice.*

1814 European allies invade France, capturing Paris and forcing Napoleon into exile.

1818 Mary Wollstonecraft Shelley publishes her Gothic novel *Frankenstein.*

1819 King Kamehameha the Great of Hawaii dies. The people of the islands mourn his loss as the first chief of a united Hawaiian people.
■ After freeing his native Venezuela from Spanish rule, Simon Bolivar liberates Colombia.

III. A NATION GROWS, A NATION GROWS APART

Above: This illustration shows a wagon train of white settlers moving westward through the Rockies. Local natives appear to wave them a welcome. In real life, the journey was a long and dangerous one. Many settlers died along the way, either from illness, or from attacks by Indians, who were less than happy about the new visitors.

WITH THE RISE of Andrew Jackson, a new era arrived in American history. Unlike all presidents who came before him, he was neither from Virginia or Massachusetts—the two states that had led the rest of the original American colonies into revolution and then into a new national government. Nor did he reach adulthood during the nation's founding years. Although Jackson had defeated the British in a heroic victory at the Battle of New Orleans, his real interest was in clearing Indians from the western frontier. And it was that growing frontier that captured the minds of America. And by 1850, the borders of the United States had stretched clear to the Pacific Ocean.

While the country's borders expanded westward, the dividing lines between North and South began to split wide open. A string of compromises over the slavery issue kept the peace for a time, but by 1850, national fear and mistrust over the issue had led the country to the brink of war.

New Factories and New Frontiers

Lucy Larcom, a farmer's daughter from New England, was one of America's first factory workers. She left her family to labor in the Lowell textile mills of Massachusetts when she was 12 years old.

"I went to my first day's work in the mill with a light heart," Lucy wrote to her family. "The novelty [newness] of it made it seem easy . . . I liked it better than going to school and 'making believe' I was learning when I was not."

The factory owners of the early 1800s preferred young girls like Lucy. They were more obedient than adults. They could be paid less. Their small hands fit inside the complicated machines.

Soon, however, Lucy changed her mind about the work. "I never cared much for machinery. The buzzing and hissing of pulleys and rollers and spindles and flyers around me often grew tiresome . . . I began to reflect upon life rather seriously for a girl of twelve or thirteen. What was I here for? What could I make of myself?" Like most of the Lowell Mill girls, Lucy left the factory after a couple of years and returned to her family and school.

Lucy and the Lowell Mills were part of the early Industrial Revolution. Things that were once made by hand were now made by machine. The rhythms of nature were replaced by the time clock. For some, growing food for one's family changed to earning a paycheck in factories.

Four things were needed for factory production: labor, money, technology, and resources. Some new workers, like Lucy, came from the countryside. Others were immigrants flooding into the country from Europe. The great potato famine in Ireland during the 1840s would send nearly a million poor Irish men and women to America.

The money came from rich New England and New York merchants. They were looking to invest the profits they made in trade. One of them, Francis Cabot Lowell, built the mill town that was named after him.

The earliest technology came from England. England was the first nation to industrialize. Other nations wanted to use these machines, but England made it illegal to export textile machines. In 1789, Samuel Slater, an apprentice to the inventor of one of the first mills, disguised himself with a fake beard and snuck out of the country with instructions for building English textile machines. When he got to New York, he met a merchant named Moses Brown. Together, the two men built the nation's first textile in Providence, Rhode Island, in 1790.

The Cotton Gin

The cotton that the textile mills wove into cloth came from the South. Two kinds of cotton were grown, long staple cotton and short staple cotton. Long staple cotton got its name because its fibers were long and silky, and this cotton could only be grown in warm, wet climates, like the Sea Islands of South Carolina and Georgia. Short staple cotton could be grown across the South, but it had one disadvantage. It contained seeds, and it took workers a long time to remove them to make the cotton ready for market.

Slavery was on the decline in the South by the 1780s and many people expected it to die out. Then, in 1792, a New England teacher, Eli Whitney, moved to Georgia. He wanted to do something about the short staple cotton problem. Within a year, he had invented his cotton gin, a machine that pulled the seeds from the cotton quickly and easily. This meant that plantation owners had more need for slaves. The cotton gin, changed the face of the South. Over the next 30 years, cotton plantations and slavery spread across the region from the Carolinas to Louisiana. Cotton production jumped from 10,000 bales a year in 1793 to a half million in 1820.

"There are more than 5,000 females employed in Lowell, and when you come to see the amount of labor performed by them, in superintending the different machinery, you will be astonished . . . Some of the girls attended three looms, and they make from $1.75 to $3 per week, after paying their board. These looms weave 55 yards per day, so that one person makes 165 yards per day. Everything moves on like clockwork, in all the variety of employments; and the whole manufacture appears to be the very best."

—DAVY CROCKETT, *on a visit to Lowell, Massachusetts, during an 1835 Northwest tour*

Above: Eli Whitney, who invented the cotton gin in 1792. His invention helped spread slavery throughout the entire South.

America's Industrial Revolution

While cotton cultivation spread across the South, industry grew in the North. New England was the first region to industrialize. By the beginning of the Civil War, factories had spread to the mid-Atlantic states and the midwest. Machines were also invented for production in other industries. Soon, the nation's shoes, farming equipment, and iron were being made in great factories.

The first factories were built near waterfalls in the countryside. The force of rushing water was used to power the machines. When steam engines, using wood and coal for fuel, replaced waterpower,

Above: Barges move their way along the Erie Canal in 1836. The opening of the canal eleven years earlier linked the Great Lakes with New York Harbor for the first time, and allowed goods to travel faster then ever before.

Right: The West Point, built in 1831, was the second train made in the United States for actual use on the rails.

factory owners were able to move their factories into the cities. After England, where the industrial revolution began, the United States was soon the world's leader in factory work and production.

A Transportation Revolution

It was cheaper and easier to make things with machines. But making things was one thing. Getting them to customers was another. With the industrial revolution came the transportation revolution. First came the turnpikes, made of dirt and corduroy, or logs laid side by side. Some were built by the government, like the great National Road across the Cumberland Gap from Maryland to

Kentucky. Others were built by private companies. Tolls were charged to pay for the roads.

The Erie Canal

Travel on canals, the next stage in the industrial revolution, was faster and cheaper. There were many canals built in the early 1800s, but none were longer than 30 miles. In 1817, New York governor Dewitt Clinton came up with a plan for something much bigger: a canal stretching from Buffalo to Albany. Eight years later, the Erie Canal was completed. Clinton opened the 363-mile long canal by pouring a bucket of water from the Great Lakes into New York Harbor. "The Big Ditch," as it was called, included several locks to raise and lower the boats over hills. Horses and mules pulled the boats from footpaths alongside the canal.

The Erie Canal, an instant success, helped make New York the largest city in America. Now farm and factory goods could be shipped all the way from the Midwest to New York Harbor. In 1800, it cost farmers 30 cents to ship a ton of grain one mile by wagon. Forty years later, it cost them less than a penny by canal.

Fulton's Steamboat

River transportation was changing, too. In 1807, a New York inventor named Robert Fulton built his first steamboat. For a few years, however, the cost of running the boats was too high. Gradually, lighter wood and more efficient engines helped make it less expensive. Steamboats were widely used on upriver routes by the 1820s. Twenty years later, they began to sail the oceans, though they wouldn't completely replace sailing ships until the early 1900s.

Water transport had several problems, however. Rivers and canals sometimes froze in winter, ran dry in summer, and flooded in the spring. "Rivers," wrote a St. Louis newspaper, "run only where nature pleases." A new form of transportation that could "run wherever man pleases" was needed.

The Railroads

It was not long in coming. The English invented the steam locomotive in the early 1800s. In 1829, the Delaware and Hudson canal company imported two, but the engines were too heavy for American rails. A New York manufacturer named Peter Cooper decided to try his hand at it. His first locomotive, the Tom Thumb, was named after a famous circus midget of the day. To test it, Cooper had the Tom Thumb race a horse. The locomotive lost, but that didn't stop Cooper. He was soon building bigger and faster engines.

With their noise, smoke, and speed, the first railroads thrilled and scared people. A group of Boston doctors warned that bumps at 20 miles an hour would produce "concussion of the brain."

The first railroads were built mostly in the Northeast and Midwest. In 1830, America's first rail line, the Baltimore and Ohio, opened for business. It was only 13 miles long. Three years later, South Carolina's 136 mile-long Charleston and Hamburg became the longest in the world. By 1840, America had over 2,800 miles of track. Still, the great railroad-building era did not begin until after 1850.

Jacksonian Democracy

Industry was not the only thing expanding in the 1820s and 1830s. Democracy was, too. When the Constitution was drafted in 1789, only six states allowed all white men to vote. The rest restricted the vote to those with property. By 1800, however, things had already begun to change. New western states entered the union without property rules for voting, older

"Low bridge, Everybody down!
Low bridge! We're a-comin' to your town
You'll always know your neighbor
You'll always know your pal
If you've ever navigated on the Erie Canal."

—*from "Low Bridge, Everybody Down," a popular folk song. Although the song was not actually published until 1913, many believe it to be much older. The cry "Low Bridge, Everybody Down" was used by barge drivers to warn passengers of upcoming bridges.*

states began to drop them, and by 1830, only six out of 25 states still had them.

As more people were allowed to vote, American politics changed. Before the voting changes, political parties, like the Federalists and Democratic-Republicans, were small. There were no big election campaigns.

In the 1824 election for president, there were five candidates, all calling themselves Democratic-Republicans. Andrew Jackson, hero of the War of 1812, won the most votes. John Quincy Adams, a Massachusetts congressman, former secretary of state under President Monroe, and son of former President John Adams, came in second. Henry Clay, a powerful senator from Kentucky, was third. Clay did not like Jackson, however, and gave his votes to Adams. Jackson and his supporters said the election was stolen.

Jackson began to prepare for the 1828 elections. With millions now voting, Jackson's men began to build a bigger party through campaign parades and rallies. They said Adams only served the interest of rich eastern merchants and bankers, while Jackson was a man of the people. In fact, he was a rich Tennessee plantation owner, with far more money than Adams.

Voters believed Jackson stood for the regular folk and elected him in both 1828 and 1832. Jackson did many things that pleased farmers and workers. He invited thousands to the White House on inauguration day. He also destroyed the official Bank of the United States. Many common people believed that the bank served the rich and powerful.

Black Hawk's War

Sadly, another popular issue was Indian removal. Jackson had been a famous Indian fighter in the army and he continued the wars against Indians as president. The latest Indian-white struggle was over lands in the Midwest and Southeast.

White settlers were pushing into western Illinois territory in the 1820s. The land belonged to the Sauk and Fox Indians, whose leader was chief Black Hawk. In 1829, government agents told Black Hawk his people would have to move farther west. "I refused to quit my village," he later said. "It was here, that I was born—and here lie the bones of many friends and relatives. For this spot I felt a sacred reverence, and never could consent to leave it without being forced."

Below: Andrew Jackson, the seventh president of the United States

ANDREW JACKSON (1767–1845)

Born to Irish immigrant parents on the Carolina frontier, Andrew Jackson was orphaned at 15. He left his home and traveled the frontier, taking one odd job after another to survive. Though he had little formal schooling, he eventually became a successful lawyer. Shortly after Tennessee became a state, Jackson was elected to the House of Representatives.

When war broke out with the British and their Indian allies in 1812, Jackson quickly joined the army. He was sent west to fight the Creek Indians. At the battle of Horseshoe Bend, Jackson was victorious and the Creeks surrendered much of the Mississippi Territory to him. He then marched his troops to New Orleans, where despite the odds stacked against him, he defeated the British.

Jackson's success on the battlefield made him a national hero. In 1828, he was elected president. Even in the White House he was a fighter. He took government money away from the Bank of the United States, disobeyed the Supreme Court, fired many government employees, and argued constantly with his advisors. Still, his popularity remained untouched. To the common people, he remained a hero until his dying day.

When Jackson sent troops, Black Hawk said he would not fight. "If he [the army commander] determined to fight, [the Indians] remain quietly in their lodges, and let them kill them if he chose." The troops refused Black Hawk's surrender and chased him from Illinois to Wisconsin. On August 3, 1832, the army caught up with the Sauk and Fox people at Bad Axe. After the massacre was over, only 150 of Black Hawk's 1,000 warriors were still alive.

The Trail of Tears

In the Southeast, the struggle to remove the Indians took longer. The region was inhabited by the Cherokee, Chickasaw, Choctaw, Creek, and Seminole, who were called the "five civilized tribes" because they had adopted white ways. They farmed and owned slaves, and many converted to Christianity. An Indian scholar named Sequoyah even created a written language for the Cherokee and published a newspaper.

Whether or not the natives adopted white ways did not matter much to the white men who wanted Indian land for cotton farming. In 1830, Jackson pushed the Indian Removal Act through Congress. When the state of Georgia tried to drive the Cherokee out, the Indians followed U.S. laws by taking their case to

the Supreme Court. Chief Justice John Marshall ruled in their favor, but Jackson refused to obey the court. "Marshall has made his decision," he said, "now let him enforce it."

Another treaty demanded the Cherokee leave Georgia by 1838, but when the deadline came, only 2,000 of the 17,000 had left. The army was sent in to place the Indians in government camps where many died. Then in the middle of winter, the Cherokee were forced to march 1,200 miles to Oklahoma. Four thousand died on the way. The Cherokee called this forced removal "The Trail of Tears."

The Seminole War

One tribe remained in the Southeast and fought on. The Seminole, a mixed tribe of runaway African slaves and Indians, used the Florida swamps to hide from the army. Under their leader Osceola, they won several battles.

Eventually, however, most were starved out and sent to Oklahoma. Osceola died in an army prison in South Carolina. A small group remained deep in the Everglades, where their descendants still live. They are proud that they have never signed a treaty of surrender with the United States government.

"The sick and feeble were carried in wagons . . . a great many ride on horseback, and multitudes go on foot—even aged females, apparently ready to drop into the grave, were traveling with heavy burdens attached to the back— on the sometimes frozen ground, and sometimes muddy streets, with no covering for their feet except what nature had given them . . . We learned from the inhabitants on the road where the Indians passed, they buried fourteen or fifteen at every stopping place."

—eyewitness account of the Trail of Tears, 1838

Above: One of the key battles of the Seminole War took place at Lake Okeechobee in Florida on Christmas Day, 1837. Future President Zachary Taylor was promoted to brigadier general following the battle.

*"You are gazing now
at old Tom Moore,
A relic of bygone days;
'Tis a bummer too
they call me now,
But what care have I
for praise?
It's oft to I repine,
For the days of old,
when we dug out
the gold
In the days of '49."*

—*from the song, "Days of Forty-Nine," a popular song about the California Gold Rush*

Below: This map shows the main westward trails of the 19th century, including the 2,400-mile-long Oregon Trail stretching from Missouri to Oregon's Willamette Valley. Wagon trains moved at a pace of about 15 miles a day, which meant the whole trip took six months to finish.

Westward Ho!

When James W. Marshall, a 36-year-old carpenter, was put in charge of building a new sawmill in the winter of 1848, he thought it would be a routine job. His employer, a Swiss-born immigrant named John Sutter, needed the wood for his ranch in the California foothills of the Sierra Nevada mountains.

On the morning of January 24, Marshall was inspecting the stream that would provide the water power for the mill. He noticed some bright yellow specks in the water. At first, he dismissed the stuff as iron pyrite, or "fool's gold," which breaks when hit with a hammer.

"I then tried it between two rocks and found that it could be beaten into a different shape but not broken." He stopped and turned to his work crew. "Boys, by God," he said, "I believe I have found a gold mine."

The Gold Rush

Sutter had mixed feelings about the find. Gold might make him rich, he knew, but it would put an end to the peaceful ranch life he loved. He tried to keep things quiet. On March 15, however, a San Francisco newspaper published the first news of the discovery. Within two weeks, the paper was forced to shut down

after the staff left for the gold mines. The final edition declared, "The whole country, from San Francisco to Los Angeles . . . resounds with the sordid [dirty] cry of Gold! Gold! Gold! while the field is left half-planted, the house half-built, and everything neglected but the manufacture of picks and shovels." The great California gold rush was on.

In 1849, over 80,000 men poured into California. Some came by ship around Cape Horn, South America. Others took steamers to Panama, crossed it on mules, and then sailed up the Pacific Coast. Most, however, made the five-month journey by wagon from across the country. Many used the Beckwourth pass through the Sierra Nevada mountains, a path into California first discovered by the African-American fur trapper James Beckwourth.

Miners, called Forty-Niners, came from Latin America, Europe, Australia, and China. In July 1850, sailors abandoned over 500 ships in San Francisco harbor. The city's population jumped from less than 500 to over 20,000 in a few months.

As for Sutter, his worries proved true. People stole his land without paying for it. He lost his ranch and moved to Pennsylvania. When he died in 1880, he was still begging Congress to pay him for the losses he suffered in the gold rush.

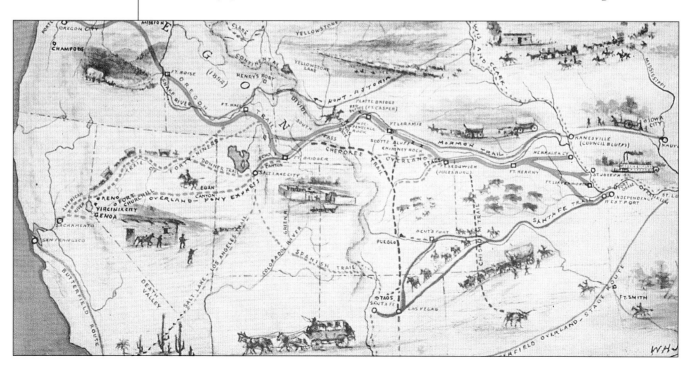

Sutter wasn't the only one to lose in the gold rush. Most miners came away with nothing. The Indians of California were massacred in a few years. And Californians of Mexican descent, known as Californios, lost their lands and were turned into second-class citizens.

For over three centuries, California and the Southwest had been ruled by Spain. In 1810, a priest named Miguel Hidalgo y Costilla led a revolt against Spanish rule. The uprising was put down but it started Mexico's war of independence from Spain. In September, 1821, Mexico won its independence, and in the process inherited all the land claimed by Spain in the Southwest, from Texas to the Pacific Ocean, including California. During the 1820s, American settlers began pouring into Texas territory. By 1830, the 30,000 American settlers outnumbered the original Mexicans seven to one.

The Americans came to plant cotton and they brought their slaves with them. Mexico, however, had outlawed slavery and, in 1830, it passed laws to prevent more from coming in. Texan protests quickly turned into rebellion. On March 2, 1836, General Sam Houston proclaimed Texas's independence. Mexico sent in the army.

The Alamo

At first, the war went Mexico's way. At the Alamo, a fort in San Antonio, 183 settlers, including Jim Bowie and Davy Crockett, tried to fight off a 10,000-man Mexican force under General Antonio López de Santa Anna. The Alamo defenders were all but wiped out.

News of the battle spread across America. Thousands of settlers were offered land in Texas if they fought for its independence. Recruits poured in and turned the tide of battle. On April 21, the settlers defeated the Mexican army for good at the Battle of San Jacinto. The Texans immediately applied for statehood, but were turned down by the American government. President Martin Van Buren did not want another slave state in the Union. He also worried that

Top: San Francisco, 1849

Above: This flag, designed by settler William Todd, features a red star and a grizzly bear as symbols for the Republic of California. California was an independent state only briefly before being admitted into the United States.

making Texas a state would lead to war with Mexico.

He was right. Americans had been moving to the Oregon Territory in the Northwest as well as to Texas in the Southwest. Pioneers had been crossing the continent on the Oregon Trail since 1836 and settling the Willamette Valley. In 1844, the Democrats elected James Polk, a Tennessee planter, as president. Polk wanted America to stretch from coast to coast. His campaign slogan was "54-40 or Fight," or in other words, "Oregon territory or Fight!" Fifty-Four-Forty was the latitude and longitude, or geographical location, of the northern border of the Oregon territory.

But Britain claimed the Oregon territory just as Mexico claimed Texas. The United States was risking war with both countries. Although both sides prepared for another war, Americans did not want to fight with Britain. In 1846, the two countries decided to split the difference and divide the territory along the 49th parallel.

The Mexican War

Mexico was not nearly as powerful as Britain. In 1845, Polk accepted Texas into the union. The Mexican government warned Washington that this would lead to war. Instead of compromising, Polk sent in troops. Mexico claimed the border between the two countries should be the Nueces River. The United States said it should be 150 miles south on the Rio Grande. A young army officer named Ulysses S. Grant, later head of the Union forces in the Civil War, said later, "We were sent to provoke [pick] a fight, but it was essential that Mexico should commence [start] it."

On April 25, 1846, the Mexicans did just that, crossing the Rio Grande and attacking American forces. On May 8, the Americans retaliated with a victory at the Battle of Palo Alto. Three days later, Polk asked Congress to declare war. "Mexico," he announced, "has passed the boundary of the United States, has invaded our territory, and shed American blood on American soil."

The war was an uneven match. The Americans attacked on three fronts. In June 1846, settlers in California declared independence for their Bear Flag Republic. An American force under a former fur trapper named James Fremont was sent in

Below: Joshua Abraham Norton

THE EMPEROR OF THE UNITED STATES

One of the most colorful characters among the citizens of gold rush-era San Francisco was an Englishman named Joshua Abraham Norton. Arriving in San Francisco with just $40,000 in 1849, Norton quickly turned his money into a fortune. Within a few years, he seemed ready to become one of the richest men in America. In 1853, however, he made the mistake of investing his money in the rice market. When the price of rice collapsed, he lost all of his money. He was forced to move into a small room at the Eureka Lodging House, with no possessions except a worn carpet, broken furniture, and a collection of portraits of foreign leaders.

In time, Norton began to lose his sense of reality. Declaring himself Emperor Norton I of the United States, he began appearing on the streets of San Francisco dressed in a gold-braided uniform and plumed hat. The people of San Francisco were fond of Norton I, and he became a familiar sight following the police in their duties, checking up on any new construction, and presiding over the growth of his fair city. Norton even went so far as to print up his own money, which shopkeepers, bartenders, and restaurant owners happily accepted.

When he died in 1880, several prominent citizens stepped forward offering to pay for the services. More than 10,000 people attended his funeral, mourning him as they would a true emperor.

Above: The Battle of Palo Alto, May 8, 1846

to defend the Californians. At the same time, Colonel Stephen Kearny led a force into territory that is today's New Mexico. He captured Santa Fe in August.

The main American force, under General Zachary Taylor, defeated the Mexican army on the Rio Grande and marched south. His forces captured the Mexican city of Monterrey, and an American naval force took the port of Tampico on the Gulf of Mexico. Still, the Mexicans refused to surrender. Although they counterattacked at Buena Vista, American forces held the line.

President Polk and Winfield Scott, commander of all American forces, decided to strike at the heart of Mexico. In March 1847, a large force of Marines landed at Veracruz. After six months of fighting, leaving 4,000 Mexican and 1,000 American soldiers dead, the Marines captured the capital of Mexico City.

The American victory was total. Mexico was forced to sign the treaty of Guadalupe-Hidalgo on February 2, 1848. Under the treaty, Mexico gave up the entire southwest from Texas to what is today the California-Oregon border. In exchange, America offered Mexico $15 million, the same figure it had paid France for the Louisiana Purchase 45 years before. Like Louisiana, the land was well worth the money. Ten years after gold was discovered in California, the world's largest deposit of silver was found in Nevada. Called the Comstock Lode, it started a silver rush of its own.

Still, the war with Mexico divided the country. Many northerners feared that slavery would spread to the new territory. If new slave states from this territory entered the union, then slaveholders would form a majority in Congress and thus take control of the federal government. The new territory would help slavery spread. Henry David Thoreau, a Massachusetts philosopher, refused to pay his taxes because he said they paid for an unjust war. He spent a night in jail for an action he called "civil disobedience."

Most Americans, however, were excited by the outcome of the war. They believed that the continent belonged to the white man, not the Indian or Mexican. A newspaper editor named John O'Sullivan wrote that it was America's "manifest [clear] destiny to overspread the continent allotted [given] by Providence for the free development of our yearly expanding millions." Manifest destiny became the slogan of a growing America.

Below: Following his capture, John Brown is led away by federal troops to be executed.

The Roots of Civil War

Many Americans called him a madman and a murderer. Others said he was a hero. His name was John Brown. Born in Connecticut in 1800, Brown, a white man, was raised to hate slavery.

In church, he learned that slavery was "a sin against God; a high-handed trespass on the rights of man; a great physical, political, and social evil, which ought to be immediately and universally abandoned."

Brown took these words seriously. A failure in business, he dedicated his life to the destruction of slavery. In 1856, he moved to Kansas where proslavery and antislavery settlers were fighting for control. The proslavery forces wanted Kansas to become a slave state, while the antislavery farmers wanted it to be a free state. The region became known as "Bloody Kansas." After proslavery forces attacked the antislavery town of Lawrence, Brown

decided to avenge the murders. It was time, he told his followers, "to fight fire with fire."

On the night of May 23, Brown, two of his sons, and several other men snuck into the houses of five slave owners on Pottawatomie Creek. They pulled the men from their beds, dragged them out of their homes, and murdered them in cold blood.

Brown avoided capture and soon turned up in the East. He met with leading antislavery businessmen in Boston and told them of his new plan. He needed money, men, and arms, he explained, to start a slave rebellion in the South. The men listened and gave him what he wanted.

On Sunday, October 16, 1859, Brown and 21 recruits, including five free blacks, launched their attack on Harpers Ferry, Virginia (now West Virginia). Brown planned to take the federal arsenal, or weapons storehouse, and arm the slaves.

The idea was doomed to failure. Few slaves lived in the mountainous region. Brown's force was soon surrounded by Virginia troops, led by Robert E. Lee, the future commander of Southern forces in the Civil War. Most of Brown's men were killed in the raid. A few got away. Brown was captured.

He was quickly put on trial. White southerners were angry, while most northerners agreed with Abraham Lincoln. "[Brown] agreed with us in thinking slavery wrong," Lincoln said. But that did not "excuse violence, bloodshed and treason."

In court, Brown's courage inspired many northerners, but it didn't stop him from being hanged. His body was shipped north. In Philadelphia, the corpse was removed from its slave-made coffin and put in one crafted by free blacks. He was buried on his upstate New York farm.

What led a man like Brown to take such action in the name of fighting slavery? The struggle over slavery was as old as America itself. In the first version of his Declaration of Independence, Thomas Jefferson, a slave owner himself, had said England forced slavery on America. Other slave owners at the Second Continental

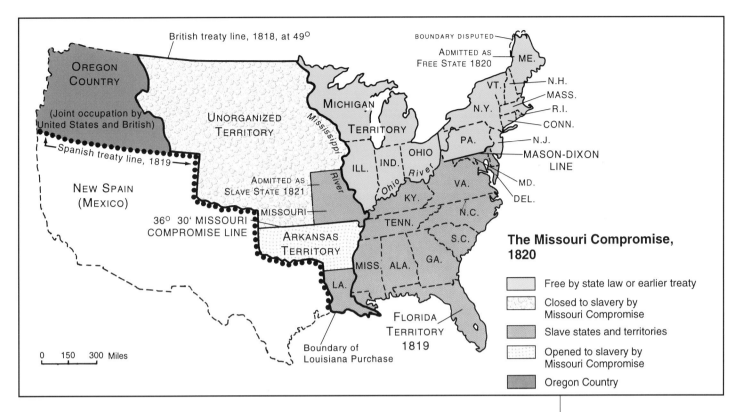

The Missouri Compromise, 1820

Free by state law or earlier treaty

Closed to slavery by Missouri Compromise

Slave states and territories

Opened to slavery by Missouri Compromise

Oregon Country

Congress made him take this paragraph out.

The Constitution legalized slavery. Northerners at the Constitutional Convention were opposed to slavery, but the southern delegates to the convention were almost all slaveholders. This division shaped the nation from the very start and shaped the Constitution as well. According to the Constitution, a state's number of delegates to the House of Representatives would be determined by the number of residents living in that state. Southern planters wanted slaves counted, and naturally, northerners did not. Southerners threatened to leave the convention unless they got their way. To prevent this from happening, northerners agreed to a compromise. To figure out how many representatives would go to Congress from each state, the government decided to count each slave as three fifths of a person. This gave southerners more power in Congress. They could vote down any antislavery laws that northerners tried to pass.

As pioneers moved west and territories became new states, the conflict over slavery rose time and time again. The government tried to keep a balance between slave and free states. In 1820,

proslave Missouri was admitted, along with free-state Maine, and a line was drawn to the Pacific Ocean. Slavery would be permitted below the line, but not above it. The Missouri Compromise, Congress hoped, would put the slavery issue to rest forever.

The Abolitionists

It didn't. On January 1, William Lloyd Garrison published the first issue of his newspaper, *The Liberator.* "I will be as harsh as truth," he declared, "and as uncompromising as justice. On this subject [ending slavery], I do not wish to think, or speak, or write with moderation . . . I will not excuse—I will not retreat a single inch—AND I WILL BE HEARD."

Garrison was an abolitionist. While most northerners wanted to keep slavery out of the West, abolitionists wanted to end it everywhere immediately. They published newspapers, petitioned Congress, and held meetings. Frederick

Above: The Missouri Compromise helped to keep the peace for four decades.

Below: Frederick Douglass, a former slave, published an abolitionist newspaper called The North Star.

Above: Harriet Tubman was sometimes called "the Black Moses" for helping to lead so many slaves to freedom on the Underground Railroad.

Below: Henry "Box" Brown arrives in Philadelphia.

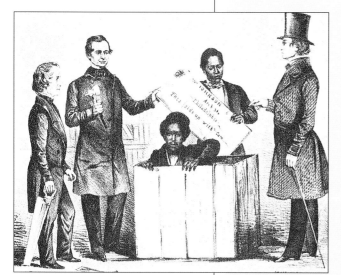

Douglass, a runaway slave from Maryland, became the most famous abolitionist. He published an antislavery newspaper called *The North Star* in Rochester, New York.

Abolitionists, both white northerners and free blacks, also helped slaves escape from the South. Their system was called the "underground railroad." Abolitionist homes, called "stations," had secret rooms for runaways to hide in. "Conductors" would lead the slaves from station to station until they could cross the border into free Canada. Harriet Tubman, a runaway slave from Maryland, was the most famous conductor. She risked her life and freedom 19 times to rescue her fellow Africans held in bondage.

There were never very many abolitionists, but they made a lot of noise. They kept the slavery issue alive when politicians and other Americans didn't want to talk about it. This often got them into trouble, even in the North. In 1835, mobs attacked Garrison in Boston. The police had to take him to jail for his own protection. Two years later, the antislavery editor Elijah Lovejoy was murdered in Illinois.

In 1832, South Carolina nearly seceded, or left, the Union. Led by Jackson's former vice president, Senator John C. Calhoun, South Carolinians did not believe they had to pay a tax they did not want. President Jackson threatened to send troops and South Carolina backed down. Most historians, however, believe that the real issue was slavery.

Nat Turner's Rebellion

By 1832, many southerners believed that northerners were abolitionists. Events

HENRY "BOX" BROWN IS DELIVERED TO FREEDOM

A slave living in Richmond, Virginia, Henry Brown longed for his freedom. As was true with almost all slaves, however, he had few connections, no money, and almost no chances to escape. He also knew that if he was caught trying to run away, he would be punished severely. But despite these odds against him, Brown had a plan. He decided he would mail himself to freedom.

With the help of a friend, Brown built a box 2'8" deep, 2' wide and 3' long. He then climbed inside and his friend nailed the box shut, writing "This Side Up" on the top. The box was mailed to the Anti-Slavery Office in Philadelphia, where abolitionists anxiously awaited its arrival.

The journey was a long one, and very rough. The box was jostled about, and at one point was even left upside down for several hours! Henry Brown was exhausted when he arrived in Philadelphia 26 hours later. The silence from inside the box caused the abolitionists to fear that he had died. They carefully placed his box on the floor and stood, their faces solemn, around it. Then, one stepped forward and knocked on the wooden lid.

"All right?" he asked, hesitantly. There was a silence before a voice spoke from inside. "All right, sir!" said Henry Brown, and a great cheer went up at the bravery of the slave who had mailed himself to freedom. Brown went on to join the abolitionist cause, and even toured Great Britain, giving lectures about his great escape.

THE FAMOUS JARRETT & PALMER LONDON COMPY CONSOLIDATED WITH SLAVINS ORIGINAL AMERICAN TROUPE

UNCLE TOM'S CABIN.

Above: Harriet Beecher Stowe's Uncle Tom's Cabin *helped to rally the north against slavery. This poster advertises a stage production of the book.*

had also helped to make them nervous. Southerners were very nervous in 1832. The year before, Nat Turner, a Virginia slave preacher had led the biggest slave uprising in American history. Before Turner and his followers were captured by the militia, they had killed over 60 slave owners and their families. Whites responded by killing hundreds of slaves in Virginia. Turner was also captured and hanged. The South passed a law banning abolitionist newspapers from the mail. Southern politicians also enacted the "gag rule" that made it almost impossible to discuss ending slavery in Congress.

Trouble over slavery was also brewing in the West. The Mexican War brought new territories into the Union. Would these become free or slave states? The arguments began even as the war was being fought. In August 1846, a young congressman from Pennsylvania named David Wilmot introduced his proviso, or amendment. It said that slavery would not be permitted in any territories taken from Mexico. Many southerners were outraged and the proviso was defeated in the Senate.

The California gold rush, two years later, pushed the issue back into the news. California wanted to come into the union as a free state, but there was no new slave state to keep the balance of power. For almost a year, Daniel Webster, the antislavery senator from New Hampshire, and the dying John Calhoun of South Carolina led Congress in a great debate. In 1850, Henry Clay, the senator from Kentucky, came up with a complicated bill. The Compromise of 1850 included four minor laws, and two important ones.

For the North, California would be admitted as the 16th free state, to the slave states' 15. In return, a law called the Fugitive Slave Act was passed. This made it a federal crime to help runaways. Abolitionists said this really legalized slavery in the whole United States. Many northerners agreed. When marshalls came to arrest conductors of the underground railroad, crowds now turned on the lawmen instead of the abolitionists.

One woman who saw the suffering of runaways was Harriet Beecher Stowe. The

Above: Henry Clay, one of the leading figures of 19th century American politics, speaks on the floor of the Senate. The Compromise of 1850 was Clay's idea.

Above: Sojourner Truth

SOJOURNER TRUTH (1797?-1883)

Born a slave in Ulster County, New York, Sojourner Truth remained in bondage until she was set free by the New York Emancipation Act of 1827. Little is known about her early childhood, except that she bore the name Isabella Van Wagener in 1843, when she changed her name to Sojourner Truth and became a traveling preacher. She spoke of many things, but mostly she spoke of the great need for equal rights, for the end of slavery, and for a woman's right to vote.

"Children, I talk to God and God talks to me!" she would announce over and over from podiums all across the northern states. She was a fiery speaker, capturing and mesmerizing her audiences with her powerful message. As very few women spoke publicly in those days, some people thought Sojourner Truth was surely a man! For what woman could express herself so well, and affect so many people's lives?

But Sojourner Truth didn't care what other people thought. She just cared about spreading her message of equal rights. When a Washington streetcar conductor pushed her against the wall and yelled for her to make room for a lady, she refused to be treated like a second-class citizen.

She just proudly lifted her head and said, "I'm a lady, too."

daughter of an antislavery preacher, Stowe published her book *Uncle Tom's Cabin* in 1852. It described the cruelties of slavery and became an instant bestseller in the North. Many Americans read the book and rallied to the antislavery cause. When President Abraham Lincoln later met Stowe in the White House during the Civil War, he said "so you're the little lady who started this great big war."

Two years after *Uncle Tom's Cabin* was published, a new problem arose. The territories of Kansas and Nebraska asked to join the union as new states. Above the Missouri Compromise line, they should have come in as free states. However, Stephen Douglas, a powerful senator from Illinois, pushed the Kansas-Nebraska Act through Congress in 1854. The law left the decision up to the settlers themselves.

Proslavery farmers poured in from Missouri. Abolitionists and antislavery men emigrated from New England. The two sides were soon fighting one another. The newspapers called the fighting "bleeding Kansas." They didn't know it yet, but Kansas was a small version of what would face the whole country in a few years.

In 1856, the bloodshed moved from Kansas to the floor of Congress. It started when Charles Sumner, an abolitionist senator from Massachusetts, insulted Senator Andrew Butler of South Carolina in a speech on the Senate floor. A few days later in the Senate chamber, Preston Brooks, a congressman, and Butler's nephew, beat Sumner with a cane until he was knocked out. Sumner did not return to the Senate for three years. His empty chair became a symbol for antislavery politicians.

The Kansas-Nebraska Act showed that Congress could not solve the slavery issue. In 1857, the Supreme Court tried to settle it. In a complicated case, a former slave named Dred Scott who lived in the North sued to keep his freedom. The court decided for his master. Chief Justice Roger Taney, a southerner, ruled that African-Americans were not citizens and "had no rights which any white man was

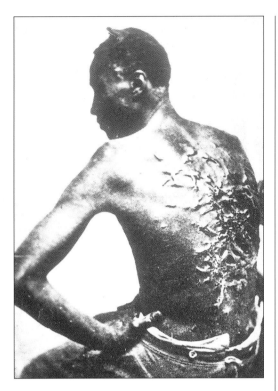

bound to respect." The ruling outraged northerners. They believed it legalized slavery everywhere.

The following year, the struggle over slavery shifted to Illinois. In the race for Senate, the Democrats nominated Stephen Douglas and the new antislavery Republicans put up a former congressman named Abraham Lincoln. The two debated each other up and down the state. Lincoln said slavery must be kept out of the West by federal law. Douglas disagreed. If people didn't want slavery there, they could settle it for themselves. Douglas won the election, but Lincoln made a national name for himself.

Two years later, the two men faced each other for the presidency, along with two other candidates. Lincoln's three opponents divided the proslavery vote. This gave Lincoln the edge, but he was elected with less than 2,000 votes in the entire South.

Lincoln was no abolitionist. He simply wanted to stop the spread of slavery. But that's not how southerners saw him. Lincoln's election, they said, was a total victory for the abolitionists. The federal government, no longer represented them. As in 1776, it was time, they said, to declare their independence.

"Those who deny freedom to others deserve it not for themselves."

—ABRAHAM LINCOLN, *during a speech in 1856*

Left: According to the law, slaves were property of their owners. This meant that masters and their white "overseers" were free to treat slaves any way they wanted. Although some slave owners treated their slaves kindly, that may have been because a badly injured slave was not able to work as hard. This photograph shows the badly scarred back of a slave who had been whipped repeatedly.

AMERICAN TIMELINE

1824 Crow Indians show Jebediah Smith the path through the Rockies, and in February he crosses the Continental Divide.

1825 Workmen complete the 363-mile-long Erie Canal, which connects the Atlantic Ocean with the Great Lakes.

1826 Thomas Jefferson and John Adams, both signers of the Declaration of Independence, die within hours of each other on the Fourth of July.

1830 Passing into law the Indian Removal Act, President Jackson gives Indians land west of the Mississippi, provided they leave the eastern states.

1831 Nat Turner, a Virginia slave, leads a revolt which results in the death of 50 whites and his own hanging.

1834 The first set of rules for "Rounders" or "Baseball" is published in the United States. These rules will gradually evolve into modern baseball.

Above: The Erie Canal, in 1836

WORLD TIMELINE

1824 In an effort to prevent revolution, Britain grants workers the right to organize unions and to strike for better conditions.
■ Antonio de Sucre of Peru defeats the Spanish at Ayacucho, making Peru an independent nation.

1825 Czar Nicholas orders his troops to open fire on an angry mob in St. Petersburg, Russia. Rebels in southern Russia are also quickly suppressed.
■ Egyptian ruler Mohammed Ali captures the Sudan.

1827 Austrian composer Ludwig van Beethoven dies. He was completely deaf at the time of his death.

1828 Uruguay, a new nation between Brazil and Argentina, is founded.

1830 Dutch troops withdraw from Belgium, granting the Belgians their independence.
■ Threatened by a wave of the deadly disease cholera, many wealthy Europeans flee their cities in fear.

1833 Dismayed by terrible working conditions, British Parliament passes a law making it illegal for children under 13 to work more than 9 hours a day.

■ Isabella ascends to the throne of Spain, sparking an outbreak of civil war.

1834 With the passage of the Emancipation Act, all slaves in the British colonies are freed.

1837 French-Canadian Louis-Joseph Papineau and Scotsman William Lyon Mackenzie organize uprisings against the British government in Canada.

1839 Using silver iodide on a copper plate, the French government demonstrates Louis Daguerre's invention of the photograph.

1835 Ringing to commemorate the death of Chief Justice John Marshall, the Liberty Bell in Philadelphia cracks and is silenced forever.
■ Revolutionaries declare the Republic of Texas independent from Mexico. Sam Houston is called upon to lead the Texan army into battle.

1836 After a 12-day siege, Mexican general Santa Anna gives the battle cry as his troops storm the Alamo. Although the Texan defenders fight bravely, not one survives the attack.

1837 The newly independent Republic of Texas applies to the U.S. government for admission into the Union. Their application is denied.
■ Michigan enters the Union as the 26th state.

1838 Although the Supreme Court ruled it unconstitutional, the U.S. Army rounds up the Cherokee and forces them to march from Georgia to Indian Territory west of the Mississippi. Many die of starvation, disease, and exhaustion in what has become known as the "Trail of Tears."

1841 Just 43 days after taking office, President William Henry Harrison dies from pneumonia. He fell sick after speaking for two hours at his inauguration in the cold without an overcoat or hat.
■ France breaks ties with the Republic of Texas because of its refusal to punish a man who killed some pigs belonging to a French official.

1843 Dorothea Dix issues a protest against the treatment of the insane. Asylums, she says, are like "cages, closets, cellars, stalls, and pens."

1845 Ex-slave Frederick Douglass, fearing recapture, moves to England where he hopes to gain support for the freeing of American slaves.
■ The Republic of Texas is accepted into the Union.

1846 Mexican troops attack Americans south of the Nueces River in Texas. American President James Polk declares war.
■ The United States acquires Oregon Territory south of the 49th parallel from Britain.

Above: In 1839, the Boers and Zulus went to war in South Africa. This photograph shows Zulu warriors in 1879.

■ Boers and Zulus clash at South Africa's Blood River, leaving 3,000 Zulus dead.

1840 After three years of rebellion, Canadians are awarded the right to self-government.
■ War is declared between China and Britain as a result of numerous clashes over the British right to trade opium in the Chinese nation.

1841 Afghan ruler Shah Shuja al-Mulk is assassinated.

1842 The Treaty of Nanjing ends the Opium War. China is forced to open her ports to the British.

AMERICAN TIMELINE

1847 The capture of Mexico City ends the war with Mexico.

■ Maria Mitchell is awarded a gold medal for her discovery of a new comet.

■ After spending two years living in a hut at Walden Pond near Concord, Massachusetts, writer Henry David Thoreau leaves the woods. *Walden*, an account of his experiences, is published in 1854.

1848 In the Treaty of Guadalupe-Hidalgo, Mexico gives Texas, New Mexico, California, and other parts of the Southwest to the United States.

1849 After President Polk announces the discovery of gold in California, thousands of prospectors begin the move west in the hopes of getting rich quick.

1850 Henry Clay develops the Compromise of 1850, momentarily stalling the threat of civil war.

■ In a rally for women's rights, a thousand people vote to form a political and civil organization designed to promote the cause.

1852 Harriet Beecher Stowe publishes her antislavery book, *Uncle Tom's Cabin*, and sells a record-breaking 300,000 in the first year.

1853 The first potato chips are made in an exclusive resort in Saratoga, New York.

1854 The Kansas-Nebraska Act, which allows the states to choose whether they will be free soil or slave states, sparks a series of bloody conflicts.

1855 New York passes prohibition laws, making it illegal to make or sell alcohol within the state.

Right: Henry David Thoreau

WORLD TIMELINE

1844 Alexandre Dumas publishes *The Three Musketeers* and *The Count of Monte Cristo*.

1845 A continuing potato famine in Ireland causes a huge migration of poor farmers to America.

1846 With the help of French and British astronomers, German J. G. Galle discovers the planet Neptune.

Left: In 1845, Ireland underwent a great famine, which drove thousands to leave their home country for America. This newspaper recounted the story.

1848 Exiled German workers Karl Marx and Friedrich Engels join together to write a pamphlet calling for the revolution of the workers of the world, launching revolts and political reformation across Europe.

1851 In New South Wales, gold is discovered, beginning an Australian gold rush.

■ Backed by the populace, Louis Napoleon seizes power of the French government.

1856 Abolitionist John Brown is accused of the murders of five proslavery settlers in the Kansas Territory. Two weeks later, Representative Preston Brooks of South Carolina severely beats Massachusetts Senator Charles Sumner in the Senate chamber after the abolitionist senator insulted Brooks' uncle, Senator Andrew Butler, in a speech.

1857 In the Dred Scott case, the Supreme Court rules that people of African descent born as slaves are not citizens, and are therefore not protected by the Constitution.

1858 Minnesota joins the Union as the 32nd state.

1859 The ninth annual National Women's Rights convention, led by Susan B. Anthony, is held in New York City.

■ John Brown leads a group of slaves in an attack on Harpers Ferry. The revolt is unsuccessful, and Brown is executed.

1860 Abraham Lincoln is elected president.

■ Political leaders in Charleston vote to secede from the Union, declaring their relationship with the United States "hereby dissolved."

Above: A decade after the California gold rush of 1849, gold and silver were found at Cripple Creek, Colorado, near Pikes Peak.

Above: Karl Marx, founder of communism

1852 Frenchman Henri Giffard makes his first appearance in his invention, a steam-powered balloon, over the city of Paris.

1853 Ottoman warships, resting in the Black Harbor of Istanbul, are attacked and destroyed by the Russian fleet.

1854 Allying themselves with the Turks, Britain and France declare war on Russia, marking the beginning of the Crimean War.

1855 An enormous earthquake and resulting fires destroy Tokyo.

1856 In a Paris peace conference, the nations of Europe sign a treaty ending the Crimean War.

1857 In a revolt against colonialism, Indian soldiers capture Delhi and slaughter British residents.

1859 Emperor of France, Napoleon III, declares war on Austria.

IV. DIVIDED AND REUNITED

Above: The 54th Massachusetts regiment reaches the edge of Fort Wagner, yards from Confederate fire. Sergeant William Carney, who grabbed the regiment's flag as the flag bearer fell dead, became the first of 16 black Civil War soldiers to win the Medal of Honor.

B Y 1820, following the passage of the Missouri Compromise that year, Thomas Jefferson was struck with fear. "This momentous question, like a [fire alarm] in the night," he wrote, "awakened me and filled me with terror." Jefferson knew this compromise could not heal the growing wound made by slavery. Forty more years and a string of new compromises only delayed the first cannon fire instead of preventing it. In 1861, a war unlike any other in history was unleashed. More than 600,000 were killed.

In the years right after the war, many new laws were written to give African-Americans rights that had been denied for so long. But the anger still lingered. Some northerners, inspired by revenge and greed, prevented the nation from truly coming back together. And some southerners, bitter in defeat and fearful of what freedom for slaves would mean for them, ignored the new laws and used violence and terror to win back what they had lost. One thing had changed forever, though. When writing about the country before the war, people used the phrase, "The United States *are* . . . " After the war, that phrase became, "The United States *is* . . . "

The Civil War

In June 1861, a 19-year-old boy named Elisha Hunt Rhodes said good-bye to his family in Pawtuxet, Rhode Island. He was leaving to fight for his country as a soldier in the Union Army.

When Rhodes came home in the summer of 1865, he returned as the commander of a regiment. He had fought in every major eastern battle in the war. And for four long and terrible years, he had kept a diary. "On reaching the clearing . . . we were saluted with a volley of musketry [round of rifle fire]," he wrote after the first battle of Bull Run in 1861. "I remember that my first sensation was one of astonishment at the whir of the bullets."

Two years later at Gettysburg, the greatest battle of the war, little surprised him. "Soon the rebel yell was heard, and the rebel General Pickett made a charge," he wrote. "Our lines of Infantry . . . rose up and poured in a terrible fire."

Although Elisha Rhodes grew used to the sound of battle, he never got used to the horrible costs of war. "The firing gradually died away, and but for an occasional shot all was still," he wrote of Gettysburg. "But what a scene it was. Oh, the dead and dying on this bloody field."

The Civil War was the bloodiest war in American history. By the time the Confederacy surrendered in the spring of 1865, over 600,000 soldiers on both sides were dead. That's almost as many as in all other American wars put together. The war left millions more wounded and much of the South in ruins. What started this war? Why was it so bloody?

Slavery Divides the Nation

Since the beginning of the republic, the North and South had disagreed about many things. Most especially, the two regions had disagreed about slavery. Long before the start of the war, slavery had been outlawed in the North, first in New England, and eventually, in the Middle Colonies.

"All we ask is to be left alone."

—JEFFERSON DAVIS, *President, Confederate States of America*

Below: This map shows a divided nation in 1861— the slave states of the Confederacy and the free states of the Union with the dates in which slavery was outlawed. Missouri, Kentucky, Maryland, and Delaware were all slave states, but each stayed in the Union.

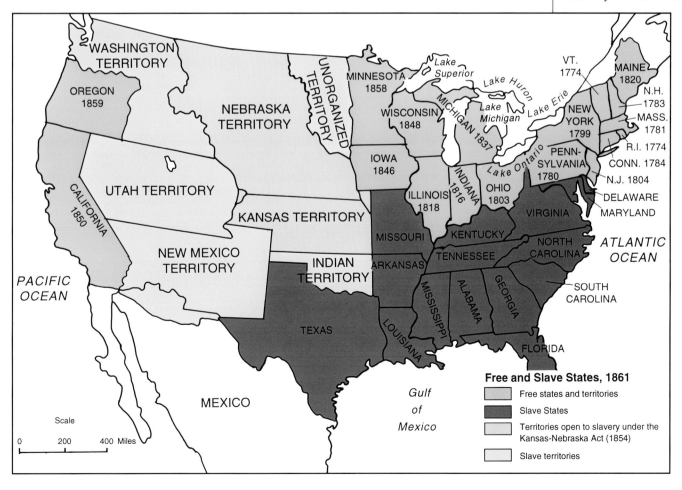

Free and Slave States, 1861
- Free states and territories
- Slave States
- Territories open to slavery under the Kansas-Nebraska Act (1854)
- Slave territories

"A house divided cannot stand. I believe this government cannot endure, permanently, half slave and half free. I do not expect the union will be dissolved; I do not expect the house to fall; but I do expect it will cease to be divided. It will become all one thing or the other."

—ABRAHAM LINCOLN, 1858

Although abolitionists had long been active in the North, there were more practical reasons that slavery was abandoned in the North. For one, the growing season was short. Besides, northern crops like wheat and corn did not need a lot of labor, except at harvest time. It made no sense to provide for slaves year-round and then only use them for a short time.

While conditions in the North helped end slavery there, the southern climate did not pose any such problems. The industrial revolution created an ever-growing appetite for resources like cotton. By 1860, cotton exports were worth more than all other American exports put together. The slave population of the South stood at nearly 4 million, out of a total southern population of 13 million.

Slaves were expensive, especially after importing slaves directly from Africa was outlawed in 1808. For this reason, only about 10 percent of white southerners actually owned slaves. But almost every white southerner supported slavery. Some said it was a "necessary evil." Africans, they argued, could not take care of themselves on their own. They needed whites to provide them with food, clothing, and shelter. Others believed slavery was a "positive good." It offered a way, they said, for black people to become civilized and become Christians.

No matter how white Americans felt about slavery, it was clear that slavery had to keep growing to survive. Cotton, tobacco, and other southern products drained the soil. Growers always needed fresh new lands.

Even poor southerners without much land had reasons to hope for the spread of slavery. Only if slavery spread would they have opportunities to obtain and

ABRAHAM LINCOLN (1809–1865)

A master of diplomacy and a great humanitarian, Abraham Lincoln will always be remembered as one of the greatest presidents this country has ever known. But he was also a family man.

Lincoln and his wife, Mary, had four sons: Robert, Edward, William (Willie), and Thomas (Tad). "His children did much as they pleased . . ." Lincoln's friend, William Herndon, once said. "He restrained them in nothing." Indeed, Tad, the youngest, was often seen playing loudly in the halls of the White House, pestering his father's guests, and even bringing goats in to dirty the carpets! But Abraham Lincoln did not protest. He loved his boys, and frequently took them with him on his trips about town. When asked why he continued to carry the youngest in his arms after the child got big, Lincoln replied "don't you think his little feet get tired?"

Then, in February of 1862, tragedy struck. Willie came down with a mysterious fever. Lincoln spent many hours at his son's bedside, stroking his hair, reading him stories, and bathing his fevered forehead. Yet all his efforts were in vain. On February 20th, Willie died.

Gaunt and hollow-eyed, Lincoln joined the funeral procession to Oak Hill Cemetery, where he bid a last good-bye to his son. Then, he buried his grief in the work of the presidency. The loss of his son and the sons of so many others on the nation's battlefields caused Lincoln to declare that the only justification for such death and sorrow could be the absolute end of slavery. It was an end that he pursued with a grim determination.

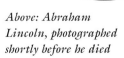

Above: Abraham Lincoln, photographed shortly before he died

farm large tracts of new inexpensive land. Planters realized, too, that if poor whites couldn't get their own lands out west and buy their own slaves, they might cause trouble back home in the South. And finally, without a growing number of slave states, which would allow the black population to spread out over wider territory, many feared that blacks might one day outnumber whites in the South, making escapes and rebellions impossible to stop.

The only place where slavery could grow was in the West. The northerners, however, also wanted those lands. If slavery spread west, slave plantations would dominate the land, leaving no room for the small farms of poor northern farmers.

Both sides believed that free and slave labor could never prosper in the same place. Southerners believed that anti-slavery people would allow slaves to escape. Northerners felt that free farmers could not compete economically with slaves.

Even so, for 40 years, the two sides had tried to resolve their differences in peace. With the Missouri Compromise in 1820, they had drawn a line to the Pacific Ocean, allowing slavery to the south, but banning it to the north. They had also tried to strike a balance in Washington. But by the mid-19th century, the North had more people, and therefore controlled the House of Representatives. After California came into the Union as a free state, antislavery states controlled the Senate as well.

By the mid-1850s, the only branches of government controlled by the South were the presidency and the Supreme Court. With the election of Illinois's Abraham Lincoln, the South lost the presidency. And since the president selected the judges, it was bound to lose the court, too. White southerners were both frightened and angry. Just six weeks after the election, a group of radical southerners called the "fire-eaters" decided they had had enough. It was time to secede from, or leave, the Union.

The Confederacy Is Born

On December 20, 1860, South Carolina became the first state to secede. At a state convention, delegates voted to dissolve "the union now subsisting between South Carolina and other states." Within six weeks of their secession, South Carolina was joined by the other states of the Deep South: Florida, Mississippi, Alabama, Georgia, Louisiana, and Texas.

In early February, even before Lincoln could take office as U.S. President, representatives from these states met in Montgomery, Alabama. They adopted a temporary constitution. They elected a former senator from Mississippi named Jefferson Davis as president of their new nation, which they called the Confederate States of America, or the Confederacy, for short.

Meanwhile, the upper South (Arkansas, North Carolina, Tennessee, Virginia) and border states (Delaware, Kentucky, Maryland, and Missouri) were divided. In January, 1861, Virginia and Tennessee voted not to secede but stated that they would resist a Union invasion of the Deep South. In Congress, Kentucky Senator John Crittendon tried a last compromise. His plan would have redrawn the line between slavery and freedom in the West. It was rejected by Lincoln and other Republicans. They did not want to compromise on slavery in the West. They also believed secession was illegal and unconstitutional.

Meanwhile, the new Confederate states in the Deep South faced some big problems. If their new nation was going to be truly independent, it had to capture the Union forts on its territory. By April, all Union forts had surrendered without fighting, except for one—Fort Sumter, in Charleston, South Carolina's harbor.

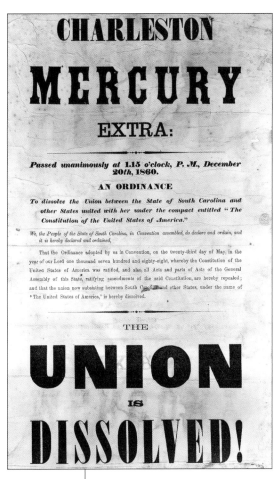

Above: On December 20, 1860, The Charleston Mercury *announced South Carolina's secession with this full-page headline.*

Below: Confederate cannons pound Fort Sumter on the morning of April 12, 1861.

The War Begins

Fort Sumter, built on a small island, was commanded by Major Robert Anderson. In early April, Anderson alerted the War Department in Washington that he was running out of supplies. President Lincoln faced a tough decision. If he sent supplies, the South would try to stop him. If fighting broke out, the upper South and even the border states might also secede. Lincoln's generals told him that a united South would be almost impossible to defeat militarily. Lincoln also worried that northerners might not support a war. If there was to be a war, the new president wanted the South to take the blame for starting it.

On the other hand, Lincoln could not let the last fort in the South surrender without a fight. Lincoln came up with a clever plan. He told the South he was resupplying the fort with food, but not ammunition. He felt that even anti-war Northerners would accept sending food to hungry soldiers. And with enough food, the fort would not have to surrender.

On April 8, the Confederates learned of Lincoln's plan. President Davis ordered General P. G. T. Beauregard to take Fort Sumter by force. On April 12, 1861, Beauregard's troops opened fire from cannons on the mainland. Two days later, Anderson was forced to surrender Fort Sumter to Confederate forces. Although the first battle of the Civil War left no one dead, that kind of luck would not last long.

Within a week of the battle, Arkansas, North Carolina, and Tennessee had voted to leave the Union. On the other hand, Virginia, the most populated southern state, was divided. Its western half was mountainous, with few slaves. Most people there were pro-Union. When Virginia seceded from the Union, western Virginians seceded from Virginia. Two years later, West Virginia was admitted to the Union as the 35th state.

Lincoln sent troops into the border states of Maryland and Missouri to keep them in the Union. The situation in Kentucky was trickier. The state was evenly divided between pro-secession and pro-Union citizens. Lincoln promised Kentuckians that he was not fighting the war to end slavery, but to preserve the Union. Kentucky slaveholders agreed not to push the state government to secede.

Both North and South thought their side would win the war quickly. Most of the best trained military officers were Southerners and the region had a long tradition of soldiering. Southerners also knew that they only had to defend their region against attack, a much easier thing to do than capture territory.

Finally, the Southern leaders knew they had "King Cotton" on their side. While the South had few weapons factories, its leaders believed they could buy what they needed with money from cotton sales. And since Britain was one of

their biggest customers, the Confederates also thought Britain would side with them.

On the other hand, the North had the numbers on its side. It had more farms, more factories, and more railroads. And most importantly, the North had far more people.

From Bull Run to Antietam

Heading into the war, people on both sides looked forward to quick and easy victories. When Lincoln and Davis called for volunteers, thousands of young men jumped at the chance to come to the aid of their region. At Manassas, Virginia, or Bull Run, those new recruits would get their first taste of war.

The Confederates had moved their capital from Montgomery, Alabama, to Richmond, Virginia, just 100 miles from Washington. Lincoln hoped capturing the Confederate capital would end the war quickly. In July, 1861, he sent 30,000 troops into Virginia. With blankets and picnic baskets in tow, a crowd of politicians and their families followed, expecting to watch a quick defeat of the rebels.

The spectators were in for a shock. The Confederates charged the Union troops and sent them running back

Above: During the war, supplies were carried to the front lines in long wagon trains. Here, a chain of Confederate supply wagons arrives at Manassas, where the Battle of Bull Run marked the first rebel victory.

Below: General George McClellan, commander of the Union's Army of the Potomac, was loved by his men, but hated by Lincoln. Lincoln eventually fired him for being too slow to move his troops into battle.

Above: Many Union soldiers were actually recent immigrants, less interested in freeing slaves than in getting paid for their services. The Third Irish regiment saw early action at the First Battle of Bull Run.

to Washington, with the picnickers a few steps behind. It was a humiliation for the Union. Clearly, the war would not be as quick and easy as everyone thought.

After the loss, Lincoln appointed a new general to command his troops. George McClellan was a great organizer. He spent the winter of 1861-62 training and equipping the 150,000-man Army of the Potomac in Washington. In the spring, he transported 100,000 of them up the James River toward Richmond. Before he could attack, however, a Confederate army under Thomas "Stonewall" Jackson marched up the Shenandoah Valley in Virginia toward Washington. Lincoln had to recall 30,000 of McClellan's men to defend the capital.

When McClellan did attack on June 26, beginning a week of heavy fighting on the Virginia Peninsula known as the Battle of Seven Days, the Confederates held firm. That summer, the new Confederate commander, Robert E. Lee, also tried a quick end to the war. In August, 1862, he marched 50,000 men into Maryland. His men met McClellan's Union troops near the small town of Antietam on September 17, 1862. In the bloodiest single day in American military history, over 8,000 men were killed. Lee was forced to retreat.

A Naval War

Capturing capitals was only one part of the war. The two sides had other strategies as well. The North's overall plan was simple. First, they would use the navy to blockade the South, and prevent imports and exports. Second, they would capture control of the Mississippi River and divide the Confederacy. The South's plan was even simpler: to stop them.

CLARA BARTON (1821-1912)

Clara Barton was born in Oxford, Massachusetts, the youngest of five children. At the age of 15 she became a teacher, and soon afterward started a school in New Jersey. The school grew so quickly that authorities didn't feel it was proper for a woman to run it, and she was forced to resign.

Then, in 1861, Barton received a new calling. After the first battle of Bull Run, she witnessed the terrible conditions the wounded were forced to endure. Infection and disease spread quickly throughout field surgeries and hospitals, as few surgeons sterilized their equipment, rooms were not kept clean, and the same dressings were used repeatedly. The wounded were feverish and dying from disease. There were few nurses to ease their pain. Barton quickly organized a network of contributors to purchase food and supplies. She gained permission to pass through battle lines tending the wounded. Her post, she said, was "the open field between the bullet and the hospital." Through her hard work, the number of deaths from disease and infection greatly decreased.

As a military nurse, Clara Barton came to realize the importance of providing aide to the wounded. It was she who founded the American Red Cross, and who convinced more than a dozen nations to recognize the neutrality of the Red Cross flag.

Above: Clara Barton, who founded the American Red Cross after serving as a nurse

By 1862, the Union warships had blocked access to the Confederate coast and captured the Sea Islands of South Carolina and Georgia. To get supplies in and cotton out, the South built smaller and faster ships that tried to sneak through the blockade. They also purchased "rams," iron-clad ships, from Britain. One of these vessels, the *Alabama*, sank more than 100 Union ships before the war was over.

The Confederacy and the Union also built their own ironclads. The Confederacy's was named the *Merrimack* and the Union's was called the *Monitor*. On March 9, off Fort Monroe, Virginia, the *Monitor* and *Merrimack* fought each other to a draw in the first battle of iron-clads in world history.

A New Kind of War

The use of iron-clad ships was not the only military first of the Civil War. The war was also the first time that either railroads or telegraph communications were used. The telegraph allowed a commander to gather information from battlefields across the country, and railroads made it easier to move weapons and troops from place to place.

The Civil War was also the first in which hot air balloons were used to spy behind enemy lines. And it was the first war to be heavily photographed. People back home could now see the horrors of war in local exhibits.

For the average soldier, however, the most important, and deadly, invention was something much simpler: the grooved barrel musket. The grooved barrel made bullets spin as they fired. Like a pitched baseball, a spinning bullet goes straighter and farther. Before the Civil War, the best guns could fire straight for about 100 yards. The grooved barrel made them accurate to 300.

It took some time for the generals on both sides to realize this. They would send men into battles in rows, as they had during the Revolution and Mexican War. But faced with guns with grooved barrels, soldiers would be mowed down

like grass. This was one reason why there were so many killed at places like Antietam and the place that became known as "Shiloh, bloody Shiloh."

The War in the West

The site of a tiny church in northern Mississippi, Shiloh became the site of the deadliest battle in the western part of the Civil War. And it was a battle that started by accident. In April, 1862, a young Union general named Ulysses S. Grant was moving his army toward the Mississippi River as part of the plan to split the South.

Grant's forces ran into a large Confederate army that wasn't supposed to be there. After two days of fighting, Grant won the battle, but the cost was enormous. In his memoirs, Grant later wrote that the large battlefield was "so covered with dead that it would have been possible to walk over the clearing in any direction, stepping on dead bodies, without a foot touching the ground."

The same month that Grant won

Above: The bodies of dead Confederate soldiers lie piled together along "Bloody Lane," a sunken farm road where the men had gone for safety during the Battle of Antietam.

Below: Shown is an example of a typical Union infantry uniform.

"It is rather for us to be here dedicated to the great task remaining before us—that from these honored dead we take increased devotion to that cause for which they gave the last full measure of their devotion—that we here highly resolve that these dead shall not have died in vain—that this nation, under God, shall have a new birth of freedom—and that government of the people, by the people, for the people shall not perish from the earth."

—from ABRAHAM LINCOLN's *Gettysburg address, 1863*

Above right: This illustration, created shortly after the Emancipation Proclamation was issued, celebrates Lincoln as the man who freed the slaves.

Above: In order to pay for the war, the Confederacy needed money. Early in the war, the government issued loans, and promised to pay them back with interest. By 1862, most Southerners had to settle for paper money like the bill shown here. Even before the war's end, however, Confederate money had become almost worthless.

Shiloh, Commander David Farragut of the Union Navy captured New Orleans. With these victories, the Union's control of the Mississippi River was half-complete. Encouraged by these successes, President Lincoln decided to make his boldest move of the war.

The Emancipation Proclamation

Although he felt slavery was immoral, Lincoln hoped to win the South back through diplomacy. Ending slavery, he knew, would make this impossible. Events soon forced him to change his mind. During the summer of 1862, abolitionists in Congress passed the Confiscation Act, which declared all slaves escaping from Confederate territo-

ries "contraband," the word for enemy property captured in war.

As the war dragged on, many northerners began to ask what would be the point of all the fighting if the South was allowed to keep slavery—the very cause of the war in the first place. Lincoln knew that if he did not lead the move toward emancipation, the more radical Congress would do it themselves. On September 22, 1862, he issued one of the most important acts in American history, the Emancipation Proclamation. The Proclamation declared that all slaves in the 10 states that had seceded were now free.

The Proclamation changed everything. The Civil War was no longer a war to save the Union only. It was now a war to end slavery—at least in the Confederacy. The Proclamation did not free the 440,000 slaves in the border states that had remained in the Union. Even so, the Proclamation had a very important effect. Nations around the world, many of which had favored the South, came over to the North's side. Great Britain stopped supplying ships to the Confederacy as it had been doing since the start of the war.

Yet the war was far from over. Not until July, 1863, would the tide turn the North's way on the battlefield. Since May, the Union army had surrounded the town of Vicksburg, Mississippi, and bombed it with artillery. Vicksburg's citizens were forced to move into caves to protect themselves. Finally, on July 4, with food and water running out, they surrendered. The capture of Vicksburg meant the Union now controlled the entire Mississippi River. Arkansas, Louisiana, and Texas were cut off from the rest of the Confederacy.

The Battle of Gettysburg

Meanwhile, in the East, Lee decided to march north into Union territory to force Lincoln to ask for peace. He got as far as the small town of Gettysburg, Pennsylvania. There he met up with a huge Union force. For three days, the Confederate and Union armies fought a

desperate battle. On July 5, Lee was forced to retreat to Virginia.

Later that year, Lincoln would visit the bloodied battlefield to dedicate the cemetery to the Union soldiers that had died there. In his Gettysburg Address, Lincoln said that the fallen had made the "supreme sacrifice" so that a nation "of the people, by the people, and for the people shall not perish from the earth."

Not all eligible men, however, proved willing to make such a sacrifice. By 1863, both the North and the South, desperate for new soldiers, began to draft them, or force them into the army. Not all had to serve, however. Planters with more than 20 slaves were excused. In response, many poor white Southerners complained, "It's a rich man's war, but a poor man's fight."

The Draft Riots

In the North, men could buy their way out of the draft for $300, about a year's wages for a working man. This angered many working people in New York City. In early July, they rioted, and soldiers who had barely finished fighting in Gettysburg were rushed to the city. The rioters burned down the draft office. Next

they marched on the fancy mansions on Fifth Avenue, but police stopped them. Last, they turned their anger on the city's African-Americans. Dozens of blacks were murdered and the city's Colored Orphan's Asylum was burned down. Over 100 people died before soldiers from Gettysburg could bring peace to the city.

Many poor immigrants and working people in New York blamed blacks for the war. They feared that the end of slavery would bring blacks to the North to take white working people's jobs away. In fact, many African-American men were more than ready to fight for their freedom and to save the Union. Lincoln and many in government, however, were not ready to let them. Some didn't think blacks were brave enough to be soldiers. Others didn't like the idea of giving black men guns and telling them to kill white people, even if the white people were the enemy.

Above: Union and Confederate forces clash at Gettysburg, July 3, 1863. The Union victory at Gettysburg was to be the turning point of the war.

Below: General George Pickett was the commander of one of the divisions involved in the attack known as Pickett's Charge. On the third day of the battle of Gettysburg, Confederate troops failed to break through Union lines by charging directly at the enemy.

"If the people [of Georgia] raise a howl against my barbarity and cruelty, I will answer that war is war, and not popularity-seeking."

—GENERAL WILLIAM TECUMSEH SHERMAN, during his March to the Sea

When the first black soldiers were recruited in early 1863—first, free blacks from the North, then former slaves from the South—they were not allowed to fight. Most were kept in training camps far away from the battlefield or used as cooks and workers. They were paid less than white soldiers. By early 1864, the black soldiers had had enough. They began to protest. They even went on strike.

After several months, the army gave in. The black soldiers' pay was raised and, by the middle of 1864, they were sent into battle. By the end of the war, over 200,000 soldiers, or ten percent of the Union army, were black. Lincoln said that without African-American soldiers "we [the Union] would be compelled to abandon the war in three weeks."

Along with the help from black soldiers, the Union was also aided by new leadership. In March 1864, Lincoln asked Ulysses Grant, the hero of Shiloh and Vicksburg, to command all Union armies. Grant followed a simple plan. He would use the North's greater power and numbers to wear the South down.

Sherman's March

Grant sent an army under William Tecumseh Sherman south into Georgia. Sherman's forces captured Atlanta during the summer of 1864 and then made their famous "March to the Sea." Their job was to destroy everything in their path, thus making it impossible for the South to

Below: Belle Boyd, Confederate spy

BELLE BOYD (1844-1900)

Some called Belle Boyd a colorful, eccentric woman, more interested in public attention than the Confederate cause. She loved the press and spent hours preparing to be interviewed and photographed.

Her boastful tales of spying escapades were told repeatedly, and often with more spirit than caution. Most spies avoided the limelight, as their very safety depended on remaining anonymous.

Nevertheless, Belle Boyd was able to provide useful Union intelligence to more than one Confederate general. In 1861, she became a courier for P. G. T. Beauregard and Stonewall Jackson, smuggling medicine and messages through Union lines. Sometimes she would do her work quietly, sneaking through the shadows past the enemy, but other times she threw caution to the wind. Once she even dashed through open fields waving her bonnet to bring a message to the Rebels!

In 1862, Belle Boyd once again braved the Union lines to bring information about enemy movements in the Shenandoah Valley to Stonewall Jackson. This time, the secrets she revealed caused Jackson to move, and move quickly. Distracting Union troops with cavalry, he marched his infantry across Massanutten Mountain and joined with Richard Ewell's forces. Then, he struck the Union troops in the rear, capturing almost 1,000 men. This victory forced the Union to retreat northward, and eventually to leave the Shenandoah Valley altogether.

The Battle of Front Royal caused the press to go wild, calling Belle Boyd the "Siren of the Shenandoah," and "the Rebel Joan of Arc." Her fame as a spy became so great that she was arrested six times and, in 1864, was deported to Canada.

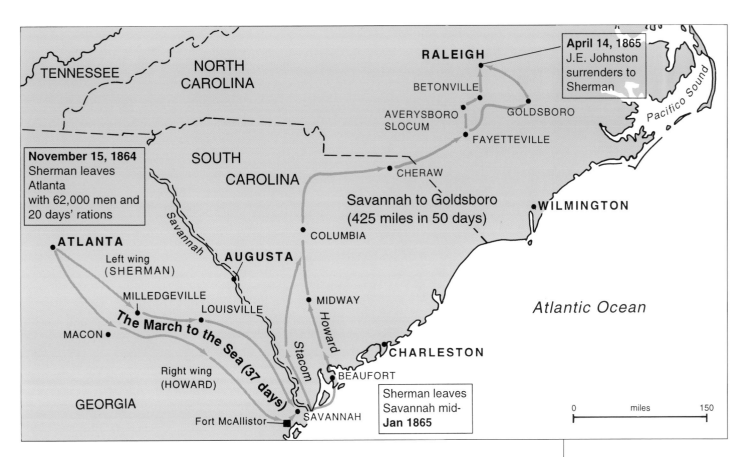

November 15, 1864
Sherman leaves
Atlanta
with 62,000 men and
20 days' rations

April 14, 1865
J.E. Johnston
surrenders to
Sherman

Savannah to Goldsboro
(425 miles in 50 days)

Sherman leaves
Savannah mid-
Jan 1865

*Above: During the final
stages of the war, the Union
Army attacked the
Confederacy in two places.
General William Tecumseh
Sherman led his men into
Georgia, where they cap-
tured and then burned the
city of Atlanta.*

*Continuing the attack,
they charged through
Savannah and then up
the Atlantic coast, leaving
a trail of destruction.*

*Left: Meanwhile, further
north, General Philip
Sheridan and his men swept
through the Shenandoah
Valley of Virginia.*

keep fighting. During the fall of 1864, Sherman's armies burned towns and tore up railroad tracks. They destroyed plantations and even poured salt into the fields so nothing could grow.

Sherman captured Savannah, Georgia, on Christmas, 1864. In February, he turned north toward South Carolina, set-ting fire to the city of Columbia and then marching into North Carolina.

Sheridan's Ride

Grant also sent General Philip Sheridan into the rich Shenandoah Valley. Grant told Sheridan that he wanted him to turn the valley into "a barren

Above: The Union army reduced the Confederate capital of Richmond, Virginia, to rubble.

waste . . . so that crows flying over it for the balance of this season will have to carry their provender [food] with them."

In Virginia, Grant sent waves of Union soldiers against Confederate defenses. Between May 1864 and April 1865, the Union Army of the Potomac and the Confederate Army of Northern Virginia fought at least eight major battles and many smaller ones.

Thousands of troops on both sides died in the battles of the Wilderness, Chancellorsville, Spotsylvania, Cold Harbor, and Petersburg. Grant knew that each battle brought him closer to victory. He had plenty of supplies and could recruit new soldiers to join his cause much more easily than Lee could. The South's population was smaller, and most Confederate men were already fighting.

By early April, 1865, Lee and his now tiny army of 25,000 men were in full retreat. They were forced to give up Richmond and head west. Just after the Confederates left their capital, Lincoln visited the city and was cheered by thousands of newly freed slaves.

The Confederates Surrender

For the Confederates States of America, time was running out. When Grant captured an important railroad junction near Richmond, Lee was trapped. On April 9, the Confederate commander sent messengers to Grant. Lee was ready to surrender. The two generals met at the courthouse in the small town of Appomattox, Virginia.

According to locals, as Grant and Lee rode up, it was hard to tell who was the winner and who was the loser. Grant showed up in a wrinkled jacket and muddy pants, while Lee wore a fancy dress uniform and a polished sword. All the same, Grant was generous in victory. He allowed Lee to keep his sword and let his troops return home. It was spring and time for planting crops, Grant said.

The Civil War was a strange and bloody conflict. The North had gone to war to save the Union. It ended the war by freeing the slaves. In January, 1865, Congress passed the Thirteenth Amendment to the Constitution, outlawing slavery forever.

The South began the war to save slavery. In early 1865, however, the Confederate Congress passed a law that gave slaves their freedom if they fought for the Confederacy! In the end, the South was fighting not to save slavery but to protect its own union.

All of this came at a terrible cost. Billions of dollars of property were destroyed in the war and much of the South lay in ruins. Over 600,000 soldiers died and more than two million were wounded.

During his trial before the war began, the abolitionist John Brown had made a terrible prediction. The evil of slavery, he said, would only come when America was "purged . . . with blood." He probably never imagined just how much blood it would take.

There could not have been two great generals more different than Ulysses S. Grant and Robert E. Lee. Son of an aristocrat, Lee's strong dignity won him the admiration of even his enemies. Grant was shy and awkward. His shabby appearance often caused people to think he was drunk. Perhaps it is for this reason that the Union was slow to make him a general.

As soon as war broke out, both the Union and Confederate governments asked Lee to be commander of their forces. Grant, on the other hand, was forced to prove his worth on the battlefield. It was not until 1864 that he was appointed general-in-chief of Union forces. In Grant, Lee finally had met his match.

Left: The opposing heroes of the Civil War, the Union's Ulysses S. Grant and the Confederacy's Robert E. Lee, are shown here at Appomattox Courthouse.

Reconstruction

In the 1930s, almost 70 years after the Civil War, a group of historians headed to the South. Their job was to search for the last living people who had been born as slaves and talk to them. They asked the 80- and 90-year-old survivors to recall what happened after the Civil War.

Above: After the war, some northern businessmen invested money in the South, hoping to sell products like cotton and tobacco. Shown here is an advertisement for "Reconstruction" brand tobacco.

Right: Some of the Union's African-American troops came home to the North. According to General Benjamin Butler, the Union's black troops had "with their bayonets . . . unlocked the iron-barred gates of prejudice, and opened new fields of freedom, liberty, and equality of right." In reality, although slavery had ended, the struggle for equality for blacks had not.

"Soldiers, all of a sudden, was everywhere, coming in bunches, crossing and walking and riding," Felix Haywood of North Carolina remembered about emancipation. "Everyone was a-singing. We was all walking on golden clouds. Hallelujah!"

"After freedom," recalled Lee Guidon of South Carolina, "a heap of people say they was going to name themselves over . . . Some of the names was Abraham, and some called themselves, Lincum [sic]. Any big name, 'cepting their master's name."

Some had less happy memories. "I worked for Massa 'bout four years after freedom," said Toby Jones of South Carolina, "'cause he forced me to. Said he couldn't 'ford to let me go . . . So I goes on working for him till I gits the chance to steal a hoss [horse] from him. The woman I wanted to marry, Govie, she 'cides to come to Texas with me. Me and Govie, we rides the hoss 'most a hundred miles, then we turned him a-loose and give him a scare back to his house, and come on foot the rest the way to Texas."

The Civil War and emancipation turned southern society upside down. The old way of life was gone forever. Slavery was dead. The South was in ruins.

The Confederate government had fallen. Southern money was worthless. The Civil War destroyed the old. Now, it was time to build something new.

Rebuilding the South

There were important things to be done. The economy had to be rebuilt. New governments had to be set up. Big questions surrounded these tasks. Who should control those new governments? Should rebels be punished? And, most importantly, what should happen to all the newly freed slaves? Historians call the period after the Civil War, Reconstruction.

In fact, the Reconstruction period began well before the war was over, in areas conquered by Union forces. For example, when the Union Navy landed on the Sea Islands of Georgia and South Carolina in 1861 and 1862, the white planters fled. Some took their slaves, but many African-Americans remained behind.

The newly freed slaves destroyed the cotton gins and looted the island homes of their former masters, but they didn't hurt those whites who stayed behind. The former slaves divided up the land and began to grow their own crops.

Eventually, the Union government would allow them to keep the land they took from the masters. Abolitionists would come to the islands and start schools. Under slavery, blacks had not been permitted to read and write. Now, on the Georgia and Carolina Sea Islands, they flocked to the schools, adults and children alike.

When the North began winning the war, Lincoln had to start thinking about what would come after. In December 1863, the president announced his plans for the postwar South. He would offer pardons to all Confederate citizens, except top officials of the government and army. Southerners would have to sign their names to loyalty oaths. They would have to accept the government's laws passed during the war, including the Emancipation Proclamation. Once 10 percent of the citizens of a state did this, they could begin to organize a new government.

Lincoln's plan was easy on the South.

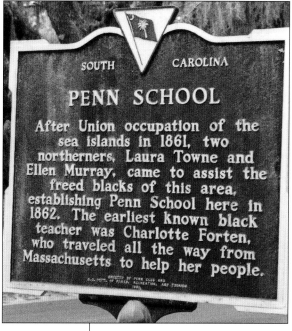

Above: The Penn School, built in 1861 on Union-occupied St. Helena's Island off the South Carolina coast, was founded by abolitionists who came to the island to teach newly freed slaves to read and write.

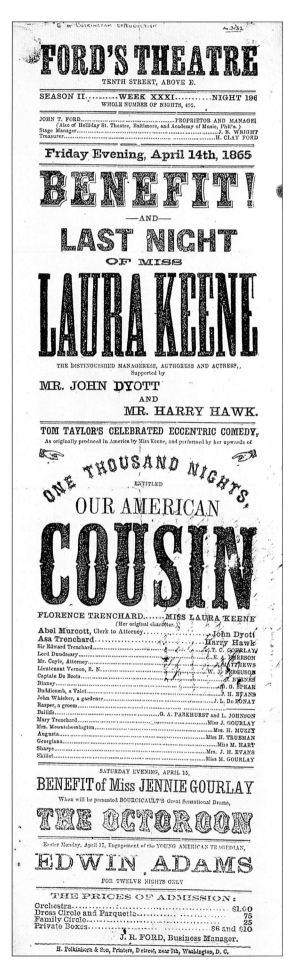

During his second inaugural address in early 1865, Lincoln said he wanted a peace "with malice [bad feelings] toward none; with charity for all."

Lincoln's Assassination

We will never know if Lincoln's plan would have worked. On the evening of April 14, just five days after the Confederate surrender, Lincoln decided he needed some rest. He and his wife Mary Todd went to Ford's Theatre in Washington to see a popular English comedy called *Our American Cousin*.

An angry Confederate actor named John Wilkes Booth was waiting for him. In the middle of the play, Booth entered Lincoln's box and shot the president in the head. Breaking his leg while jumping onto the stage, Booth shouted "Sic semper tyrannis," which meant "this is the fate of tyrants" in Latin. Lincoln was carried back to the White House where he died later that night. On hearing the news of Lincoln's death, Secretary of War Edwin Stanton said, "Now he belongs to the ages."

"Looking upon African slavery from the same standpoint held by the noble framers of our Constitution, I have ever considered it one of the greatest blessings (both for themselves and for us) that God ever bestowed upon a favorite nation."

—JOHN WILKES BOOTH, *in a letter to his sister*

The North went into mourning. Millions of weeping citizens stood by the side of railroad tracks, as a nine-car train carried the dead president's body across the countryside from Washington back to his home in Springfield, Illinois.

Booth had not acted alone. He was the leader of a group of southerners who planned to kill not just Lincoln, but also Vice President Andrew Johnson, and Secretary of State William Seward. The man assigned to kill Johnson got scared and never carried out the attack. Seward was stabbed, but survived.

It took Union troops almost two weeks to find Booth. On April 26, they found him in a barn in northern Virginia. They set the barn on fire and then shot him as he tried to escape. Four other members of Booth's group were hanged, including Mary Surrat, the owner of the boardinghouse where the plan was hatched. Samuel Mudd, a doctor who treated Booth's wounded leg, was given life imprisonment, even though he was not part of the group.

Meanwhile, the government had to go on. The day after the president's assassination, Vice President Johnson was sworn into office as president. Oddly, Johnson, a Democrat, had been a senator from Tennessee, but had stayed loyal to the Union. Lincoln had picked him as his vice president in 1864, hoping that this would make Southerners feel more welcome in the Union after the war.

Andrew Johnson Becomes President

Johnson, like Lincoln, wanted to restore the southern states to the Union easily and quickly. During the summer of 1865, he offered an amnesty, or pardon, plan. Southerners only had to sign a loyalty oath and ratify the amendment that outlawed slavery. By December, all southern states had met the requirements. They then elected to the United States Congress nine members of the old Confederate Congress, four generals from the Confederate Army and even the Confederacy's Vice President Alexander Stevens.

Below: After the war, the federal government began the Freedmen's Bureau to help feed both freed slaves and hungry whites. Shown here is a group of white Alabamians lining up for food rations.

Above: General Tom Thumb, P. T. Barnum's star attraction

Below: P. T. Barnum

Despite Johnson's demands being met, the new southern state governments also passed a group of laws known as the "Black Codes." These new laws were very unfair to the former slaves. Under these laws, a black person who wasn't working could be convicted of vagrancy. If he couldn't pay the fine, he was hired out to an employer, often his former master. Sometimes the Black Codes were no different than the old laws that governed slavery, except that the word "slave" was replaced with the word "Negro."

The Black Codes outraged many northerners. Four years of war and 600,000 dead, they argued, now meant nothing. Southern planters were back in power and African-Americans were practically slaves again. At first, however, there was little they could do. Congress was not in session until December.

The Radical Republicans

During the war and Reconstruction periods, the Republican Party controlled the Congress. Although Lincoln was also a Republican, midway through the war, he began to argue with the Congress about who should shape the laws of Reconstruction. In 1864, Congress passed the Wade-Davis Bill. It was much harsher than Lincoln's plan. It said that no one who had fought for the Confederacy could help organize the new governments of the South. It also permanently took the vote away from military and government

P. T. BARNUM, THE GREATEST SHOWMAN ON EARTH

If anyone was a true showman, it was P. T. Barnum. As a young man, he made his living doing various odd jobs. Then, in 1835, inspiration struck. At a small show in Philadelphia, Barnum saw a woman named Joice Heth being displayed as George Washington's 160-year-old nurse. "Impossible!" he thought, but he also noticed that the people around him were fascinated. It seemed that Americans had a taste for the truly bizarre.

In 1841, Barnum decided to cash in on this fascination. He started Barnum's American Museum in New York. Among the museum's attractions were the bearded lady, the Siamese twins, Fiji cannibals, woolly horses, and the dwarf, General Tom Thumb. Admission to the museum was only 25¢, but it soon became so popular that Barnum was making money hand over fist. In 1871 he realized that the museum was too small to fit his showman dreams. He opened "The Greatest Show on Earth," that became the Barnum and Bailey circus ten years later when James Bailey became his partner. There he exhibited an elephant that he called "the last surviving mastodon" and developed the three-ring show that soon became famous around the nation.

Barnum easily admitted that the show was all a big sham. It doesn't matter, he said. Americans like a little deception to take their minds away from reality. And the fabulous success of "The Greatest Show on Earth" proved him right.

Johnson got drunk and told supporters the radicals were out to assassinate him. News of violence against blacks in the South made Congressional Republicans angrier. In April 1866, they passed the nation's first civil rights bill. The law gave former slaves the right to own and rent property, make contracts, and sue in court. Johnson vetoed this bill, too, but the Republicans were able to override the veto this time. The following month, they began to write a new amendment to the Constitution.

The Fourteenth Amendment, which officially became law in 1868, was complicated and had many parts. Its most

"Is this great conquest to be in vain? That will depend upon the virtue of the next Congress. To Congress alone belongs the power of reconstruction—of giving law to the vanquished . . . If a majority of Congress can be found wise and firm enough to declare the Confederate States a conquered enemy, reconstruction will be easy and legitimate; and the friends of freedom will long rule in the councils of the nation."

—SENATOR THADDEUS STEVENS *of Pennsylvania, 1865*

officials of the Confederacy. Lincoln refused to sign it.

In March 1865, Congress also organized the Freedmen's Bureau. The Bureau was put in charge of feeding and clothing both white and black war refugees. It rented land taken from planters to poor farmers. Working with charities, the Bureau sent missionaries and teachers to the South.

President Johnson had tried to destroy the Freedmen's Bureau. He told the head of the bureau, General O. O. Howard, to take back lands given to freed slaves on the Sea Islands. "Why do you take away our lands?" one of the island's new black landowners asked Howard. "You take them from us who have always been true, always true to the Government! You give them to our all-time enemies! That is not right!"

When the Republican congressmen returned to Washington at the end of 1865, they were angry. They refused to seat new representatives and senators from the South. They also tried to pass a new Freedmen's Bureau bill, but Johnson vetoed it. Celebrating his victory,

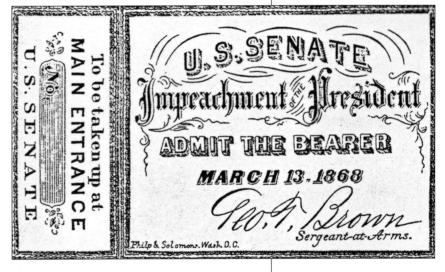

important section, however, gave full citizenship rights to all Americans. It also said that the federal government would actively protect those rights for the first time.

In the congressional elections of 1866, the Republican party swept to victory, winning a three-to-one majority over Johnson and the Democrats. A group of Republicans, known as the Radicals, took control of Congress. The Radicals wanted to punish the South and protect its former slaves.

First, they dissolved the state govern-

Above left: Thaddeus Stevens, the leader of the Radical Republicans

Above right: The admission ticket above was given to spectators who wished to watch Congress vote to impeach President Andrew Johnson.

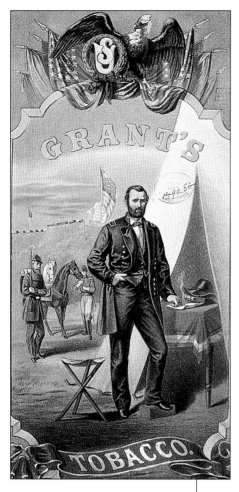

Above: Civil War hero Ulysses S. Grant joined the Radical Republicans after the war, and won election as president in 1868. While Grant was a great general, he was totally unqualified to be president. He is shown here in an 1874 advertisement for tobacco.

Although Grant had been the top Union general in America's bloodiest war, the actual sight of blood made him sick. For this reason, he rarely ate meat, and when he did, it had to be cooked black. During the war, one of his favorite breakfast meals was cucumbers soaked in vinegar.

ments of the South, except in Tennessee, and then divided the entire region into five military districts. The commander of each district was required to register all black men to vote, while preventing former Confederate officials from doing the same. The commander then supervised an election for delegates to state conventions where new constitutions would be written. These constitutions had to legalize voting for black men and had to be approved by Congress. Johnson vetoed the Reconstruction Act of 1867, but was overridden by Congress once again.

In 1868, six states—Alabama, Florida, Arkansas, Louisiana, and North and South Carolina—were readmitted into the Union under their new constitutions. By 1871, the rest of the old Confederate states had also been accepted back into the Union.

Johnson Is Impeached

The Radicals went after Johnson, too. At the same time they passed the Reconstruction Act of 1867, they voted for the Tenure of Office Act. This law said that the president had to get the approval of Congress to dismiss a member of his cabinet. The Radicals were trying to protect Secretary of War Edwin Stanton, who shared their goals and ran the military in the South. The law also said that all presidential orders to the army had to go through the commander Ulysses Grant, who was a Radical himself. The Radicals were trying to reconstruct both the South and the presidency.

Johnson stood quietly by at first, but he believed that the Tenure of Office Act was unconstitutional. As soon as Congress adjourned in August, 1867, he suspended Stanton and replaced him with Grant. Then, in February, 1868, he fired Stanton. Three days later, the House voted to charge Johnson with "treason, bribery, or other high Crimes and Misdemeanors."

Under the rules of the Constitution, this meant Johnson would stand trial, or impeachment hearings, by the Senate. This was the first and only impeachment trial of a president in United States history. To avoid the humiliation of losing the presidency, Johnson secretly promised to let Congress have its way with Reconstruction. On May 16, 35 senators voted for conviction, one short of the necessary two-thirds majority.

The Grant Administration

Later that year, Grant was elected president, and the Radicals swept to power again. They passed yet another amendment to the Constitution. The Fifteenth Amendment made it illegal to prevent someone from voting because of their race or previous condition of slavery.

Meanwhile in the South, political leadership had shifted from Democrats to Republicans. More importantly, the old planter class had been replaced by a mixed group, of whites and blacks.

Many of the whites in government came from the North. Most were businessmen and politicians. Many were honest, some were not. Many brought needed skills and money. Others came to make their fortunes by buying land cheap or stealing from the government. White southern Democrats hated them all and called them "carpetbaggers." A carpetbag was a cheap suitcase that people who had to leave in a hurry might use. The name was meant to show that these northerners came South to take advantage of the region and then leave.

Some southern whites joined the northerners. They recognized that a new era of racial equality had come to the South. They wanted to help rebuild the South from inside the government. White southern Democrats had a name for them, too. They called them "scalawags," an old Scottish term for a worthless animal.

Blacks Are Elected to Congress

Being governed by carpetbaggers and scalawags may have taken some getting used to for white southern Democrats, but when black men began winning election to Congress, the shock was almost too great to bear. In 1860, almost all southern blacks were slaves, without any rights or freedoms. Ten years later, the South had two African-American U.S. senators, 16 members of the House of Representatives, and 20 statewide officeholders. They even controlled one of the branches of the South Carolina legislature, the state that first seceded from the Union ten years before. Just as important, blacks served in local offices like sheriff, judge, and mayor across the South.

The Republican Party encouraged black voting and officeholding. After all, they knew that the freed blacks would vote for their party, the party of Lincoln. Republican officials even recruited former slaves to run for office. Most blacks in government, however, were free blacks from before the war. Both of the black senators from Mississippi, Blanche Bruce and Hiram Revels, had left the South before the war and been educated at schools and colleges in the North.

New leaders were only part of the picture. The Reconstruction governments offered all kinds of new programs and laws. Before the Civil War, the South lagged behind the North in its number of schools, hospitals, asylums, and other public services. It also had fewer railroads and factories. The Reconstruction governments tried to change that. South Carolina's new government offered medical care for the poor of both races. In Alabama, the government provided free legal advice. All the state governments built new railroads.

To pay for all of this, the Reconstruction governments passed new taxes on property and luxuries. This angered many of the old planters, who believed that Reconstruction politicians were stealing tax money for themselves. There was some truth to these charges, but crooked politicians were a problem all over the country, not just in the South. Nevertheless, the South's economy was in a shambles,

which made it easier for dishonest men to profit.

For Southern blacks, freedom and citizenship meant the chance to leave plantations behind. Tens of thousands of blacks moved to southern cities or to find jobs on the railroads. Freedom also meant rebuilding families torn apart by slavery. Thousands of blacks searched the South for loved ones in the years after the Civil War.

Most African-Americans, however, stayed on the lands where they lived as slaves. But many also moved their cabins away from the planter's house and the planter's eyes. Most refused to work for their old masters, even for pay. They did not want to work in gangs as they had under slavery.

This led to a new system of farming after the Civil War, called sharecropping. Under this system, the planter provided the land. The tenant, or cropper, provided the work. Tools and seeds were sometimes given by the planter and sometimes paid for by the cropper. At the end of each growing season, the two would share the crop half-and-half.

In the beginning, sharecropping offered African-Americans more freedom. They could work on their own land at their own pace. It also helped the planters. Most of them had no money to pay wages. Sharecropping offered a cheap way to keep their former slaves working their land.

Because the Civil War had disrupted the cotton supplies, prices were high. In addition, local black politicians made sure that the croppers did not get cheated by their landlords. Under Reconstruction governments, a black cropper could sue his

Above: Grant hated being president. Although he was honest himself, many of his advisors were not. Here he is depicted as a drunken fool.

Below: This cartoon shows Grant struggling under the weight of a "world of care and responsibility."

landlord in court or leave to find a better deal with another planter.

The new political power and economic independence of the blacks angered many of the white Democratic southerners. While most white Democrats won back their right to vote, they were outnumbered by white and black Republicans. They felt they had lost not just their governments, but also control over their lives. Since they could not win power through elections, they used other methods. One of these was terror.

The Ku Klux Klan

Since the earliest days of Reconstruction, some white southerners had begun to meet secretly. One of these men was a Tennessee farmer and former Confederate colonel named Nathan Bedford Forrest. In 1867, he joined a secret organization in Memphis called the Ku Klux Klan. He soon became the Klan's Grand Wizard, or leader, and turned the organization into a major force across the South.

The members of the Ku Klux Klan had a simple goal. They wanted to overthrow the Reconstruction governments and put the black man back in his place, below the white man. The Klan attacked anyone who stood in its way. They threatened Republican politicians and teachers in black schools. Their main target, however, were the blacks who demanded the right to vote and the right to get a fair price for their crops. During Reconstruction, the Klan lynched, or hanged, thousands of innocent blacks across the South.

The governments responded with anti-Klan laws. Federal army troops tried to chase down Klan members and put them in jail. But this was hard. The Klan operated in secret. Members of the Klan always wore hoods and masks when

PAP SINGLETON AND THE EXODUS OF '79

Above: Benjamin "Pap" Singleton

Right: This poster, printed by "Pap" Singleton's company, advertises available land in Kansas.

After the war, thousands of newly freed slaves moved north and west in search of a better life. While many headed for the cities, others found that the West offered the best start toward a new life. Among these was Benjamin "Pap" Singleton. An escaped slave, Singleton traveled the plains, scouting out locations for blacks who wanted to leave the South. Soon, he was leading settlers to Kansas. Like Harriet Tubman before him, Singleton earned the nickname Black Moses, and his followers Exodusters, after the Bible's Exodus, in which the real Moses lead his people out of slavery. One of the first new colonies was Nicodemus, which remains the only all-black town in Kansas.

Singleton went on to found the Edgefield Real Estate and Homestead Association, and was invited to testify before a Senate committee in 1880 about the causes of black migration from the South. As he told the committee, he had first started leading people out of the South in 1869. "I have been fetching people," he said. "I believe I have fetched out 7,432 people." When asked why so many blacks would leave the warm South for the cold of northern cities and western plains, another witness before the committee put it this way: "We believe life, liberty, and happiness to be sweeter in a cold climate than murder, raping, and oppression in the South."

they attacked. Many blacks were too scared to face arrested Klansmen in court. And many whites cheered what the Klan was doing.

The Ku Klux Klan created a climate of terror and violence across the South. The Klan made it hard for Republicans to run for office or even to vote. By 1876, the Reconstruction governments in all but three states—Florida, Louisiana, and South Carolina—had been replaced by white Democratic governments.

The End of Reconstruction

This change helped make the presidential election that year a close one. The Democratic candidate, Governor Samuel Tilden of New York, won the popular vote with 51 percent. He also received 184 of the 185 electoral votes needed to win. Rutherford B. Hayes, the Republican candidate, had just 164 votes. The remaining 21 votes—20 in Florida, Louisiana, and South Carolina, plus one in Oregon—were still up in the air at the end of the year.

Under the Constitution, receiving more votes from the people than your opponent is not enough to become president. Instead, winning candidates must win more electoral votes than their opponents. And in 1876, electoral votes were not actually counted until the January after the election. For two months, Republicans and Democrats in Washington fought over these 21 votes. Finally, they set up a special committee to decide the question. The members included seven Republicans and seven Democrats. The chief justice of the Supreme Court, Salmon P. Chase, was the chairman and 15th vote. Appointed by Lincoln, Chase went with the Republicans and gave all 21 votes to Hayes.

Democrats were outraged. Before they would accept the decision, they decided to demand something in return.

A secret deal was worked out. The Republicans would get the presidency, but all remaining Federal troops would be removed from the South. By 1877, Reconstruction was over. Florida, Louisiana, and South Carolina elected nearly all-white Democratic Party governments.

As quickly as southern blacks had gained political and economic power, they lost it. Without the courts and soldiers to stop them, white planters were free to cheat their black sharecroppers. Most sharecroppers fell into debt to their planters. Laws were soon passed that made it illegal for indebted sharecroppers to leave their plantations.

Over the next 20 years, many other laws were passed to keep black men from voting. Segregation became the order of the day. White southern governments passed laws that made it illegal for blacks to go to school with whites, eat in the same restaurants, or ride in the same train cars. Slavery had not returned, but discrimination and racism had.

It took almost another 100 years and a new civil rights movement to regain the rights African-Americans had briefly won during Reconstruction.

Above: The first African-Americans to serve in Congress are shown above. Although some white politicians welcomed them, they were not always welcomed by the press and public. One Illinois newspaper worried about "semi-barbarians [making] laws to govern millions of intelligent Caucasians [whites]."

Above: Early members of the Ku Klux Klan

AMERICAN TIMELINE

April 12, 1861 In Charleston Harbor, Fort Sumter is shelled by Confederate forces. His supplies cut off, Union commander Major Robert Anderson is forced to surrender.

April 18, 1861 General Robert E. Lee is offered a position as commander of the Union forces. He declines, and the position is offered to George McClellan. Lee is later appointed general in the Confederate Army.

July 21, 1861 Union forces under General Irwin McDowell attack the Confederates at Manassas. They are routed in what becomes known as the first Battle of Bull Run.

March 9, 1862 Two iron-sided warships, the *Monitor* and the *Merrimack,* meet in battle. Although they fire at one another throughout the morning, neither suffers serious damage.

September 17, 1862 In the bloodiest day of the war, 23,500 men are killed and wounded at the Battle of Antietam.

September 22, 1862 Lincoln issues the Emancipation Proclamation, declaring that all slaves will be free with the coming of the new year.

November 5, 1862 Tired of the frequent losses and fearing a lengthy war, Lincoln removes McClellan as general-in-chief, replacing him with General Burnside.

Above: The ironclad ships Monitor *and* Merrimack *do battle on March 9, 1862.*

WORLD TIMELINE

February 25, 1861 A French force captures forts around Saigon, extending French rule into present-day Vietnam.

March 3, 1861 Russian Czar Alexander II issues a decree freeing 20 million serfs. The act is regarded with some skepticism as the penniless serfs are required to buy their own land or continue working for the landlord.

May 13, 1861 Britain declares it will not take sides in the American Civil War.

Above: Alexander II

May 5, 1862 After invading Mexico in an attempt to force the government to pay their debts, French troops are forced to retreat at Puebla.

November, 1862 The only survivor of a two-year expedition, John King returns from his exploration of the Australian outback.

August 28, 1862 In a failed effort to make Rome the capital of a new united Italy, Italian revolutionary Giuseppe Garibaldi attempts to take the city from the Catholic Church.

December 13, 1862 Ambrose Burnside leads his troops to slaughter at Fredericksburg, ordering them to dislodge the Confederates from the impenetrable Marye's Heights.

January 26, 1863 Abolitionists aid in the formation of the 54th and 55th Massachusetts, the first African-American regiments organized for the Union cause.

May 1, 1863 The Confederate Congress passes a law permitting the enslavement or execution of captured African-American Union soldiers.

May 6, 1863 Stonewall Jackson is mistakenly wounded by North Carolina soldiers at the Battle of Chancellorsville. Although his arm is successfully amputated, he is overcome by pneumonia and dies.

June 20, 1863 West Virginia joins the Union as the 35th state.

July 4, 1863 General Ulysses S. Grant wins the strategically located Vicksburg, Mississippi, effectively splitting the Confederacy in two.

July 5, 1863 With heavy losses, Lee's army is forced to retreat at Gettysburg, marking the turning point in the war.

July 17, 1863 Angry at Lincoln's Conscription Act that allows the wealthy to buy their way out of the draft, the poor of New York erupt in four days of rioting.

February 17, 1864 After several failed attempts, the Confederate navy's secret weapon, the submarine *Hunley* successfully sinks a Union ship.

March 8, 1864 Lincoln appoints Grant commander of the Union Army.

August 5, 1864 Union Admiral David Farragut cries "Damn the torpedoes—full speed ahead!" as he leads his fleet in the capture of Mobile Bay, Alabama.

October 31, 1864 Nevada enters the Union as the 36th state.

November 6, 1864 By an overwhelming majority, Lincoln is elected to a second term as president.

November 16, 1864 General William Tecumseh Sherman captures Atlanta, burns the city, and begins his march to the sea.

Above: Opening ceremonies on the London subway

September 24, 1862 Otto von Bismarck becomes minister-president of Prussia. He is known as the "Iron-Chancellor."

January 10, 1863 The first subway opens in London.

April 10, 1864 Napoleon III declares Archduke Maximilian emperor of Mexico, violating the Monroe Doctrine, but Lincoln is unable to present any opposition.

September, 1864 Britain, France, and Holland attack Japan in an attempt to force the Japanese to open trade with foreign nations.

AMERICAN TIMELINE

December 24, 1864 Sherman sends a telegram to the president. "I beg to present you as a Christmas gift," he writes, "the city of Savannah."

April 9, 1865 Surrounded and cut off from the rest of his troops, Lee accepts Grant's terms for surrender at Appomattox Courthouse.

April 15, 1865 While attending a performance at Ford's Theatre, Lincoln is shot in the back of the head and killed.

May 10, 1865 Confederate president Jefferson Davis is captured, putting an official end to the rebel government.

December 18, 1865 The Thirteenth Amendment is officially ratified, thus abolishing slavery in the United States.

April 9, 1866 Congress passes the Civil Rights Act, making all African-Americans citizens of the United States.

December 21, 1866 A force of Sioux, angered by white settlement in tribal lands, attacks Fort Phil Kearney in Idaho Territory.

April 9, 1867 At the urging of Secretary of State Seward, the United States purchases Alaska at the price of two cents an acre.

July 19, 1867 Congress passes the third Reconstruction Act. Under these acts, the South is governed by military governors and required to allow freedmen to vote.

May 26, 1868 Impeachment proceedings initiated by Congress end. President Johnson is acquitted of all charges.

July 28, 1868 The Fourteenth Amendment is ratified, making African-Americans full citizens.

September, 1868 The Georgia legislature expels all 28 of its African-American members, stating that although they may have the right to vote, they do not have the right to hold office.

November 27, 1868 Troops under Colonel Custer attack and massacre a village of Cheyenne and Arapaho Indians.

February 27, 1869 The Fifteenth Amendment to the Constitution is passed, granting African-American men the right to vote. Women are still denied that right.

May 10, 1869 Tracks of the Union Pacific and Central Pacific railroads meet in Utah, completing the first transcontinental railroad.

WORLD TIMELINE

May 1, 1865 Brazil, Argentina, and Uruguay join together to fight the Paraguayan forces of Francisco López. López sealed his doom when he declared war on the three nations in an attempt to establish a Paraguayan empire.

October 4, 1865 In a secret meeting in Biarritz, Napoleon III agrees to remain neutral when Prussian forces under Bismarck invade Austria.

March 29, 1867 Canada is given the right to self-government under the British crown.

Above: French Emperor Napoleon III and Prussian Prime Minister Otto von Bismarck

Above: Chicago in flames, 1871

December 10, 1869 Women in Wyoming territory are given the right to vote.

October 8, 1871 A fire ravages Chicago, burning most of the city to the ground.

June 10, 1872 The Freedmen's Bureau, designed to protect African-Americans in the South and to provide them with necessary services, is closed.

September 1, 1875 Four members of the Molly Maguires, Irish miners agitating for better working conditions, are convicted of murder.

May, 1876 At the Centennial Exposition in Philadelphia, Alexander Graham Bell displays his new invention, the telephone.

June 25, 1876 In a poorly timed attack on Sioux warriors, General Custer and all 265 of his troops are killed at Little Big Horn.

May 1, 1877 The last federal troops withdraw from the South, effectively ending Reconstruction.

June 19, 1867 French-appointed Mexican emperor Maximilian is seized and executed by forces under Benito Juarez.

January 3, 1868 The Japanese Shogun, whose family had ruled Japan for 200 years, is ousted by 16-year-old Emperor Meiji. Meiji is determined to open the country to Western trade and influence.

July 19, 1870 France declares war on Prussia.

September 2, 1870 After 44 days of warfare, French forces clash with the Prussians at Sedan. Bismarck emerges victorious, a unified Germany behind him, and Napoleon surrenders.

September 7, 1872 The League of the Three Emperors, or Dreikaiserbund, is formed by the emperors of Russia, Austria, and Germany in an attempt to maintain peace in Europe.

November, 1875 Fearing bankruptcy, the ruler of Egypt decides to sell his shares in the Suez Canal to Britain.

Above: Mexican emperor Maximilian I

November, 1876 Porfirio Díaz, former supporter of war hero Benito Juarez, is elected to the Mexican presidency.

V. A NATION TRANSFORMED

During the late 19th century, most Americans believed that it was the nation's duty to tame the Wild West by settling it. The painting shown here is called Progress. *It shows an angel of progress guiding white settlers—with their wagon trains and railroads—westward. Note the telephone wire that the angel carries with her across the Plains.*

OST PEOPLE DON'T remember much about Rutherford B. Hayes. Few can list highlights in the life of Chester A. Arthur. Nor do James Garfield, Benjamin Harrison, or Grover Cleveland ring many bells. Yet each of these men was president of the United States during a time of enormous change —a time in which the nation's population almost doubled, a time when everyday objects like the lightbulb, the telephone, and the automobile were first developed.

Out west, dusty frontier towns grew into large centers of commerce. By 1900, natives who had lived for centuries on wide, open plains and in secluded mountain valleys now scraped out lives on crowded reservations—fenced in like cattle by white men who used their sacred lands for railroads, gold mines, and cow towns.

In 1876, most Americans were farmers and craftsmen living in small towns and in the countryside. By 1900, most worked not for themselves but for companies, often in factories and usually in or near large cities. During these years, the United States became the most powerful industrial nation in the world. And as the century came to a close, America stretched its might overseas—to Hawaii and the Philippines in the Pacific, and to Cuba and Panama in the Caribbean. Only a few years later, America would again flex its muscles, but this time toward Europe, as that continent found itself torn by world war.

The Wild West

Shaggy and horned, the huge animals once numbered in the millions. Their stampedes, it was said, "would most likely wake the dead." A single passing herd once held up a Kansas Pacific locomotive for eight hours. Their scientific name was the bison, but Americans called them "buffalo."

To the Native Americans of the Great Plains, the buffalo was like a supermarket on four hooves. They ate its meat. They wore its hide as clothes and they lived in buffalo skin tepees. They even used the dung, or "buffalo chips," as fuel for their fires.

To the white man, however, the buffalo was a nuisance and an obstacle. While its meat helped feed crews building the transcontinental railroad, most Americans preferred cattle. If the Great Plains were to serve as farms and ranches, many said, the buffalo must go.

Buffalos were easy targets. For several years in the 1870s, white hunters killed them by the millions, until there were hardly any left. "I have seen their bodies so thick after being skinned," said hunter W. Skelton Glenn, "that they would look like logs where a hurricane had passed through a forest."

White men had other reasons for slaughtering buffalos. It wasn't just the buffalos that white settlers wanted to get rid of. "These [buffalo hunters] have done in the last two years . . . more . . . to settle the vexed [troubled] Indian question, than the regular army has done in the last 30 years," hunter John Cook told the Texas legislature.

"[The hunters] are destroying the Indians' commissary [food supply]," he added. "For the sake of a lasting peace, let [the hunters] kill, skin, and sell until the buffalos are exterminated. Then your prairies can be covered with speckled cattle." With the buffalo gone, huge herds of cattle would later be driven by cowboys up cattle trails, from Texas to Kansas.

A Way of Life Ends

Until the Civil War, the prairies of the Great Plains were simply a place to pass through on the way to California and Oregon. They were not a place to settle. The weather was harsh. There were no trees. White Americans called the region "the great American desert."

Until 1860, the only sign of the white man marking the vast plains was a few army forts and the wagon trails to the Pacific. Then came the Pony Express, a

Ever since the 1830s, when the "Five Civilized Tribes" of the southeastern United States had been pushed from their lands and forced to march west to Oklahoma on the "Trail of Tears," Oklahoma had been set aside as Indian territory. In 1889, however, the federal government finally opened the land to white settlers. Seen above is an advertisement for land in Indian territory.

Left: Natives of the Great Plains relied on the buffalo for much of their food and clothing. In this painting, several natives, disguised with wolf skins, sneak up on a herd of unsuspecting buffalo.

"I have come to kill Indians, and I believe it is right and honorable to use any means under God's heaven to kill Indians."

—COL. JOHN M. CHIVINGTON, *before ordering the massacre of over 250 Cheyenne at Sand Creek, Colorado, on November 24, 1864. Most of Chivington's victims were unarmed women and children.*

mail delivery company that built stations housing fresh horses about every 20 miles.

Relay teams of young riders raced from Missouri to California in just ten days, changing horses at each station. The Pony Express had the fastest riders and horses in the country. Although the invention of the telegraph would put it out of business just a short time after it was begun, the Pony Express would become famous around the world.

While there were few white men in the prairies, mountains, and deserts of the West before the Civil War, those that were there caused problems for the Native Americans. Among the greatest trouble spots were Arizona and New Mexico. For years, Mexican settlers and soldiers had battled the Pueblo and Navajo Indians there.

When the United States took control of these lands after the Mexican War, new problems arose. White settlers on their way to California stole sheep and cattle from the Navajo people. The Navajo fought back. In response, the U.S. government established Fort Defiance in Arizona. In 1851, the government and the

Navajo signed a peace treaty, agreeing to put an end to the fighting.

By 1860, however, trouble over stolen horses had led to new fighting. In 1863, the army sent former fur trapper Kit Carson to round up the Navajo. In order to starve the Navajo into surrendering, the army destroyed the Indians' orchards, flocks, and crops. The Navajo were then forced to move hundreds of miles to Fort Sumner in eastern New Mexico. The Navajos called this forced move "The Long Walk."

The army's idea was to make peaceful farmers of the Navajo, but the new lands were too dry and rocky. Away from their sacred lands in Arizona, the Navajo continued to starve. After four years, the army allowed them to return to Arizona.

The Cheyenne people of Colorado were not so lucky. In 1859, gold was discovered near Pikes Peak. Thousands of white miners poured in. The nearby town of Denver grew quickly on Cheyenne and Arapaho land. Fighting broke out between the settlers and the Indians. Colorado militia commanders decided to move the Indians out.

THE UNITED STATES CAMEL CORPS

Although he is best remembered as the one and only president that the Confederate States of America would ever have, Jefferson Davis also played a major role in one of the stranger chapters in the history of the American West.

In 1855, Davis was serving as secretary of war in the administration of President Franklin Pierce. It was in that role that Jefferson Davis helped to convince Congress to pay $30,000 to bring a small number of camels to America to test how they might help the U.S. Army. Two shipments, containing fewer than 100 camels, arrived in San Antonio, Texas, in 1856 and 1857. In 1857, a 25-camel caravan made a four-month journey from San Antonio to Los Angeles, led by specially hired Turkish, Greek, and Armenian camel drivers. After that first test, however, the government lost interest, and soon the Civil War arrived to end the project forever. And what became of the camels? Some were stationed for a while at various U.S. Army forts in the West, but most were sold off. Some joined circuses, while others were used by freight hauling and road construction teams. Others were just left in the desert to fend for themselves. How many survived is a mystery, but for years, stories traveled the west about camels showing up in strange places with no explanation.

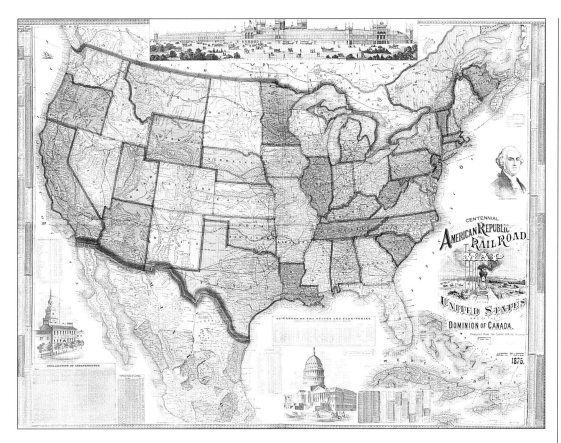

Before the age of railroads, settling the West was not really possible. In the eastern United States, goods could be shipped by boat along the ocean, rivers, or lakes. In the West, however, rivers and lakes were few and far between, and distances were much greater. Only railroads could carry the wheat, lumber, cattle, and metals. The map at left shows the major rail routes that crisscrossed the frontier.

Below: William H. Bonney, who was also known as "Billy the Kid," was a legend in his own time. During his short, violent life, Billy was thought to have killed 21 people. His first murder may have come when he was just 12 years old. He died in 1881, at the age of 21, shot to death by his one-time friend, Sheriff Pat Garrett.

They used a plan they had used before and would use again. They paid some local Indians to sign a peace treaty. The militia called these Indians chiefs, even though they really were not. The Cheyenne and Arapaho peoples refused to listen to the fake chiefs. When the Native Americans refused to move, the militia said they were violating the treaty.

One of the real chiefs of the Cheyenne, a man named Black Kettle, wanted peace. He settled his people near Fort Lyon for protection. When several of his warriors stole some army cattle, Black Kettle raised the white flag of surrender over his village of Sand Creek. Sadly, this didn't stop the the local militia, led by Colonel J. M. Chivington, from attacking. Over 250 Cheyenne, mostly unarmed women and children, were massacred in their tepees.

The Transcontinental Railroad

After the Civil War, white settlement of the West increased rapidly. Peace between the Union and Confederacy brought miners, farmers, ranchers and, most importantly, the railroads. Since the 1850s, Americans had talked of building a railroad to California. But the South and North argued over the route. When Southern politicians left the government during the Civil War, a northern route was chosen.

In 1862, Congress granted two companies the right to build a transcontinental railroad. The Union Pacific would lay track westward from Omaha, Nebraska, and the Central Pacific would build eastward from Sacramento, California. The government agreed to pay the companies $16,000 for each mile of track on flat land and $48,000 in the moutains. More valuable was the land. For every mile of track laid, the Union Pacific and Central Pacific received 20 square miles.

Employing thousands of Chinese, Irish, and other immigrant laborers, the two railroads raced each other to earn land and money. Hundreds of workers died in mountain avalanches and dynamite explosions. Seven years later, on May 10, 1869, the two lines met at Promontory Point, Utah. To celebrate the event, Central Pacific President Leland Stanford drove in a golden spike. "[He]

General George Armstrong Custer (above) was one of the nation's most famous Indian fighters by the time he met the combined forces of Chief Crazy Horse's Ogala Sioux warriors and Chief Sitting Bull's Hunkpapa Sioux, at the Battle of Little Big Horn. The battle lasted just half an hour, and the only survivor among Custer's forces was a horse named Comanche. Chief Sitting Bull is shown below.

took the sledge [hammer]," a witness recalled, "and the first time he struck he missed."

The transcontinental railroad bill was one of two important western bills passed during the Civil War. The other was the Homestead Act, which gave each settler 160 free acres of government land in the West. The settlers had to improve the land and live on it for five years. Thousands of pioneers used the Homestead Act to earn their first farms.

Gunslingers and Lawmen

Not all westerners, however, wanted to make a living the hard way. The West was full of violent men who felt they could make a fortune by robbing and killing. The Clancey gang tried to control the town of Tombstone, Arizona, through terror. William Bonney, known to history as Billy the Kid, was said to have first killed a man when he was 12 years old. In the 1870s, he became a hired killer for a group of cattle ranchers trying to take control of land and water in New Mexico.

Other criminals, like Jesse James and his brother Frank, formed gangs to rob banks and trains all over the West in the 1880s. The Dalton family gang, who were relatives of the James family, continued the tradition in Oklahoma in the 1890s.

Crime, however, didn't always pay in the Old West. The Clanceys were killed by Marshall Wyatt Earp at the O.K. Corral in 1881. Billy the Kid was killed by Sheriff Pat Garrett that same year. Jesse James was shot for a reward on his head in 1882, while Emmet Dalton was captured and spent 15 years in Leavenworth prison.

While criminals like Jesse James and Billy the Kid broke the law, the U.S. government was breaking treaties with the Indians. In 1867, Congress came up with a new way to remove the Indians. It would set up special areas called reservations and move the Indians there.

In 1868, Red Cloud, the leader of the western Sioux people, signed a treaty to settle his people on a reservation that covered all of western South Dakota. Not all the Sioux agreed to it, however. Some continued to hunt the buffalo off the reservation. The army, including the African-American cavalry the Indians called "buffalo soldiers," were sent in to round them up.

Custer's Last Stand

In 1873, things got worse. Gold was discovered in the Black Hills of South Dakota, land that was holy to the Sioux. As miners poured onto the Sioux's sacred lands, fighting broke out. A cavalry officer named George Armstrong Custer went looking for the Sioux and their chief, Sitting Bull. On July 25, 1876, he found them on the Little Big Horn River in Montana. Custer expected a small camp, but Sitting Bull had over 2,500 warriors. The battle only lasted as one Indian reported, "as long as a hungry man needs to eat his dinner." When it was over, Custer and his entire force of 256 men were wiped out.

The Sioux were warriors, but the Nez Perce of Oregon had always tried to live in peace. In 1877, their leader, Chief Joseph, agreed to move his people from their homeland to the Lapwai reservation of Idaho. Just before they left, however, nearby settlers stole their horses. This was the final insult for several young warriors. Disobeying Joseph, they killed 18 whites.

The army went after them. For six months, Joseph led the soldiers on a chase across the Northwest. Even though he had women and children with him, he got to within 40 miles of Canada and safety. When he surrendered, he told the army commander, "Joseph will fight no more forever." Brokenhearted about losing his people's land, he asked the U.S. Congress many times to allow him to return. Congress refused.

Life for Sitting Bull, the victor of Little Big Horn, was even sadder. After the battle, he took his people to Canada. With no land of their own, they were forced to take handouts from the Canadian government. When the government refused to feed them anymore, Sitting Bull and his people returned to the United States in 1881.

The Old West Disappears

To help feed his people, Sitting Bull took a job with a frontier circus called Buffalo Bill's Wild West Show. Founded by William Cody, a famous Indian fighter and buffalo hunter, the show toured the world. It was the beginning of the Wild West as entertainment.

Sitting Bull, however, felt embarrassed to be on display, like an animal in a zoo. He eventually quit and rejoined his people on their South Dakota reservation. Things had changed by the late 1880s. Congress had passed the Dawes Act. Under this law, the communal lands of the Indians were divided up and given to individual families. The government hoped to turn Indians into small farmers. It didn't work. Many Indians were forced to sell their lands. Living alone on a small farm was not the Indian way.

Native Americans like the Sioux grew desperate. Then great news came from Nevada. A Paiute Indian shaman, or spiritual leader, named Wovoka had a vision. By performing the Ghost Dance, he preached, Indians could drive out the white man and bring their dead ancestors and the buffalo back to life.

The Ghost Dance religion spread like wildfire through the Indian reservations of the West. White traders and missionaries did not like the dance. They felt it might make the Indians go to war. They also felt it was un-Christian. Local whites called in the army. On December 14, 1890, the soldiers, along with Indian police, marched onto the Sioux reservation. They thought Sitting Bull was leading the ghost dance and they came to arrest him. Shots rang out and Sitting Bull was dead.

This didn't stop the Ghost Dancers. On December 28, the army moved in on a camp at Wounded Knee Creek, South Dakota. When they started to disarm the people, someone fired a gun. In the massacre that followed, over 250 Sioux men, women, and children were murdered. Wounded Knee marked the last battle between Indians and whites in the Old West.

The Old West was disappearing in other ways, too. In 1889, even though the United States had promised the Cherokee people that they could live in Oklahoma forever after they were forced from their homeland in the southeast during the 1830s, the government opened the land up to white settlers.

On April 22, 1889, thousands of whites waited for a government agent to fire a gun. When he did, they rushed in to claim their land. Some hadn't waited. They snuck in days before, thus giving Oklahoma its nickname: the Sooner State.

Oklahoma was the last great land rush in the history of the West. The following year, the U.S. Census Bureau made it official. Since the first census was conducted in 1790, the bureau had noted a frontier line between settlement and Indian land. One hundred years later, the 11th census said that line had disappeared. White settlers had filled in the lands between the Atlantic and the Pacific oceans.

William "Buffalo Bill" Cody probably did more than any other figure to keep the legends of the Wild West alive in the minds of the public. Forming Buffalo Bill's Wild West Show, he toured the nation, and even traveled to Great Britain in 1887 to perform for Queen Victoria. Above: A poster for the show features Buffalo Bill himself.

Above: One of the most popular performers in Buffalo Bill's Wild West Show was the sharpshooter Annie Oakley, who joined Cody's act in 1885.

The Age of Industry

July 4, 1876. America was going through troubled times. Sitting Bull had wiped out General Custer's troops at the Little Big Horn. Reconstruction was dying in the South and blacks were being murdered by the Ku Klux Klan. Officials in the administration of President Ulysses S. Grant were charged with corruption. Millions of unemployed wandered the nation in the third year of the worst economic depression in history.

But for nearly 10 million visitors to Philadelphia, it could all be forgotten at the fair, the great Centennial Exhibition. America was celebrating its birthday where it had all begun 100 years earlier. The Liberty Bell was on display and Independence Hall had been redecorated.

This being America, however, it was the future on display more than the past. Visitors from all over the country and the world marveled at new inventions like the telephone, the typewriter, and a "new floor-cloth called linoleum."

The most popular attraction was the Corliss engine. Over 700 tons and 40 feet high, it was the largest steam engine in the world. Within a few years, however, the Corliss would already be out of date. Electricity would replace steam power. Yet for the visitors at the fair, the Corliss engine represented all that was powerful and new in an industrializing America.

An Empire Made of Steel

America's first factories appeared before the Civil War. Driven by water-power, they were located near waterfalls in the countryside of New England. Most produced thread and textiles. With the factories came new forms of transportation. Canals and steamboats offered cheaper ways to move goods and people over water. Railroads did the same for overland routes. By 1860, America's 30,000-mile railroad system was the largest in the world.

Below: Carrie Nation

CARRIE NATION (1846-1911)

Life was not easy for Carrie Nation. Her father, a Kentucky landowner, lost all of his money to the Confederate cause. Brokenhearted at the defeat of his beloved South, he took his family to Missouri. It was there that Nation met Dr. Charles Gloyd. They fell in love and were soon married. Shortly after the wedding, Nation discovered that her new husband was an alcoholic. Despite her gentle pleading, he refused to reform his ways. His love for liquor destroyed their marriage, ruined his health, and finally killed him.

This tragedy roused Nation to a fury. Alcohol was a great evil, she said, and needed to be destroyed. At this time, the sale of liquor was illegal in Kansas, but saloons ignored the law. She decided it was time somebody did something about this. With a Bible in one hand and a hatchet in another, she traveled to saloons across Kansas. She harassed customers, threatened bartenders, and hacked liquor crates to pieces. Although she was frequently arrested, fined, and shot at, Nation didn't let this stop her on her mission. For Carrie Nation, no threat was too great and nothing was too violent in the war against alcohol.

Still, most people lived on farms. They grew most of what they ate and made much of what they needed themselves. The Civil War began to change all that. To win the war, the government needed huge amounts of weapons, ammunition, and supplies. Manufacturers jumped at the opportunity of money-making government contracts. Many grew very rich and used their profits to build great business empires after the war. Andrew Carnegie, a poor immigrant who became the greatest steel manufacturer of the late 1800s, opened his first iron mill in 1865 with money he made during the war.

During the years following the Civil War, new industry spread across the country. While U.S. companies mined 20,000 tons of coal in 1870, by 1910, they dug over 400,000 tons. Iron and steel production increased from less than 1,000 tons to over 24,000. In 1870,

about $100 million worth of machinery was built. By 1910, America's manufacturers were making five times that much. By 1900, the nation had pushed ahead of Great Britain to become the greatest industrial power in the history of the world.

Numbers alone don't capture how much America was changing. New technologies made workers more productive and created new industries. One of the most important was steel. Until the Civil War, iron was the metal of choice for machinery and railroad track. Iron, however, was brittle and rusted easily.

Steel, a stronger metal made of iron, carbon, and other elements, had been around for centuries. But it was slow and expensive to make. In 1856, a British inventor named Henry Bessemer found a way to make steel cheaply and quickly. In 1872, Andrew Carnegie brought the Bessemer system to America.

Above: The Remington Arms Company of Connecticut was the nation's largest gun manufacturer. In 1875, Remington bought the rights to a new invention called the typewriter. The typewriter helped create a huge demand for office workers, positions that more and more were filled by women.

New sources of raw material, like iron ore mines in Minnesota, helped America industrialize as well. But perhaps the greatest natural resource discovery of the century was oil. In 1859, Edwin Drake sank his first oil well in Pennsylvania. By 1890, America was producing over 50 million barrels of oil a year. Over 90 percent of this was pumped, refined, and sold by one man and one company—John D. Rockefeller's Standard Oil.

New Inventions

The late 19th century was also the heyday of American invention. In 1876, Alexander Graham Bell designed the first telephone. In 1884, George Eastman invented paper film and portable cameras called Brownies to use it. With the creation of the Brownie, nonprofessionals could take pictures of their families.

The greatest inventor of the era was Thomas Alva Edison. In the 1870s and 1880s, he produced the first electric light bulb, the phonograph, the electric street car, and the movie camera. Edison turned the creation of inventions into an industry in itself. He built a laboratory in Menlo Park, New Jersey. The "Wizard of Menlo Park" said his laboratory would produce a new small thing every week and a really big invention once a month.

New inventions and industries of this age made possible another development—the city. Cities, of course, were not new. They have existed throughout history as places of trade, production, culture, and government. For the most part, however, they were small. Before the Civil War, people could walk across New York or Philadelphia, America's two largest cities, in half an hour.

Between 1870 and 1910, New York's population grew from less than a million to almost five million. In 1870, a year before its great fire, Chicago had 300,000 residents. By 1910, it boasted two million. The new inhabitants came from the American countryside and as immigrants from abroad.

As cities grew in size, the people in them needed better ways to get around. "The only trouble about this town," the writer Mark Twain wrote in 1867 about New York, "is that it is too large. You cannot accomplish anything in the way of

The last quarter of the 19th century was sometimes called "The Gilded Age" after the style in which the rich lived. While working people struggled to earn enough to live on, wealthy men like William Astor, shown at right with his daughters, Helen and Gussie, built giant palaces and lived like kings.

business, you cannot even pay a friendly call, without devoting a whole day to it."

Two inventions solved that problem. Telephones made for instant communication. The electric street car and elevated railway (the "el") allowed commuters to make their way around. New York, divided by rivers, completed the Brooklyn Bridge in 1883, the largest in the world up to that time.

Cities were not just growing outward, they were growing upward as well. Older brick and iron buildings rarely went above six stories. The building material wasn't strong enough. The use of cheap steel and the invention of the steel skeleton allowed for the modern skyscraper.

The first was the 12-story Home Insurance Company building of Chicago, finished in 1885. Less than 30 years later, New York's Woolworth building soared 60 stories high, which made necessary another invention. Nobody could possibly climb a stairway over 750 feet high to go to work every day. Elisha Otis's development of the safety brake made the modern elevator possible.

Elevators, light bulbs, streetcars—the new cities ran on electricity. The question was how to make it available. In 1882, Edison built his first power station in New York. Unfortunately, it used direct current (DC), an unreliable and dangerous form of power. When George Westinghouse, the millionaire inventor of the modern railroad brake, tried to start up his own electric system, Edison fought him in court. But Westinghouse's alternating current (AC) was safer and less expensive. It soon became the standard.

New technology and money were two important ingredients to America's growing industries. The third was labor. In the handicraft shops before the Industrial Revolution, owners and workers labored together. They often lived in the same neighborhoods and socialized together. Workers owned their own simple tools and had special skills. The pace of work was slow and production was limited.

The Industrial Revolution changed all that. Machines began to set the pace of

work. Owners left the workroom for the front office and moved into richer neighborhoods. Machinery replaced tools and the skills of individual workers mattered much less. Workers were no longer craftspeople who had the skills to make an entire product. They became workers charged with doing a single task. By the end of the century, millions of Americans were working for pay in huge factories, under bosses they never even met.

The Birth of the Labor Movement

The new working class had a hard time of it. One individual worker was nearly powerless in the face of factory owners who had millions of dollars behind them. What made things even worse was that competition among factories meant that owners had to keep prices low. And to keep prices low, owners kept the money paid to their workers low as well.

Many workers felt that the solution was to organize—to form labor organizations, or unions. They realized that groups of workers acting together had greater power than individual workers acting alone. Owners did not want their workers joining together in unions and certainly didn't want to talk to union representatives about wages and working conditions.

Many workers felt that they had only one option: to go on strike. Unfortunately for them, it was easy to replace unskilled striking workers with new unskilled workers. Union workers called these replacement workers scabs, and often would surround factories to prevent scabs from going to work. In response,

As the end of the 19th century neared, two new features changed America's cities. The elevator allowed buildings to reach new heights. Also, elevated railways helped move crowds from one section of the city to another more quickly. The artist of the drawing above used his imagination to combine both inventions into one.

owners would call the police to arrest the strikers.

Late 19th century America was filled with labor violence. In 1877, railroad workers went on strike after the owners cut their pay by 30 percent and fired half the workforce. Demonstrations spread across the country. In Chicago, police shot at demonstrating workers, killing over 30 of them. The army, recently returned from Reconstruction duty in the South, came in to break the strike. In the end, over 100 workers were killed. The newspapers talked of a new civil war— not between free states and slave states, but between owners and workers.

Despite the difficulty of organizing, labor unions managed to grow. One union, called the Knights of Labor, signed up almost a million members by the mid-1880s. The organization welcomed skilled and unskilled, men and women, black and white. Its slogan was "an injury to one is an injury to all."

During the 19th century, most factory workers had to work very long hours each day. Members of the Knights and other workers demanded a law that prevented owners from making work days longer than eight hours. In 1886, they organized the first labor day marches. Police watched them closely. At the McCormick reaper plant in Haymarket Square, Chicago, somebody threw a bomb that killed four policemen. The government and businessmen attacked the union and it soon collapsed.

This didn't stop workers from fighting against what they called "wage slavery." In 1892, the workers at Andrew Carnegie's steel plant in Homestead, Pennsylvania, near Pittsburgh, went on strike. But Carnegie and his factory manager Henry Frick were ready for them. They hired Allan Pinkerton, a Civil War spy who later started an anti-strike security agency. Pinkerton rented his private police force to factory owners. At Homestead, Pinkerton's men even used cannons against the workers. Two

Below: A turn-of-the-century advertisement for Kellogg's Corn Flakes

CORN FLAKES AND THE KELLOGG BROTHERS

In Battle Creek, Michigan, everybody knew Dr. John H. Kellogg. People would shout delightedly and wave to him as he strolled through the grounds of his health sanitarium. Sometimes, if they were fortunate, he would pause to shake their hands, or to speak a few words. After he left them, they would murmur about what a charming man he was. But nobody noticed the man who walked beside John Kellogg, frantically scribbling notes on a pad of paper.

Unlike his brother John, Will Keith Kellogg was unfriendly and awkward. His contribution to the sanitarium unacknowledged, he spent many quiet hours attempting to develop a breakfast food that was both nutritious and delicious. After some success with wheat flake cereals, the Kelloggs had a major breakthrough with the invention of Corn Flakes. Soon, all of the residents in the sanitarium were eating the new cereal. Will thought that they should start advertising in order to increase their sales.

"Certainly not!" John said. He felt that such advertisements would be frowned upon in the medical community. It was then that Will's resentment of his brother boiled over. He secretly began to buy up stock in Corn Flakes. When he finally owned the business, he smugly planted his signature on every box and launched an aggressive advertising campaign. Corn Flakes cereal was an immediate success. Will Keith Kellogg had finally escaped from the work of the sanitarium, with a fortune in his pockets.

years later, the workers at George Pullman's railroad car factory near Chicago faced the same violence. Both strikes were broken and the workers returned to work.

For the most part, the unions that tried to organize at Homestead and Pullman were made up of unskilled workers. Another union, founded in 1886, had a more successful, but limited, plan. Led by an immigrant cigarmaker named Samuel Gompers, the American Federation of Labor (AFL) organized skilled workers only. Since it was more difficult for owners to replace skilled workers, the union had better success in strikes.

Factory workers weren't the only ones fighting for their economic rights in the late 1880s. Farmers were organizing, too. In the South, the sharecropping system had forced both black and white sharecroppers into debt. Many had to sell their cotton to planters for whatever price they could get. They also had to buy their goods from planter-owned stores that charged high prices.

The Populists

Out west, farmers fought the railroads. In most western states, railroads charged farmers high rates to ship crops to market, sometimes more than the crop was even worth. In both the South and the West, farmers organized into a new political party called the Populist Party. One of their demands was that the government take over ownership of the railroads. The Populists also wanted the government to buy their crops and lend them money at a fair rate. One populist organizer named Mary Lease told Kansas farmers "to raise less corn and more hell!"

By 1896, the Populists led by William Jennings Bryan had captured control of the Democratic Party. Bryan crisscrossed the nation, speaking to more crowds than any candidate for president had ever done before. The Republicans far outspent Bryan, and their candidate, William McKinley, won anyway.

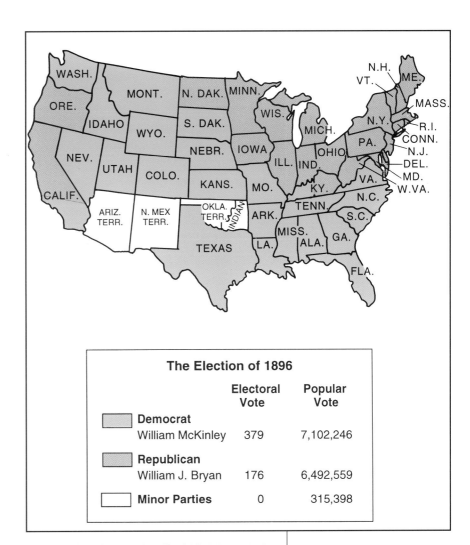

The Election of 1896

	Electoral Vote	Popular Vote
Democrat William McKinley	379	7,102,246
Republican William J. Bryan	176	6,492,559
Minor Parties	0	315,398

Above: The election of 1896 was one of the most hotly contested in history. William Jennings Bryan, a 36-year-old Democrat from Nebraska, crisscrossed the nation stirring up Populist Party voters against the East Coast business interests and the Republican Party's William McKinley. McKinley, who campaigned almost entirely from his front porch in Ohio, won anyway.

Left: Many labor unions tried to convince shoppers to avoid non-union-made products. This advertisement was created by the Missouri State Federation of Labor during the 1890s.

123

The Immigrants

Between 1880 and 1920, over two and a half million Jews came to the United States. Many were fleeing anti-Semitic, or anti-Jewish, violence in Europe. Others came for the job opportunities America offered. Most settled on the Lower East Side of Manhattan in New York City.

Life in the New World was not easy for them. Immigrant families lived in crowded tenements that were poorly built and poorly maintained apartment blocks. They worked long hours in dangerous factories, known as sweatshops because of their poor condition. Even young children had to work to make ends meet.

To help his people, a Jewish editor named Abraham Cahan started a Yiddish, or Jewish-language, newspaper called the *Daily Forward.* One of the most popular features was called the bintel brief (bun-

THE ISLAND OF TEARS

Over 16 million people entered the United States through Ellis Island between 1892 and 1954. Fleeing the poverty of their homelands, most came with little more than the clothes on their backs. "What did we take with us? Our clothes, our pillows, our big, thick comforters made from pure goose feathers . . . and a barrel of pickles," said a Polish Jewish immigrant in 1921.

Passage across the Atlantic took about three weeks. Although conditions aboard ships were crowded and unsanitary, immigrants had other things to worry about: such as the inspection at Ellis Island. Called the "Isle of Tears" in many European languages, Ellis Island was the inspection point for people wishing to enter the country. For some, landing there meant being told that they would have to turn back again. After having saved their money for years and years, they would be forced to return home.

Upon arrival, immigrants were sent to the registry room. There they were inspected by doctors who checked their eyes, scalp, and general appearance. Those who looked sick were marked with a letter in chalk and were forced to undergo further medical inspection, detainment, and perhaps would even have their entry denied. But most immigrants eventually passed the medical inspection and went on to an interview where questions were rapidly fired at them: "What's your name, where are you from, can you work, how much money do you have, can you read?"

If all the inspection officials were satisfied, the immigrants were finally given permission to enter the country. They walked down a hallway to a door labeled "Push to New York" and started their new lives.

dle of letters). People wrote in about their problems. Cahan published the letters, with a few words of advice.

Readers, using made-up names, talked of their money difficulties. "I had to work all day in the shop and my sick wife lay alone at home," wrote someone called "The Newborn." "But how could I think of work . . . when my wife was so ill? Yet without the job what would happen? There would not be a penny coming into the house."

Many complained about children who had become too American and forgotten about the traditions of their home countries, a common problem in Jewish immigrant families. "When [my husband and I] opened the door and went into the living room [of our son's house]," wrote 'A Reader from the Bronx,' "we saw a large Christmas tree . . . When my husband saw this he turned white . . . He is so angry that he doesn't want to cross the threshold [entrance] of their home again."

America's "Golden Door"

The readers of the *Daily Forward* were part of the greatest wave of immigration in world history. Between 1880 and 1920 alone, over 36 million people came to America. Many came from countries that had a long tradition of immigration to America, like England, Ireland, and Germany. Even more came from countries in eastern and southern Europe. Over three million arrived from Russia, four million from Austria-Hungary, and over five million from Italy.

Some, like the Jews, came because they were persecuted at home. In the late 1800s, groups of Russian soldiers would rob and murder Jewish villagers. These attacks were called pogroms. Most, however, came looking for work. Many peasants in Italy and Poland were losing their lands to larger farmers. Usually, they migrated to the large cities of their own countries looking for work. But these countries were poor and there was little to do.

פריִע קלאסען איז ענגליש!

לערנט רעדען שריִבּען און רעדען
די שפּראך פוו איִערע קיִנדער.

פארבערטונג צו
ווערען א בּירגער
אלע סקוֹל געגעוען
שטעענדע.בּפעצעעלע
קלאסען פאר געביִל-
דעטע איִמיגלענדער.

איִנפארמאציע וועמעו די קלאס
עו העט טרינעו איִ...

FREE CLASSES IN ENGLISH!
LEARN TO SPEAK,READ
&WRITE THE LANGUAGE
OF YOUR CHILDREN.
NATURALIZATION PREP-
ARATION.ALL SCHOOL

INFORMATION & CLASSES AT

Above: This poster advertises English-language lessons for newly arrived Jewish immigrants.

For many, the only alternative was to leave for new lands, such as Canada, Argentina, and Australia. But most came to America. America had the most jobs, and it also did the most advertising. Railroads, factories, and steamship companies passed out millions of flyers in dozens of European countries and languages. They wanted new customers, new travelers, and new workers. The ads spoke in glowing words about the good life in America. Soon an expression grew up about America: "The streets are paved with gold."

Most immigrants, of course, had no gold. And without it they had to travel to America in steerage class, where the luggage was stored. Packed into the holds of ships, with little fresh air and clean water, many became both seasick and homesick. Describing the long journey to America, a Russian immigrant named Alexander Rudnev wrote, "First [the immigrant] has a hard enough time at the borders [in Europe] then with the [ticket] agents. After this he goes through a lot till they send him, like baggage, on the train to a port. There he lies around in the immigrant sheds till the ship finally leaves. Then follows the torment on the ship, where every sailor considers a steerage passenger a dog."

Immigrants poured into ports throughout the United States, with many coming through Boston and New Orleans. Most immigrants, however, came through New York City. As they entered New York harbor, they eyed the towering skyline of Manhattan in the distance. Closer up, they saw two small islands. One had a welcoming statue and the other a not so welcoming set of brick buildings.

On the first island stood the Statue of Liberty. A gift from France in honor of America's 100th birthday, the statue was designed by Frédéric-Auguste Bartholdi and finished in 1886. In 1903, a poem by Emma Lazarus was inscribed on the statue's pedestal. It read:

> Give me your tired, your poor,
> Your huddled masses yearning to
>   breathe free,

> The wretched refuse of your teeming
>   shore.
> Send these, the homeless, tempest-
>   tost to me,
> I lift my lamp beside the golden door!

The second island was called Ellis Island. Opened in 1892, Ellis Island was used as New York's immigrant processing center until 1924. In those 32 years, more than 16 million people passed through its gates. It was a frightening place. Doctors checked all immigrants for disease and mental illness. If they didn't pass the tests, they were sent back home.

After making it through Ellis Island, the immigrant was free to go where he or she pleased. Some bought railroad tickets and left directly for other cities or the countryside. Many, however, stayed in Manhattan.

Life in Urban America

The busy streets of New York were a scary place for the many immigrants who came from farms. Most settled in poor and crowded neighborhoods favored by other people from home. These were called ghettoes. In the ghettoes, immigrants found the foods they liked and others who spoke their languages.

Whole families packed themselves into crowded tenement apartments, with bathrooms in the backyard. People from different countries tended to find jobs in one or two industries. Many Italians and Jews went into the clothing business. Poles and Russians, many of whom settled in Chicago and other cities, worked in steel mills, coal mines, and meat-packing factories. And immigrants of all nationalities opened small businesses that served their communities.

Families and friends were not the only form of support for new immigrants. In 1889, a wealthy, college-educated woman named Jane Addams gave up her life of ease to open Hull House in the immigrant ghetto of Chicago. Hull House offered classes in English, sports programs, and childcare. Soon others opened "settlement houses" in other immigrant ghettoes across the country.

City governments also played a role in helping the new citizens. In many cities, a new form of political organization, called a "machine," offered immigrants a trade-off. If the immigrants helped elect the local machine's candidates, they would be taken care of in times of need. Local politicians, known as aldermen, helped immigrants find new apartments after fires, gave out turkeys to poor families on Christmas, and even offered jobs on new building projects. Although most local machines were dishonest, they were welcome friends to immigrants fresh off the boat.

Poverty, overcrowding, and new lifestyles were not the only problems facing immigrants. Many native-born Americans blamed the new immigrants for not acting American enough. They felt that if new immigrants wanted to become good citizens, they had to give up their old ways first. Immigrants, they believed, should speak American, dress American, and eat American.

Other native-born Americans were less welcoming. Not only did they feel that the new immigrants were not smart enough to become good citizens, but that they shouldn't even be allowed in the country. They believed that the new immigrants were inferior and that they could never become good citizens. A new political movement to stop immigration began to build in the early 1900s.

In 1921 and 1924, two laws were passed that limited immigration. Limits on the number of people allowed into the United States from different countries were established. Immigrants from England, Germany, and Ireland, the countries where the ancestors of most native-born Americans came from, could enter. But Jews, Italians, Poles, and other people from Eastern and Southern Europe were kept out. These quotas would last until 1965, when a new general limit for all nationalities became the law of the land.

Above: An immigrant family in their one-room tenement apartment, located in a New York City neighborhood known at the time as "Poverty Gap." This photograph was taken by Jacob Riis, whose book of photographs, **How The Other Half Lives,** *showed Americans just what kind of life many of the nation's new citizens faced once they arrived here. According to Riis, this family all lived together in one room, and all slept together on "a heap of old rags." In a good week, the father earned about five dollars shoveling coal.*

"This country needs a war!"

—THEODORE ROOSEVELT, *in 1895*

Below: On February 18, 1898, the American battleship Maine *blew up in Havana harbor in Spanish-ruled Cuba. Although the explosion was probably an accident, American newspapers immediately called for the United States to invade. In April, President McKinley declared war on Spain. Four months later, the war was over and the United States had won.*

America Looks Overseas

"Russia has sold us a sucked orange," the editors of the *New York World* wrote in 1867. "What remains of the Russian fur trade is not of sufficient importance to justify the expense of the naval protection."

What made these newspapermen so mad? Secretary of State William Seward had just paid $7 million for the territory of Alaska. People called the purchase "Seward's Folly" and they labeled Alaska "Seward's Icebox."

Supporters of the sale, the editors continued, grow excited about "the vastness of the territory—ten or twelve times as large, they say, as the state of New York. But the greater part of it is of no more human use than so many square miles of ice in the Arctic Ocean by which it is bounded."

While immigration was bringing millions of people from around the world to the United States in the late 19th and early 20th centuries, America itself was reaching farther outside of its own borders toward the rest of the world.

It began with trade. Between 1870 and 1914, American exports jumped from $500 million a year to over $2 billion in value. Products like the Singer Sewing Machine—with its slogan "the Singer seam unites the continents"—were familiar in countries as far away as Russia, Australia, and Argentina.

While America was becoming an economic giant, it still remained politically isolated and militarily weak. The United States spent less on its army than any major country in the world. After all, it had two oceans to protect it from any potential enemies.

Toward an American Empire

Things began to change toward the turn of the century, however. In 1890, U.S. Navy captain Alfred Mahan published *The Influence of Seapower Upon History*. In his book, Mahan said that all great nations in history were built on overseas trade. To defend that trade, a great nation needed a great navy.

Mahan published his book just at the

right time. It was read by many business and government leaders. These men worried that America's western frontier was now closed. The nation, they believed, needed new markets and new sources of raw materials. In 1890, Congress voted to build three battleships and a two-ocean fleet. "The sea will be the future seat of empire," wrote Secretary of the Navy Benjamin Tracy. "And we shall rule it as certain as the sun doth rise."

While the United States had remained isolated during the late 1800s, the nations of Europe had been busy carving up Asia and Africa. Americans began to worry that Britain, France, and other European countries would block American trade around the world. After losing its American colonies in the 18th century, Great Britain went on in the 19th century to build an even larger empire of colonies across the world. France had also founded colonies in Asia, Africa, and elsewhere.

And although Britain had ended slavery before the United States had, many in Britain and throughout Western Europe believed, as the British writer Rudyard Kipling said, that Britain must take up "the white man's burden" to civilize the darker races of the world.

The United States focused on two parts of the world: the Pacific Ocean and Latin America. Back in 1853, Commodore Matthew Perry had sailed his fleet to Japan and forced the emperor to open up the country to American trade. But in China, Europeans were carving out "spheres of influence," areas where only one European country could trade. In response, America promoted the "open door" policy. Under this program, all countries would have the right to trade in all parts of China.

America's interest in Latin America was even older. In 1823, President James Monroe issued his famous Monroe

Among those volunteering for the Spanish-American War was Theodore Roosevelt, who would later become president. He is shown above leading his men, nicknamed "The Rough Riders" in the Battle of San Juan Hill.

"Remember the Maine!"

—popular slogan during the Spanish-American War

Doctrine. The nations of Latin America had just broken free of Spain. Monroe warned Europe not to try and make new colonies there.

Europeans didn't take colonies in Latin America, but they did expand trade and loans. Many Latin American countries owed lots of money to European banks. In 1895, Britain nearly attacked Venezuela over unpaid debts until the American president, Grover Cleveland, warned them to stay out.

The Spanish-American War

In that same year, the people of Cuba, still a colony of Spain, rose up in a war of independence. Spain reacted with a brutal campaign that cost over 200,000 Cuban lives. American newspapers, trying to increase their sales, published horrifying accounts of the war. This type of newspaper reporting became known as "yellow journalism," after the color of the paper used on the front page.

In 1897, William Randolph Hearst, the most powerful newspaper owner in the country, sent artist Frederic Remington to Cuba. Hearst wanted war pictures, but Remington telegraphed back that he couldn't find any. Hearst answered, "You furnish the pictures and I'll furnish the war." Hearst did. Across the country, his newspapers demanded that America take action. A new form of patriotism, called "jingoism," was born.

In early 1898, President William McKinley sent the battleship *Maine* to Havana Harbor in Cuba. On the night of February 17, it blew up, killing 260 sailors. Even today, nobody knows if the explosion was an accident or an act of war. It didn't matter at the time. Most Americans believed the Spanish were behind it. Headlines screamed, "Remember the *Maine!*" and called for war.

SCOTT JOPLIN AND THE COMING OF JAZZ

Below: Scott Joplin, the father of ragtime piano

Before there was jazz, there was ragtime. During the 1890s, ragtime grew out of piano styles practiced by musicians along the Mississippi and Missouri rivers. It combined a minstrel show dance called the cakewalk with black banjo songs and European-styled waltzes to form its own offbeat sound. After a little-known musician from the Texas-Arkansas border town of Texarkana released "Maple Leaf Rag," a ragtime music craze swept the country. Almost overnight Scott Joplin became a success, his name spreading like wildfire across America.

Ironically, Joplin's first musical love was opera. His music teacher, a German immigrant, taught him Bach, Beethoven, and other European composers. Even at the height of the ragtime craze, Joplin hoped to be recognized as a "serious" composer. Using money earned from ragtime, Joplin soon began composing for opera and ballet. In 1907, he wrote the opera *Treemonisha*. Although *Treemonisha* was eventually performed in 1915, it met with little success. The public was not yet ready for a ragtime opera produced by a black composer.

Despite this disappointment, Joplin broke ground for black composers. While his operas may not have won him success, he was the first black composer to create music with a national audience. When Dixieland jazz hit big in the 1910s, Scott Joplin had already paved the way for its acceptance.

On April 11, they got it. McKinley sent a message to Congress. "In the name of humanity, in the name of civilization, in behalf of endangered American interests which give us the right and the duty to speak and to act," Spain must leave Cuba. Two weeks later, Spain declared war on the United States and McKinley called for 125,000 volunteers. Among those was Undersecretary of the Navy Theodore Roosevelt, who organized a regiment of "Rough Riders."

From the beginning, the war was not an even battle. Spain was economically weak and its military was very out-of-date. Its sailing ships were no match for America's new coal-powered, steel battleships. In August, Admiral George Dewey sank Spain's fleet in the Philippines without losing a single man.

In Cuba, Theodore Roosevelt led his troops up San Juan Hill and captured the city of Santiago. Meanwhile, during the war, McKinley asked Congress to annex, or add, Hawaii to the Union. Five years earlier, American-born sugar planters had overthrown the queen of Hawaii.

In less than four months, Spain had been defeated. During the war, far more American soldiers died from tropical disease than in battle. When it was over, the United States had an empire that stretched from Cuba and Puerto Rico in the Caribbean to Guam and the Philippines in the Pacific.

Now came the great debate. Should America, a country started in revolution, have colonies of its own? Cuba, it was quickly decided, should be freed. On the other hand, the Senate decided to keep the other territories.

This led to a new war in the Philippines. For years, freedom fighters under the leadership of Emilio Aguinaldo

WELL, I HARDLY KNOW WHICH TO TAKE FIRST!

had been struggling for independence from Spain. Aguinaldo welcomed the Americans at first. He thought they would help Filipinos win their freedom. He was wrong. Americans fought a long and bloody war against Aguinaldo.

America was now a great power, with colonies in two far-flung corners of the world. The new president, Theodore Roosevelt, believed that America should protect her interests all over the world. "Speak softly and carry a big stick" was his motto.

To help the American navy get from the Atlantic to the Pacific, Roosevelt wanted to build a canal in Panama. At that time, Panama belonged to Colombia. When Roosevelt offered $10 million for a strip of land across Panama, Colombia demanded more. In 1903, Roosevelt helped Panamanians get their independence. Soon after, he got his strip of land and began to build the canal. Eleven years later, the "big ditch" was finished.

Above: In this cartoon, President William McKinley offers Uncle Sam his choice of new territories —Cuba, Puerto Rico, the Philippines, or Hawaii, which appear in the cartoon as the Sandwich Islands. The Sandwich Islands is the name given to Hawaii by British explorers in honor of the earl of Sandwich.

AMERICAN TIMELINE

1877 Angered at the injustice of increased paycuts, railroad workers across the nation go on strike, effectively putting a stop to transcontinental service.

1878 Yellow fever strikes New Orleans in May and rapidly spreads throughout the South, taking more than 14,000 lives before finally abating.

1879 Thomas Edison demonstrates his newest invention, the 13-hour lightbulb.

1880 James Garfield is elected president.
■ Ira Remsen discovers saccharin, a white crystalline compound that is so sweet it can be substituted for sugar.
■ **November 2** Entering a polling booth for the national election, Susan B. Anthony and Elizabeth Cady Stanton are told that they cannot cast a ballot, as they are not legally entitled to vote.

1881 Booker T. Washington founds the Tuskegee Institute in Alabama, for the industrial education of African-Americans.
■ Clara Barton establishes the American Red Cross.
■ **July 2** Charles Guiteau shoots President Garfield, who dies several months later. Some argue it wasn't the bullet that killed him, but poor medical care.

1882 Congress passes the Chinese Exclusion Act, prohibiting Chinese immigration to the United States for the next ten years.

1883 The U.S. Supreme Court overturns the Civil Rights Act of 1875, which had prohibited the segregation of blacks and whites in all public accommodations.

Above: The Washington Monument

WORLD TIMELINE

1878 British warships arrive at the port of Istanbul to support the Ottomans in the war against Russia. They are too late: The treaty of San Stefano is signed and Russia acquires much of Bulgaria. In order to avoid further warfare, the Balkans are divided among the European nations.

1879 In South Africa, violence in opposition to British rule erupts. Zulus and Boers both attempt to assert their independence by attacking British troops.

1880 In an attempt to open Patagonia to settlement, Argentinian president Julio Argentino Roca orders the massacre of the Patagonian Indian tribes.

1881 British forces are overwhelmed by the Boers at Majuba Hill.

1882 Blamed for the execution of Russian czar Alexander II, Jews are herded into ghettos in Moscow and St. Petersburg. Many flee, seeking refuge in Europe and the United States.

1883 Chile wins the War of the Pacific, gaining Bolivia's coastal lands and large portions of Peru.

Above: William Gladstone, Prime Minister of Great Britain

1884 Despite Republican claims that he is a man of low moral character, Grover Cleveland is elected president.

1885 At 585 feet the world's tallest stone monument, the Washington Monument is completed. It took 36 years and $1.3 million to build.
■ Anti-Chinese sentiment erupts in violence in Wyoming territory, leaving 28 Chinese dead and 15 wounded.

1886 During a labor rally in Chicago's Haymarket Square, a bomb explodes, killing seven police officers. Despite a lack of evidence, eight labor activists are convicted of the crime.
■ After 15 years of fighting, Apache leader Geronimo and his soldiers surrender to U.S. troops in Arizona Territory.

■ In a quiet ceremony at the White House, President Cleveland marries his ex-partner's daughter, Fanny Folsom.

1887 The American Federation of Labor, or AFL, is formed to protect the interests of the workingman and to unite the labor unions.

1888 A cyclone hits Illinois, killing 35, and a blizzard hits the eastern seaboard, killing 400.

Above: Settlers pour into Oklahoma after it is opened to white settlement.

1885 Fifteen nations meet in Berlin to divide up the African continent. France, Germany, and Britain get the majority of the land.

1886 Germany's Karl Benz patents the first automobile.
■ Great Britain's Prime Minister William Gladstone is brought down after he proposes the Irish Home Rule bill, which would have established a parliament and cabinet in Dublin, with the power over defense, foreign affairs, currency, customs, and the post office remaining in the hands of the Parliament in London.

Above: European leaders gather at the Berlin Congress.

AMERICAN TIMELINE

1889 In an attempt to settle the west, two million acres of Oklahoma territory are opened to white settlement, causing the first of several land rushes.
■ Benjamin Harrison is inaugurated president.

1890 The Sherman Antitrust Act is passed, limiting the power of huge corporate monopolies by preventing them from fixing prices and forcing smaller companies out of business.
■ Over 250 Sioux Indians, half of them women and children, are killed in an attack on a village at Wounded Knee, South Dakota.

1891 President Harrison orders the U.S. Navy to begin preparations for war against Chile. Conflict is avoided when the Chilean government publicly apologizes for its slow investigation of the deaths of two American soldiers in a Chilean saloon.
■ In an attempt to find some entertainment for bored college students in Massachusetts, Dr. James Naismith invents basketball.

1892 First lady Caroline Harrison dies of tuberculosis, shortly before her husband loses reelection to Grover Cleveland.

1893 Queen Liliuokalani of Hawaii is ousted by American merchants. Although an application for admittance to the United States is submitted to the president, Hawaii does not become a state until 1898.
■ The stock market crashes and the economy plunges as more than 15,000 businesses fold.
■ Colorado grants women the right to vote.

Above: Queen Liliuokalani, the last queen of Hawaii

WORLD TIMELINE

1888 The crown prince of Austria, depressed because of an arranged marriage to the princess of the Belgians, commits suicide.

1889 Germany, the United States, and Britain sign a treaty granting the Samoan Islands their independence.
■ Pedro II, King of Brazil, is forced to flee the nation as armed forces seize the throne.
■ To commemorate the centennial of the French Revolution, Gustave Eiffel's wrought-iron tower is built in Paris. Many Parisians protest that it is hideously ugly.

Left: A poster showing the French actress Sarah Bernhardt as Medea

1890 German chancellor Otto von Bismarck is forced to resign.
■ After French troops open fire on striking miners, workers across the nation rally in protest.

1891 French actress Sarah Bernhardt begins a world tour, traveling to South America and Australia.

1892 Britain passes the Indian Councils Act, allowing Indians to be elected to office.

1894 The Pullman railroad strike in Chicago turns violent as federal troops cross picket lines and escort trains to safety outside of the Chicago stockyards.

1896 The Supreme Court rules that "separate but equal" facilities for whites and blacks are constitutional.
■ **June 4** In a barn behind his house, Henry Ford completes his first automobile, the "Quadricycle."
■ William McKinley is elected president.

1898 Angered by the unexplained explosion of the USS *Maine* in the port of Havana, Congress declares war on Spain.

1899 Filipino rebels attack U.S. troops in Manila.
■ Spanish-American War ends with the ratification of the Treaty of Paris. Spain is forced to grant Cuba independence and to give the Philippines, Guam, and Puerto Rico to the United States.

1900 To save foreign diplomats from persecution, U.S. forces invade China and crush the Boxer Rebellion.

*Below: This issue of **Scribner's** magazine reported on the Battle of San Juan Hill.*

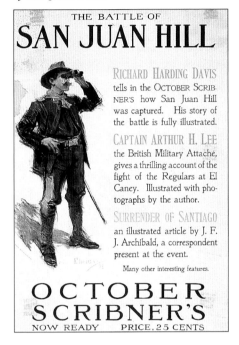

1893 New Zealand puts the Electoral Act into effect, becoming the first country to allow women to vote.

1894 Driving through the streets in his open carriage, French president Sadi-Carnot is fatally stabbed by an Italian anarchist.

1895 China is forced to surrender to Japanese forces after a devastating year-long war over Korea.

1896 The first modern Olympic games are held in Athens, as the nations of the world meet in sporting competition.

■ Queen Victoria of Great Britain celebrates her sixtieth year on the throne.

1899 Rising tensions between British and Boers in South Africa erupt in warfare.

Left: Queen Victoria, photographed on her Diamond Jubilee, 1897

VI. A NEW WORLD POWER

During the administration of President Theodore Roosevelt, the United States took a much larger role in international affairs. From managing the construction of the Panama Canal to helping negotiate peace between Russia and Japan, Roosevelt moved America to the center of the world stage. The cartoon above is based on the president's view that the United States should "speak softly and carry a big stick" when dealing with other nations.

THROUGHOUT MUCH of the 19th century, the United States had remained a land apart. Although Europe was largely at peace, many of its citizens left home for a new land of promise. In 1900, America was still a vast land that spread wide with rich soil, growing cities and industries, and a people who saw the future as always better than the past.

During the next two decades, this hope would be tested. Although Americans led the world in new inventions and American factories were the world's busiest, life wasn't easy for everyone. Many workers made very little money, and many of the machines they ran were quite dangerous. Most blacks were prevented from voting, almost 40 years after laws were written giving them the right to do so. Women couldn't vote at all. If America was truly to be a democracy, some things would have to change. In the years between 1900 and 1920, hundreds of new laws were written to improve the lives of America's people.

Before 1920, another big change would occur. For the first time, Americans would fight and die in Europe in a war that most Americans wanted to ignore when it started. But as Europe's war dragged on, and the United States was slowly pulled into it, it became a world war. The United States would never be a land apart again.

The Progressive Era

They had marched in countless parades since 1913. They had written to their representatives in government. They had authored dozens of articles in the nation's press. But it had done no good. Woodrow Wilson refused to support their cause. The voting booth, the president said, was no place for a woman.

On a cold winter's morning in 1918, a dozen or so members of the National Women's Party chained themselves to the iron fence around the White House, refusing to leave until the president would speak to them. They were sent to jail instead.

"If this thing is necessary, we will naturally go through with it," wrote Rose Winslow, an immigrant woman from Poland, from her cell. "Force is so stupid a weapon."

The women called themselves suffragists because they believed in women's suffrage, or voting. After being jailed, they went on a hunger strike. The prison authorities responded with solitary confinement and force-feeding.

"I had a nervous time of it, gasping long afterward, and my stomach rejecting during the process," Winslow continued. "I spent a bad, restless night, but otherwise I am all right. The poor soul who fed me got liberally besprinkled during the process. I heard myself making the most hideous sounds. One feels so foresaken [alone] when one lies prone [on one's back] and people shove a pipe down one's stomach."

Winslow's belief in the cause kept her going during the long months in solitary. "All the officers here know we are making a hunger strike [so] that women fighting for liberty may be considered political prisoners. God knows we don't want other women ever to have to do this over again," she closed one of her letters.

Two years later, Winslow's dream came true. After passing both houses of Congress and being ratified by two-thirds of the states, the Nineteenth Amendment was added to the Constitution. It read simply: "The right of citizens of the United States to vote shall not be denied . . . on account of sex."

An Age of Reform

The Nineteenth Amendment was the last, and perhaps the most important, reform in a great age of reform. Between 1900 and 1920, laws and amendments

"'We the people of the United States.' Which 'We, the people'? The women were not included."

—Lucy Stone

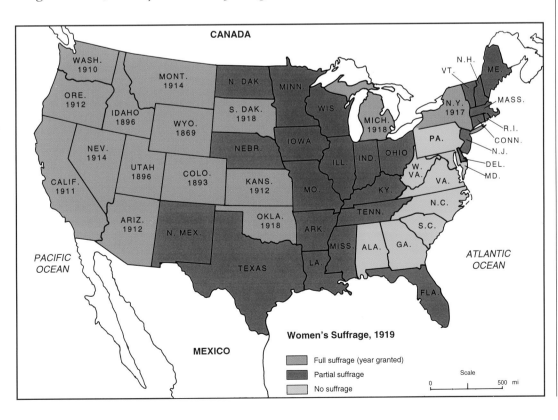

Women's Suffrage, 1919

Full suffrage (year granted)
Partial suffrage
No suffrage

Before the passage of the Nineteenth Amendment in 1920, New York and Michigan were the only states in the eastern half of the country that allowed women full voting rights. Wyoming, on the other hand, gave women the vote in 1869, just four years after the Civil War ended.

137

*"The true republic—
men, their rights,
and nothing more;
women, their rights,
and nothing less."*

—SUSAN B. ANTHONY

were passed that changed the way Americans voted, worked, and lived. Never before had the government and private citizens worked harder to improve the lives of their fellow Americans. As the new century opened, America looked toward the future with optimism. During the years between the Civil War and 1900, the country had become the greatest industrial nation in the history of the world. America had settled a continent and was absorbing millions of new immigrants. The country now had an empire that stretched from the Caribbean to the Pacific.

On the other hand, all this new growth had brought new problems with it as well. Millions of immigrants were crowded into unhealthy ghettoes. Workers, including thousands of children, were underpaid and labored in dangerous conditions. Products made by these workers were often unsafe and unhealthy. The environment was being used up without much thought for the future.

Many believed that it was time for a change. Those who believed most strongly in change were called Progressives. The years between 1900 and 1920 have become known as the Progressive Era. While most historians date the Progressive Era from the turn of the century, signs of the changing spirit of America began in the 1880s. In 1881, President James Garfield was killed by a frustrated office seeker. Under the old political system, known as "the spoils system," government jobs were rewarded to those who helped elect the candidate. It didn't matter if the person was qualified for the position or not.

Many reformers believed the spoils system was one of the causes of bad government. They wanted qualified people in civil, or government, service. They believed that every job seeker should pass a civil service examination. President Garfield's assassination helped convince Congress to pass the Pendleton

SUSAN B. ANTHONY (1820-1906)

Above: Susan B. Anthony

One of the greatest heroines in the long struggle for women's suffrage was Susan B. Anthony. Born in Adams, Massachusetts, in 1820, Anthony received an excellent education, which was rare for a girl at that time. So good was her education that she began teaching school herself by age 15. In 1850, Anthony came to know a group of women that would fight along with her throughout her life. Among them were Elizabeth Cady Stanton, Lucretia Mott, Amelia Bloomer, and Lucy Stone.

In 1852, Anthony launched an alcohol temperance group for women, and in 1856, she joined the Anti-Slavery Society. In 1868, she helped found the National Women's Suffrage Association, and when the Fifteenth Amendment gave blacks the right to vote, Anthony tried to have the law include women. Although her effort failed, Anthony decided she would vote anyway, and did so in the election of 1872. She was convicted of breaking the law and charged with a fine, which she refused to pay. Over the next 30 years, Anthony never stopped campaigning for women's right to vote, traveling endlessly throughout the United States and in Europe. Along the way, men angrily made fun of her and her cause. Although Anthony died before seeing women across the country legally vote, her lifelong efforts paid off at last in 1920.

*Left: Women suffragettes
protest for the right to vote.*

Act. The new law created a Civil Service Commission.

The Populist Party also had an impact on reform. As farmers who had to ship their crops to market, the Populists disliked and distrusted the railroads. They believed that these great national corporations charged too much and had too much power over people. They wanted the railroads to be taken over by the government.

That didn't happen, but some reforms did. Instead of taking over the railroads, the federal government moved to regulate them. In 1887, Congress passed the Interstate Commerce Act. The law established a commission that would regulate railroad rates and make sure they were fair.

These new laws, however, were not always effective. Sometimes they weren't even enforced. For example, the Civil Service Commission examined less than 10 percent of applicants. It took decades before most government workers would have to pass an exam to enter the civil service. And the Interstate Commerce Commission did little to regulate the railroads for several decades.

Often, the reforms that came directly from citizens worked better. Many of these citizen reformers were women. In 1889, Jane Addams started Hull House, a community center in Chicago's immigrant ghetto. Another, Josephine Shaw Lowell of New York, came to the conclusion that charity wasn't enough. "It is better to save [the poor] before they go under," she wrote, "than to spend your life fishing them out afterward."

In 1890, Lowell founded the New York Consumers League. Her goal was to improve the wages and working conditions of the city's female store clerks. To do this, the League issued a "white list." Stores that paid a decent wage and treated their workers well would be put on the list. The League then told shoppers to buy at those stores. Under the leadership of Florence Kelley, the organization went nationwide in 1899.

Beginning around 1900, a new generation of journalists added their voices to the call for change. In a series of magazine articles, journalists like Lincoln Steffens and Ida Tarbell began to expose the corruption of business and government. They were called "muckrakers" because they stirred up the muck [dirt] of politics and industry.

In his 1903 article "The Shame of Cities," Steffens argued that corrupt politicians were destroying America's cities for their own profit. "Such then, is the boodling [corruption] system as we see it in St. Louis," he wrote. "Everything the city owned was for sale by the officers elected by the people . . . [As] long as the members of the [government] got the proceeds they would sell out the town. Would? They did and they will."

Tarbell focused on big business. In 1902, she published a magazine article called "The History of the Standard Oil Company," which attacked the business practices of Standard Oil's owner John D. Rockefeller. "[He] was willing to strain every nerve," she wrote, "to obtain for himself special and illegal privileges [favors] from the railroads which were bound to ruin every man in the oil business not sharing them with him."

Some in the government were serious about reform as well. Beginning with Hazen Pingree in Detroit in 1889, a new breed of politicians began to fight the spoils system and win office. By the turn of the century, mayors like Samuel "Golden Rule" Jones in Toledo, Ohio, and Mark Fagan in Jersey City, New Jersey, promised governments that would be more efficient and less corrupt. They called their efforts the "good government" movement. Their corrupt enemies labeled them "goo-goos" for short.

Teddy Roosevelt's "Bully Pulpit"

Far and away the most important progressive politician of the era was Theodore Roosevelt. The former police

Above: John Muir, the father of the conservation movement, helped persuade the government to expand the National Park System.

commissioner of New York City and governor of New York State, Roosevelt was picked to be President William McKinley's vice presidential running mate in 1900. After McKinley was assassinated while visiting the Pan-American Exposition in Buffalo, New York, on September 6, 1901, Roosevelt became president.

Roosevelt was eager to make changes quickly, but because he was not elected himself, he had to move carefully at first. Powerful people in the government and industry wanted to keep things as they were. His first moves were cautious and concerned conservation of natural resources.

Roosevelt's interest in the environment began years before. As a boy, he had suffered from asthma, and his parents had sent him to a ranch in the Dakota territories. They hoped hard work and dry air would cure him. Since that time, Roosevelt had been an enthusiastic outdoorsman and hunter.

When he became president, Roosevelt inherited a small Forest Service and National Park System. Yellowstone, the first national park, had been established in 1872. Pushed by the naturalist John Muir, Congress had added Yosemite and two other parks in California to the system in 1890. Roosevelt believed the nation's natural resources had to be preserved for future generations. During his presidency, he added over 120 million acres to the national forest reserve.

The first real test of the Roosevelt presidency, however, occurred in the area of labor relations. In the fall of 1902, the United Mine Workers and the coal companies could not reach a settlement over wages and working conditions. John Mitchell, president of the miners' union, was willing to go to arbitration, or third-party settlement, but the owners were not. With winter approaching, the nation badly needed coal. Roosevelt called a conference on October 1, but no agreement was reached. Other presidents might have warned the miners to go back to work, but Roosevelt warned the coal owners instead. He told them to reach an agreement or have the government take over the mines. The owners were furious, but were forced to give in. "Of all the forms of tyranny," Roosevelt wrote in his diary, "the most vulgar is the tyranny of mere wealth."

Like the muckrakers, Roosevelt was very concerned about the power of big business. Corporate power had been growing ever larger since the end of the Civil War. The depression of the 1890s had forced these corporations to lower prices, and many had lost a lot of money. They wanted an end to what they called "destructive competitive." When recovery came in 1897, they used their profits to combine into even larger business enterprises. Several companies would combine under a single board of directors. They were called "trusts."

These large corporations could be efficient, but they were also dangerous. With their huge power, they could and did destroy competitors and force any sales price on the American people. By 1910, 1 percent of the nation's manufacturers produced 44 percent of the nation's goods. Many Americans saw this as a threat to free enterprise and democracy.

Years earlier, in 1890, Congress had passed the Sherman Anti-Trust Act. The act made it illegal for people or organizations to conspire, or work together, to prevent free trade. For the most part,

however, the act had been used against trade unions, not corporations. If a union called a strike, its leaders could be and were found guilty of interfering with the owner's right to free trade.

Roosevelt decided to use the act against corporations. In 1902, he ordered the Justice Department to prosecute Northern Securities, which owned a number of railroads in the Midwest and Northwest. Two years later, the Supreme Court agreed that the company had engaged in anti-free trade practices. The justices ordered the corporation broken up into smaller companies. Roosevelt also set up a new organization called the Bureau of Corporations to investigate big business wrongdoing. It wasn't until after his landslide victory for reelection in 1904 that Roosevelt really started going after big business. Roosevelt promised a "square deal" for America. He promised that his government would become even more active in protecting the people's interests. Roosevelt called the presidency a "bully pulpit" (bully was slang for great) for focusing public attention on social problems and protecting its interests.

Immediately after his reelection, Roosevelt ordered the Bureau of Corporations to begin investigating 45 trusts. Roosevelt was not against all big businesses, but he felt that some businesses abused their power. The worst of these, most Americans agreed, was Rockefeller's Standard Oil. After a long battle that

According to an usher named Ike Hoover, who worked at the White House during Roosevelt's administration, the president often would get up from his desk at the end of a long and busy day, sneak out the back door and run several times around the Washington Monument to work off extra energy. As Roosevelt himself remarked, "No president has enjoyed being president as much as I."

Left: President Theodore Roosevelt

141

Collier's
THE NATIONAL WEEKLY

A G A I N !!!

Above: **Collier's** *was one of the Progressive Era's most popular muckraking magazines. This 1912 issue warned of the dangerous drugs used in patent medicines.*

Below: Booker T. Washington

Above: W. E. B. DuBois

lasted until 1911, after Roosevelt had left office, the oil giant was broken up.

The Roosevelt administration did not begin every reform of big business on its own. Sometimes it had to be pushed. In 1905, a muckraking journalist named Samuel Hopkins Adams published an article about the patent medicine business. Patent medicines were untested drugs that promised to cure anything that ailed the sufferer. America spent $75 million a year on such medicines. "In consideration of this sum," wrote Adams, "it [the American public] will swallow huge quantities of alcohol, an appalling amount of opiates and narcotics, a wide assortment of drugs ranging from powerful and dangerous heart depressants to insidious [evil] liver stimulants; and in far excess of all other ingredients, undiluted fraud."

The following year came an even more frightening story. In 1906, Upton Sinclair published his classic novel *The Jungle* based on his experiences working in the meatpacking plants of Chicago. Sinclair exposed the dangerous working conditions in the factories. The book became an instant best-seller.

Readers, however, were less interested in the meatpacking workers than in the products they made. Sinclair showed how the sausages and packaged meats Americans ate were made with rotten meat and in filthy conditions. "It seemed [the packinghouses] must have agencies all over the country, to hunt out old and crippled and diseased cattle to be canned," the hero of the novel explains. "There were cattle which had been fed on 'whiskey-malt,' the refuse of the breweries, and had become what the men called 'steerly'—which means covered with boils."

Roosevelt had not been very interested in consumer issues. But the public out-

BOOKER T. WASHINGTON AND W. E. B. DUBOIS

When Reconstruction ended in 1876, African-Americans lost many gains they had made after the Civil War. Rising violence, laws aimed at preventing blacks from voting, and the poor quality of black schools all worked against African-Americans hoping to improve their lives. Despite these roadblocks, many organizations were launched to improve the lives of African-Americans. In 1881, a former slave named Booker T. Washington founded the Tuskegee Institute, an educational center that stressed industrial training for blacks as a means to success. In 1895, Washington argued in a speech in Atlanta that blacks needed to gain the trust of whites through hard work and education instead of fighting for civil rights. "It is at the bottom of life we must begin," he said, "and not at the top." Washington was praised by whites and even invited to the White House by Theodore Roosevelt. Many blacks, however, disagreed with him.

One was W. E. B. DuBois, who called Washington's 1895 speech "The Atlanta Compromise." In 1903, DuBois published his book, *The Souls of Black Folk.* In it, he sarcastically called Washington "the most distinguished Southerner since [disgraced Confederate president] Jefferson Davis." Although DuBois respected Washington's many achievements, he wrote, "Is it possible . . . that nine million men can make effective progress in economic lines if they are deprived political rights. . . ?" Throughout his life, DuBois fought for social equality for blacks. In 1909, he cofounded the National Association for the Advancement of Colored People (NAACP), and edited its magazine *The Crisis* for the next 24 years.

John D. Rockefeller's Standard Oil Company was perhaps the most powerful corporation in America at the turn of the century. Formed in 1863, Standard Oil controlled 90 percent of the oil refined in America by 1882. This cartoon at left shows Standard Oil as an octopus grabbing up anything and everything in its path. In 1911, the Supreme Court finally broke up the company into smaller pieces.

rage started by Adams and Sinclair forced him to act. He ordered an investigation and proposed the Pure Food and Drug Act and the Meat Inspection Act. When probusiness opponents tried to block him in Congress, he threatened to publish the results of the investigation. Industry backed down and Congress passed the bill. Under the meat act, the Department of Agriculture sent inspectors into meatpacking plants. The Food and Drug Act established the Food and Drug Administration to approve and regulate other foods and drugs.

By 1908, Roosevelt's actions had divided the Republican Party. Deciding not to run again, Roosevelt hand-picked his secretary of war, William Howard Taft, as his successor. After seeing Taft win the election, Roosevelt believed his work would be carried on and he left the country for a year-long safari in Africa. Taft was a progressive, but not a very active one. In fact, it was the Supreme Court that did more for reform than the president. In 1911, it broke up the Standard Oil Company and issued its *Muller* v. *Oregon* decision. With that case, the court agreed for the first time that the government had the right to regulate the conditions of female labor.

Labor reforms did not just occur on the national level. On May 25, 1911, a fire broke out in the Triangle Shirtwaist Factory in New York City, killing 146 mostly young, female workers. An investigation later proved that the women had been locked into the factory and that there were no fire escapes. Two months later, New York established the Factory Commission. Over the next four years, it issued 56 laws to prevent fires, outlaw unsafe machines, and improve wages and hours for women and children.

The NAACP Is Born

At the same time, black Americans were also beginning to organize. Even as Progressives were fighting for the rights of consumers, workers, and immigrants, racial violence was reaching its peak in America. National politicians did almost nothing about lynching. President Taft assured southern whites that the "the federal government has nothing to do with social equality." In 1909, a group of African-American leaders, including educator and historian W. E. B. Dubois, founded the National Association for the Advancement of Colored People (NAACP), now the oldest and largest civil rights organization in America. The NAACP pushed for anti-lynching laws in the South and published a newspaper called *The Crisis*.

When Theodore Roosevelt returned

Shown above is a 1929 edition of The Crisis, *the newspaper published by the National Association for the Advancement of Colored People.* The Crisis *was first published 20 years earlier, in 1909.*

from Africa, he was disappointed by the slow pace of the Taft administration's reforms. In 1912, he decided to challenge Taft for the presidency. To do this, Roosevelt formed the Progressive, or Bull Moose (one of Roosevelt's nicknames) Party. In the end, Roosevelt only took away votes from Taft, thus helping the Democratic candidate, Woodrow Wilson, win election.

A former history professor at Princeton University and Governor of New Jersey, Wilson was an active Progressive like Roosevelt. In his campaign, he lashed out at corporate power. "This is a struggle for emancipation," he declared. "If America is not to have free enterprise, then she can have freedom of no sort whatsoever."

The reforms of the Wilson administration were even greater than those of Roosevelt's. One of the first was the Federal Reserve Act. For the first time since the 1830s, the United States had established a government institution to regulate private banking. The act established a Federal Reserve Board that would decide how much money would be released by the government. This helped to regulate the economy and limit the power of wealthy bankers.

In 1914, Wilson established the Federal Trade Commission, which gave the government even more power to regulate business and trade. Wilson also passed the Federal Workmen's Compensation Act to help people injured on the job, a federal child labor law, and the eight-hour work day for all railroad workers.

On top of that, four amendments to the Constitution were ratified during Wilson's two terms as president. The Sixteenth Amendment legalized income taxes. The Seventeenth Amendment called for the direct election by the voters of U.S. senators. Previously, senators were elected by state legislatures. The Eighteenth Amendment banned the possession, use, and sale of alcohol, and the Nineteenth Amendment gave women the right to vote.

In just a few short years, both reformers in the government and outside of it had brought more changes to American life than had taken place since at least the Civil War. For the first time, the federal government had taken responsibility for regulating and controlling big business. New laws and amendments to the Constitution helped make the country more democratic and improved the lives of millions.

But there was one reform that the government was not willing to make. Workers still did not have the right to freely organize into trade unions to

President Wilson worked to pass federal child labor laws, including a minimum age of 14 for most work, and an eight-hour day. The Supreme Court, however, ruled that these laws were unconstitutional since they violated states' rights and personal freedom. Not until 1938 would the federal government pass its first laws restricting child labor. Above, a young girl at work in a North Carolina textile mill. Right, President Wilson (front row, smiling) taking in a baseball game.

This paper has been paid for, if not by you, then by some one who wants you to read it.

No. 241 If No. 242 appears on your address label, your subscription expires next week. Do not fail to renew.

AMERICAN ⬤ SOCIALIST

Death, the hand maiden of war, is coming closer. The government has ordered 200,000 coffins to be used as required.

VOL. III. No. 49. ⬤ 304 CHICAGO, SATURDAY, JUNE 16, 1917. 25 CENTS FOR SIX MONTHS; 50 CENTS PER YEAR; $1 PER YEAR OUTSIDE UNITED STATES

Registration Day Shows Overwhelming Vote Against War By Men Of Draft Age; Help Repeal The Conscription Law Now!

demand better wages and working conditions on their own. Courts continued to use the Anti-Trust Act against workers more often than against their bosses. The courts also issued injunctions, or temporary stoppages, of strikes. If workers continued striking, they risked jail. The nation's leading union, the American Federation of Labor, had a hard time protecting even its skilled union members. For the unskilled, there was almost no protection at all.

The Wobblies and the Socialists

Out of frustration and anger, many skilled and unskilled workers turned to radical politics and radical unions. In the election of 1912, nearly a million workers voted for the Socialist candidate Eugene V. Debs. Thousands of others joined the Industrial Workers of the World (IWW). Calling itself "one big union," the IWW, or Wobblies as they liked to call themselves, had been organized in 1905.

The Wobblies had founded their union in the mining and lumber camps of the West, where working conditions were very bad. They tried all kinds of ways to improve the working conditions of their members. When a strike was called in a town, hundreds of outside organizers would pour in from around the West. They would give speeches on the streets and get arrested. The jails would fill up so quickly that before long, local police would often have to let them out. In San Diego, however, business and government leaders put strikers in railroad cars and sent them to the desert where they left them to die.

In time, the Wobblies moved eastward. Their first target was the giant American Woolen mill in Lawrence, Massachusetts. Most of the company's 40,000 workers were immigrants. Many were women. Half were under 18 years old. Working conditions were terrible and pay was very low. When the company tried to cut wages even further, the union went into action. Led by IWW leaders William "Big Bill" Haywood and Elizabeth Gurley Flynn, the strikers stayed out of the plants for months. The Socialist Party raised funds for the striking workers across the country. The company, however, was too powerful. It hired strikebreakers to beat up union organizers.

Still, the Wobblies continued to organize local workers into unions. And they continued to organize strikes against business for several more years. By the end of the decade, however, the United States had begun to inch closer to entering a growing war in Europe. The Wobblies and the Socialist Party were against this war. The government said that the union was helping the enemy and it put many of the two organization's leaders in jail. There would be little union organizing until after the war.

The Industrial Workers of the World, or Wobblies, were closely allied to the American Socialist Party. The Wobblies united many of the nation's smaller unions and helped to organize strikes across the country during the 1910s. As World War I approached, both the Wobblies and the Socialists publicly opposed it. Shown at top is an antiwar headline from the American Socialist *newspaper, and above a recruitment poster for the IWW.*

"The War to End All Wars"

Nothing like it had ever been used in war before.

"The soldier's clothes soon becomes impregnated [soaked] with the stuff as he brushes through the undergrowth, and the burns develop through the help of moisture . . . The burns are extremely painful, but in general not fatal unless the gas has been inhaled or (as with other surface burns) a third or more of the total skin area has been affected."

As a medic in the American Expeditionary Force (AEF) in World War I, Frederick Pottle learned firsthand about the terrible effects of mustard gas. "[M]ustard gas cases were probably the most painful we had to witness in all our service."

Both the Allies (the United States, France, and England) and the Germans used mustard gas during the war. "[It] . . . is a heavy liquid, which, though fairly volatile [gaseous], will remain for some time clinging to grass and undergrowth, and will burn any flesh with which it comes in contact," Pottle continued.

"It is especially adapted for use by a retreating army. By soaking down with mustard gas the area through which the pursuing American troops had to advance, the Germans made sure that a large number of the advancing force would be incapacitated [injured]."

Mustard gas was such a terrible weapon that the world's nations agreed to end its use in warfare after World War I. It would not be unleashed again for another 70 years, until President Saddam Hussein of Iraq used it in his war against Iran in the 1980s.

A Divided Europe

World War I followed a century of great change in Europe. Led by England, many of Europe's greatest nations had built strong economies, powered by the Industrial Revolution. Across the globe, Great Britain, France, Holland, Portugal, and Belgium had established colonies, ruling over people in just about every corner of the globe. Although a number of small wars broke out from place to place, Europe's great powers ruled a stable world.

The first signs that a much larger war was coming had emerged in the 1860s

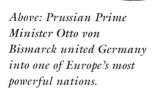

Above: Prussian Prime Minister Otto von Bismarck united Germany into one of Europe's most powerful nations.

Right: Archduke Ferdinand, the heir to the throne of Austria-Hungary, was assassinated by a Bosnian Serb gunman moments after this picture was taken. His death led directly to the start of World War I.

and 1870s. A new country was forming in Central Europe. For a thousand years, Germany had been made up of dozens of tiny kingdoms. Under the leadership of Prime Minister Otto von Bismarck, these ministates were brought together to become the most powerful country on the continent. This new German power was used in a short war against France, when it took Alsace-Lorraine, a territory along the two countries' borders with a population of both German and French people.

While Germany was expanding, the Ottoman Empire was dying. Almost 500 years earlier, the Ottoman Turks had captured the Balkan region in the southeast of Europe. By the late 1800s, however, the Ottoman Empire was known as the "sick man of Europe." As it slowly collapsed, Germany and other countries—including Britain, France, Russia, and the Austro-Hungarian Empire—competed for new power. No country wanted another to get an advantage.

This competition led to a series of alliances or partnerships. Some were public, and others were kept secret. Sometimes one country would make an open deal with another, and a secret deal with a third. It got so complicated that even diplomats did not always know which country was secretly allied with another. By 1900, however, the continent was roughly divided into two sides. On one side were the English, French, and Russians. On the other were the Germans, Austro-Hungarians, and Ottoman Turks. Each of these countries had agreed that if one country on its side was attacked, the other allies would come to its defense.

Although these alliances were meant to protect each country, they actually helped push them toward war. Each of the leading allies began to build more and more weapons to use in case war did break out. Looking back, it does not seem surprising that expanding alliances and growing armies were the fuel for war. The spark came in the form of assassination. The place was Sarajevo, Bosnia, which has also been the scene of so much fighting in the 1990s.

Above: French troops charge at the Battle of the Somme, in 1916.

"No nation is fit to sit in judgment upon any other nation."

—WOODROW WILSON, *in 1915, urging that the United States stay out of the war in Europe*

"The world must be made safe for democracy."

—WOODROW WILSON, *in 1917, while declaring war on Germany*

In 1915, a German submarine sank the British luxury liner Lusitania. *The* Lusitania *was secretly carrying weapons for England. Over 1,200 passengers died.* **The New York Times** *headline shown (right) announces the news.*

"All the News That's Fit to Print."

The New York

VOL. LXIV...NO. 20,923.   NEW YORK, SATURDAY, MAY 8, 1915.—TWENTY-FOUR PA

LUSITANIA SUNK BY A SUBMARINE, PROB TWICE TORPEDOED OFF IRISH COAST; S AMERICANS ABOARD INCLUDED VANDE WASHINGTON BELIEVES THAT A GR

HOCKS THE PRESIDENT

Washington Deeply Stirred by Disaster and Fears a Crisis.

BULLETINS AT WHITE HOUSE

Wilson Reads Them Closely, but Is Silent on the Nation's Course.

HINTS OF CONGRESS CALL

Loss of Lusitania Recalls Firm Tone of Our First Warning to Germany.

CAPITAL FULL OF RUMORS

Reports That Liner Was to be Sunk Were Heard Before Actual News Came.

Death in Sarajevo

In 1908, the Austro-Hungarian Empire seized the territory of Bosnia from the Ottomans. This angered the nearby country of Serbia, a nation of Slavic peoples allied with Russia, another Slav country. Many Serbians lived in Bosnia and didn't like being ruled by the Austro-Hungarians.

On June 28, 1914, a Bosnian Serb assassinated Archduke Ferdinand, heir to the Austro-Hungarian throne, as he rode through the streets of Sarajevo in his carriage. The Austro-Hungarians demanded that Serbia give up all claims to Bosnia. Serbia refused and the Austro-Hungarians declared war a month later.

Now all the alliances came into play. Germany immediately backed Austria and the Russians sided with Serbia. As the three powers prepared for war, France declared war on Germany. On August 2,

the German general Helmuth von Moltke demanded that Belgium, a tiny country between Germany and France, allow his army to pass through on its way to attack France. When Belgium refused, Germany attacked. Britain, the last great power to enter the conflict, quickly declared war on Germany.

Both the Allies (Britain, France, and Russia) and the Central Powers (Germany, Austria-Hungary, and the Ottoman Empire) thought the war would end quickly. Germany's invasion of France, however, was stopped at the First Battle of the Marne in late 1914. A stalemate followed. The two sides dug trenches and defended the "no-man's land" between them with machine guns, barbed wire, and mines. For the next three years, huge and bloody battles were fought as the two sides tried to gain a few hundred yards of territory. At the battles of the

ONE CENT In Greater New York, Jersey City and Newark. { Elsewhere TWO CENTS.

LY 1,000 DEAD;
S IN 15 MINUTES;
ILT AND FROHMAN;
E CRISIS IS AT HAND

SOME DEAD TAKEN ASHORE

Several Hundred Survivors at Queenstown and Kinsale.

STEWARD TELLS OF DISASTER

One Torpedo Crashes Into the Doomed Liner's Bow, Another Into the Engine Room.

SHIP LISTS OVER TO PORT

Makes It Impossible to Lower Many Boats, So Hundreds Must Have Gone Down.

ATTACKED IN BROAD DAY

Passengers at Luncheon—Warning Had Been Given by Germans Before the Ship Left New York.

This was a new kind of warfare. Submarines could not warn ships before they sank them or rescue their survivors. To many, this violated all the rules of civilized behavior. On May 7, 1915, a German submarine, or U-boat, sank the British luxury liner *Lusitania*. Over 1,200 passengers died, including 128 Americans. The Germans claimed the ship was secretly carrying weapons for England (which it was). Americans were furious. Wilson sent warnings to the Germans, who then stopped the submarine attacks. America had gone to the edge of war, but backed off. The following year Wilson won reelection with the slogan, "Who keeps us out of war?"

To break the war stalemate in Europe, however, Germany warned the United States it would begin attacking all ships again on January 31, 1917. Three days later, Wilson cut off all ties with Germany. The situation was made even more tense after American newspapers published a strange telegram from Germany to

After the Lusitania *was sunk, President Wilson demanded that Germany apologize, pay the United States for damages, and promise not to use submarines again. Germany did apologize and pay damages, but refused the last demand. Kaiser Wilhelm of Germany is shown in the cartoon below tossing spare coins at Wilson, as an American eagle hangs its head in embarrassment.*

Somme and Verdun in 1916, nearly two million men were killed or wounded. After the Battle of the Somme, British poet Siegfried Sassoon wrote, "I am staring at a sunlit picture of Hell."

The United States Stays Out of War

Americans, meanwhile, were horrified by the news coming out of Europe and wanted no part of it. Shortly after the war broke out, President Wilson declared Americans were "neutral in fact as well as in name, impartial in thought as well as in action."

In actual fact, many U.S. farmers and businesses were making money trading with both sides. But a British naval blockade stopped trade with the Central Powers. To stop American supplies getting to England and France, Germany launched a submarine war against shipping in the Atlantic.

Mexico. In the communication, German ambassador Alfred Zimmerman asked Mexico to attack the United States. In return, Germany promised Mexico help in regaining territories lost in the Mexican-American war 70 years earlier.

Americans Join the War

The Zimmerman telegram was more than the United States could stand. On April 2, just a month after taking office with the promise of peace, Wilson asked Congress to declare war on Germany and the Central Powers. In May, General John J. Pershing sailed for Europe to ask the Allies what America could do for them. "Men, men, and more men" was French Marshall Joseph Joffre's answer.

While Pershing was in France, Congress passed the Selective Service Act. By early June, over nine million men between the ages of 21 and 30 were processed for the draft.

In order to fight a war, the United States needed more than just men. It needed supplies. In July 1917, Wilson organized the War Industries Board. Under banker Bernard Baruch, the agency shifted factories from domestic to war production. It took over railroads and used them to ship troops and war materiel. The government launched a massive propaganda, or advertising, campaign to win support for the war and sell bonds to pay for it.

New taxes were imposed on business, and unions agreed not to strike. With men off fighting, women went to work in war factories. Many southern blacks who were not in the military moved north to find better-paying jobs in the war industry.

America's entry into the war came just in time for the Allies. On the eastern front, Russia was collapsing. In March, 1917, an army mutiny led to the downfall of the emperor, or czar, Nicholas II. The new democratic government, headed by Alexander Kerensky, promised to continue fighting. But Russian peasants and workers were sick of the war and

JEANNETTE RANKIN (1880-1973)

Although most states in the western United States granted women the right to vote before the Nineteenth Amendment was passed in 1920, Montana was among the last to do so. Montanan women might have had to wait until 1920 if it hadn't been for women like Jeannette Rankin. Rankin became active in the women's suffrage movement in 1910, and by 1914, had become a legislative secretary for the National American Women Suffrage Association. Two years later, in 1916, before women in many states were allowed to vote at all, Rankin became the first woman elected to the U.S. House of Representatives.

While in that position, Rankin continued to fight for national women's suffrage. But it was her opposition to America's entry into World War I that gained her national attention. Her strong antiwar views may have cost her election to the U.S. Senate, but defeat did not lead her to change her mind about the evils of war. She spent the 1920s and '30s as a social worker, and then was reelected to the House in 1940. After the Japanese attacked Pearl Harbor, Rankin shocked the nation by again voting against sending U.S. troops to war. "You can no more win a war than you can win an earthquake," she once said. Later in life, Rankin founded a cooperative women's homestead in Georgia, and led marches on Washington to protest the Vietnam War.

Above: Jeannette Rankin

Left: Captain Eddie Rickenbaker was America's greatest World War I ace. In battle after battle, he emerged victorious. By the end of the war, he had shot down 26 aircraft. When peace came, he returned to the United States a hero.

Below: American soldiers train for battle at Fort Dix, New Jersey, before being sent to Europe.

the food shortages at home. They were ripe for another revolution and the Germans knew it.

The Russian Revolution

In April, the Germans helped ferry Communist leader Vladimir Lenin back to the Russian capital of St. Petersburg. Lenin and his Bolshevik party rallied the Russian people with promises of "peace, land, and bread." On November 6, 1917, the Bolsheviks overthrew Kerensky and established the Soviet Union. Less than six weeks later, the new Soviet government agreed to a cease-fire with Germany. In March 1918, the two countries signed the Brest-Litovsk peace treaty, giving a huge piece of the former Russian Empire to Germany.

This did not end the fighting in the Soviet Union, however. A civil war soon broke out between the communist government and anticommunist forces. In June 1918, Britain, the United States, and others sent troops to fight the Bolsheviks.

Meanwhile, peace with the Soviets allowed Germany to transfer its troops to the western front against Britain, France, and the United States. In the spring and summer of 1918, Germany launched several massive attacks in France, including the Second Battle of the Marne. Each was driven back with the help of Americans. One soldier, Sergeant Alvin York, became

an American hero after he killed 25 Germans and captured 132 more in France's Argonne Forest.

By September, more than 500,000 American troops, known as "doughboys," were on the attack. The fresh recruits turned the tide of war and the Germans were forced to surrender. At 11 minutes past 11 in the morning, on the 11th day of the 11th month, the guns of World War I fell silent. The timing was not accidental. The number 11 symbolizes the last possible moment as in the "eleventh hour." Many believed that continued warfare would mean the end of European civilization.

UNITED STATES ARMY RECRUITING SERVICE

Above: In this famous recruiting poster created by artist James Montgomery Flagg, Uncle Sam issues the call for troops.

Right: In June 1918, gas-masked American marines defeated Germans at the Battle of Belleau Wood, in France.

The League of Nations

Now it was time to shape the peace. In January 1919, Allied leaders met at Versailles, a palace outside Paris, to sign the official peace treaty and decide the shape of postwar Europe. Wilson arrived with a Fourteen Point peace program. It included independence for the people of Europe (though not for the European colonies in Asia and Africa), an end to secret alliances, and arms reduction. Wilson's most important point was the formation of the League of Nations, an international organization dedicated to solving disputes between countries peacefully.

Most of these points were accepted by the other allies. On one point, however, there was sharp disagreement. Wilson did not want to punish Germany too strongly for the war. Britain, and especially France, did. After all, much of the fighting had been on French soil and much of the country's industrial heartland was in ruins. They wanted Germany to pay billions in reparations, or rebuilding, costs.

For six months, Wilson and the other allied leaders worked on the Versailles Treaty. In the end, the president got most of what he wanted, except for light German reparations. But an even greater fight awaited him when he returned home in June 1919. Many members of Congress, and the American public, were disgusted by the peace. They felt that Britain and France were seeking revenge on Germany, not a fair peace treaty for Europe, and that 100,000 American soldiers had died only to help make Britain and France more powerful. They wanted no part of the League of Nations or European politics.

All that summer, Wilson traveled the country trying to win support for American membership in the League. The effort broke his health. In late September, he collapsed in Colorado, the victim of a stroke that left half his body paralyzed. For the rest of his term, his wife and advisors oversaw the government. We will never know if a healthy Wilson could have won Congress over. In November, Congress voted against U.S. membership.

Trouble at Home

The years after World War I were troubled ones for America. Relations between black and white Americans reached a new low. As blacks poured into the cities during the war, riots broke out in St. Louis, Houston, and Philadelphia over jobs in war factories.

The defeat of Germany and its allies led to the birth of a number of new European countries, including Poland, Czechoslovakia, and Yugoslavia. Shown at left are Europe's borders before the war, and then after it.

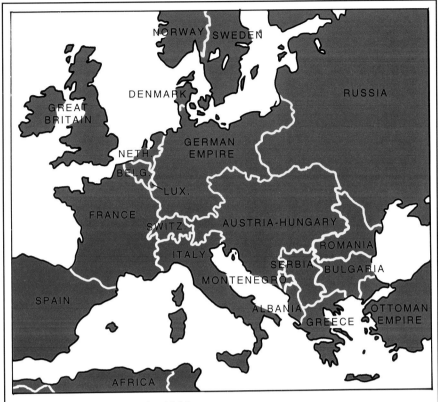

Europe in 1914

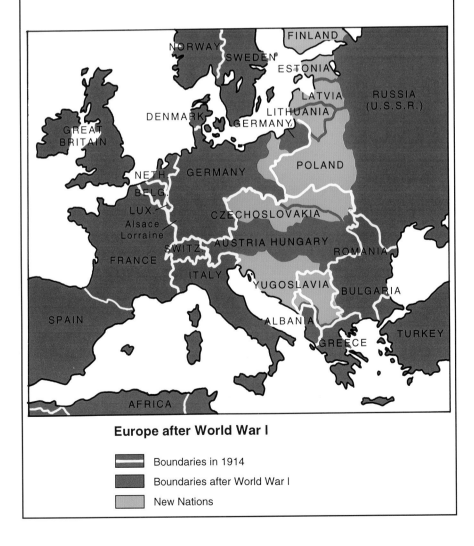

Europe after World War I

- ▬ Boundaries in 1914
- ▬ Boundaries after World War I
- ▬ New Nations

With the end of the war, America was ready to celebrate. The above lapel ribbon was produced for a Hackensack, New Jersey, welcome-home parade.

Tensions grew worse when the war ended and many factories closed down.

In 1919, over 75 blacks, including several in military uniform, were lynched by white mobs. Then in July 1919, a black teenager named Eugene Williams swam toward a Chicago beach reserved for whites. Somebody hit him with a rock and the boy drowned. The incident touched off five days of rioting that left 23 blacks and 15 whites dead.

Troubles between business and workers also exploded. Many union leaders had hoped that wartime cooperation with factory owners would continue. But when workers asked for more pay to cover the 77 percent inflation rate, business leaders refused. More than four million workers, or one-fifth of the nation's workforce, went on strike in 1919, the highest number before or since in American history.

The wave of strikes began in the shipyards of Seattle and spread to a general strike of all workers in that city. Soon, the strike spread nationwide.

In Boston, even the police force went on strike. Massachusetts Governor Calvin Coolidge, later president, declared, "There is no right to strike against the public safety by anybody, anywhere, anytime."

Coolidge's words captured the mood of the nation. All during the war, there had been a propaganda campaign against German Americans. Many native-born Americans began to blame all foreigners for the war and the troubles that followed. Because many labor leaders and industrial workers were foreign born, many saw unions and union leaders as dangerous alien radicals who were disturbing the American way of life. They blamed worker demands for rising prices. With so many Americans angry at unions and workers, business owners were able to crush the strikes.

The anger against foreigners and labor leaders reached a peak in 1920. Many had already been jailed when they spoke out against the war. Now, they were being blamed for all the strikes. In May

The town of Rosewood was located in northwestern Florida. Totally destroyed in 1923, it no longer exists today.

TRAGEDY AT ROSEWOOD

One of the worst cases of mob violence against blacks took place in 1923, in the all-black town of Rosewood, Florida. On New Year's Day, a married white woman named Mrs. Taylor from the neighboring town of Sumner reported that she had been attacked by a black man. Several witnesses later said that they had seen a white man enter her home that morning, but no black men. However, Mrs. Taylor's story spread throughout the area. An angry mob of Sumner men soon gathered looking for revenge. Over the next several days, many of Rosewood's citizens were murdered in cold blood and many more fled into the surrounding wooded swamp land for protection.

Before the week was over, four blacks and two whites were dead, and every structure in Rosewood—homes and churches included—had been burned to the ground by angry whites who had come to the town from all over the surrounding region.

When the violence stopped, a grand jury investigated the events. Despite the widespread destruction, the jury found that there was not enough evidence to find anyone guilty of any crime. Although newspapers at the time mentioned the story, few people remembered it over the years, and survivors refused to discuss it. Only in 1996 did the story attract national attention once more, when a major motion picture retold the story. In 1997, the Florida State Legislature agreed to pay $7 million in damages to the victims of the destruction and their families.

1919, postal workers discovered 34 letter bombs addressed to government officials. The public blamed communists and other radicals. In June, a bomb went off outside Attorney General A. Mitchell Palmer's Washington house. Nobody was hurt and the identity of the bombers was never discovered.

On November 6, the second anniversary of the Russian Revolution, the government struck back. In a series of raids called the "red scare," Palmer arrested thousands of legal immigrants who were suspected of membership in radical and Communist organizations. In December, a ship nicknamed the "Soviet Ark" forcibly carried 294 radicals to Russia.

The raids continued. On New Year's Eve, Palmer conducted an even bigger sweep, arresting 6,000 people in one night. The arrests made Palmer a national hero. In the spring of 1920, Palmer revealed a radical plot to take over the U.S. government by force. It was scheduled, he said, for May 1, the international holiday of workers. The attorney general ordered out state militia units and police to guard government buildings. But when nothing happened, people began to calm down and the red scare died out.

Still, the fears would linger through the 1920s, especially around the case of Nicola Sacco and Bartolomeo Vanzetti. Arrested in the Palmer raids, the two Italian-American workers were found guilty of robbery and murder. They were sentenced to death. Many people, both in America and around the world, believed the two were convicted only because they were foreigners and radicals, not because they were guilty. For seven years, they sat on death row as lawyers appealed their case and protesters demanded a new trial. In August 1927, the two men were executed in the electric chair.

The anger at foreigners came out in less obvious ways, too. Since the early 1800s, a political movement known as "temperance" had tried to get people to stop drinking alcohol. During the Progressive Era, their activity shifted to banning alcohol by law. The "prohibitionists," or "drys," believed that alcohol was a source of crime and public disorder.

Many members of the Women's Christian Temperance Union and the Anti-Saloon League were native-born Protestants who lived in the countryside. They were suspicious of both immigrant Catholics and city life. To them, drinking was a problem caused by foreigners. By the beginning of World War I, 19 states had banned alcohol. In December 1917, the drys persuaded Congress to pass the Eighteenth Amendment, outlawing the selling, possessing, and drinking of alcohol, except for medical use and religious services. By 1919, every state but two had ratified the amendment. It went into effect on January 16, 1920.

While the Sacco and Vanzetti case led to protests, Prohibition led to an explosion of organized crime in the 1920s. The government could ban alcohol, but it couldn't stop people from wanting to drink it. Criminal gangs soon rose up to supply the demand. The illegal trade in alcohol would be one episode in the violent and colorful decade people called "the Roaring Twenties."

Fear of foreigners grew after World War I. In one of the most famous criminal trials of the 20th century, Nicola Sacco and Bartolomeo Vanzetti (center) were convicted of murder. Some felt that the two men were denied a fair trial because they were immigrants.

AMERICAN TIMELINE

1901 President McKinley is shot in Buffalo, New York. Eight days later, Theodore Roosevelt is sworn in as the 26th president.
■ The U.S. Supreme Court rules that inhabitants of Puerto Rico and the Philippines are American nationals, not American citizens, and are not entitled to all the rights enjoyed by citizens.

1902 In the first federal government action on behalf of labor, President Roosevelt threatens to take over coal mines if mine owners don't listen to strikers' demands.

1903 Flying for 12 seconds and traveling 120 feet, an airplane made by Orville and Wilbur Wright makes its first flight.
■ After encouraging their revolution, President Roosevelt officially recognizes Panama as a nation independent of Colombia.

Above: Orville Wright takes to the air in the first airplane.

1904 Roosevelt is elected president, easily defeating Democrat Alton B. Parker.
■ The ice-cream cone is invented at the St. Louis World's Fair.

1905 In Portsmouth, New Hampshire, President Roosevelt meets with Japanese and Russian leaders to negotiate an end to the Russo-Japanese War. He is awarded a Nobel Peace Prize for his successful efforts.

WORLD TIMELINE

Above: American cavalrymen in front of the Great Wall of China during the Boxer Rebellion

1900 American troops are sent to China as part of a multinational force to protect westerners during the Boxer Rebellion.

1901 Queen Victoria dies, ending 63 years of reign over the growth of an enormous empire.
■ The six states of Australia unite under one government.

1902 Signing the peace of Vereeniging, the Boers surrender to the British in South Africa and agree to recognize British rule.

1903 With Jewish persecution on the rise, delegates of the Zionist

1906 Over 700 die and 250,000 lose their homes when an earthquake and fire ravage San Francisco.

■ When revolutionaries attempt to overthrow the Cuban government, Roosevelt orders U.S. troops under William Howard Taft to restore order and to oversee the appointment of Nebraska lawyer Charles Magoon as governor.

1907 The Indian and Oklahoma territories are merged and are admitted into the union as the state of Oklahoma.

■ After filming one reel of *The Count of Monte Cristo* on Lake Michigan, the Selig Company directors begin to search for a warmer place for filming. They eventually decide on Los Angeles.

Right: In 1906, the city of San Francisco was rocked by a giant earthquake.

1908 William Howard Taft is elected president and tells his wife: "Now I'm in the White House; I'm not going to be pushed around anymore."

1909 Commodore Robert E. Peary becomes a national hero after he reportedly plants the American flag on the North Pole. Years later, reports would surface questioning whether Peary ever actually reached the pole.

■ President Taft establishes the Payne-Aldrich Tariff on imported goods to limit imports and bolster business at home.

Above: British soldiers fighting in the Boer War are seen here, posing with a howitzer, a short cannon.

Congress meet in Switzerland to discuss the possibility of a Jewish state in Uganda.

■ Hearing of a planned uprising in opposition to their rule, Turkish Ottomans massacre 50,000 Bulgarians.

1904 In a surprise attack, Japanese warships torpedo and destroy three Russian ships sparking the Russo-Japanese war.

1907 Fifty-seven women demonstrating for the right to vote are arrested in London and thrown in prison.

1909 Bulgaria is officially recognized as an independent nation.

1910 After watching growing political unrest in Persia, Britain and Russia finally decide to intervene and restore order.

■ Slavery is abolished in China.

AMERICAN TIMELINE

Above: As this cartoon shows, after the Japanese government tried to buy Mexican land for military purposes, a new law was passed forbidding Japanese-Americans from owning American land.

1911 One hundred and forty-six women are killed in a fire in a New York clothing factory. This tragedy brings unsafe working conditions to national attention.

1912 New Mexico and Arizona are admitted to the union as the 47th and 48th states.
■ Woodrow Wilson defeats Taft, Roosevelt, and Socialist candidate Eugene Debs in the race for the presidency.
■ Arizona, Kansas, and Oregon give women the vote.

1913 The Sixteenth and Seventeenth Amendments are passed, creating a national income tax and ensuring that senators are elected by popular vote rather than by state legislatures.
■ After the Japanese government attempts to purchase land from Mexico to use for military pur-

poses, Congress passes the Webb Alien Land Holding bill, which prevents Japanese immigrants from owning land in the United States. Many Japanese Americans have their lands seized as a result.

1914 The United States declares its neutrality in World War I and offers to negotiate peace between the warring nations.
■ After ten years of construction, the Panama Canal opens to water traffic.
■ After several American sailors are arrested in the Mexican port of Tampico and President Wilson learns that German weapon ships are sailing for Mexico, the U.S. Marines invade Mexico and occupy the city of Varacruz.

1915 Wilson orders U.S. Marines to restore order in violence-racked Haiti. In 1916, troops move in to

WORLD TIMELINE

1911 Mexican dictator Porfirio Díaz is overthrown by revolutionaries, led by Francisco Madero.

1912 The "unsinkable" *Titanic* sinks in icy waters off the coast of Newfoundland.

1913 Mexican rebel leader Francisco Madero is killed by a competing faction of rebels, led by Victoriano Huerta. Huerta names himself ruler of Mexico.

1914 On their 14th wedding anniversary, the Austrian Archduke Franz Ferdinand and his wife, the duchess of Hohenburg, are assassinated by a Serbian nationalist in

Sarajevo. Austria-Hungary, backed by Germany, demands justice and Russia, France, and Britain come to the support of the Serbs. World War I breaks out.
■ Germans attack the Russian Army at Tannenberg and win a decisive victory, taking 100,000 prisoners.
■ Germany captures Belgium and invades France.

1915 British, Australian, and New Zealand forces retreat from Gallipoli after failing to rout the Ottomans.

Left: Pancho Villa (center), one of the heroes of the Mexican Revolution, is seen here with some of his men.

occupy the Dominican Republic as well, and remain there until 1934.

■ **May 7, 1915** A German submarine sinks the British ocean liner *Lusitania* off the coast of Ireland. The attack marks the turn of American sentiment in favor of entering the war.

1916 In response to repeated submarine attacks on American merchant vessels, Wilson breaks off diplomatic ties with Germany.
■ A U.S. expeditionary force is sent into Mexico to attempt to capture the Mexican revolutionary Pancho Villa, after Villa led his men on several raids into U.S. territory.

1917 The United States declares war on Germany.
■ The Supreme Court rules that a Kentucky ordinance enforcing segregation is unconstitutional.

■ The United States purchases the modern-day U.S. Virgin Islands from Denmark for $25 million.

1918 President Wilson proposes his Fourteen Point program for an end to World War I. "The program of the world's peace is our only program," he says.

1919 The Treaty of Versailles ends World War I. Germany is required to pay $130 million in reparations and to dismantle its armed forces. Wilson proposes a League of Nations dedicated to the preservation of peace.
■ Wilson suffers a near-fatal stroke and his wife and advisors carry out his duties for the remainder of the term.
■ With the passage of the Eighteenth Amendment, Prohibition becomes law, making the sale of alcoholic beverages illegal.

Above: President Wilson, right, met (l-r) Georges Clemenceau of France, Vittorio Orlando of Italy, and David Lloyd George of Great Britain at the Versailles Peace Conference in 1919.

■ Italy enters the war after signing a secret treaty with the Allies guaranteeing Italy land.
■ In August, Austrian and German troops take Warsaw, followed shortly afterward by Poland.
■ The Greeks join the Allies against Germany and Austria-Hungary.

1916 Germany declares war on Portugal and Romania.
■ At the Second Battle of Verdun, French troops break enemy lines.

1917 Led by Vladimir Lenin, Bolsheviks overthrow the Russian government, seize power, and open peace talks with Germany and Austria.
■ Australian forces seize Jericho and force the Ottomans to retreat.
■ China declares war on Germany and Austria.

1918 In Britain, married women over 30 win the vote.
■ Russia signs a peace treaty with Germany.
■ Hammered by the Allies, the German line finally breaks near Amiens, and German troops retreat.

■ British officer Lawrence of Arabia liberates Damascus from Ottoman rule.

■ The Ottomans surrender. Germany and Austria sign an armistice.

1919 World leaders meet at Versailles to discuss the terms of surrender. Germany is forced to bear the costs of the war.
■ Benito Mussolini founds the Fasci di Combattimento party to fight Communism.

VII. BETWEEN THE WARS

Above: Painter Thomas Hart Benton's City Activities with Dance Hall *shows one artist's idea of life in the 1920s.*

THE GREAT WAR HAD ENDED. U.S. troops had returned from Europe as winners, having helped make the world "safe for democracy," they thought. The country was ready to celebrate.

The 1920s brought new fashions, dance crazes, and music, all fed by illegal drink and a booming stock market. Radio brought popular programs into the nation's living rooms. Automobiles, once reserved for the rich, became cheap enough for average Americans to afford. America was on the move.

In October 1929, it all came grinding to a halt. When the stock market crashed, banks and factories across the nation closed, throwing millions out of work. The Great Depression had begun. The government, led by Herbert Hoover, couldn't do a thing about it. "In Hoover we trusted," signs read, "and now we're busted."

Hoover was defeated in 1932 by Franklin Delano Roosevelt, who, despite a privileged background, promised quick action to help the poor. Launching program after government program, he tried to lift the country out of the Depression. Not all of his "New Deal" plans worked, but in the course of his efforts, FDR changed the way Americans looked at Washington. For the first time, the federal government accepted responsibility for caring for the basic needs of its people. That responsibility would not come into question again for another 50 years.

The Roaring '20s

"When I was a boy, about 50 years ago . . ." wrote advertising executive Earnest Elmo Calkins in 1928, "mother used to buy a bar of Castile soap half a yard long . . . The cake was hard as Stonehenge, the corners sharper than a serpent's tooth.

"Today, we have a cake of toilet soap—a great many of them, in fact—just the right shape to fit the hand . . . scented if we like, tinted to match the bathroom decorations if we prefer, reasonable in price; and when we want another cake we go to the nearest grocery or drugstore, and there it is.

"And not only toilet soap," he continued. "We have seen the evolution of shaving creams, safety razors, and toothpastes, as well as soap powders . . . washing machines . . . vacuum cleaners—everything, in short, that constitutes [makes] the difference between our mothers' kitchens and our wives'."

What had brought about these wonderful changes? Calkins offered a surprising answer. "These things did not come into existence because women demanded them. Women did not know that they were possible. They exist because there was a method of distributing them, of teaching possible buyers what a help they would be." In short, he said, the changes were "due directly and indirectly to advertising."

In the 1920s, advertising became big business. As each new product was introduced, advertising agencies tried to convince people that something they had never seen or heard of before was something that they had always needed. Many advertisers hired psychologists to figure out how best to reach new customers. Psychologists soon found one surefire sales tool—the fear of being laughed at. The makers of Listerine, for instance, turned "halitosis" (bad breath) from a scientific term into a household word.

The Jazz Age

Most people call 1920's America the "Roaring Twenties" and the "Jazz Age" because of its excitement and fast pace.

As jazz music developed, wild new dance crazes developed with it. Clothing styles changed, too. Some young women, called flappers, began wearing skirts so short that their legs were visible, which shocked the older generation who had never seen such behavior in public.

Many historians consider the 1920s the period in which "the modern age" began. But this modern age was about more than new products, clothes, and dances. It started with a new way of thinking. For centuries, most Americans had lived by certain principles: thrift, self-reliance, and sacrifice. These values had conquered a continent and turned the United States into an industrial giant. During the Jazz Age, however, many

By the 1920s, many working women had risen to positions of responsibility on the job. This 1924 advertisement for the Ford Motor Company (below) was aimed at these new customers.

er habit of measuring time in terms f dollars gives the woman in business een insight into the true value of a rd closed car for her personal use.

his car enables her to conserve min-es, to expedite her affairs, to widen e scope of her activities. Its low

first cost, long life and inexpensive operation and upkeep convince her that it is a sound investment value.

And it is such a pleasant car to drive that it transforms the business call which might be an interruption into an enjoyable episode of her busy day.

DOR SEDAN, $590   FORDOR SEDAN, $685   COUPE, $525   (All prices f. o. b. Detroit)

Ford
CLOSED CARS

Although it was illegal for bars to serve alcohol openly during the 1920s, illegal bars, known as "speakeasies" popped up throughout the country. Shown above is an advertisement for one of them.

Above: This cartoon satirizes Charles Darwin's theory that human beings evolved from apes.

Americans started to feel that these values were no longer so important. After all, by 1920, more Americans lived in cities than in rural areas. Self-reliance, a way of life for the American farmer, was more difficult to maintain in the city. For many, having fun had become more important than making sacrifices.

Thrift, or careful spending of one's money, gave way to free spending and rising debt. While the average worker's income rose some in the 1920s, the amount of products he or she purchased skyrocketed. This was made possible by a new kind of buying: the installment plan. Before World War I, Americans had purchased everything with cash, except their homes. Now, manufacturers and retailers encouraged people to buy cars, radios, and refrigerators on the "buy now, pay later" system, or as critics put

it, "a dollar down and a dollar forever." By 1929, consumer borrowing reached $7 billion, and the business of lending money became the 10th largest in America.

Americans on the Move

By far the most important new product of the day was the automobile. Invented in the late 1800s, the automobile was handmade and expensive at first, a product only the rich could afford. Henry Ford, a self-educated engineer from Michigan, changed all that. By using the assembly line, where parts came to the worker instead of the other way around, Ford reduced the time it took to make a car from over 12 hours to 90 minutes. When it was introduced in 1908, Ford's basic Model T, popularly called the "tin lizzy," sold for $1,000. By 1929, it could be purchased for $260, less than six months' income for the average worker. The number of cars on the road jumped from 8.5 million in 1920 to 23 million in

THE SCOPES TRIAL

In 1925, one of the most famous trials in history took place in the tiny Tennessee town of Canton. John Scopes, a biology teacher, was arrested after he broke a state law that banned teaching any theory of creation other than the Bible's version. Scopes taught his class Charles Darwin's theory of evolution—which states among other things that human beings evolved from apes. The case pitted two of the country's top lawyers against each other— William Jennings Bryan, the longtime candidate for president, and Clarence Darrow, a brilliant lawyer provided to Mr. Scopes by the American Civil Liberties Union (ACLU). The ACLU believed that the Tennessee law violated the right of free speech, as well as the constitutional separation of church and state.

Although the issues involved were serious ones, the atmosphere at the trial took on the air of a circus. Crowds from around the country showed up to witness the debate. Salesmen sold Bibles, toy monkeys, and refreshments to the crowd. Around the country, people tuned in to the trial, thanks to a nationwide radio broadcast.

Bryan immediately had the advantage, since the judge opened each day of trial with a prayer, and refused to allow any experts to testify about evolution. Since he could not use experts, Darrow decided to use just one witness—Bryan himself. Darrow then led Bryan through a number of Bible passages, getting him to admit that many of them were illogical and contradicted each other if they were read literally. Although the jury found Scopes guilty and fined him $100, the judgment against him was later overturned. The debate about the teaching of evolution continues to this day.

1929. Americans owned 80 percent of the world's cars.

The automobile changed how Americans lived in many ways. Henry Ford, the son of a farmer, had hoped the automobile would give new freedom to rural folk. It certainly did. As one Indiana resident asked researchers looking into small town life, "Why on earth do you need to study what's changing this country? I can tell you what's happening in four letters: A-U-T-O!"

One of the biggest changes cars brought was allowing people to live farther from work. People could now live in the suburbs and drive to city jobs. This, in turn, helped lead to another feature of modern life that we take for granted today. In 1924, the Country Club Plaza, the world's first shopping center, opened in Kansas City.

The car also changed the way Americans spent their time away from work. "We've been away from church this summer more'n ever since we got our car," reported one housewife. By 1929, 45 million Americans, nearly a third of the population, took vacations in their cars.

While the car made it easier to leave home, new appliances like the vacuum cleaner, refrigerator, and toaster made the home a very different place. On the one hand, kitchens became smaller and housewives spent less time preparing food. On the other hand, advertisers convinced women to keep their houses spotless, which meant more time cleaning.

Radio Reaches the Home

If the car helped Americans see more of the world, the radio brought the world home. On November 2, 1920, KDKA in Pittsburgh went on the air. The first commercial radio broadcast covered that year's presidential elections.

Soon, stations all over the country were broadcasting news, concerts, and popular serials like *Amos 'n' Andy*. People changed their schedules to gather around the huge tube receivers to listen to their favorite shows, and the advertisements that paid for them. In Europe, radio stations were owned by the government, but in America, people listened to privately owned networks like the National Broadcasting Company (NBC), formed in 1926, and the Columbia Broadcasting Service (CBS), founded two years later. Not everyone approved of the new habit. "One of the bad features of radio," said a

"A Chicken in Every Pot, a Car in Every Garage."

—Republican National Committee's advertising slogan for the 1928 election

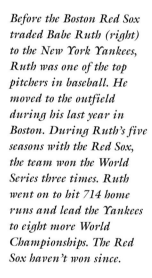

Before the Boston Red Sox traded Babe Ruth (right) to the New York Yankees, Ruth was one of the top pitchers in baseball. He moved to the outfield during his last year in Boston. During Ruth's five seasons with the Red Sox, the team won the World Series three times. Ruth went on to hit 714 home runs and lead the Yankees to eight more World Championships. The Red Sox haven't won since.

schoolteacher, "is that children stay up late at night and are not fit for school next day."

Popular Culture in the 1920s

Sports were among the most popular radio broadcasts. Boxing was especially popular. Millions "tuned in" (a new phrase in the 1920s) to the 1927 match between Jack Dempsey, the "Manassas Mauler," and "Gentleman Gene" Tunney. Dempsey knocked Tunney out but, after what became known as the famous "long count," Tunney got up and defeated Dempsey in 15 rounds. All across the country, people said the fight had been fixed.

Radio broadcasts also covered baseball, which became the true national sport in the 1920s. It, too, had a scandal to live down. In 1919, gamblers bribed seven members of the Chicago White Sox to lose the World Series on purpose. The players were angry that the Sox's owner wouldn't pay them a World Series bonus. To clean up the sport, the owners hired Judge "Mountain" Landis for the new job of commissioner. But what really saved the game was a new hero. George Herman "Babe" Ruth thrilled audiences with his incredible feats of homerun hitting that were matched by his larger-than-life personality.

Movies, another popular form of mass entertainment in the 1920s, dated back to the late 1800s. During their early years, they were viewed not in theaters but in "nickelodeons." Customers would pay five cents to look into a machine that would play a one-reel feature. The first full-length feature, *The Great Train Robbery*, was produced in 1903. Soon millions were attending "picture shows," featuring favorite stars like Charlie Chaplin, Lillian Gish, and Douglas Fairbanks Sr. Throughout those early years, movies were silent, making it easier for non-English-speaking immigrants to follow along. In 1927, the first "talkie" was released, starring Al Jolson in *The Jazz Singer*. Within a couple of years, almost every movie had sound.

The title of the first talkie is not surprising. Jazz was the most popular new music of the day. Created by African-American musicians in New Orleans in the early 1900s, jazz spread north with the great black migration of the 1920s. Musicians like Louis Armstrong and Edward "Duke" Ellington played in nightclubs, including some like Harlem's Cotton Club, which were for white customers only.

While the Cotton Club was a legal establishment, millions of other night-

Left: Few captured the spirit of the 1920s as well as cartoonist John Held Jr. did. His drawings of flappers and their admiring boyfriends graced magazines like the New Yorker *and* Life. *Held's drawings earned him a fortune. Although he arrived in New York City from his home state of Utah with four dollars in his pocket, he soon earned $2,400 a week.*

Below: Nicknamed "The Empress of the Blues," Bessie Smith was one of the most popular African-American singers of her day. Her emotional blend of blues and jazz singing made her a legend.

spots were not. Known as "speakeasies," they were places people could go for an illegal drink. Prohibition, the national ban on alcohol, went into effect at the beginning of the 1920s, but it didn't stop people from drinking.

Some people made their own liquor called "bathtub gin." Most alcohol, however, was smuggled into the country from Mexico or Canada. Criminal gangs, like Al Capone's in Chicago, soon took over the sales and distribution of liquor. Gangs often fought wars over territory. But as with the drug trade today, the government found it almost impossible to stop the flow of alcohol and the violence it caused. Liquor could be bought, Attorney General William Mitchell said in 1929, "at almost any hour of the day

*"There ain't nothin'
I can do
Or nothin' I can say
That folks don't criticize.
But I'm going to do just
as I want to anyway
And I don't care if they
all despise me.
If I should take a notion
To jump into the ocean
T'aint nobody's business
if I do."*

*—from "T'aint Nobody's
Business If I Do,"
as sung by Bessie Smith*

or night, either in rural districts, the smaller towns, or the cities."

Not all Americans, of course, were breaking the law by visiting speakeasies. For many, the new culture was upsetting and confusing. Many turned to religion for answers. Religion was changing with the times, too. Radio did not replace going to church, but it created a new kind of preaching and a new kind of preacher. Billy Sunday, a former professional baseball player, became one of the most popular figures of the day after he became a preacher and began delivering his sermons over national radio.

A return to religion was not the only reaction to changing times. Many turned to hate instead. In 1915, a new version of the Ku Klux Klan was formed, inspired by the Reconstruction-era group of the same name. Unlike the old Klan, which attacked blacks in the rural South, the new one targeted immigrants in the nation's cities. In fact, much of the new Klan's strength came from the Midwest instead of from the South. The Klan

burned crosses to scare people they didn't like and sometimes lynched blacks and immigrants. But after anti-immigration laws were passed in 1921 and 1924, membership in the Klan fell sharply.

Many of America's artists did not like what they saw happening in America in the 1920s and left for Europe. Called the "lost generation," the group included Ernest Hemingway, who wrote about World War I, and F. Scott Fitzgerald, who published books that mocked the rich and famous. Closer to home, African-American writers like Langston Hughes and Zora Neale Hurston were gaining recognition as they criticized America's double standard on race. They were part of a movement called the "Harlem Renaissance."

Other African-Americans reacted to racism in a different way. The United Negro Improvement Association preached black separatism, suggesting blacks would succeed more easily if they separated themselves from whites. Founded by

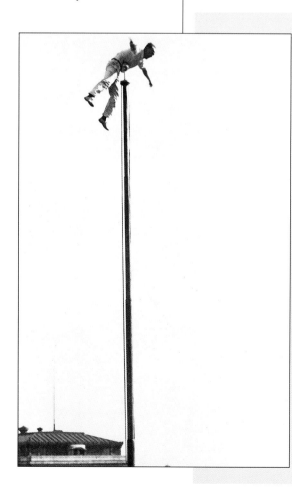

Below: As can be seen in this photograph from 1924, some flagpole "sitters" did quite a bit more than sit. The man seen here is John Reynolds, who also earned himself the nickname "The Human Fly."

THE FLAGPOLE SITTING CRAZE

One day in 1924, a little known man named Alvin "Shipwreck" Kelly decided he needed "some fresh air," and he didn't just step out into the Los Angeles sunshine to get it. Instead, he climbed to the top of a flagpole and sat down. The air was so fresh, and he was so comfortable, that Kelly stayed sitting on top of the flagpole for 13 hours.

Soon, people all over the country were taking up the strange craze of flagpole sitting. In Denver, a young man named LeRoy Haines sat on top of a flagpole for 12 days. In Chicago, Bennie Fox flagpole-sat for 18 days, and Bobby Mack stayed aloft for 21 days in Los Angeles, until police officers forced him to climb down. Some people even built platforms and tents on top of flagpoles, to make their stays more comfortable. In Memphis, flagpole sitting became so popular that the chief health officer, Dr. L. M. Graves, felt it necessary to warn people against excessive flagpole sitting. Such foolishness, he said, could result in colds, grippe, and even the flu.

Despite this concern, the strange fad did not stop. No one could cure "Shipwreck" Kelly of the need for fresh air. In 1930, he set the flagpole sitting record by remaining on top of a flagpole for 49 days in Atlantic City. The record has never been broken.

*Left: Panicked crowds
gather outside the New
York Stock Exchange on
October 29, 1929, following
the collapse of the stock
market.*

Marcus Garvey, a Jamaican immigrant, the organization promoted black businesses. It eventually started a steamship company to help resettle blacks in Africa. After Garvey was convicted of mail fraud and deported to Jamaica in 1927, however, the movement died.

The Harding and Coolidge Administrations

During the 1920s, most Americans believed that business provided the answer to the country's problems. After twenty years of Progressive reforms, people felt that government was interfering too much in their lives. Republicans like Harding, who became president in 1920, were elected on the slogan of returning the country to "normalcy." Despite Harding's promises, his administration got caught up in scandal. In 1923, it was learned that oil companies had bribed his

secretary of interior for the national oil reserves at Teapot Dome, Wyoming.

Harding, however, died before the scandal became public. He was replaced by his vice president and former governor of Massachusetts, Calvin "Silent Cal" Coolidge. Coolidge had a reputation for honesty. He shared Harding's belief that government should interfere as little as possible in the nation's economy. "The business of America," he said, "was business."

Perhaps the most famous politician of the decade was Herbert Hoover. Secretary of commerce under Harding and Coolidge, Hoover hoped government could help big business grow and prosper, but only if business wanted the help. Hoover was elected president in 1928, promising that America was "nearer to the final triumph over poverty than ever before in the history of any land."

The Stock Market Crash, the Depression, and the New Deal

After Franklin Delano Roosevelt was first elected president in 1932, letters from around the nation poured into the White House. Hard times had come to America. The writers spoke of suffering and want across the country. Some wrote in perfect English; others could not spell very well. Letters came from cotton farmers and from unemployed steel workers, from housewives and from schoolteachers. The saddest, perhaps, came from children.

"Dear Mr. President," one child wrote, "I'm a boy of 12 years. I want to tell you about my family. My father hasn't worked for five months. He went plenty times to relief [welfare], he filled out [an] application. They won't give us anything. I don't know why. Please you do something. We haven't paid four months' rent . . . Everyday the landlord rings the door bell . . . we don't open the door for him. We are afraid that [we] will be put out, [we've] been put out before, and [we] don't want [it] to happen again."

Others wrote to the First Lady. "Dear Mrs. Roosevelt," a girl from Ohio began. "I am writing you a little letter this morning. Are you glad it [is] spring? I am, for so many poor people can raise some more to eat. You know what I am writing this letter for? . . . I thought maybe you had some old clothes. You know, Mother is a good sewer, and all the little girls are getting Easter dresses. And I thought that you had some. You know Papa could wear [President Franklin] Roosevelt's shirts and clothes."

The Stock Market Crash

The 1930s were the decade of the Great Depression, the worst economic disaster in American history. What had happened? Why had the Roaring Twenties come to a screeching halt?

In fact, there were plenty of economic warnings in the 1920s, but people had tended to ignore them. For one thing, the 1920s was a difficult decade for the nearly half of all Americans who lived on farms. Crop prices fell throughout the decade. Even in the cities there were problems. Corporations were making huge profits, but workers weren't always sharing in them. Many were going deeper into debt each year. By 1927, consumer spending and housing construction were going down and workers were being laid off.

The final blow, however, came in 1929. While the economy was getting weaker in the late 1920s, the stock market was skyrocketing. People all over the country were borrowing money to take their chances on Wall Street. Nobody worried because stock prices kept going up. People thought they could pay back the loans with their profits. One magazine article, written by a stockbroker, was

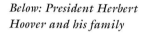

Below: President Herbert Hoover and his family

entitled, "Everyone Ought to be Rich." On "Black Tuesday" —October 29, 1929—the bubble burst. More dark days followed. In just a few weeks, stock values fell from $87 billion to $55 billion. Millions of people went broke in what came to be called the "Great Crash." Companies lost millions of dollars and began laying off workers they could no longer afford to pay. With fewer people working, there were fewer consumers to buy new products. Falling sales meant even more layoffs. The economy went into a downward spiral.

The Great Depression

Soon, the banks began to fail. First the small ones in the countryside went broke. Since they had borrowed from the big city banks, the Depression brought down those as well. People began to panic, pulling their money out, and hiding it under mattresses. With less money in banks, there was less money for investment.

The numbers were terrible. Between 1929 and 1933, the gross national product, an economic term meaning the total worth of all goods and services produced in America, fell by almost one half. One hundred thousand businesses, including

9,000 banks, closed their doors. Corporate profits fell 90 percent. One out of four workers lost his or her job. Employed workers saw wages fall and feared for their own jobs.

Numbers only capture part of the story. As one historian said, "Mass unemployment is both a statistic and an empty feeling in the stomach. To fully comprehend [understand] it, you have to both see the figures and feel the emptiness."

Very few average citizens escaped the fear and hopelessness of the Great

Although the Depression was not caused by Herbert Hoover, many Americans blamed him for it. Many who had lost their homes were forced to build temporary villages. These villages became known as "Hoovervilles." The children seen above lived in one of them.

Depression. "What is going to become of us?" said an Arizona man. "I've lost twelve and a half pounds this last month, just thinking. You can't sleep, you know. You wake up at 2 A.M. and you lie and think."

Many were too embarrassed or proud to accept help. One social worker cried when she remembered a visit to an unemployed railroad man's house. "If the family needed clothing, I was to investigate how much . . . they had. So I looked into this man's closet . . . He said 'Why are you doing this?' . . . He was so deeply humiliated [embarrassed]. And I was too." Not that there was much relief to go around. New York, which paid out more in relief per family than most states, offered each family just $23.50 per week in current dollars.

Farmers in the Midwest had an especially hard time. They were hit by both falling crop prices and the worst drought of the century. The most extreme part of the drought was centered in Oklahoma, but throughout much of the Midwest, the soil dried up and turned to dust. When the wind picked up, it sent huge clouds of dust that darkened the skies. One dust storm left a film of dirt as far away as New York City.

Many of the farmers owed money to the banks. When they couldn't pay, the banks foreclosed, and took their farms away. Known as "Okies" because many, but not all, came from Oklahoma, they packed up their belongings on old trucks and headed west along Route 66 to California. Once they arrived, they lived in shacks, and moved up and down the state—when they could find work—picking crops on the giant farms of the Central Valley. Their sad stories were captured in John Steinbeck's *The Grapes of Wrath*, one of the decade's most popular novels.

Above: One of the many new agencies started by Roosevelt was the Federal Communications Commission (FCC).

FRANKLIN DELANO ROOSEVELT (1882-1945)

Franklin Delano Roosevelt did not seem like the man to bring America out of the Depression. He had never known what it was to be poor and hungry. Born an only child to a wealthy Hyde Park, New York, family, Roosevelt had toured Europe eight times before he was 16, and had attended only the fanciest schools.

For this golden boy, the world was an easy place. But in August 1921 while on vacation in Canada, Roosevelt went for a swim in icy waters and his life was changed forever. That evening he suffered stabbing pain and chills. The next morning, when he awoke, Roosevelt was unable to stand. Diagnosed with polio, he was told that he would never be able to use his legs again.

Roosevelt, however, was determined to prove that he did not need to live as a helpless invalid. He spent long hours doing special exercises for his legs, learned how to use a wheelchair, and built up the strength in his upper body so that he could get around without assistance. "Maybe my legs aren't so good," he once laughed, "but look at these shoulders!" Perhaps it was this stubborn optimism and sense of humor that convinced the American people that he was the man to end the Depression. They elected him president in 1932 by a landslide.

Above: Franklin Delano Roosevelt

As the Depression continued, people wanted to know why the government wasn't doing more to help them. They blamed President Herbert Hoover for the nation's problems. They called the shacks homeless people built in city parks, "Hoovervilles." And an empty pocket turned inside out was called a "Hoover flag."

In fact, Hoover spent over $700 million in public works to provide jobs, but it wasn't nearly enough. He gave loans to banks, railroads, and insurance companies to keep them from going broke. Hoover, however, did not believe that the government should give money directly to the poor. People said he only cared about his friends in big business.

Things got worse for President Hoover in 1932 when World War I veterans marched on Washington. The former soldiers had been promised a bonus, to be paid in 1945, but they hoped to get it sooner. Instead of talking with them, Hoover sent troops to break up the Bonus Army's camps. When people saw government troops attacking veterans, Hoover's popularity went down even further.

Others were furious with big business. In 1932, workers, angry at wage cuts, marched on the Ford Motor plant in Detroit. Police and Ford security guards opened fire on the marchers, killing three and injuring 50. Over 40,000 people attended the funeral for the dead workers and carried banners reading, "Ford Gave Bullets for Bread."

FDR Takes Office

Despite the hard times, people hoped for peaceful change. Surprisingly, America's struggling working class found what it was looking for during the election of 1932 in a wealthy New Yorker who had attended the country's finest private schools as a boy and never gone without in his life. Perhaps people saw something in this man that reminded them of his distant cousin, Theodore Roosevelt. Perhaps, they hoped, Franklin Delano Roosevelt would fight for regular people just like President Roosevelt had 30 years earlier.

Little in his early years would give people the idea that this Roosevelt, or FDR, as he would become known, would become the workingman's friend. In 1905, he married Eleanor Roosevelt, another distant cousin, and won a seat in the New York legislature in 1910. He served as undersecretary of the navy in World War I, then ran unsuccessfully for vice president in 1920. During these years, FDR lived a carefree life and was often seen sailing on his yacht.

It was after one voyage in 1921, that his life changed forever. FDR was stricken with polio, a once-common disease that killed or crippled its victims. Polio left Roosevelt paralyzed from the waist down. But it also made him a stronger and more serious person. "If you had spent two years in bed trying to wriggle your toe," he once said, "after that anything would seem easy."

In 1928, Roosevelt won election as governor of New York and served there during the early years of the Depression. Unlike President Hoover, Roosevelt believed strongly in spending government money to help the poor. His record helped win him the Democratic Party nomination for president in 1932.

One of the most controversial New Deal agencies was the National Recovery Administration (NRA). The NRA set policies on wages, hours, and working conditions, and employers who agreed to these policies were given the chance to display the NRA blue eagle, with its slogan "We Do Our Part." In the cartoon above, Uncle Sam is seen with twin Roosevelts representing employers and workers.

During the Dust Bowl years, photographer Dorothea Lange traveled the country photographing America's poor. Seen at right is one of Lange's most famous photographs.

Ben Shahn was both a photographer and an artist. He painted the poster below for Roosevelt's Resettlement Administration.

YEARS OF DUST

RESETTLEMENT ADMINISTRATION
Rescues Victims
Restores Land to Proper Use

During his campaign, Roosevelt only made general statements about what he was going to do, but he captured the mood of the times. "The country needs and, unless I mistake its temper, the country demands bold, persistent experimentation," he said. Yet it was more than his speeches, and the public's dislike of Hoover, that won him the election in a landslide.

Roosevelt was full of hope and optimism. Although photographers rarely showed him in his wheelchair, people knew he was disabled and liked him for it. If he could overcome such personal hardship, they thought, he could help the country overcome its economic troubles.

On March 4, 1933, FDR took the oath of office. In his inaugural address, he tried to raise America's spirits. He told the country that "the only thing we have to fear is fear itself." From that day forward, Roosevelt used his ability to lift people's spirits. His famous "fireside chats," which were broadcast nationwide over the radio, were listened to by millions.

FDR had promised quick action in his first hundred days in office, and he delivered on that promise. He asked Congress to give him emergency powers "as great as the power that would be given to me if we were in fact invaded by a foreign foe." While he acted quickly, he made sure not to promise easy answers. "I have no expectation of making a hit every time I come to bat," he once told reporters. "What I seek is the highest possible batting average."

The day after taking office, he declared a "national bank holiday" and convinced Congress to pass the Emergency Banking Act. After checking each of the nation's banks to find out which ones were strong enough to avoid collapse, the government reopened them a week later. With new confidence, people began to take their savings out from under their mattresses and put them into banks where they could be used for loans that would help rebuild the economy.

The New Deal

Among the things that Franklin Roosevelt is best known for is the huge number of new government agencies that he established to help pull the country out of the Depression. Together, these programs were called the "New Deal."

For example, to help make banks safer, Roosevelt began the Federal Deposit Insurance Corporation (FDIC) to insure up to $2,500 of people's savings. Another new law, the Glass-Steagall Act, stopped commercial banks from investing in the stock market. In 1935, Congress began the Security Exchange Commission (SEC) to regulate the stock market and prevent wild speculation like the kind that had led to the crash of 1929.

FDR also tried to help the nation's farmers. Under the Agricultural Adjustment Act (AAA), the government paid farmers not to grow certain basic crops. With less produced, prices went up. Unfortunately, most of the benefits went to the nation's biggest farmers. Many landlords in the South pushed sharecroppers off the land to take advantage of government payouts.

For business, which was also suffering from deflation, the New Deal offered the National Recovery Administration (NRA). Led by Bernard Baruch, who had

This government poster above advertises the Social Security Act, one of the longest-lasting New Deal programs. Began in 1935, Social Security continues to provide all Americans with a monthly check after they retire.

While the Dust Bowl was at its worst in Oklahoma, its effects were felt around the country. As the map below shows, winds blew dust as far east as New York.

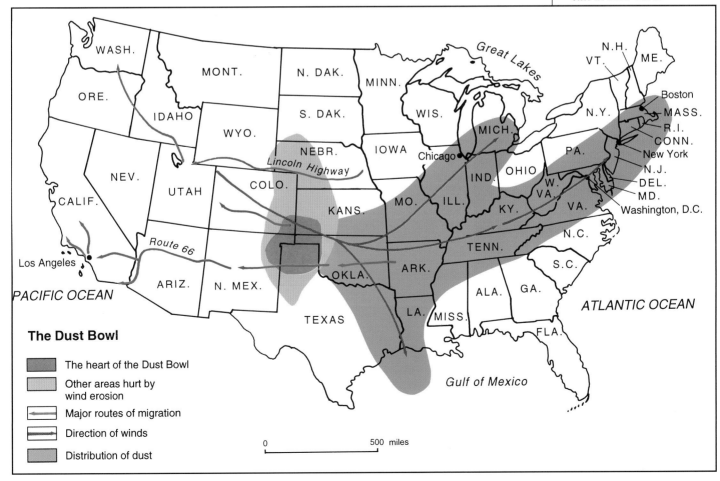

The Dust Bowl

- The heart of the Dust Bowl
- Other areas hurt by wind erosion
- Major routes of migration
- Direction of winds
- Distribution of dust

0   500 miles

organized industry during World War I, the agency worked with business to regulate prices. Over 600 industries were covered, from major ones like steel and coal, to small ones like dog food makers and theaters. To sell the idea of government direction of industry, participating businesses placed posters in their windows with the slogan "We Do Our Part." One of the most important parts of the NRA act was Section 7(a). For the first time, the Federal government guaranteed workers the right to organize unions and to bargain collectively "through representatives of their own choosing."

The biggest problem facing the nation when Roosevelt took office in 1933 was hunger and joblessness. FDR immediately established the Federal Emergency Relief Administration (FERA). Harry Hopkins, a New York social worker, was put in charge of FERA and gave out $5 million in his first two hours in office. He put people to work doing anything he could think of. When critics said some of the projects were not useful in the long run, Hopkins replied, "People don't eat in the long run—they eat everyday." Over the next two years, FERA spent $1 billion.

A larger and more long-term project was the Public Works Administration (PWA). Over $3 billion was spent on new public buildings throughout the country. Part of that money went to the Civilian Conservation Corps (CCC), which sent thousands of young men (and a few women) to fix up the nation's parks. By June 1933, the first hundred days had come to an end. There was renewed hope in America. Unfortunately, the economy refused to go along.

Roosevelt was soon challenged by leaders with more radical plans. A

WOODY GUTHRIE (1912–1967), DUST BOWL BALLADEER

Very little rain fell in the Southwest. The pounding sun caused the earth to dry out and crops to die. Great swirls of dust blew across the plains, covering everything in a thick layer of dirt. Without the money from their crops, many farmers were unable to pay their debts and were forced off their land. They had little choice but to leave their drought-ridden states and head to California where they might find work.

A young man from Oklahoma named Woodrow Wilson "Woody" Guthrie joined the steady stream of farmers as they traveled across the country. What he saw on the road touched him deeply. He watched as the "Okies," or migrant farmers, struggled to feed their families while the California landowners took advantage of their hunger. Then he began to write songs about what he saw.

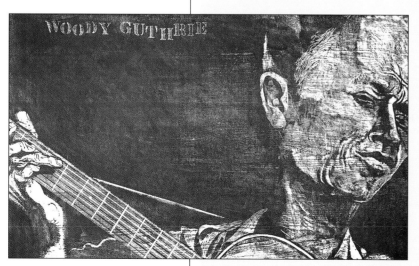

"I am out to sing songs that will prove to you that this is your world . . . [and] that make you take pride in yourself and your work," Guthrie once said. He wrote songs like "This Train Is Bound for Glory" and "My Uniform's My Dirty Overalls." After the Depression, Guthrie continued singing at labor union halls and worksites across the nation. He was so well loved that many suggested his most famous song, "This Land Is Your Land," should be the national anthem.

Above: Woody Guthrie

FDR is seen at left signing the National Labor Relations Act in 1935. The new law set up a government board to settle arguments between workers and employers, and outlawed unfair business practices, such as spying on workers or forcing them to sign anti-strike contracts.

Below: In 1932, violence broke out between hungry strikers and Ford Motor Company security guards at Ford's Dearborn, Michigan, plant.

California doctor named Francis Townshend spoke up for the nation's elderly, demanding that the government pay every citizen over 60 years of age $200 a month. A popular radio priest from Michigan named Father Charles Coughlin insisted that the government take over the nation's banks directly. When the president refused, Coughlin started calling him Franklin "Double-Crossing" Roosevelt and organized the National Union for Social Justice. Coughlin's 40 million listeners wanted him to run for president. Because he was born in Canada, he could not.

A more serious challenge to FDR's leadership came from the South. Huey Long, who served as both senator and governor of Louisiana, had made a career attacking big business. He passed new state taxes on corporations and used the money to pay for new hospitals, roads, and schools. He also used some of the money to make himself rich. Long had a simple solution

The poster above advertises an exhibition of Federal Art Project works.

The poster above was produced to promote the WPA.

Among the most popular books published by the WPA's Writers' Project was a series of guides to American cities. Shown above is a recent edition of one of those books.

THE WORKS PROGRESS ADMINISTRATIO

"One morning as I was in the kitchen of the rooming house fixing my breakfast," recalled writer Anzia Yezierska, "the radio broadcast a special news item about the WPA: a headquarters had just been set up for the new Writers' Project."

Yezierska was broke and desperately needed a job. A Hollywood screenwriter in the 1920s, she had lost almost all of her savings in the stock market crash of 1929.

"I hurried to the address, eager to work," she wrote. "Ever since I had marched with the unemployed I was full of ideas for stories. All I needed to begin writing again was the security of a WPA wage to get my typewriter out of the pawnshop."

At the "huge barracks-like Writers' Hall," she joined dozens of other fiction writers, historians, and playwrights. "We were as ill-assorted as a crowd on a subway express," she remembered, "spinster poetesses . . . youngsters with school magazine experience, veteran newspaper men . . . people of all ages, all nationalities, all degrees of education, tossed together in a strange fellowship of necessity." An old writer dressed in "rags" told Yezierska, "Roosevelt will go down to posterity [future generations] as the savior of art in America."

"'The savior of art!' I laughed. 'At the bargain price of $23.86 per artist.'"

Like steelworkers and cotton farmers, artists were hard hit by the Depression. Fewer books were published, theaters closed down, and advertisers needed fewer commercial artists. When the WPA began spending billions of dollars on public works, some of the money was spent on the arts.

The program was called "Federal One" and there had been nothing like it in American history. The purpose of the program was to support America's artists by helping them to bring the arts to America's poor and working people. Never before had the federal government helped artists in such a way, nor had the

to the Depression. He wanted to place a 100 percent tax on all incomes over $1 million and guarantee every family a $2,000 annual salary. Long had his eyes on the White House and established his Share Our Wealth Society to help his campaign. In 1935, however, an assassin's bullet ended his career.

Townshend, Long, and Coughlin criticized FDR for not doing enough. Business and Republicans blamed him for doing too much. In 1935, the conservative Supreme Court ruled that the NRA, along with its Section 7(a), was unconstitutional, saying it interfered with free trade and competition.

In 1935, Roosevelt responded to his critics by coming up with a whole new set of even bigger programs called the "second New Deal." With the NRA and its Section 7(a) gone, the nation's unions wanted new protections. Roosevelt was nervous about giving them too much power but agreed to sign the National Labor Relations Act, also known as the Wagner Act. The new law set up the National Labor Relations Board (NLRB) to help settle disputes between workers and employers. The law also outlawed unfair labor practices by business. Employers could no longer spy on workers, force them to sign antistrike contracts, or blacklist (ban) union organizers.

ND THE FEDERAL ONE PROJECT

arts reached such a large new audience. The New Deal slogan was "Art for the Millions."

Artists were hired to paint huge murals for the new public buildings going up across America. Government-sponsored orchestras toured the country, offering free concerts of classical and popular music. Aaron Copland, one of the great composers of American history, wrote his "Billy the Kid" and "Rodeo" suites for the WPA.

Writers were hired to produce fiction and nonfiction. Among the most popular books was a series of guidebooks to cities and regions across the country. The government also hired students of the social sciences to study different communities around America. Zora Neale Hurston, an African-American writer from Florida, wrote her famous novel *Their Eyes Were Watching God* with WPA money. Historians were sent across the country to collect oral histories of America's past.

Perhaps the most popular of the WPA arts program was the Federal Theater Project (FTP). Theater companies were organized and toured the country, offering free and low-cost plays. Among the most famous productions was Orson Welles's all-black version of Shakespeare's *Macbeth,* performed by the FTP of Harlem. New plays by Arthur Miller and T. S. Eliot were also produced by the FTP.

Some FTP productions were very critical of the government and big business. This angered many critics who already saw not just the Federal One Program but much of the New Deal as a waste of taxpayer dollars. It was bad enough, complained some, that FDR insisted on throwing taxpayer money at every road or bridge construction project that crossed his desk, but funding art projects that criticized the government was too much for FDR's critics to bear. In 1939, Congress ended the Federal One project.

Above: Novelist Eudora Welty also took photographs for the WPA.

Above: Writer Zora Neale Hurston

Above: Playwright Arthur Miller

The Wagner Act set off the greatest wave of union organizing in the nation's history. For years, the nation's largest union, the American Federation of Labor (AFL), had stuck to organizing skilled craftsmen like carpenters and locomotive engineers. John Lewis, head of the United Mine Workers, decided it was time to organize industrial workers. In 1935, he launched the Congress of Industrial Organizations (CIO).

On December 31, 1936, the CIO began its campaign against the largest industrial corporation in the world, the automotive company, General Motors. Instead of going on strike, which would allow strikebreakers to take their jobs, the workers sat down in the factories. After 45 days, the "sit-down" strikes forced General Motors to bargain with the United Auto Workers, a union connected with the CIO.

The CIO's next target was the steel industry. In 1937, U.S. Steel agreed to recognize the Steel Workers Organizing Committee. Other steel companies, however, refused to go along. When striking workers held a Memorial Day picnic and rally outside the gates of Republic Steel in Cleveland, things turned violent. Rocks were thrown and police opened fire, killing 10 strikers. All were shot in the back. It took four more years for the companies called "little steel" to accept the union.

Above: Police stand at attention as steelworkers go back to work after the Republic Steel strike in Cleveland in 1937.

Meanwhile, in 1935, FDR was tackling other problems. To get more people working, the president and Congress set up the Works Progress Administration (WPA). Between 1935 and 1943, when the program ended, over eight million Americans were put to work constructing 651,087 miles of roads, 125,110 public buildings, and 853 airports. Artists were hired to decorate the buildings with murals and other public art projects.

To help the nation's elderly, FDR pushed for the Social Security Act, perhaps the most important program of the whole New Deal. Under the new law, workers and employers contributed to a fund that took care of workers and their families when they retired or were unable to work. It also provided funds for blind, deaf, and disabled people.

Other New Deal programs included the Rural Electrification Administration and the Tennessee Valley Authority. Under the latter act, a series of government-owned dams and power plants were built in a seven-state area of the South.

Roosevelt's only major defeat during his first term was on taxes. The president wanted to sharply hike taxes on wealthy individuals and corporations. Called a

Above: Huey Long

THE BREAD LINE   Reginald Marsh

In the charcoal sketch at left, by Reginald Marsh, unemployed men wait to receive free handouts of bread.

THE 1930s: HOLLYWOOD'S GOLDEN AGE

Above: Groucho Marx

Above: Shirley Temple

Above: Clark Gable

The 1930s are remembered as the golden age of both radio and film. Perhaps that is because the national radio networks and Hollywood movie studios put out radio programs and popular films that allowed people to escape their troubles. Radio was certainly the cheapest form of entertainment. Despite hard times, the number of radios in America doubled during the 1930s, from 13 million to 27 million sets.

Listeners enjoyed radio shows like the *Lone Ranger, Superman, The Shadow*, and *Dick Tracy.* Radio also offered helpful shows like *The Betty Crocker Hour,* which helped housewives stretch their budgets. Variety shows with Jack Benny and George Burns were popular, as were broadcasts of classical and jazz concerts from the big cities.

The power of radio to influence people's thinking was demonstrated by a bizarre broadcast of 1938. On a Sunday night in October, Orson Welles produced a radio play based on science fiction writer H. G. Wells's book, *War of the Worlds.* Welles's actors went on the air to announce that the Earth was being attacked by invaders from Mars. Using make-believe news bulletins and on-the-air reports, Welles convinced millions the story was true. Thousands fled their homes.

Movies, however, were by far the most popular form of entertainment during the Depression. Ticket prices were low enough to allow more than 60 percent of Americans to see at least one movie a week.

Americans flocked to W. C. Fields and Marx Brothers comedies, including *The Bank Dick, Animal Crackers,* and *Duck Soup.* The most popular star of the decade, however, was a little girl named Shirley Temple. She made her first big hit *Stand Up and Cheer* in 1934 (at the tender age of six), and before long, she was the world's top box-office star.

Not all of the movies of the 1930s were appropriate for children. Some of the first talking pictures were very bold in the way they treated sexual topics. This led to talk of government censorship. Instead, the film industry started its own Production Code Administration to make movies cleaner. Before the code went into effect, however, Hollywood produced several very popular films about gangsters, including *Little Caesar* with Edward G. Robinson, *Scarface,* the story of Al Capone, and *The Public Enemy* with James Cagney.

The year 1939 saw the release of two of the most famous movies of all-time. *Gone with the Wind,* starring Vivien Leigh and Clark Gable, told the story of the last days of the Confederate South during the Civil War. The other, starring the teenage actress Judy Garland, featured such fantastic characters as a cowardly lion, a heartless tin man, and a scarecrow with no brain. The movie's name? *The Wizard of Oz.*

"soak the rich" tax by critics, Congress passed only a minor tax increase in its place.

Though the economy was still weak and unemployment was still almost 17 percent, Americans felt more hopeful in 1936. They elected FDR and a Democratic Congress by an even bigger landslide than they had in 1932.

FDR and the Supreme Court

Still, FDR faced a major obstacle in the Supreme Court. It had already overturned the NRA, and was threatening other New Deal programs. In early 1937, FDR decided to act. His plan worked like this: For every Supreme Court justice who failed to retire after the age of seventy, the president could appoint a new justice, up to a total of six. While the Constitution does not set the number of Supreme Court judges, tradition had put the total number at nine. If Roosevelt were able to add six more justices to the court, he could have ensured that his New Deal programs would be safe.

Although President Roosevelt tried to convince Congress that his plan was a way to help older justices with their heavy workloads, almost everyone knew that what Roosevelt really wanted was a Supreme Court that would do what he wanted. Even his vice president, John Nance Garner, came out against the plan. Garner, who was 79 years old himself, felt insulted by the suggestion that people over seventy needed extra help doing their jobs. Many critics feared Roosevelt was becoming a dictator. His plan failed, and although FDR remained as popular as ever with the public, his power to push programs through Congress was weakened.

Below: Marian Anderson

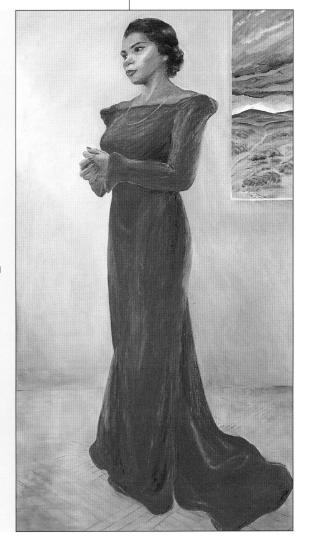

MARIAN ANDERSON AND THE DAR

Marian Anderson had a voice "that comes once in a hundred years," said the great Italian conductor Arturo Toscanini. He was not the only one who thought so. When Anderson was a child in a poor neighborhood in Philadelphia, her community was so proud of her voice that they got up a collection to pay for voice lessons. After years of hard work, she won a national singing contest, and was asked to perform at Carnegie Hall. Anderson also toured Europe and South America, where she became an instant sensation.

Then, in February 1939, Anderson prepared for a performance at Washington D.C.'s Constitution Hall. The Daughters of the American Revolution, a women's organization that operated the Constitution Hall, refused to allow Anderson to perform, saying that it was not proper for the hall to be used by someone who was African-American. Hearing of this slight, First Lady Eleanor Roosevelt was furious. A DAR member herself, she quickly resigned and set to work helping Anderson find another place to perform.

On Easter Sunday, Anderson stood on the steps of the Lincoln Memorial and looked out over Washington. Over 7,000 people listened as her warm contralto voice swelled across the Mall.

Sixteen years later, Anderson broke another racial barrier. In January of 1955, she became the first African-American to sing at the Metropolitan Opera House.

Right: First Lady Eleanor Roosevelt

By the middle of 1937, the economy was making a slow but steady recovery. The gross national product was growing at 10 percent a year, while industrial output was back to 1929 levels. For years, the government had been borrowing and spending more than it took in. This was called deficit spending or "pump priming" since it was designed to help get the economic pump working again.

Right: Mary McLeod Bethune served as director of the Office of Minority Affairs of the National Youth Administration.

FDR decided it was time for the government to spend less. Millions of workers were laid off from government jobs and billions less were spent on public relief and public works projects. The results were a disaster. The stock market collapsed and unemployment rose again to 19 percent. Protests and strikes jumped as well. Pump priming was started up again in 1938.

Many people worried that despite all of the New Deal programs, not all Americans were being helped equally. One of these people was the president's wife, Eleanor Roosevelt.

Eleanor Roosevelt, just like her husband, was a strong-willed and independent person. She was also the first president's wife to publicly make statements about the affairs of the government. In fact, Mrs. Roosevelt wrote a daily newspaper column while she was in the White House, held regular press conferences of her own, chaired public works committees, and made many of the trips around the country that her wheelchair-bound husband was unable to make. FDR called her "my eyes and ears." In fact, Eleanor Roosevelt was so active that she earned the nickname "Public Energy Number One."

On the occasions that Mrs. Roosevelt felt that her husband was not doing enough to solve a particular problem, she would tell him so. For instance, she demanded that more women be hired for public works projects. She also pushed for fairer treatment of African-Americans. Working with her was Mary McLeod Bethune, director of the Office of Minority Affairs of the National Youth Administration. Bethune had founded the National Council of Negro Women, an organization dedicated to improving the social, political, and economic standing of African-American women. She had also founded a college for African-American women, which was later named Bethune-Cookman College. Together, she and Mrs. Roosevelt fought to end discrimination in government programs.

Opportunities for poor southern blacks were especially limited during the Depression. Many types of jobs remained closed to African-Americans. Shown at left is a black-only store during the 1930s.

One of the poorest regions of the nation during both the Depression and today is the Delta region of northwest Mississippi. As can be seen from the Depression-era photograph below, paved roads and automobiles were uncommon luxuries for most Delta residents.

The New Deal changed the way Americans lived forever. It set up huge new agencies and bureaucracies. It made Washington an important player in the nation's economy. And, for the first time in the nation's history, people looked to the Federal government in times of economic trouble.

As for actually ending the Depression, the New Deal was not entirely successful. Even after seven years of new programs and government spending, 15 percent of America's workers remained out of work in 1940. Roosevelt had declared war on the Depression and had, in some ways, lost. It would take a real war to end the Depression for good.

AMERICAN TIMELINE

1920 After the passage of the Eighteenth Amendment, Prohibition goes into effect, making it illegal to make, sell, import, or export liquor.
■ The Nineteenth Amendment is ratified, giving women the right to vote.
■ Seven players on the Chicago White Sox baseball team accused of throwing the 1919 World Series are officially banned from the game. Third baseman Buck Weaver, who had not participated in the scheme but knew about it, is also banned.

1921 Italian anarchists Nicola Sacco and Bartolomeo Vanzetti are found guilty of murder and are executed. Many Americans believe their conviction was based more on their political beliefs than any actual guilt.
■ The Emergency Quota Act is passed, limiting immigration to only 358,000 a year, less than half the number admitted in 1920.

1923 Suffering a stroke after an exhausting cross-country tour, President Warren Harding dies. Vice President Calvin Coolidge takes office.
■ Rising membership in the Ku Klux Klan sparks racial violence in Oklahoma. The black section of Tulsa is burned to the ground. Despite death threats, Oklahoma governor J. C. Walton calls out the National Guard to protect minorities.

1924 With the passage of the Snyder Act, all Native Americans become citizens.
■ Calvin Coolidge is elected president, defeating Democrat John W. Davis and Progressive Robert "Fighting Bob" LaFollette.

Above: Calvin Coolidge

1925 Thousands flock to Florida to purchase land. Many sign deeds without inspecting the property, and find themselves the owners of swamps.

WORLD TIMELINE

Above: Mahatma Gandhi

1920 Angry at Germany's failure to pay for World War I damage, French troops occupy the Ruhr Valley on the border between the two countries.

1921 Nonviolent activist Mahatma Gandhi is arrested in India for stirring up opposition to the British government that occupies the country. He pleads guilty to all charges but refuses to stop his protests.

1922 Benito Mussolini seizes control of Italy and declares himself dictator.
■ Archaeologists uncover the remains of the tomb of King Tutankhamen, and gain important insight into the lives of the Egyptians 3,000 years ago.

1923 The price of bread in Germany skyrockets from a mere 250 marks to 3,465 marks.

1925 Adolf Hitler's *Mein Kampf* is published.

1927 Nationalist leader Chiang Kai-shek hires a gangster to rid China of any Communist opposition to his government.
■ Britain formally recognizes the independence of Saudi Arabia with the signing of the Treaty of Jeddah.

1926 In a record-breaking 14 hours and 31 minutes, Miss Gertrude Ederle of New York swims the English Channel.

1927 Charles Lindbergh and his plane, *Spirit of St. Louis,* make the first solo flight across the Atlantic.
■ Secretary of Commerce Herbert Hoover gives a speech from his Washington office to New York bankers with the help of a new invention—the television.

1928 Fifteen nations, including the United States, sign the Kellogg-Briand Pact, banning war as a technique for resolving international conflict.
■ Herbert Hoover is elected president with his campaign promise "A chicken in every pot and a car in every garage."

Above: Charles Lindbergh

1929 In what becomes known as "Black Tuesday," the stock market crashes. In the New York Stock Exchange alone, losses are reported at $9 billion.

1930 A drought hits the nation and banks close to prevent further withdrawals. Although the government spends $45 million to help drought victims, the number of jobless climbs higher.

1931 Congress passes a bill to officially recognize "The Star Spangled Banner" as the national anthem.
■ After making thousands of dollars on bootlegged booze and murdering many of his rivals, Al Capone is sentenced to 11 years in prison and $50,000 in fines for tax evasion. His arrest is a direct result of a crusade by treasury agent Eliot Ness.

Above: Adolf Hitler, in a photograph that appeared in his book **Mein Kampf**

1928 Bolshevik Joseph Stalin gains control of the USSR, sending his opponents into exile. He also seizes private farm lands, declaring them property of the state.
■ Mexican president Alvaro Obregon is reelected. He is assassinated a few weeks later.
■ British scientist Alexander Fleming discovers a mold that kills bacteria. He calls it penicillin.

1929 Fighting breaks out as Arabs and Jews clash across Palestine.

1930 Hitler's Nazi Party rises to power in national elections. Only Germany's Socialist Party wins more seats in the government.

1931 Japanese forces invade civil war–torn China. When the League of Nations condemns the invasion, Japan quits the League.

Above: Chinese leader Chiang Kai-shek

AMERICAN TIMELINE

Above: World War I veterans camp out in Washington D.C.

1932 Seventeen thousand World War I veterans, most of them victims of the Great Depression, arrive in Washington to ask for early payment of their bonus pay. They are forcibly removed by the U.S. Army under General Douglas MacArthur.

■ Charles Lindbergh's 20-month-old son is kidnapped and later found dead. German immigrant Bruno Hauptmann is arrested and convicted of the crime. He continues to proclaim his innocence all the way to his execution.

■ Angry with President Hoover's failure to end the Depression, Americans elect Franklin D. Roosevelt to the presidency.

1933 Thirteen years after it began, Prohibition ends.

■ The first wave of Roosevelt's "New Deal" programs go into effect, creating federally funded jobs and businesses aimed at ending the Depression.

1934 The FBI takes a bite out of crime when the criminal careers of gangsters John Dillinger, "Baby Face" Nelson, "Pretty Boy" Floyd,

WORLD TIMELINE

1932 Paul von Hindenburg is elected president of Germany. After appointing several others to the position of chancellor, all of whom are ineffective, Hindenburg finally gives the job to Adolf Hitler.

■ In a series of riots, Britain's unemployed protest their hunger.

1934 After the death of Hindenburg, Hitler seizes control of the German government. He begins executing or replacing his opponents and burning books and magazines that he decides are threatening.

1935 Mussolini invades Ethiopia. Although Ethiopian Emperor Haile Selassie asks for help from the

Above: Hitler announces Germany's takeover of Austria.

League of Nations, it does not get involved.

Above: Wanted: John Herbert Dillinger

and Bonnie and Clyde all end in shootouts.

1935 Roosevelt starts the Works Progress Administration, giving work to 367,000 unemployed within the year.
■ The Social Security Act is passed.

1936 At the Olympic Games in Nazi Berlin, African-American Jesse Owens sets three world records and wins four gold medals.
■ Margaret Mitchell publishes her best-selling Civil War novel, *Gone with the Wind.*

1937 After leaving the United States to make a historic flight around the world, Amelia Earhart disappears over the South Pacific. She is never found.
■ While on a rescue mission in China, U.S. gunboat *Panay* is bombed by Japanese warplanes. Japan's formal apology and agreement to pay $2 million in damages only slightly appeases Americans as tensions rise.

1938 Fearing the spread of Communism and Fascism, Congress forms the House Committee of Un-

Above: Amelia Earhart

American Activities to investigate organizations or citizens who might betray the nation.

■ The Nuremberg Laws are passed in Germany, denying Jews their basic rights.

1936 Spanish Fascists led by General Francisco Franco try to overthrow the popularly elected Socialist government. Civil war breaks out.
■ England's King Edward VIII gives up the throne in exchange for the hand of a twice-divorced American, Wallis Warfield Simpson.

1937 Hitler sends German bombers to Spain in order to help Franco destroy opposition.
■ After heavy fighting, the Japanese seize Nanking, China.

1938 In a violation of the Versailles Treaty that ended World War I, Hitler unites Germany and Austria and seizes the Sudetenland in Czechoslovakia. Although the Czechs are prepared to fight, France and Britain refuse to back them and they are forced to lay down their arms.
■ In what later became known as *Kristallnacht,* Nazis smash and burn Jewish homes, shops, and synagogues.

Right: During the early 1930s, many Jewish-owned shops in Germany were boycotted. As the decade wore on, many of them were simply destroyed.

VIII. WORLD WAR II

Weary American troops rest between battles in the painting above.

A S AMERICANS BATTLED THE Depression of the 1930s with New Deal experiments, Europe had its own hard times. While Americans elected— and then reelected—Franklin D. Roosevelt—European dictators denied their people the freedom to vote. In 1923, Benito Mussolini and his Fascist Party took over Italy. And the same month that FDR became president, Adolf Hitler became Germany's chancelor.

As the 1930s wore on, Hitler's army moved into more and more territory— first Austria and then Czechoslovakia. European leaders did nothing, and few Americans wanted to get involved. Even after Poland and France were overrun by the Nazis, and Britain was bombed, many Americans continued to believe that the United States should not take sides.

Everything changed on December 7, 1941, when the United States was directly attacked by Japan, another expansion-minded nation. Japan had conquered the Chinese region of Manchuria in 1931, and had come to dominate the Western Pacific. When the Japanese launched an all-out attack on the American naval base at Pearl Harbor, Hawaii, there could be no turning back. America was at war, again.

The Road to War

"We interrupt this broadcast to bring you a special news bulletin from Hawaii. The Japanese Empire launched a surprise attack this morning on the U.S. naval base at Pearl Harbor, Oahu."

It was Sunday, December 7, 1941—10 in the morning on the West Coast, 1 P.M. in Washington—when the news crackled over the nation's radios. Though the attack occurred thousands of miles away, most Americans knew it meant war.

For Stephen Bowers Young, a mess cook on board the battleship U.S.S. *Oklahoma*, it *was* war. "The bugle tore the air," he recalled. "Now it was general quarters! A voice boomed throughout the ship—'All hands, man your battle stations!' What . . . was this? Drills on Sunday? The harsh, excited voice on the PA system froze us in our tracks. . . 'This is no drill! Get going—they're real bombs.'"

Japanese planes sunk the *Oklahoma*. Young and some of his shipmates were trapped in the ship's hull for hours. The men joked with each other to keep their fears away. "Join the Navy and see the world," one sailor laughed, "from the bottom of Pearl Harbor."

Over a day later, a rescue team brought the men to the surface. "Standing on the upturned hull," Young remembered, "I gazed about me. It was the same world I had left 25 hours before, but as I looked at the smoke and wreckage of battle, the sunken ships *Tennessee, West Virginia,* and *Arizona* astern [behind] us, I felt that life would never be the same,

not for me—not for any of us."

Young was right. A few days after the attack on Pearl Harbor, the United States was officially at war with the Axis Powers of Japan, Germany, and Italy. But as had been the case during World War I, the United States didn't get directly involved in the war until several years after it had begun.

In many ways, World War II was a product of World War I. The Allies, particularly France and Britain, used the Versailles Peace Treaty of 1919 to punish Germany. The treaty demanded that Germany pay $33 billion in war reparations, or repayments. The debt crippled the German economy.

In 1923 the economy became so bad in Germany that people had to carry money in wheelbarrows just to buy groceries. Many people lost their entire savings

Below: The Honolulu Star-Bulletin *spreads the news of war.*

Bottom: Japanese planes bomb Pearl Harbor.

and fear gripped the country. By the late 1920s, reparations were cut back and new loans from the United States helped Germany get back on its feet. The Great Depression, however, caused a new collapse in the economy of Germany, and much of Europe.

The Versailles Treaty also contained a "guilt clause" that blamed Germany for starting the war. Most Germans believed that reparations and the guilt clause were unfair. They were angry at the new German government for accepting the terms of the treaty.

The Rise of Fascism

In the 1920s, a political movement called Fascism began to gain influence in various countries around the world. A small group of German Fascists, called Nazis, was formed by Adolph Hitler. The Nazis promised to end the national humiliation of defeat by restoring German power. In 1923 the Nazis failed at an attempted

coup (attack) on the government.

In 1922, a newspaper editor and politician named Benito Mussolini seized power in Italy, and within a few years had created a Fascist dictatorship there.

Fascism was a political system opposed to both Communism and democracy. Fascists argued that the state was more important than individual people. All Italian organizations—from labor unions to corporations and even the Catholic Church—were required to obey the Fascist Party and Mussolini. Although Italy under Mussolini would never grow strong enough to threaten Europe militarily by itself, the philosophy of the Fascist party became a great influence on Hitler.

In Asia, another Fascist government was also coming to power. Fascists in Japan believed that their nation and their people were superior to others and that strong nations had the right to conquer weaker ones. The Japanese government said that the European colonial empires

Below, right: Jesse Owens outruns the competition.

JESSE OWENS AND THE 1936 OLYMPICS

Adolf Hitler was ready for the Olympics. He had a magnificent new stadium built in Berlin that would serve as a temple to the Aryans, or northern Europeans, a race that Nazis believed was superior to all others. His posters promoting the games reflected the Nazi idea of a superior race. And, when the stadium doors opened in August of 1936, 110,000 spectators gathered to see the great showcase of Nazism.

Jesse Owens, a young African-American from Alabama, quickly stole the show. Breaking three world records, he won the gold in four different track-and-field events: the 100- and 200-meter dashes, the broad jump, and the 400-meter relay. Newspapers heralded him as the "world's fastest athlete." Following Owens's broad jump victory, Lutz Long, a competing German athlete, hugged Owens in admiration and offered congratulations.

Hitler was furious. He had planned sweeping victories for the German Aryans followed by dramatic parades. Owens was an embarrassment to the Nazi theory of a master race. When the time came to present the athletes with their medals, Hitler left the stadium. He could not stand to recognize an African-American who was taking home the gold.

in Asia should give way to a Japanese one. They called their plan the Greater Asia Co-Prosperity Sphere.

In 1931, Japan launched a massive attack against Manchuria in northern China. When China complained to the League of Nations, Japan simply dropped out of the organization. The League took no action against Japan, a sign of the League's weakness and lack of unity.

Halfway across the world, in Germany, Hitler was organizing his National Socialist German Workers', or Nazi, party. By 1928, the party already had over 100,000 members who were totally loyal to Hitler. Hitler had written of his plans to conquer the world in his book *Mein Kampf* (My Struggle). The Great Depression would give Hitler the chance to make his move.

The Depression hit Germany especially hard. Almost half the population was unemployed. Working people went hungry, and the middle class feared a

Communist revolution. Hitler promised to destroy Communism and make Germany rich and strong again.

In the elections of 1930 and 1932, the Nazis became the largest party in the Reichstag, or German parliament. In January 1933, President Hindenburg appointed Hitler to be chancellor, Germany's version of a prime minister. On March 23, about two weeks after FDR was inaugurated as president of the United States, the Nazis pushed through the Enabling Act, giving Hitler the powers of a dictator.

Hitler, who had himself called the "Führer" (German for leader), did not waste time using those powers. He quickly dissolved all other parties in Germany. Big business, labor unions, publishing houses, artists, and professional organizations were put under Nazi control. Those opposed to the Nazis were jailed. In June 1934, Hitler's Special Police, or Gestapo, destroyed the anti-Nazi leadership of the last independent organization in Germany, the army.

At first, Hitler was popular with many Germans. The economy had improved and government service was opened up to the poorer classes. At the same time, the Nazis brutally attacked those they considered enemies, including Communists, gypsies, gay people, and especially Jews. In 1935, the Nuremberg laws stripped all Jews of citizenship. In 1938, the Gestapo burned down the Reichstag building. Blaming the arson on Jews, Hitler launched an attack against Jewish homes, businesses, and synagogues. The assault is called *Kristallnacht*, German for "night of broken glass," because of the high number of Jewish-owned shop windows broken.

Above: Germany's Adolf Hitler

Below: Italy's Benito Mussolini

DER DEUTSCHE STUDENT

KÄMPFT FÜR FÜHRER UND VOLK

IN DER MANNSCHAFT DES NSD-STUDENTENBUNDES

Above: A poster for a Nazi government-sponsored student group

While all of this was going on, the former Allies of World War I did nothing. The U.S., French, and English governments refused to help the Spanish republic fight off the Fascists, although individuals from these countries joined in the fight. A group of Americans, called the Abraham Lincoln Brigade, fought the Fascists for almost three years in Spain.

In September 1938, Hitler demanded the Sudetenland, a German-speaking part of neighboring Czechoslovakia. The prime ministers of France and England flew to Germany and met with Hitler. Czechoslovakians were not invited. After agreeing to give Hitler what he wanted, British leader Neville Chamberlain returned to London and declared that he had obtained: "Peace with honor . . . peace for our time."

The policy was called "appeasement." After such huge losses in World War I, the British and French desperately wanted to avoid war. They believed that appeasing, or giving in to, Hitler would keep war from returning to Europe. They were wrong. In March 1939, Hitler marched into the rest of Czechoslovakia. France and Britain had learned their lesson, but still did nothing to stop Hitler.

Fearing that Germany would turn on his country next, Joseph Stalin, the premier of the Soviet Union, signed a nonaggression pact with Hitler. Publicly the pact said neither country would attack the other. Secretly, the two countries agreed to divide Poland between them.

With the Soviet Union out of the picture, Hitler invaded Poland on September 1, 1939. The Germans used a new kind of warfare. It involved quick and massive tank and bomber attacks, called *blitzkrieg*, or "lightning war." Two days later, France and England finally declared war on Germany. World War II had begun.

The following spring, Germany conquered Norway, Denmark, Belgium, Holland, and finally France. By June 1940, the only country in Western Europe still free from foreign domination was Great Britain. That month, the Germans began a long campaign called the

All three Fascist powers—Germany, Italy, and Japan—wanted to expand in size and were willing to fight wars to do so. Year by year, they became more ambitious and more aggressive. In 1935, Italy invaded Ethiopia, the last independent kingdom in Africa. When the League of Nations tried to impose sanctions, or penalties, against Italy, Mussolini dropped out of the organization. That same year, Hitler tore up the Treaty of Versailles, pulled out of the League of Nations, and began to rearm Germany.

Nazi Aggression

In 1936, the German army moved into the Rhineland, an area of the country that bordered France and was supposed to have no military forces. Later in the year, Fascists in Spain rose up against the republican government. In 1937, Japan invaded the rest of China, and in 1938, Germany took over neighboring Austria without firing a shot.

Battle of Britain, during which Nazi planes rained bombs on London night after night.

Hitler's real interest, however, was in the east. In *Mein Kampf*, he had spoken of giving the German people *Lebensraum,* or "living room," by conquering the "inferior" Slavic people of Eastern Europe and Russia. In June 1941, Hitler tore up his nonaggression pact with Stalin and launched the largest invasion in history against the Soviet Union. Millions of Soviet citizens would be killed over the next few years, but the Nazi invasion would fail.

American Isolationism

Protected from the Japanese and the Nazis by two oceans, most Americans did not believe that the country should get involved in another European war, although the vast majority stood opposed to Hitler and Japan. These people were called isolationists, or "America Firsters." American involvement in World War I hadn't stopped Europeans from fighting, they argued. How would another war solve anything?

A minority of Americans, including FDR, believed that events in Europe and Asia directly affected the United States.

They wanted to help fight the Fascists. Unfortunately for FDR and the interventionists, the American Firsters controlled Congress.

In 1934 and 1935, isolationist Senator Gerald Nye of North Dakota opened an investigation into why America went to war in 1917. He concluded that it was caused by weapons makers, whom he called "merchants of death." The 1935 Neutrality Act banned arms sales to countries at war. And because Americans dying on foreign ships that had been sunk had helped pull the country into the First World War, the new law said all Americans traveling on the ships of countries at war did so at their own risk.

In 1936, Congress banned loans to nations at war, as well. And in 1937, it added a "cash and carry" part to the law. If a country at war wanted to buy supplies from the United States, it would have to pay cash and pick them up with its own ships.

Preparing for War

The Fascist victories of 1940, however, began to change some American minds. A poll taken after the fall of France found that 69 percent of Americans believed a

Ideas not approved by the Nazi government were not permissible under Hitler. Above a group of pro-Nazi Germans burn books.

German victory would be dangerous for America. FDR set up two government committees to help America prepare for war or, at least, to help countries at war with Hitler and Japan.

During the summer of 1940, FDR brought two Republicans onto his cabinet to get wider support for his foreign policy. He also agreed to trade 50 World War I destroyers to Britain in exchange for use of British bases in the Atlantic. In October, Congress voted to increase defense spending and draft soldiers into the military. Believing the country was in a grave situation, FDR also agreed to run for a third term, the only president ever to do so. He won, though with a smaller majority than in his first two campaigns.

In March 1941, FDR got Congress to pass the Lend-Lease Act. The law gave the president the power to "lease, lend, or otherwise dispose of" arms to any country whose defense was important for America. Lend-Lease was mainly aimed at Britain, and, after it was attacked on June 22, 1941, Russia, too.

In a fireside chat, FDR used a story to explain Lend-Lease to Americans. "If my neighbor's house is on fire," FDR said, "I don't say to him, . . . 'Neighbor, my garden hose cost me $15; you have to pay me $15 for it.'" The President continued, "I don't want $15—I want my garden hose back after the fire is over." In short, said FDR, America must become the "arsenal of democracy."

But who would work in this "arsenal?" In 1940, only 240 of the nation's 100,000 aircraft workers were black. A. Philip Randolph, head of the largest black union in the country, demanded the government end this discrimination. Roosevelt, worried about upsetting southerners in his own Democratic party, did nothing. Then Randolph threatened a massive march on Washington. That did the trick. Roosevelt agreed to set up the Fair Employment Practices Committee and outlawed racial discrimination in defense plants.

In August 1941, Roosevelt and British prime minister Winston Churchill met aboard a cruiser off the Canadian coast.

Above: British prime minister Neville Chamberlain cheerfully returns from meeting with Hitler.

Right: The ruins of Warsaw, Poland, following the Nazi invasion in 1939

Left: Young Americans show their support for staying out of the war in Europe.

They agreed that defeating Hitler was the most important immediate goal of the war. By the fall, American ships were fighting a secret and undeclared war against Nazi submarines. In October, Congress allowed merchant ships to arm themselves. Roosevelt, however, still did not think he could ask Congress to declare war against Germany.

In the end, it was not Germany that pushed the United States into war, but Japan. America's relations with Japan went from bad to worse in the late 1930s, especially after the Japanese sank a U.S. gunboat during its 1937 invasion of China. In 1940, Japan signed the Tri-Partite, or Axis, pact with Italy and Germany and, by the fall of 1941, began invading Indo-China.

The Bombing of Pearl Harbor

The United States responded by cutting off trade with Japan, including America's most important export at that time, oil. Japan's leaders knew they would have to expand farther into Asia and the Pacific to get needed oil and other resources. They also knew this would probably lead to war with the United States.

In September 1941, Japanese prime minister Hideki Tōjō began secretly planning for war with the United States. On December 7, his forces attacked Pearl Harbor. Japanese leaders hoped that destroying this critical base would make it impossible for the United States to fight back for several years. This would allow enough time for Japan to become stronger.

The attack almost did the job. In just a few hours, the Japanese damaged or destroyed 18 ships, and killed 2,403 American military men and civilians. Fortunately, America's most important fighting ships, its aircraft carriers, were out to sea on December 7.

FDR, calling the day of the attack "a date which will live in infamy," asked and got a declaration of war against Japan from Congress. Within the week, Germany and Italy had declared war on the United States and the United States declared war on them. As mess cook Stephen Bowers Young said, "Life would never be the same." He was right. America would never be isolated from world affairs again.

Above: A proud Frenchman reacts to the sight of Nazi troops marching into Paris in 1940.

Life on the Homefront

They were nicknamed "Rosie the Riveters." They built airplanes, tanks, machine guns, jeeps, and just about anything else needed in a modern war. They were America's women.

Most had never been inside a factory before. "I was awed, really awed," said a Los Angeles housewife, Helen Studer. "Well, you can imagine how big it would have to be to have that big airplane [inside]. And all these fluorescent lights . . . Really, it takes you several hours almost to quit looking. I had never been inside anything like that."

With American men off at war, the government and the nation's businesses urged women to take war production jobs. Many men, and women, were worried that factory work was not fit for women. Recruiters promised that running factory machines was as easy as using "electric cake-mixers and vacuum cleaners."

"I applied for a job at Rohr aircraft," recalled Winona Espinosa of Grand Junction, Colorado, "and they sent me to a six-week training school. You learned how to use an electric drill, how to do precision drilling, how to rivet. I hadn't seen anything like a rivet gun or an electric drill before . . . But I was an eager learner, and I soon became an outstanding riveter."

Recruiters also appealed to women's patriotism and emotion. One recruitment poster read, "Longing won't bring him back sooner . . . GET A WAR JOB!" Millions did. By war's end, women made up over a third of the labor force. When the war ended and the soldiers came home, however, women were laid off by the millions.

To fight a world war, America needed to raise money, build weapons, and draft troops. To raise money, the government increased the income tax and sold war bonds. Until World War II, income tax had been for the wealthy only. Now, it was expanded to include most working Americans. Tax revenues rose from $2.2 billion in 1939 to over $35 billion at war's end. To make collection easier, the government began withholding taxes from people's paychecks.

The government also sold war bonds. A bond is like a loan to the government. A person buys a bond and gets paid interest on his or her money after a few years. The government gets to use the money in the meantime. Despite new taxes and bonds, government debt skyrocketed during the war. By 1945, the American government owed over $258 billion.

Above, right, and opposite page: During the war, the U.S. government printed hundreds of posters that encouraged Americans to do their part in the war effort.

Building enough weapons to fight a world war was another part of the government's job during World War II. Less than two weeks after Pearl Harbor, Congress passed the War Powers Act, giving FDR enormous power over the economy.

As in World War I, the War Production Board was established. It helped businesses switch from peacetime to wartime manufacturing. Automobile and appliance factories became weapons and munitions plants.

The Office of Price Administration and Civilian Supply (OPA) was created to guide the economy. In April 1942, the OPA froze most prices and rents. The agency also set up a complicated rationing system for everything from gasoline to food. Americans received ration stamp books from the government. If they wanted to buy something, they had to have a ration coupon to do so. Many people bought things on the black, or underground, market without coupons.

Lastly, the government needed troops to fight the war. The armed forces grew from a few hundred thousand members to over 15 million by war's end. About two-thirds were in the army, including the Army Air Corps (today's Air Force), and the rest were recruited into the Navy, Marines, and Coast Guard.

Minorities in the Armed Forces

While women were not drafted, nearly 300,000 enlisted, including a third of the nation's nurses. Some were even trained as pilots and given the job of flying planes to where they were needed, though not in combat.

One of the most highly decorated groups in the military was the Tuskegee Airmen, a group of black fighter pilots. Despite their bravery, and the bravery of other minority soldiers, racial discrimination continued in the armed forces. While nearly 700,000 blacks served in the armed forces, they were kept in segregated units. Most were assigned the lowest jobs, like mess cooks. The army even had blood banks kept separate, though scientists knew black and white people have the same blood types.

The National Association for the Advancement of Colored People (NAACP), the largest civil rights organization in the country, argued "a Jim Crow [segregated] army cannot fight for a free world." Jim Crow was the term in the South for anything segregated. The military, however, did not listen.

The War at Home

In the States, people from all classes volunteered and served in the war effort. The government also needed office and factory workers in America. The number of civil servants grew by four times during the war. At the height of the fighting,

civil service exams were given three times a day. Some of these government employees were called "dollar a year men." These were business executives who agreed to work for a dollar a year to help convert factories from peacetime manufacturing to weapons production.

Labor unions, which had grown tremendously in the 1930s, grew even larger during World War II. By 1945, nearly one-third of America's nonfarming workers belonged to unions. Two weeks after Pearl Harbor, America's trade union leaders pledged that their members would not strike for the rest of the war.

Pay increased greatly during the war, although many workers resented that wages were not going up as fast as business profits. Workers would often hold "minute strikes" at defense plants. The workers knew that the owners were making lots of money from war contracts and would not want to see strikes last very long. They were right. Most strikes were

AMERICA GOES ON WAR RATIONS

Below: A gasoline ration stamp

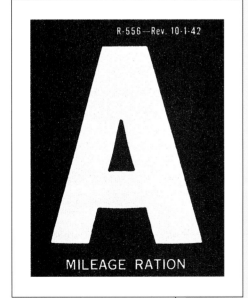

After the bombing of Pearl Harbor, America went to war. Almost overnight, weapons factories sprang up, civilian ships and aircraft were converted for wartime use, and food and supplies began to be shipped overseas. This caused a shortage of raw materials.

In 1942, rationing began. Americans were given ration tickets that limited the amount of gas, meat, sugar, and even shoes they could buy. Gas rationing caused stores to stop home delivery and milkmen to use horses and wagons. Car pooling became popular and some people rode their bikes or skated to work. Food rationing caused people to begin growing their own vegetables in "Victory Gardens." By 1943, people's backyard gardens produced more than one-third of the nation's needs.

Americans also were anxious to supply factories with the materials to build weapons. Junk that would be thrown away in peacetime might be the very thing necessary to build a plane. "At school we had drives collecting metal, and people brought pots and pans right out of their kitchens," says Mary Bristow, an elementary school English teacher. Tin cans, rubber tires, and newspapers were gathered from all over the country. Even bacon fat was worth saving. "Save waste fats for explosives," said posters at butcher shops. Housewives even collected their grease to make ammunition.

Left: American women at work in an aircraft factory during the war

Below: Movie star Rita Hayworth encourages people to donate their car bumpers to the war effort.

PLEASE DRIVE CAREFULLY. MY BUMPERS ARE ON THE SCRAP HEAP

settled in the workers' favor in a few minutes. In 1942, the National War Labor Board agreed to give industrial workers cost-of-living increases. Still, a coal miner strike during the war angered many Americans and hurt the image of unions for years after the war.

For those who didn't lose family or friends in the fighting, life was pretty good in America during the war. After Pearl Harbor, there was no fighting in Hawaii or on mainland U.S. soil. And while rationing forced people to drive their cars less, life continued almost as usual. People went to more movies than ever, and Hollywood began producing patriotic films like *Thirty Seconds over Tokyo* and *Mission to Moscow* to keep up the spirit of people back home.

One important difference in people's lives was the spread of recycling and gardening. To preserve resources, children conducted scrap metal and newspaper drives. Many families grew their own vegetables in "Victory Gardens," to help free up food for the soldiers.

Perhaps the most important change the war brought was migration. Millions of Americans moved around the country during the war, mostly to work in defense plants. California, which turned out one-sixth of the nation's weapons, saw its population jump by three million during the war.

Discrimination and Racism

The housing shortages caused by migration led to competition between blacks and whites. In Detroit, rioting broke out in 1943 between the city's blacks and immigrant whites leaving 34 people dead, mostly blacks. There were riots in 47 other cities that summer.

The NAACP used the war, and the fighting against Fascism and racism, to organize at home. By war's end, 450,000 blacks had joined the organization. A. Philip Randolph launched the Congress of Racial Equality (CORE), which used direct action against racism. When restaurants in Washington refused to serve black diners, CORE protesters picketed with signs that read: "Are you for Hitler's way or the American way? Make up your mind."

In Los Angeles, fear of juvenile delinquency often led to discrimination against the Mexican Americans, or Chicanos.

During the war, Chicano youth formed pachuco, or youth, gangs. Their unofficial uniform was the "zoot suit," with long coat, baggy pants, and watch chain. Angry white soldiers, sailors, and marines, on shore leave in Los Angeles, got into fights with the zoot suiters. In July 1943, a four-day riot broke out. White servicemen entered Mexican-American neighborhoods and beat up young Chicanos, while police did nothing.

Japanese Internment Camps

More than any other minority group, however, it was the country's Japanese Americans that suffered during the war. With the attack on Pearl Harbor, anti-Japanese racism spread up and down the West Coast. "A Jap's a Jap," an army general said. "It makes no difference whether he is an American citizen or not." In March 1942, Roosevelt approved a War Department plan to move over 100,000 Japanese Americans to internment, or prison, camps away from the Pacific Coast.

Japanese Americans were given just a few days to sell their homes and other possessions and turn themselves in to the

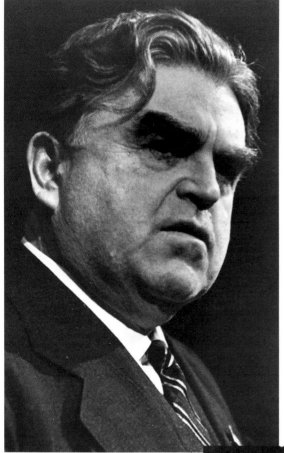

Above: Union leader John L. Lewis

In June 1943, U.S. soldiers, sailors, and marines wandered Los Angeles attacking any Mexicans they found wearing zoot suits. In the photograph at right, a mob of soldiers stops a streetcar to look for anyone wearing a zoot suit.

Opposite page, top: A Japanese-American family waits to be taken to an internment camp in 1942. Below: Civilian Exclusion Order No. 41 officially commanded that all Japanese Americans living on the West Coast be rounded up and sent to live in internment camps.

government. Many were forced to sell at a great loss to local whites. One Japanese woman destroyed her priceless set of china, rather than sell it for a fraction of its worth. Altogether, the Japanese lost over $400 million in property.

After being rounded up, the Japanese were placed in temporary holding centers, including the Santa Anita racetrack near Los Angeles, where they were forced to sleep in horse stables. After several months, they were moved to primitive camps in the desert. Most went peacefully, though some fought their cases in the courts. In two cases, the Supreme Court ruled that the government had the right to intern Japanese during the war.

Some Japanese made it out of the camps before the war's end. Many were needed to help harvest crops in California. Others moved to the eastern United States, and a few joined the army. The all Japanese-American 442nd Infantry Combat Team fought in Italy and became the most decorated unit in the entire American Army.

Despite this bravery, no apologies were offered by the American government until 1988, when Congress voted to give $20,000 cash to each of the 60,000 survivors of the camps. "When I think back to my mother and father, what they went through quietly, it's hard to explain," recalled Peter Ota of Los Angeles. "I think of my father without ever coming up with an angry word. After all those years, having worked his whole life to build a dream—an American dream, mind you—having it all taken away, and not one vindictive [vengeful] word."

NOTICE

Headquarters
Western Defense Command
and Fourth Army

Presidio of San Francisco, California
May 5, 1942

Civilian Exclusion Order No. 41

1. Pursuant to the provisions of Public Proclamations Nos. 1 and 2, this Headquarters, dated March 2, 1942, and March 16, 1942, respectively, it is hereby ordered that from and after 12 o'clock noon, P. W. T., of Monday, May 11, 1942, all persons of Japanese ancestry, both alien and non-alien, be excluded from that portion of Military Area No. 1 described as follows:

All of that portion of the City and County of San Francisco, State of California, within that boundary beginning at the intersection of Presidio Avenue and Sutter Street; thence easterly on Sutter Street to Van Ness Avenue; thence southerly on Van Ness Avenue to O'Farrell Street; thence westerly on O'Farrell Street to St. Joseph's Avenue (Calvery Cemetery); thence northerly on St. Joseph's Avenue to Geary Street; thence westerly on Geary Street to Presidio Avenue; thence northerly on Presidio Avenue to the point of beginning.

2. A responsible member of each family, and each individual living alone, in the above described area will report between the hours of 8:00 A. M. and 5:00 P. M., Wednesday, May 6, 1942, or during the same hours on Thursday, May 7, 1942, to the Civil Control Station located at:

1530 Buchanan Street,
San Francisco, California.

3. Any person subject to this order who fails to comply with any of its provisions or with the provisions of published instructions pertaining hereto or who is found in the above area after 12 o'clock noon, P. W. T., of Monday, May 11, 1942, will be liable to the criminal penalties provided by Public Law No. 503, 77th Congress, approved March 21, 1942, entitled "An Act to Provide a Penalty for Violation of Restrictions or Orders with Respect to Persons Entering, Remaining in, Leaving or Committing Any Act in Military Areas or Zones," and alien Japanese will be subject to immediate apprehension and internment.

4. All persons within the bounds of an established Assembly Center pursuant to instructions from this Headquarters are excepted from the provisions of this order while those persons are in such Assembly Center.

J. L. DeWITT
Lieutenant General, U. S. Army
Commanding

America at War Again

"I was a rifleman, private, Company G, 273rd Infantry, Third Platoon, 69th Division, First Army," recalled Joseph Polowsky. "We were in a quiet area . . . [at] a town called Trebsen [Germany], 20 miles west of the Elbe [river]. This was April 24 [1945]."

It was near the end of World War II. Nazi Germany was about to collapse. Within two weeks, Hitler would kill himself and a new German government would surrender to the Allies.

Since 1942, the American and Russian armies had been attacking Nazi-held Europe from both the west and the east. Now, the two forces were separated by a few miles and were to meet at the Elbe River.

An American patrol was formed to move up to the river and see what the Russians were doing. Polowsky was part of it. "[We] shot up two green flares. After about ten minutes, with shouts and the wind blowing toward the east, our voices were able to carry across the river. The Russians waved at us and gave the signal to approach their lines."

But, as Joseph Polowsky had remembered, the bridge had been blown up. "Fifty yards on each side was literally covered with bodies of women, old men, children . . ."

After a while, the platoon found a rowboat and rowed across to the other side. The Americans couldn't speak Russian and the Russians didn't speak English. Fortunately, Polowsky and a Russian soldier both spoke German. "It was a very solemn moment," Polowsky remembered. "There were tears in the eyes of most of us . . . Just think of the millions who died on the Russian side and the tremendous effort on the American side, amidst all those dead . . ."

When America went to war after Pearl Harbor, it faced enemies on two fronts. There was Germany and Italy in Europe. In Asia and the Pacific, Japan was on the march. Its attack on Pearl Harbor was just part of a much greater offensive. Within weeks of December 7, Japanese forces had launched invasions of the American territories Guam and Wake Island in the Pacific. It had also conquered Hong Kong, Burma, and the Malaysian Peninsula in Asia. Japan's attack on New Guinea threatened an invasion of Australia.

In the Philippines, an American colony since 1898, Japanese forces captured nearly 10,000 American troops, as well as another 50,000 Filipino soldiers serving the American army. The captured fighting men were marched across the steamy, swampy Bataan Peninsula to a prisoner of war camp. Thousands of Filipinos and Americans died of starvation, disease, and heatstroke. The survivors called it the "Bataan Death March." "In camp," one soldier remembered, "[all] you talked about is what you wanted in

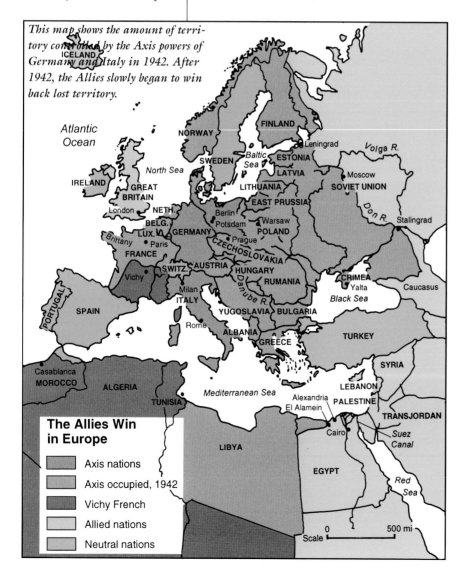

This map shows the amount of territory controlled by the Axis powers of Germany and Italy in 1942. After 1942, the Allies slowly began to win back lost territory.

The Allies Win in Europe

- Axis nations
- Axis occupied, 1942
- Vichy French
- Allied nations
- Neutral nations

your stomach. Guys would tell stories about how their mother made this . . . You'd see some of the fellas just lickin' their lips. Tasting it. You know?"

Despite the Japanese advances, however, American military leaders were more concerned with Nazi Germany. There were two important reasons for this. First, Soviet soldiers were doing most of the fighting and dying in the battle against the Nazi armies. If the USSR collapsed, American leaders feared, it would be impossible to defeat Hitler. Second, there was talk of a new and very dangerous weapon being developed by the Nazis called the atomic bomb.

The Manhattan Project

In 1939, a group of scientists had met with FDR to discuss the possibility of a powerful weapon based on the energy of atomic fission, or atom splitting. The group included many Jewish scientists who had fled the Nazis. They warned FDR that Germany was busy experimenting on such a weapon. In June

1941, six months before the United States entered World War II, the Office of Scientific Research and Development was planning studies of atomic fission.

In the spring of 1942, scientists at the University of Chicago produced the world's first atomic chain reaction. In June, they met with FDR and told him an atomic bomb was now a very real possibility. However, it would take a lot of money and personnel to build it. FDR agreed to go ahead with the plan to build an atomic bomb. It would be called the Manhattan Project and would become the most expensive, important, and top-secret military program in the nation's history.

Talk of a possible atomic bomb was welcome to FDR because the war news coming out of Europe and North Africa

Top: Japanese fighter planes during the Battle of Coral Sea in 1942. Above: Robert Oppenheimer, Manhattan Project's chief scientist

*Above: German comman-
der Erwin Rommel was
known as "the desert fox."*

*Below: Nazi spies (l-r)
Ernest Burger, Heinrick
Heinck, and Richard
Quirin, as well as four others,
were all arrested after
Burger and George Dasch
surrendered to the FBI.*

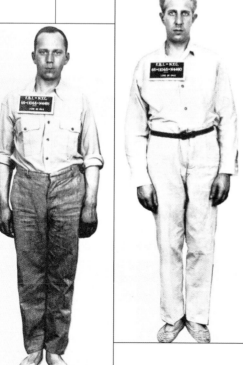

was very bad. By early 1942, the Nazi *wehrmacht*, or war machine, had reached the suburbs of Leningrad (now St. Petersburg) and Moscow, the Soviet Union's two largest cities.

The Germans were also heading toward the Caucasus region of the Soviet Union. The huge oil fields of the Caucasus could keep the German war machine running for years. Meanwhile, in North Africa, the Germans were closing in on Egypt and the very important Suez Canal. If Germany captured the canal, there would be no way to get American weapons and supplies to the Russians.

Two great battles turned the tide of war. From October 23 to November 5, 1942, Americans and British forces defeated German field marshall Erwin "the desert fox" Rommel's troops at El Alamein, Egypt. The largest tank battle in history saved the Suez Canal.

A SECRET MISSION GONE WRONG

Shortly before midnight on June 13, 1942, a German submarine silently rose to the surface just off of Long Island, New York. Four German soldiers in full mili-tary dress sneaked ashore carrying $200,000 and enough explosives to destroy defense targets across the United States. On the beach they quickly changed into civilian clothes and then headed for New York City. On June 17, four more Germans crept ashore at Ponte Vedra Beach in Florida.

Their plan was simple: to bomb railroad depots, defense plants, and essential manufac-turing centers in order to slow American defense production. Each man had memorized a map of the United States, with exact locations of key targets. Their training in Germany had taught them to find the weak points of each target, to creep in and set explosives, and then to melt into the American landscape after the sabotage was complete.

The Germans hadn't counted on one thing, however. After landing, George Dasch and Ernest Burger had changes of heart. They called FBI headquarters and turned themselves in. During a series of interrogations, they were able to provide the FBI with enough information to lead them to the capture of the other six saboteurs, who were put to death for their crimes. Dasch and Burger were deported to Germany in 1948.

Even more important, and even more bloody, was the Battle of Stalingrad in the fall of 1942 and winter of 1943. Millions of Russian and German troops battled for control of this gateway city to the Caucasus. For six months, these two huge armies fought, often from house to house and street to street. When it was over, more than 300,000 German troops lay dead, and hundreds of thousands were taken prisoner. Stalingrad is remembered as the greatest battle in human history. Together, the encounters at Stalingrad and El Alamein halted the German war machine in its tracks.

But turning the Germans back raised problems among the Allies. Because his forces were doing most of the fighting, Russian leader Joseph Stalin demanded that Britain and America open up a second front against Nazi Germany in Western Europe. British prime minister Winston Churchill argued against it. He said British and American forces weren't ready and should invade Italy, "the soft underbelly of Europe," instead.

Stalin needed to know that the United States and Britain would not sign separate peace treaties with Germany, leaving the

USSR to fight alone. To ease Stalin's worries, Roosevelt and Churchill agreed in January 1943 at Casablanca, Morroco, that they would not stop fighting until Hitler had unconditionally surrendered to the Allies. They also began daily and nightly bombing of German forces and weapons factories.

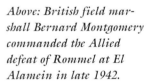

Above: British field marshall Bernard Montgomery commanded the Allied defeat of Rommel at El Alamein in late 1942.

Left: President Roosevelt (center) meeting with Prime Minister Winston Churchill of Great Britain (left) and Joseph Stalin, premier of the Soviet Union (right), at the Yalta Conference in 1945

Above: American troops landing on the coast of France during D-Day

In early 1943, American and British forces invaded Sicily and then Italy. By July, the government of Benito Mussolini had fallen. Unfortunately, the German army moved into Italy and it would take another year of fierce fighting before the Allies captured the Italian capital of Rome. Meanwhile, Russian forces were pushing the Germans back into the Ukraine on the USSR's western border and then into Poland.

Finally, in June 1944, British and American leaders felt they were ready to open the second front. On June 6, called D-Day, they launched the largest naval invasion force in military history. Within a few days, over one and a half million troops had landed on the beaches of Normandy, in northern France. By the end of the summer, the Allies had recaptured Paris and most of France. At year's end, Nazi Germany seemed close to total defeat.

Then disaster struck. Throughout the war, German scientists had been working both on an atomic weapon and a way to deliver it. By late 1944, they had

perfected the V-2, a missile that was capable of hitting England.

In December, the Nazis counterattacked through Belgium. Waiting for bad weather so Allied planes could not bomb them, they pushed American and British forces back along a wide front. The assault was called the Battle of the Bulge because the Germans pushed a bulge in the Allied front lines. Hitler hoped the Battle of the Bulge would give his scientists time to finish their atomic weapon. Carried to England by a V-2 missile, it would turn the tide of war. Fortunately, the Allies counterattacked and, after ten days of the heaviest fighting in Western Europe, they pushed the Germans back. Hitler's plan did not succeed.

By late winter 1945, British and American forces had crossed the Rhine and entered Germany from the west. At the same time, Russian troops had crossed Poland and invaded Germany from the east. On April 30, Hitler committed suicide in his bunker beneath the ruins of Berlin, the German capital. On May 8, the new German government surrendered unconditionally to the Allies. Around the world, people cheered V-E, or Victory in Europe, day.

Two things disturbed the celebrations. First, FDR never lived to see America's victory. He died of a brain hemorrhage on April 12, 1945, after serving 12 years as president.

The Concentration Camps

Second, as Allied troops marched into Poland and Germany, they made a horrifying discovery. The Nazis had not just imprisoned Jews during the war, they had tried to exterminate them. At Dachau, Auschwitz, Buchenwald, and dozens of other places, the Allied soldiers discovered Nazi concentration camps where Jews were murdered by the millions and their remains burned in ovens. The Nazis called it the "final solution" to the so-called "Jewish problem." The world remembers it as the "Holocaust."

Historians have since discovered that Roosevelt and other Allied leaders knew about the camps for most of the war. Some Jews have asked why the Allies didn't try to stop the murders by bombing the camps. But defenders of the government policy say this wouldn't have worked. Hitler was determined to destroy the Jews at any cost. Even during the final defeat of Germany, Hitler would not let his generals use the trains meant for carrying Jews to transport needed military supplies. As Churchill later said, defeating the Germans as quickly as possible was the best way to stop the Holocaust. Still, it is also known that Allied governments refused to accept Jewish refugees in large numbers, when it was still possible to get them out of Europe.

Judgment at Nuremberg

Nazi leaders would be put on trial after the war for "crimes against humanity." The Nuremberg trials would end up sending many German leaders to prison and lead to the execution of a few. Israel, a Jewish country created after the Holocaust, eventually chased down some of the Nazi murderers who got away. One, Adolf Eichmann, head of the concentration camp system, became the only man in Israeli history to be put to death.

Japan was still undefeated. Americans

"When they came for the Communists, I did not speak, because I was not a Communist. When they came for the Jews, I did not speak, because I was not a Jew. When they came for the union leaders, I did not speak, because I was not a union leader. When they came for me, there was no one left to speak."

—MARTIN NIEMULLER, *German minister, after his release from the Dachau concentration camp*

Although the Germans bombed London heavily throughout the war, historic St. Paul's Cathedral in London managed to survive. The famous church is seen at left, surrounded by clouds of smoke.

The map below shows the amount of territory captured and major battles fought by the Japanese from December 1941 to August 1942.

were preparing for a bloody invasion of its home islands.

The War in the Pacific

As it had in Europe and North Africa, the tide of war in the Pacific turned in 1942 and 1943. In May 1942, American forces halted the Japanese advance at the Battle of the Coral Sea, preventing an invasion of Australia. In June, the American and Japanese navies fought the greatest sea battle in history off the island of Midway. Using aircraft from carriers, it was the first time a sea battle was fought without the ships of the two forces ever firing on one another directly.

After Midway came a series of island invasions at Guadalcanal and Tarawa. On each of these islands, U.S. Marines and other forces fought bloody battles for tiny strips of sand and palm trees. At Peleliu, Japanese troops dug caves and waited for the American invaders. A battle that was supposed to last a few days took months. When Japanese forces refused to surren-

der, the Americans used flamethrowers, burning the Japanese soldiers to death and then sealing them in their caves. Of the 14,000 Japanese defenders on Peleliu, less than 100 surrendered.

In October 1944, General Douglas MacArthur wiped out nearly the entire Japanese navy at the Battle of Leyte Gulf, leading to the reconquest of the Philippines. Still, the Japanese were a long way from defeat. In early 1945, the Americans launched the bloody invasions of Iwo Jima and Okinawa. These two islands gave the United States air bases within reach of the Japanese home islands. American bombers began destroying one Japanese city after another.

The bloodiness of fighting in the Pacific, and the fact that the Japanese refused to surrender even when defeated, produced a feeling of racism among American troops. "I have heard many guys who fought in Europe say the Germans were damned good soldiers . . . When they surrendered, they were guys just like us,"

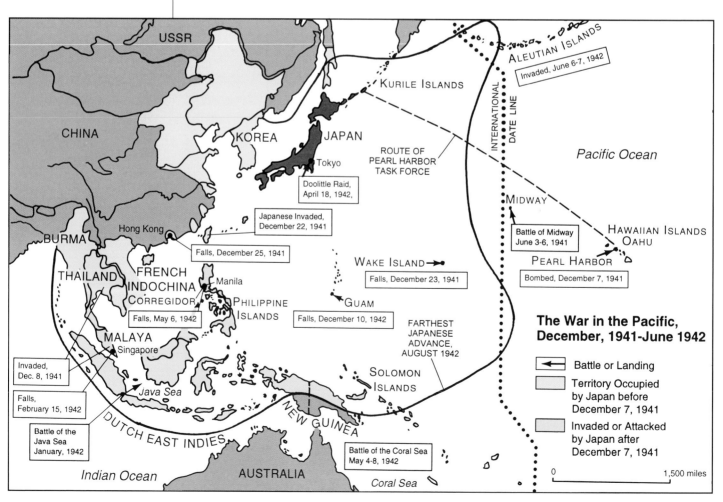

recalled Eugene Sledge, a Marine fighting in the Pacific. "With the Japanese, it was not that way . . . Our drill instructor at boot camp would tell us, 'You're not going to Europe; you're going to the Pacific. Don't hesitate to fight the Japs dirty.'"

By mid-1945, the Japanese army, navy, and air force had suffered terrible losses. The cities of Japan were in ruins. A week of firebombing had killed over 100,000 people in Tokyo alone. The Japanese were so desperate they began launching "kamikaze," or suicide, attacks. Japanese pilots would load their planes with explosives and crash them into American ships. Still, military leaders believed that an invasion of Japan's home islands might cost 100,000 American lives or more, and take over a year to complete.

Then came the news from the desert of New Mexico. In July 1945, at Alamogordo testsite, scientists and military officials of the Manhattan Project set off the first atomic blast in history. After

Japan's top diplomats to the United States are shown above shortly before their country attacked Pearl Harbor.

Left: American troops during the Bataan Death March of 1942

Right: An atomic bomb explodes over the Pacific during a test shortly before Hiroshima.

Below: The United Nations charter-signing ceremony

THE FOUNDING OF THE UNITED NATIONS

By 1943, 26 nations were at war with the Axis. No country was untouched by the fighting. The money spent, property destroyed, and millions of lives lost were enough to convince the world that a global war should never be allowed to happen again. With this thought in mind, the Allies began to consider the development of a world security organization. This organization would be given the authority to "take such action by air, naval, or land forces to maintain or restore international peace and security."

On June 26, 1945, delegates from 50 nations met in San Francisco to sign a charter forming the United Nations. "Oh, what a great day this can be in history!" declared President Harry S. Truman. The United States, Britain, China, the USSR, and France (the Allies of World War II) were appointed as the five permanent members of the United Nations Security Council. The Security Council would decide if military action were necessary to keep other nations from breaking international law. Before troops could be called in, all five permanent members would have to vote in favor of such action. It was hoped that this would lead to ruling by cooperation rather than violence, and that formation of the United Nations was a start to lasting world peace.

viewing the explosion, Robert Oppenheimer, the project's chief scientist, quoted from *Bhagavad Gita,* the Hindu Bible: "I am become Death, Destroyer of Worlds."

Now came the question: Should America use this most terrible of weapons? The new president, Harry Truman, did not hesitate and ordered American bombers at Tinian Island into action. On August 6, the *Enola Gay,* an American B-29, dropped an atomic bomb on the southern Japanese city of Hiroshima, killing 75,000 people instantly. Another 75,000 died later from radiation poisoning. On August 9, a second bomb was dropped on Nagasaki.

Many people have wondered if America really needed to use the bomb. Defenders of the action say it saved hundreds of thousands of Japanese and American lives. Critics argue that it should have been dropped on an uninhabited part of Japan first, as a warning.

Some have also argued that Japan was ready to surrender before Hiroshima was bombed, with the only remaining disputes being whether Japan's surrender would have to be unconditional, and whether Emperor Hirohito would have to step down.

Wherever the truth may lie regarding the decision to drop the bomb, once the decision was made, the war ended quickly.

Japan announced it would surrender a few days after Nagasaki. On September 2, 1945, MacArthur accepted the Japanese emperor's unconditional surrender aboard the U.S.S. *Missouri,* a survivor of Pearl Harbor, in Tokyo Bay.

World War II was the bloodiest and costliest war in the history of humanity. An estimated 60 million people around the world were killed. But these horrible losses were not distributed evenly. While much of Europe and Asia lay in ruins, America was untouched by physical destruction. American war dead stood at nearly 300,000, while Russia's amounted to over 20 million, many of them civilian. The differences between these two losses would cause many problems in the uneasy peace that followed World War II, a period that came to be called the "Cold War."

With the surrender of the Japanese, World War II came to an end. An American sailor, just home from the war, celebrates with his girlfriend (below) in New York's Times Square.

AMERICAN TIMELINE

Above: Albert Einstein

1939 Albert Einstein writes to President Roosevelt, telling him that the Germans are developing a single bomb that could easily destroy a city.

This causes Roosevelt to create the Manhattan Project for the purpose of creating an atomic bomb.

■ The New York World's Fair opens, with 60 nations participating. The opening ceremonies are shown on television by the National Broadcasting Company (NBC). Germany does not participate.

1940 Franklin Roosevelt is reelected president.

■ Twenty North and South American nations sign the Declaration of Havana, agreeing to protect American colonies from German or Japanese attack should the war spread across the Atlantic.

■ Bugs Bunny makes his debut. The cartoon character wins instant fame and popularity, as do his friends, Daffy Duck and Porky Pig.

Above: A poster for the New York World's Fair

WORLD TIMELINE

1939 Adolf Hitler forces the Czech president to surrender the rest of his country to Germany.

■ At 5:45 A.M., on September 1, Hitler's troops invade Poland. Polish forces are defeated within two weeks. Britain and France declare war on Germany.

1940 Germany captures Norway, Denmark, Holland, Belgium, Alsace-Lorraine, Luxembourg, and France.

■ Mussolini declares war on the Allies and orders his troops to march across the Ethiopian border into British Somaliland in Africa.

■ Japan officially joins Germany and Italy in the war against Britain and France.

Above: Firefighters battle blazes following the Battle of London in 1940.

Above: Mount Rushmore under construction

Above: Joe DiMaggio

1941 After 14 years of drilling and blasting with dynamite, workers complete Mount Rushmore. Gutzon Borglum, the man who designed the sculpture, did not live to see its completion.

■ In a surprise attack, Japanese air forces bomb Pearl Harbor, destroying or damaging 18 warships and killing 2,403 Americans. Roosevelt declares war on Japan, causing Japan's allies, Germany and Italy, to declare war on the United States.

■ New York Yankee Joe DiMaggio sets a new record by making a base hit in 56 consecutive games. The record is still standing almost 60 years later.

1941 German troops capture Yugoslavia and invade Greece.

■ The Soviets are surprised and almost overwhelmed by a German invasion. Although the Red Army is disorganized and outdated, the Germans are illprepared for the Russian winter, and the freezing temperatures force them to halt their march on Moscow.

1942 U.S. intelligence cracks Japanese battle codes, allowing American forces to launch a surprise attack on the Japanese navy at Midway, destroying four aircraft carriers and damaging three battleships.

■ Brazil declares war on Germany and Italy.

Below: Japanese fighter planes hit the battleship U.S.S. Yorktown during the Battle of Midway.

AMERICAN TIMELINE

Commander Jimmy Doolittle (Above: fifth from the left) and his crew

■ After Americans are forced to surrender at Corregidor and Bataan in the Philippines, a daring squadron of bomber pilots takes off under the command of Colonel Jimmy Doolittle. They bomb the Japanese cities of Tokyo, Nagoya, Osaka, and Kobe, and then escape to safety in China.

1943 Dwight D. Eisenhower is given command of the American forces in North Africa.
■ The United States Supreme Court rules that requiring students to salute the United States flag is unconstitutional.

1944 With the signing of the Serviceman's Readjustment Act, Roosevelt establishes benefits for veterans after the war.

1942 A fear of espionage causes the War Department to order the internment of Japanese Americans living on the West Coast. Over 100,000 Japanese Americans are forced into relocation camps.

WORLD TIMELINE

1943 Poorly armed Polish Jews in the Warsaw Ghetto refuse to go quietly to the concentration camps and launch a fierce fight against the Nazis.
■ The Allies slowly advance through Egypt and Libya, until German troops under "the desert fox" Erwin Rommel are forced to withdraw from northern Africa.
■ The Allies invade Italy. Although initially they meet resistance from Italian and German troops, Italian morale is low, and Italy soon surrenders.

1944 Hitler orders all children over the age of ten to arm themselves for battle.

Above: Locals cheer as the U.S. army rolls into the Italian city of Palermo in July 1943.

■ Americans under General Douglas MacArthur gain control of the Pacific as they capture the Philippines.

■ Over 30,000 young people show up outside of New York's Paramount Theatre to hear young singer Frank Sinatra. When only 4,000 are allowed inside, 700 riot police are forced to try to keep order outside.

1945 Stalin, Churchill, and Roosevelt meet at Yalta to discuss the fate of Germany and to create the United Nations.

■ President Roosevelt dies of a brain hemorrhage while resting in Warm Springs, Georgia. Vice President Harry S. Truman becomes president.

Above: Frank Sinatra

■ The American bomber *Enola Gay* releases an atomic bomb over Hiroshima. Witnessing the burst of fire on impact, copilot Robert Lewis writes, "My God, what have we done?"

■ American playwright Tennessee Williams's *The Glass Menagerie* opens on Broadway.

■ Dr. Benjamin Spock's *The Common Sense Book of Child Care* is published.

■ Operation Overlord is put into action as 150,000 Allied soldiers cross the English Channel and invade occupied France. They capture the beaches of Normandy, and the march to free Paris begins.

■ Paris, Minsk, Brussels, Antwerp, Athens, Belgrade, and Budapest are all freed by the Allies.

1945 The first Allied troops enter the concentration camp at Auschwitz and free the survivors.

■ Soviet troops enter Berlin. Amid heavy fighting, Hitler and his wife, Eva, kill themselves to avoid capture. Five weeks later, Germany surrenders.

■ Aboard the U.S. battleship *Missouri,* Japan surrenders, ending World War II.

Below: In this famous photograph, American troops raise the U.S. flag following their bloody victory at Iwo Jima in 1945.

IX. Times of Turmoil

Above: During the 1960s, thousands of college students took to the streets to protest America's involvement in Vietnam. As can be seen in this battle between protesters and police during the late '60s, these protests for peace in Vietnam often ended in violence at home.

THE WAR WAS OVER. The Allies, at terrible cost, had destroyed two enemies responsible for the submission and slaughter of millions across the globe.

Out of this victory, a new struggle would begin, pitting the United States against the Soviet Union. While the nuclear threat helped keep the peace between the superpowers, this "long twilight struggle" was played out in the mountains of Korea, the sea around Cuba, and the jungles of Vietnam.

While defending democracy overseas, America would find it tested at home. A single U.S. senator would destroy hundreds of Americans in a hunt for Communists that reminded many of Salem witch trials 250 years earlier. Governors, police chiefs, and others continued to deny African-Americans everything from good schools and the chance to vote, to the ability to sit down on the bus or drink from a water fountain. And an American president would become so suspicious of those around him that he created an official enemies list, approved burglaries, and fired investigators whose job it was to look into his behavior.

Despite these challenges, Americans won many victories in the postwar years. Communist-hunting Senator McCarthy ended his career in disgrace. African-Americans pushed the government to enact and enforce more civil rights laws than it had since Reconstruction, and President Richard Nixon was forced out of office. Almost 200 years after the nation's founding, the American people still controlled their government, and not the other way around.

The Cold War Era

Fear gripped America. During the late 1940s and early 1950s, Communism was spreading throughout the world. Many feared that there were even Communists at work in America's most important institutions, from the State Department to the universities and even that most American of places, Hollywood.

In 1947, Congress's House Un-American Affairs Committee (HUAC) decided to investigate. It called dozens of actors, directors, and producers to testify about Communists in the film industry. Screenwriter John Howard Lawson's testimony went like this:

> ROBERT STRIPLING, HUAC INVESTIGATOR: Are you a member of the Screen Writers Guild [union]?
>
> LAWSON: The raising of any question here in regard to membership, political beliefs, or affiliation . . . is an invasion of the right of association under the Bill of Rights of this country.
>
> J. PARNELL THOMPSON, HUAC CHAIRPERSON: Please be responsive to the question. The chair will decide what is in the purview [reach] of this committee.
>
> STRIPLING: Mr. Lawson, are you now or have you ever been a member of the Communist Party of the United States?
>
> LAWSON: In framing my answer to that question I must emphasize the points that I have raised before. The question of Communism is in no way related to this inquiry, which is an attempt to get control of the screen and to invade the basic rights of American citizens in all fields . . .
>
> THOMPSON (pounding gavel): We are going to get the answer to that question if we have to stay here for a week. Are you a member of the Communist Party, or have you even been a member of the Communist Party?
>
> LAWSON: I am framing my answer in the only way in which any American citizen can frame his answer to a question which absolutely invades his rights . . . I shall continue to fight for the Bill of Rights, which you are trying to destroy.

Like many other people called to testify, Lawson was blacklisted in Hollywood. Although it was never proved he was a Communist, nobody in the film industry would hire him for many years.

What had created such terrible fear in Americans? Was Congress ignoring the Bill of Rights in order to discover people's political beliefs? After all, America had come out of World War II the richest and most powerful country in history. Part of the answer lies in the early years of the 20th century.

The Red Menace

When the Bolsheviks took control of Russia in 1917 after a brief revolution, the new Communist government argued that all property and wealth should belong to the people. Businesspeople and farmers had their lands and factories taken from them. Everybody was put to work for the government.

In addition, universities, the press, and especially churches were placed under tight control. If people spoke out against the government, they were put in jail. During the 1920s and 1930s, millions

"Are you now, or have you ever been, a member of the Communist Party?"

—question asked by HUAC investigators

Senator Joseph McCarthy headed the House Un-American Activities Committee. Below, he displays a box of Northern Spies apples from the "Red Wing" orchards sent to him by the staff of a Canadian newspaper. The newspaper's editors, disgusted by McCarthy's attacks on supposed "Communists" in the government, wrote him, "Here is something for you and your committee to dig your teeth in. The woods are full of them."

During the late 1940s and 1950s, Americans feared that a nuclear war with the Soviet Union could happen at any time. Throughout the period, the federal government, as well as local governments and even individuals, built "fallout shelters" to protect themselves from nuclear blasts and the radiation that followed. Signs like the one shown on the opposite page were posted throughout the nation.

died to make a new Soviet Union out of the old Russia. Most Americans were horrified by what was happening there.

In 1919, the United States and other western powers like Britain had invaded the Soviet Union and tried to destroy the Communists. This made the Soviet government suspicious of the United States. It was not until 1933 that the Soviets and Americans exchanged ambassadors.

When Adolf Hitler rose to power in Germany, the Soviet Union and the western Allies had a common enemy. To win the war against Nazism, the two very different governments in Washington and Moscow joined forces during World War II. It was an alliance of necessity only. Neither side really trusted or liked the other.

The Yalta Conference

Three times during the war, the leaders of the United States, Britain, and the Soviet Union met to discuss global issues. The most important conference was the second one, which took place at the Soviet resort of Yalta in February 1945. At the time, Germany was on the edge of defeat and the three Allied powers were making plans for the postwar world.

British prime minister Winston Churchill, U.S. president Franklin Roosevelt, and Soviet premier Joseph Stalin each had their own interests. Churchill

wanted to keep the British Empire. Roosevelt wanted to defeat Japan and establish a new world organization called the United Nations. Stalin, whose country had been invaded by Germany twice in the 20th century, wanted security.

At the conference, a set of agreements was worked out. The most important ones concerned Eastern Europe, the war in Asia, and Germany. Stalin promised Roosevelt that the Soviet Union would declare war against Japan three months after Germany surrendered. In return, Roosevelt promised Stalin that he could have friendly governments in the Eastern European countries separating the Soviet Union and Germany. As for Germany itself, the leaders at Yalta decided it would be divided into four zones of occupation run by Britain, the United States, the Soviet Union, and France.

As soon as the war ended, it became clear that there was a big problem with the Yalta agreements. The Allies hadn't worked out how to put the agreements into effect. The Soviets felt that the terms of Yalta had given them the right to occupy Eastern Europe with troops. In response, the United States stopped sending supplies to the Soviets. Each side began viewing the other as its new enemy.

Still, the growing fear and hostility between the United States and the Soviet

Union did not stop the creation of the United Nations. In April 1945, delegates from several dozen countries met in San Francisco to establish the new international organization. Many world leaders recalled how the United States refused to join the League of Nations after World War I. So it was decided to make New York the organization's permanent home.

In July 1945, two months after Germany's surrender, the Soviet Union, Britain, and the United States met again, in Potsdam, a suburb of Berlin. The mood was very different than at Yalta. Roosevelt, who believed he could get along with Stalin, was dead. The new president, Harry Truman, had a more hostile view of the Soviet government. He believed the Communists, like the Nazis, wanted to take over the world.

During the middle of the conference, Truman received an important message from America: The atom bomb worked. Suddenly, America no longer needed the Soviet Union's help in defeating Japan. Truman believed he could now force the Soviets to do what the United States wanted.

He told Soviet Foreign Minister V. M. Molotov to leave Eastern Europe alone and to allow free elections. Molotov did not like Truman's tone and replied, "I've never been talked to like that in my life." To which Truman answered, "Then keep your agreements." The hostile exchange was a sign of the growing strain, or "Cold War," in U.S.-Soviet relations.

In the end, Stalin refused to hold elections in Eastern Europe. He believed that the people there would never vote for pro-Soviet governments. Instead, he began to install Communist governments in the capitals of Poland, Hungary, and other Eastern European countries by force.

On August 8, three months after Germany's surrender, the Soviet Union kept its Yalta promise. It attacked Japanese forces in China. But events were moving faster than armies. The United States had already dropped the atom bomb on Hiroshima. Some critics said that the decision to drop the second bomb on Nagasaki was really a message

aimed at the Soviets. It showed them the United States could build as many bombs as it needed, and would use them.

The Iron Curtain Falls

The following year, Churchill came to visit the United States. In March, he gave an important speech in Fulton, Missouri. "From Stettin in the Baltic [northeastern Europe] to Trieste in the Adriatic [southeastern Europe]," he proclaimed, "an Iron Curtain has descended across the continent."

America's leaders heard the message loud and clear. A new policy toward the Soviet Union, known as the "containment doctrine," began to take shape. In February, George Kennan, one of the U.S. State Department's Soviet experts, sent an 8,000-word telegram from Moscow. The telegram said Soviet expansion was "like a persistent toy automobile wound up and headed in a given direction, stopping only when it meets unanswerable force."

One of the first places it headed, American leaders believed, was Greece. Under Nazi occupation during World

The map below shows Europe in 1955. The Soviet Union and its Eastern European allies made up the Warsaw Pact alliance, while most of the nations of Western Europe made up the membership of the NATO alliance.

**Europe after World War II
The Iron Curtain**

During the Cold War years, Berlin was a divided city, with one half occupied by French, British, and American troops, and the other half by the Soviets. In the photograph at the right, American soldiers stand in front of a sign that is written in English, Russian, French, and German.

After the Soviets tried to seal off the non-Soviet side of Berlin in 1949, the western Allies responded by bringing in much-needed supplies by plane. In the photograph above, Berliners watch as an Allied cargo plane arrives in Berlin.

War II, Greek Communists fought a guerrilla war against the Germans. When the Nazis left, the British tried to put the king of Greece back in power. The Communists didn't want this, and a civil war broke out. In 1947, British leaders told the United States they could no longer control the situation. President Truman announced the Truman Doctrine—that the United States would help any European country trying to fight Communism.

Many in Congress, however, were still isolationists. They did not want the United States to get involved in new wars around the world. Arthur Vandenburg, a powerful senator from Michigan, disagreed with Truman. He told Truman that Congress and America would have to be scared into spending the money for defense. Truman then made a speech, declaring, "If we falter [weaken] in our leadership, we may endanger the peace of the world—and we shall surely endanger the welfare of our nation." The appeal worked. Congress voted to give Greece $300 million.

Still, many American leaders felt this would not be enough to save Western Europe from turning Communist. Nearly destroyed by war, the region suffered from hard economic times. Many American leaders feared Communists would gain support. In 1948, U.S. general George Marshall came up with a plan. America would donate billions to rebuild Europe's economy. Over the next four years, the United States would provide over $13 billion in aid to Western Europe.

Berlin: A Divided City

Another major Cold War event occurred in 1948. Like Germany itself, its capital city of Berlin was divided into a western sector controlled by the French, British, and Americans, and an eastern sector controlled by the Soviets. That year, the Soviets tried to seal off the non-Soviet parts of Berlin. Berlin itself was deep inside the Soviet sector of Germany.

The western Allies responded with the Berlin Airlift. For nearly a year, daily flights by British and American pilots, who once bombed the city, delivered over 2.5 million tons of food and fuel. In May 1949, the Soviets were forced to back down and reopen the highways and railways from western Germany to western Berlin.

That same year, France, Britain, and the United States decided to establish a new nation, West Germany (including West Berlin), by combining their zones of control. The Soviet Union soon followed by creating East Germany. To help protect West Germany and the rest of Western Europe against Soviet attack, the United States, Canada, and a number of western European countries formed a defensive alliance called the North Atlantic Treaty Organization (NATO). In 1955, the Soviets followed by creating the Warsaw Pact in Eastern Europe.

By the end of the 1940s, the lines between East and West had hardened in Europe and a cold peace set in. The same was not true in Asia. In 1949, after a long civil war, Mao Zedong and his Communist forces took power in China. The anticommunist forces fled to the island of Taiwan, forming the separate Republic of China. The United States chose to recognize Taiwan as the real China and, until 1971, refused to accept the government of the most-populated nation on Earth, the Communist People's Republic of China.

The Korean War

New troubles also arose in Korea. This East Asian country, occupied by Japan since 1910, was divided along the 38th parallel into two halves after World War II. In June 1950, Communist-controlled North Korea attacked non-Communist South Korea. Within a few

Above: President Truman and General MacArthur

weeks, North Korean forces conquered the South Korean capital of Seoul and pushed the defenders to the southern tip of the Korean peninsula.

Like most Americans, Truman believed that the Communist revolution in China and the North Korean attack of South Korea were directed by the Soviet Union. To stop the Communists winning in Korea, the UN decided to send in troops, mostly Americans. (The Soviet Union, which could have voted against this decision, was boycotting the UN. It was protesting the decision to include anticommunist Taiwan as a UN member rather than the Communist People's Republic.)

In September 1950, U.S. general Douglas MacArthur made a daring sea-launched attack against North Korea. Within two weeks, UN forces had pushed North Korea back to the 38th parallel. Then, a decision had to be made. Should UN forces push farther north? Ignoring warnings from Communist China, Truman and MacArthur sent troops over the line. They reached the Chinese-North Korean border in November.

Disaster followed. The Communist Chinese sent 300,000 troops into battle. The UN army was pushed back. Without asking Truman's approval, MacArthur

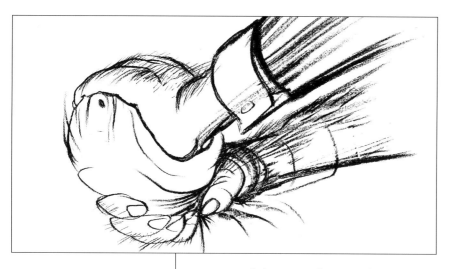

After Congress passed the Communist Control Act in 1955, over 2,500 federal workers were classified as "security risks" and fired from their jobs. In the cartoon above, the hand of government is seen stopping the free speech of one of its citizens.

Below: A campaign button for World War II hero Dwight D. Eisenhower. Eisenhower defeated Illinois senator Adlai Stevenson in both the 1952 and 1956 elections.

announced the United States should drop atom bombs on China. Truman then fired the popular general for trying to take control of the U.S. military away from the president.

Meanwhile, the UN army fought its way back to the 38th parallel. For two more years, the war continued, but the battleline did not move much in one direction or the other. At last, on July 27, 1953 the UN and the North Koreans signed a cease-fire agreement, without victory for either side.

This fighting was only one part of the Cold War between Communism and democracy. When the United States blew up its first atomic bombs in 1945, scientists believed it would take the Soviet Union at least ten years to catch up. In fact, it took just four. After the United States exploded its first hydrogen bomb (a thousand times more powerful than an atomic bomb) in 1952, the Soviets tested theirs a year later.

The Soviet atom bomb, the Communist victory in China, the Korean War—all of these things frightened and angered Americans. America seemed to be losing the Cold War. Many decided it was because Communists in America were secretly working for the Soviets.

During the postwar years, fear of Communism spread across America. The University of California, for example, demanded that all 11,000 faculty members sign a loyalty oath to the United States. UCLA fired over 150 professors who said this was unconstitutional.

The McCarthy Era

The government itself also began to suspect that there were Communists on its payroll. Back in 1947, Truman ordered the FBI to check on the backgrounds of over six million government workers.

This wasn't enough for Senator Joseph McCarthy of Wisconsin. A Republican, McCarthy charged Truman and the Democrats with selling out American interests. In 1950, he announced that he had a list of 205 Communists working in the State Department. Soon the number changed to 81, then to 57. McCarthy could never prove most of his charges, but it didn't seem to matter. If anybody disagreed, McCarthy hinted they might be Communist, too.

Some people called McCarthy's hearings "witch hunts." In 1951, the hearings led to the arrests of Julius and Ethel Rosenberg, a Jewish couple from New York. Accused of selling atomic secrets to the Soviet Union, the Rosenbergs were found guilty and sentenced to death. Because the evidence against them was slim, many people in America and around the world said they should have another trial. The climate of McCarthyism made that impossible. They were executed in 1953.

The following year, however, McCarthy went too far. He opened Senate hearings on the subject of Communists in the U.S. army. For the first time in history, Senate hearings were televised. Millions watched as McCarthy attacked witnesses without evidence. They cheered when army lawyer Joseph Welch asked, "Have you no decency left, sir?" From that moment, McCarthy's career and hysterical anti-communism began to fade away.

The Army-McCarthy hearings were not the first major TV event. In 1952, World War II general Dwight Eisenhower ran for president. He picked a young California senator named Richard Nixon as his vice presidential running-mate. When talk of illegal campaign contributions almost pushed him off the ticket, Nixon went on TV. In a half-hour speech, he explained that the only thing contributors had given him was a puppy named Checkers for his daughters. The "Checkers" speech saved Nixon's career and showed the power of the television to influence the public.

Daily Life in the '50s

Like radio before it, television spread rapidly across America. In 1947, there were less than 7,000 TVs in the whole country. By 1960, almost 90 percent of American homes had one. Television in the 1950s offered a wide variety of shows—from Westerns (like *Gunsmoke*) to varieties (*The Milton Berle Show*) to serious drama (*Playhouse 90*).

Among the most popular programs were the family situation comedies like *Father Knows Best*, *Leave It to Beaver*, and the *Ozzie and Harriet Show*. These half-hour programs featured white, middle-class homes in the suburbs. They reflected the values of the day.

Most Americans in the 1950s wanted very much to put the difficulties of the Depression and World War II behind them. Millions moved to the suburbs and spent their weekends barbequing, mowing lawns, and fixing their cars. It was a time when most people wanted to fit in, not stand out. The political fear of Communism often combined with the social fear of being different.

Of course, all this sameness was boring to many of America's artists, some of whom became "beatniks." They celebrated being different by growing their hair long, writing poetry, and refusing to accept the middle-class values of the suburbs.

For America's teenagers, there was another form of rebellion. It was called rock and roll. The phrase, invented by a Cleveland disc jockey, was used to describe a new kind of music that combined African-American rhythm and blues with white country music tunes. Its greatest performer was a former Mississippi truck driver named Elvis Presley. Presley records like "Hound Dog," "Heartbreak Hotel," and "Jailhouse Rock" sold millions of copies.

Elvis's records upset millions of adults. Many radio stations around the

country refused to play them. When Presley, who liked to swing his hips when he sang, performed on TV on *The Ed Sullivan Show*, the cameras only showed him from the waist up.

In general, however, the 1950s are looked back on as a time of calm and prosperity. Partly, this can be explained by the politics of the period. After the Communist scare of the late 1940s and early 1950s, the rest of the decade was marked by steady economic growth and the presidency of Dwight Eisenhower. The popular World War II general was elected twice. Most Americans viewed him as a stable and experienced leader.

"Ladies and gentlemen, I'd like to do a song now, that tells a story, that really makes a lot of sense—"'Awopbopoloobop, alopbamboom! Tutti-frutti! All rootie! Tutti-frutti! All rootie!'"

—ELVIS PRESLEY, in 1956, introducing his version of the Little Richard hit "Tutti-Frutti"

Left: Elvis Presley

Left: "Beat" poet Alan Ginsburg

The Fight for Civil Rights

Rosa Parks was a middle-aged seamstress from Montgomery, Alabama. A respected member of her community, Parks was a regular churchgoer and belonged to a number of civic organizations.

Right: Rosa Parks

Right: Jackie Robinson

But to the bus driver one December afternoon in 1955, only one thing about Rosa Parks mattered: her black skin. Getting off work, Parks climbed aboard her regular city bus and sat down. In 1955 Montgomery, as in most of the South, the seats in the front of buses were reserved for white passengers. Parks knew the rules and sat down in the first row behind the reserved section.

Soon more white passengers got on and the reserved section filled up. When another white man got on board, the driver demanded that Parks give up her seat. Parks refused. She was tired from a hard day's work. Besides, she thought, nobody would ask a white woman to stand. After a few minutes, the police showed up and took Parks to jail.

Jo Ann Robinson, an English professor and a member of an African-American organization in Montgomery called the Women's Political Council (WPC), described what happened next. "The news traveled like wildfire into every black home. Telephones jangled; people congregated [met] on street corners and in homes and talked."

While Parks's decision was made on the spur of the moment, what followed was carefully planned. Several African-American organizations in Montgomery, including the WPC, had been waiting for just the right moment to challenge segregation, or racial separation, on city buses. Hardworking and law-abiding, Parks presented the case they had been waiting for.

The WPC went into action. Knowing that most of the city's bus passengers were black, they printed thousands of flyers calling for a bus boycott. For months, African-American men and women, boys and girls refused to ride. They walked miles to work and school, or else they carpooled.

Ministers, traditionally the leaders of the black communities of the South, also got involved. One, the Reverend Dr. Martin Luther King Jr. agreed to lead the boycott. It took over a year, but the WPC, King, and the black community won. The Montgomery city bus company agreed to end segregation on their vehicles.

The End of Segregation

Many Americans, both black and white, date the beginning of the modern civil rights movement to Rosa Parks and

her decision to keep her seat. In fact, the movement had its origins years earlier, during World War II.

Segregation had been part of the southern, and sometimes the northern, way of life for over half a century. Most railroads, hotels, restaurants, theaters, and other institutions were reserved for either white or black patrons only.

In 1896, the Supreme Court ruled in its *Plessy* v. *Ferguson* decision that "separate but equal" facilities were constitutional. "Separate but equal," however, were just words. In fact, the places reserved for blacks either did not exist or were greatly inferior to those reserved for whites.

The fight against Nazi racism, however, began to make many Americans question their own hatred and discrimination. One event that showed that times were changing came in 1946 when the Brooklyn Dodgers became the first major league baseball team to hire a black player. His name was Jackie Robinson. Though racist fans spit on him, he proved to be one of the best players in the game. As his manager, Leo Durocher, said about him, "This guy didn't just come to play. He come to beat ya'."

The 15 years that followed the Supreme Court's **Brown** v. **Board of Education** *decision were the most dramatic years in the struggle for African-American civil rights since Reconstruction. The map below shows the locations of 16 of the most important events.*

The Struggle for Civil Rights
16 Key Places and Events, 1954-1968

1. *Brown* v. *Board of Education,* Topeka, Kans., 1954.
2. The Montgomery Bus Boycott, Montgomery, Ala., 1955-1956
3. Autherine Lucy Attends Alabama University, Tuscaloosa, Ala., 1956
4. Little Rock Central High School is desegregated, Little Rock, Ark., 1960
5. The Sit-In movement begins, Greensboro, N.C., 1960
6. James Meredith enters University of Mississippi, Jackson, Miss. 1961
7. Police violence against protesters gains nationwide attention, Birmingham, Ala., 1963
8. Civil rights leader Medgar Evers is murdered, Jackson, Miss. 1963

9. The March on Washington, Washington D.C., 1963
10. The Birmingham Church Bombings, Ala. 1963
11. Civil rights workers James Chaney, Andrew Goodman, and Michael Schwerner are murdered, near Philadelphia, Miss., 1963
12. The Selma to Montgomery March, Selma, Ala., 1965
13. Malcolm X assassinated, New York, N.Y., 1965
14. The Voting Rights Act passed, Washington, D.C.1965
15. The Black Panthers are founded, Oakland, Calif., 1966
16. Martin Luther King assassinated, Memphis, Tenn., 1968

Cold War politics also had a role in changing attitudes about race. The Cold War was partly a contest between two systems: Soviet Communism and American capitalism. As many countries in Africa and Asia became independent, they were free to develop their own forms of government. The United States tried to convince them to become democracies. The Soviets pointed to American racism as a reason for the nonwhite peoples of the world to choose Communism.

This worried President Truman. In 1948, he ordered the U.S. military to begin gradual desegregation. The sudden decision to go to war in Korea sped up the process. Truman's decision, however, angered many southern whites. In 1948,

South Carolina senator Strom Thurmond left the Democratic Party and ran for president as an independent candidate. His slogan was "Segregation Forever." He won four southern states and over one million votes.

Brown v. Board of Education

It would take six more years before another major institution was forced to integrate. In 1954, the National Association for the Advancement of Colored People (NAACP), the nation's largest civil rights organization, sued the Topeka, Kansas Board of Education. Like many other cities, Topeka had separate schools for black and white children.

Thurgood Marshall, the NAACP's

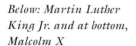

Below: Martin Luther King Jr. and at bottom, Malcolm X

MARTIN LUTHER KING AND MALCOLM X

By the 1960s, civil rights violations had come to a head. African-Americans across the country were tired of segregation, racism, and discrimination. They wanted change. Among the leaders working most actively for change were Martin Luther King Jr, a southern minister, and Malcolm X, a former petty criminal who had turned his life around after a conversion to the Islamic faith. Both men shared a similar goal. But they had very different approaches.

"The way of nonviolent resistance," said Martin Luther King Jr., "is ultimately the way of the strong man." Having studied the life of Mahatma Gandhi, who had peacefully forced Great Britain to give up its colonial empire in India, King organized bus boycotts, sit-ins, pickets, and peaceful protest marches across the South. Sometimes activists were beaten, shot, and even killed, but King was determined not to strike back. "When evil men burn and bomb, good men must build and bind," he said.

Malcolm X did not agree. After joining the Nation of Islam, an Islamic black nationalist organization, Malcolm had risen to the powerful position of representative of Temple Number 7, in New York's Harlem. He soon became well known as a powerful voice of active resistance to white racism.

"I don't believe we're going to overcome by singing. If you're going to get yourself a .45 and start singing 'We Shall Overcome,' I'm with you," he said. Malcolm X did not preach that African-Americans should use violence to gain their rights. On the other hand, he felt that blacks had every right to defend themselves if attacked.

Despite their different techniques, both men helped effect more civil rights changes than the country had seen since Reconstruction. But sadly, their words and actions threatened many people. On February 21, 1965, Malcolm X was assassinated. Three years later, on April 4, 1968, King suffered the same fate.

lawyer, and later the first black Supreme Court justice, argued in front of the Supreme Court that "separate was inherently unequal." To prove his point, Marshall brought Kenneth Clarke, a black social scientist from Harvard, to present his research to the justices. Clarke gave white and black dolls to black children and asked them which they wanted to play with. Each child chose the white doll. Clarke said this proved that separate schools made these black children feel inferior. In its famous *Brown* v. *Board of Education*, the court agreed. It ordered the nation's schools to desegregate with "deliberate [careful] speed."

But what did "deliberate speed" mean? To many whites in the South, it meant never, or close to it. In 1957, the federal government demanded that Little Rock High School in Arkansas admit several black students. When the teenagers arrived, they were attacked by white students and their parents. Local authorities said they could not do anything. President Eisenhower was forced to send in federal troops. After all, he said, the Supreme Court had to be obeyed, whether people liked it or not.

That same year, Ralph Abernathy, Martin Luther King Jr., and other black clergymen founded the Southern Christian Leadership Conference (SCLC) to fight segregation.

Still, progress was slow. In Greensboro, North Carolina, some black college students decided to take action. They were angry that the downtown Woolworth's took black people's shopping money, but wouldn't let them eat at the whites-only lunch counter.

On February 1, 1960, they sat down at the counter and demanded service. White customers poured food on their heads and pushed them off the stools. Police came and arrested them. Within a few weeks, demonstrations had spread to over 126 cities. More than 50,000 students participated and over 3,600 were arrested.

Out of the sit-down protests, a new civil rights organization was born. The Student Non-Violent Coordinating Committee (SNCC, pronounced "snick") was founded by young activists who were frustrated at the slow pace of their elders in the SCLC. The actions of SNCC

Above: Thurgood Marshall

Left: College students work on their homework during a 1962 sit-in in Little Rock, Arkansas.

Above: President John F. Kennedy

inspired the Congress of Racial Equality (CORE), a civil rights organization founded during World War II, to try direct action as well.

In 1961, CORE organized the "freedom rides." Black and white activists would ride inter- state buses through the South, refusing to obey segregation on board the vehicles or in the stations. In Anniston, Alabama, they were attacked by club-swinging members of the Ku Klux Klan. Their bus was set on fire and the freedom riders escaped just moments before it blew up. Alabama Governor John Patterson refused to get involved. "I cannot guarantee protection for this bunch of rabble-rousers," he said, meaning the freedom riders, not the Klan.

In 1963, Martin Luther King Jr. decided to take the fight against racism to Birmingham, Alabama, "the most segregated city in the United States." In April, thousands of blacks marched on downtown department stores. They were met by Police Chief Eugene "Bull" Connor, who had his men attack the marchers with cattle prods, police dogs, and high-pressure fire hoses.

As people across America watched the brutal scenes on the evening news, they grew outraged. "The civil rights movement should thank God for Bull Connor," said President John Kennedy. "He's helped it as much as Abraham Lincoln."

Kennedy might also have said that Connor helped the civil rights movement more than the federal government. Like Eisenhower before him, Kennedy was not an active supporter of the civil rights movement, at least not at first. He even had his brother, Attorney General Robert Kennedy, spy on King and the SCLC headquarters.

The March on Washington

But the scenes from Alabama, as well as the murder of Medgar Evers, NAACP activist, pushed Kennedy into supporting a major new federal law banning segregation. To help rally support for the bill, Martin Luther King Jr. and other civil rights leaders organized the March on Washington in August 1963. The 250,000 marchers, the largest political gathering in American history up to that time, listened to speeches demanding equality and freedom for all Americans.

"I have a dream," King pronounced, "that one day on the red hills of Georgia the sons of former slaves and the sons of former slaveowners will be able to sit down at the table of brotherhood." Thousands responded by singing the old black gospel song lyric, "Free at last! Free at last! Thank God almighty, we are free at last!" In September, white extremists responded by bombing a black church in Birmingham, killing four little girls.

When John Kennedy was assassinated in November and his vice president, Lyndon Johnson of Texas, became president, many feared it meant the end of civil rights legislation. In fact, it was only the beginning. A former congressional leader himself, Johnson was a brilliant manipulator of Congress. He used his talents to push through the Civil Rights Act, which banned discrimination based on sex, religion, national origin, or race.

There was, however, still one area where legal discrimination continued: voting. Many southern states used laws and fear to make it almost impossible for black people to vote. During the "freedom summer" of 1964, CORE volunteers spread out across Mississippi to register black voters. White racists responded with violence. In June, they murdered three voting organizers: two white students from the North, and a black CORE volunteer from Mississippi. The fear and violence limited registration to just 1,600 new voters.

The Selma March

King decided that he needed to bring the nation's attention to the voting rights campaign. On Sunday, March 7, 1965, he organized a 54-mile march from Selma, Alabama, to the capital in Montgomery. Governor George Wallace banned the march, but King ignored him. State troopers attacked the marchers as they crossed the Pettus Bridge in Selma.

President Johnson called "Bloody Sunday" an American tragedy. In a nationally televised speech, Johnson said, "It is wrong—deadly wrong, to deny any of your fellow Americans the right to vote." He then closed his speech with the most famous civil rights slogan "We shall overcome." The Voting Rights Act was passed the following year. It banned the literacy tests and poll taxes southern states used to prevent blacks, and other poor people, from voting.

The year 1965 was the high point of the civil rights movement in the South. It had achieved important gains. Laws that promoted segregation and discrimination were banned. But the new laws did not end racism and discrimination against black people or poverty in the black communities.

In the North, a new kind of black politics was rising. Unlike in the South, it was not aimed at promoting integration and better relations between the races. It was about black power. Its most prominent spokesman was Malcolm X. Malcolm, a former criminal, had changed his life when he joined the Black Muslim movement of Elijah Muhammed, an Islamic religious leader from Chicago, while in prison.

As a Black Muslim, Malcolm X called white people devils and said it would be best for blacks to separate themselves and build their own independent society in America. Malcolm also disagreed with Martin Luther King Jr. about violence. While King said blacks should respond to

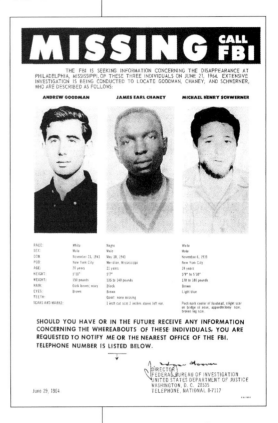

Despite the use of posters like the one above, it took the FBI several months before they found the bodies of three young civil rights workers: Andrew Goodman, James Chaney, and Michael Schwerner. Among those convicted of the murders was Cecil Price, the deputy sheriff of Philadelphia, Mississippi.

Left: A fire hose blasts demonstrators on a Birmingham street during protests in 1963.

Right: Black Panthers protest on the streets of New York in 1968. Formed in 1966, the organization had about 1,500 members by 1969.

white violence with Christian love, Malcolm said they should fight back by any means necessary.

In 1964, however, Malcolm X left the Black Muslim movement of Elijah Muhammed because he thought it was corrupt. He was also changing his beliefs. Some white people, he said, were not devils. It was possible to build a nonracist society in America. Sadly, Malcolm was assassinated in February 1965 by members of the Black Muslims before he could spread his new message.

The Black Panthers

Still, Malcolm's words had a powerful impact on other young African-Americans. In 1966, a former SNCC member named Stokely Carmichael announced, "We been saying freedom for six years and we ain't got nothing. What we gonna start saying is 'Black Power!'" That same year, Huey Newton and Bobby Seale founded the Black Panthers in Oakland, California. The Panthers mixed antipoverty programs, militant talk, and armed self-defense against the police.

Frustration among African-Americans came out in less organized ways as well. In the Watts section of Los Angeles, anger at police treatment of blacks led to

five days of violence in August 1965. The angry rioters, who attacked firemen coming to put out the flames, shouted "Burn, baby, burn!" During the summer of 1967, rioting broke out in black ghettos across the country, including in Detroit where 43 people died.

Things continued to spin out of control in 1968. On April 4, Martin Luther King Jr. was assassinated in Memphis, Tennessee. The silencing of this voice of peace and love resulted in more violence. In Washington, the National Guard had to be sent in to protect the White House and the Capitol.

The American Indian Movement

Despite the violence, the civil rights movement had a powerful impact on other oppressed Americans, inspiring them to demand equal rights. In 1968, Native Americans in Minnesota organized the American Indian Movement (AIM).

Calling for red power, they demanded more control over reservation life and special fishing and hunting rights for Indians off the reservation. They also promoted a return to the native way of life and tried to fight alcoholism and poverty on the reservation. The members of AIM often came into conflict with the older

Indian establishment that ran the reservations. And, as they did with the Black Panthers, the government tried to destroy AIM.

In February 1973, AIM led 200 Sioux in an occupation of Wounded Knee, South Dakota, site of the last Indian massacre of the 1800s. The Indians were angry that some local whites were hardly punished after killing a Sioux. The FBI quickly surrounded the village. Two months later, a gun battle broke out, leaving one protester dead, and the siege ended.

The Chicano Movement

Chicanos, or Mexican Americans, in the Southwest were also inspired by the black civil rights movement. In urban areas, they formed groups like the Brown Berets, modeled on the Black Panthers, and the political party La Raza Unida, the United Race.

But it was in rural areas that Chicanos made the biggest gains. Under the leadership of Cesar Chavez, Chicano farmworkers built a union and fought for better wages and working conditions in the fields. They organized a successful national boycott of nonunion grapes and lettuce. In 1970, the major growers of California agreed to bargain with the union.

The Women's Movement

Like the abolitionist movement 100 years earlier, the black civil rights movement of the 1950s and 1960s had its most powerful effect on women and the women's liberation movement. In 1963, at the height of the civil rights movement, Betty Friedan, a college-educated housewife from New York, published *The Feminine Mystique*. In the book, Friedan described the problem that has no name, the frustration of being a housewife who "as she made the beds, shopped for groceries . . . [drove] Cub Scouts and Brownies, lay beside her husband at night," Friedan wrote, "she was afraid to ask even of herself the silent question—is this all?"

Women by the millions bought and read the book. It inspired many to work and fight for equal rights.

In 1966, Friedan and others founded the National Organization of Women (NOW), which became the largest women's rights group in American history.

The group's marches included the freedom trash can, where women dumped makeup, curlers, and bras, as symbols of women's oppression. Many women also joined consciousness-raising groups where they met and discussed all the insults and unfairness they faced as women every day.

NOW also promoted women's political power. It organized the National Women's Caucus to help get women candidates elected

Above: Labor organizer Cesar Chavez

Left: Betty Friedan, author of The Feminine Mystique

to office. It helped win the struggle for abortion rights, as in the 1973 Supreme Court case of *Roe* v. *Wade*. But NOW also suffered defeats. The biggest was the group's failure to get the Equal Rights Amendment (ERA) added to the Constitution.

231

The Vietnam War

On June 10, 1972, Lt. Colonel John Paul Vann was flying in an army helicopter above the Central Highlands of Vietnam. The chopper was hit by enemy fire and went down. Vann was killed instantly.

It was a typical event, though Vann was no typical American casualty. In 1963, he had been one of the first American soldiers in Vietnam. Like other early recruits, he did not fight. Instead, he advised the South Vietnamese in their fight against a Communist army called the Viet Cong.

Vann was not impressed by what he saw. The South Vietnamese, he said, did not want to fight and he leaked this information to the press. This made his bosses at the Pentagon angry and Vann resigned.

But something about Vietnam drew

him back in 1965. At that moment, the number of Americans involved in the war was about to grow. Marines had just been sent in and they were starting to fight the Viet Cong directly. This would bring North Vietnamese soldiers into the conflict. Soon, there would be over 500,000 American troops in Vietnam.

Vann now worked for the American government's Agency for International Development. Its mission was to provide aid and win the hearts and minds of the Vietnamese people for America and the South Vietnamese government. Secretly, Vann questioned the war. "If I were a lad of eighteen faced with the same choice—whether to support the GVN [Government of South Vietnam] or the NLF [National Liberation Front, or Viet Cong]," he wrote to a friend, "I would surely choose the NLF."

Still, Vann believed America could

THE NIXON-KENNEDY DEBATES

As Vice President Richard Nixon and Massachusetts senator John Kennedy met for the first of four presidential debates in 1960, polls showed that the race for election was a toss-up. The debates would give the American people one more chance to decide which man deserved to win. And for the first time, many Americans would have the chance to watch the debate on television.

The debate lasted for an hour. Nixon accused Kennedy of proposing programs that would cost millions and would put a tremendous strain on taxpayers. Kennedy argued that Nixon was making campaign promises he wouldn't keep, including an increase in the minimum wage, expanding school construction, and providing medical care for the elderly. When the debate ended, TV audiences awarded Kennedy a big win, while those who had heard it over the radio declared Nixon the winner.

Before the debate, Kennedy had realized that how he looked on camera would play a big part in what voters thought of him. Nixon, on the other hand, had just gotten out of the hospital, and looked pale and uncomfortable. His dull suit blended in with the background on the set, and under the hot glare of the television lights, he began to sweat during the debate.

Some have argued that if the debates had been broadcast only on the radio, Nixon would have won the election. Ever since 1960, however, television has played a greater and greater role in how Americans choose their president.

Above: Candidates Nixon and Kennedy

win the war. But this would only happen, he thought, if the South Vietnamese government became less corrupt and helped its people more. As one journalist wrote, Vann lost his compass. He could not see that the Viet Cong were getting stronger and that the South Vietnamese government was beyond fixing.

For Vann's funeral, his wife chose two pieces of music. One was the popular march song from the World War II movie *Bridge on the River Kwai*. The other, an antiwar song from the 1960s called "Where Have All the Flowers Gone?," was for herself. One of Vann's sons hated the war so much he tore his draft card in two and placed the pieces on his father's coffin.

In many ways, Vann's life symbolized America's involvement in Vietnam. It started with great hope and ended in confusion. It divided families and set generations against each other.

The war in Vietnam was 20 years old when the first Marines hit the beach in 1965. During World War II, the Japanese occupied the country, then a colony of France. In 1945, France tried to retake control of the country after Japan surrendered. But the Vietnamese, led by a patriotic Communist named Ho Chi Minh, had other ideas. He turned to the United States for help. He had read America's Declaration of Independence and included some of its phrases in Vietnam's Declaration. But American leaders, fearful of Communism, refused to help.

For nine years, Ho Chi Minh's army, known as the Viet Minh, fought the French. Even with over $2 billion in U.S. military aid, France could not win. In 1954, the French army was surrounded by Ho Chi Minh's forces at Dien Bien Phu in the northern part of the country. France was forced to pull out.

Vietnam was then divided at the 17th parallel. The north was controlled by the Communists and the south was under the leadership of the pro-French emperor Bao Dai. The division was supposed to be temporary. Countrywide elections, which

would have brought the country back together under one government, were to be held in 1956. The United States, fearful that Ho Chi Minh would win the elections, cancelled them.

The United States then replaced the unpopular Bao Dai with Ngo Dinh Diem. But Diem, a Catholic in the largely Buddhist country, was just as unpopular. He attacked Buddhists and imprisoned anyone who criticized him. By the early 1960s, South Vietnamese Communists and other anti-Diem forces had taken to the jungle to fight Diem's government. They began receiving arms and other aid from North Vietnam.

In 1961, John F. Kennedy became president of the United States. In his inaugural address, he told Americans: "Ask not what your country can do for you, but what you can do for your country." Kennedy wanted America to play a more active role in the underdeveloped world. He started the Alliance for Progress to offer economic assistance in Latin America. He also launched the Peace Corps. This agency sent American civilians to work directly with the people in poor countries.

Kennedy believed that these programs would both help the people of the underdeveloped world and stop them

Above: Col. John Paul Vann (left), one of the first Americans to be sent to Vietnam, is seen discussing strategy with Vietnamese soldiers.

"Let every nation know, whether it wishes us good or ill, that we shall pay any price, bear any burden, meet any hardship, support any friend, oppose any foe to assure the survival and the success of liberty."

—PRESIDENT JOHN F. KENNEDY, *in his inaugural address, 1961*

*Above: Lyndon Johnson is sworn in as president on board **Air Force One,** just hours after President Kennedy's death. Jacqueline Kennedy, the president's widow, stands beside him.*

Below: President Kennedy and Soviet premier Khrushchev

tried to prevent South Vietnam from falling to the Communists. Then, in November 1963, Kennedy okayed a plan to overthrow the government of the unpopular Diem. On November 2, Diem was assassinated.

The Kennedy Assassination

Three weeks later, while driving in a parade in Dallas, Texas, Kennedy himself was assassinated. The prime suspect, Lee Harvey Oswald, was murdered several days later by Jack Ruby. The new president, Lyndon Baines Johnson, nicknamed LBJ, ordered Chief Justice Earl Warren to investigate the assassination. Over the years many have argued with the Warren Commission's conclusion that Oswald acted alone.

The War Escalates

Johnson, continuing the policies on Vietnam started by Kennedy, expanded the number of advisors. In August 1964, Johnson went on national television and announced that North Vietnamese gunboats had attacked American warships in international waters of the Gulf of Tonkin. He asked Congress to pass the Tonkin Gulf Resolution, allowing him to

from becoming Communists. But if aid didn't work, Kennedy was willing to use military force. In 1961, Kennedy launched an invasion of Cuba, which had been taken over in a Communist revolution by the forces of Fidel Castro. The mission, which took place at the Bay of Pigs in Cuba, was a disaster. The anticommunist Cuban attackers were killed or captured by Castro's forces.

Over 17,000 American military advisors

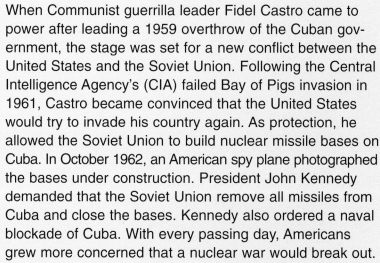

THE CUBAN MISSILE CRISIS

When Communist guerrilla leader Fidel Castro came to power after leading a 1959 overthrow of the Cuban government, the stage was set for a new conflict between the United States and the Soviet Union. Following the Central Intelligence Agency's (CIA) failed Bay of Pigs invasion in 1961, Castro became convinced that the United States would try to invade his country again. As protection, he allowed the Soviet Union to build nuclear missile bases on Cuba. In October 1962, an American spy plane photographed the bases under construction. President John Kennedy demanded that the Soviet Union remove all missiles from Cuba and close the bases. Kennedy also ordered a naval blockade of Cuba. With every passing day, Americans grew more concerned that a nuclear war would break out.

Finally, on October 28, Soviet premier Nikita Khrushchev offered to remove the missiles under supervision from the United Nations. The next day, President Kennedy ordered an end to the blockade. By November 2, the missile bases were being closed down. The Cuban missile crisis is remembered as a great Cold War victory for the United States. It is also remembered as the closest the world has come to all-out nuclear war.

take all necessary measures to repel any armed attacks against the forces of the United States. Only two senators voted against the measure. Not until later did Congress and the American people learn that Johnson had lied. There had been no attack.

Following passage of the Tonkin Gulf Resolution, Johnson sent additional forces to Vietnam to protect American bases. Soon, the Marines were under attack. The President sent more troops to protect them. When it was decided that U.S. forces should actively pursue the enemy, still more troops were sent. By the end of 1965, 150,000 Americans were fighting in Vietnam; within two years the number had climbed to over half a million.

Each time that American generals in

One of the chief strategies used by the United States in the Vietnam War was the bombing raid. Shown above is a B-52 bomber in action.

Left: American troops jump from a helicopter to search for hidden enemy bunkers.

Vietnam told the president that a few more troops would turn the tide, Johnson would send them. But Vietnam was a different kind of war than any America had fought before. The enemy Viet Cong avoided direct combat, preferring ambushes, or surprise attacks, before disappearing back into the jungle.

In response, the United States dropped millions of gallons of Agent Orange, a chemical herbicide, or plant killer. By the end of the war, Americans

had burned or killed more than 10 percent of Vietnam's jungles. Agent Orange came back to haunt American troops. The chemical caused cancers and other diseases both to the troops who dropped it, and the Vietnamese it was dropped on.

To stop North Vietnam from helping the guerrillas, the United States began a massive bombing campaign against its cities and ports. The campaign failed and North Vietnam continued to send supplies and troops into South Vietnam.

Above: Two South Vietnamese soldiers man guns over Saigon during the Tet Offensive in 1968.

Perhaps most frustrating for U.S. soldiers and military planners was the attitude of many Vietnamese peasants. Angry at American bombs and napalm, a sticky gasoline that burned its victims alive, many supported the guerrillas. This made it hard for Americans to know who the enemy was. In March 1968, a group of soldiers led by Lieutenant William Calley in a search for guerrillas murdered hundreds of Vietnamese civilians at the village of My Lai. While Calley was eventually found guilty of war crimes, many Americans had had enough. More and more Americans felt that the war itself was not only unwinnable but unjust.

The Antiwar Movement

The first antiwar protests began at American universities like Berkeley in California and Columbia in New York. Opponents of the war were called doves; these young men and women said the war was immoral. Supporters of the war were called hawks. Soon, demonstrations spread across the country. Millions began to march and protest.

The antiwar demonstrators were against the war for a variety of reasons.

Some believed that the fighting should be left to the Vietnamese themselves, and that the war was no threat to American security. Some believed that Ho Chi Minh and his forces were fighting a just cause— to rid themselves of foreign domination.

Still, most Americans supported Johnson and the war at the end of 1967. Then came Tet, in 1968. Tet, in late January, is the Vietnamese New Year, and the Viet Cong used it to launch their biggest offensive of the war. They attacked cities across the country. They even took over the U.S. embassy in Saigon, South Vietnam's capital, for a few hours.

The Viet Cong were eventually pushed back. American military experts said the offensive cost the Viet Cong lots of men and matériel. But the effect on America was just what the Viet Cong had hoped it would be. For years, U.S. generals told the American people there was a light at the end of the tunnel, that the war would soon be over. Tet proved them wrong. Many even said the government lied. Journalists said the government had a credibility [truth] gap.

Tet turned millions of Americans against Johnson and the war. When antiwar candidate Eugene McCarthy almost beat Johnson in the 1968 New Hampshire Democratic presidential primary, Johnson announced he would not run for reelection. This encouraged another peace candidate, Senator Robert Kennedy, President Kennedy's younger brother, to throw his hat in the ring. Tragically, Robert Kennedy was also assassinated, just two months after the murder of Martin Luther King Jr.

To many Americans, it seemed like violence was spinning out of control in 1968. In August, thousands of antiwar demonstrators came to Chicago to protest at the Democratic convention that would nominate Vice President Hubert Humphrey for president. When tension rose between the police and the protesters, Chicago mayor Richard Daley ordered his police to attack. On national TV, Americans watched police beat protesters, journalists, and innocent passersby in an episode that was later called a police riot.

The War Winds Down

The troubles at the convention divided the Democrats and helped turn the election for Republican Richard Nixon, who claimed he had a secret plan to end the war.

Nixon did, but it was a gradual one. Nixon and his national security advisor, Henry Kissinger, wanted to gradually shift the fighting to the Vietnamese themselves. They also tried to stop the North Vietnamese from sending supplies to the Viet Cong via the neighboring country of Cambodia. The 1970 American invasion of that country produced new antiwar protests. At Kent State University in Ohio, National Guardsmen opened fire on protesters, killing four. This led to waves of demonstrations that closed many of the nation's colleges and universities.

As protests spread across the country and Nixon began slowly pulling American troops out of Vietnam, peace talks between North Vietnam, South Vietnam, and the United States continued in Paris. By late 1972, a deal began to emerge. Viet Cong and North Vietnamese forces would

be allowed to stay where they were in South Vietnam but there would be no fighting. The North Vietnamese, who wanted a united Vietnam, hesitated.

To force the North Vietnamese to go along, Nixon unleashed a bombing at Christmas. In just two weeks, the explosive power of several Hiroshima atom bombs was dropped on the cities and ports of North Vietnam. When Le Duc Tho, the North Vietnamese negotiator returned to Paris in early 1973, he was so angry he refused to shake Kissinger's hand. Still, a peace deal was signed. Thousands of American prisoners of war

came home, and the longest war in U.S. history was over.

A divided Vietnam, however, remained tense. In early 1975, the truce between the Communists and the South Vietnamese government broke down. Within several months, the South Vietnamese government and army collapsed. The Viet Cong takeover happened so fast that people had to flee the American embassy by helicopters from the roof. On April 30, 1975, Communist tanks rolled into Saigon. The war was finally over.

Above: American secretary of state Henry Kissinger (left) signs the treaty that ends American involvement in the Vietnam War. North Vietnamese official Le Duc Tho (back to camera) signs for his country.

The anti-Nixon poster above shows many of those arrested as a result of the Watergate scandal, but notes that Nixon remained free.

America in the '70s

Washington Post reporter Bob Woodward had just arrived at work on June 17, 1972 when his editor called him into his office. The editor told him that a security guard at the Watergate office complex had discovered several men breaking into the Democratic National Party headquarters early that morning. Police had been called and several arrests had been made.

Woodward, a new reporter at the paper, was assigned to cover local news. The editor thought the Watergate story was a routine burglary, until Woodward and fellow rookie reporter Carl Bernstein began to find strange things about the crime.

One of the burglars, for example, had connections to the Central Intelligence Agency (CIA), the federal government's main spying agency. The two reporters began to follow the story full-time. For months, recalled Bernstein, "we knocked on doors, we talked to people at the bottom, which is to say secretaries and file clerks, rather than starting at the top."

The Watergate Scandal

The two reporters began to suspect that the burglary might have been ordered by President Nixon's White House. In 1972, Nixon, a Republican, was running for reelection. Nixon's Committee to Reelect the President (CREEP) wanted inside information on the Democratic campaign.

Few people in the White House would talk to the reporters. The story was going nowhere, until one day they got a call from someone high up in the White House. He asked to meet the reporters secretly and promised to tell them what he knew, under one condition. The reporters would never reveal his identity.

Woodward and Bernstein nicknamed him "Deep Throat." For months, the two reporters met with their secret source in an underground parking garage. The arrangements were straight out of a spy novel. Deep Throat would let them know he wanted to talk to them by moving a flower pot on his apartment balcony. He would then send the reporters a copy of *The New York Times*. On the lower corner of page 20, Deep Throat drew a clock showing the time they were to meet.

Deep Throat's information, however, did not hurt Nixon's political chances. In November, the president was reelected by one of the largest landslides in presidential election history. Yet the victory did not stop the unfolding investigation.

By early 1973, Woodward and Bernstein were reporting that people in the White House planned the break-in and that White House attorney John Dean had used $400,000 to buy the silence of the burglars and cover up the crime.

In February, the Senate voted 70-0 to establish a special committee to investigate crimes in the Nixon White House. The following month, Woodward, Bernstein, and the *Washington Post* won the Pulitzer Prize, journalism's highest award, for their investigations.

A criminal investigation was begun by federal judge John Sirica that same month. Dean, the lawyer who paid off the burglars, began to get nervous. He told the president that "there is a cancer within, close to the presidency, that is growing."

In April, Nixon accepted the resignation of his two top aides, John Ehrlichman and H. R. Haldeman. Both were later found guilty of conspiracy—they tried to stop the investigation—and served time in jail. In addition, Attorney General John Mitchell was forced to resign. He was also found guilty of various crimes.

The investigation by the Senate opened in May, led by North Carolina Senator Sam Ervin. Dean, fearing he would be used as a scapegoat, pointed the finger at Nixon, saying he ordered the cover-up. Still, it was Dean's word against the president's. Then a White House aide named Alexander Butterfield told the Senate Committee that all White House conversations had been recorded on tape. Nixon refused to hand over the tapes, saying that he had "presidential immunity," or protection from the law.

By the fall of 1973, there was talk in Washington that Nixon should resign, or be impeached, or officially tried by Congress for crimes in office. (The only president ever to be impeached was Andrew Johnson, who served during the early years of Reconstruction, more than a century before Nixon.) Meanwhile, Nixon's vice president, Spiro Agnew, was facing criminal charges of his own. He was accused of accepting bribes and income tax fraud while governor of Maryland. In October, he resigned and was replaced by Michigan congressman Gerald Ford.

Nixon hoped Agnew's resignation would quiet critics. It didn't, and he was forced to appoint Archibald Cox as a special prosecutor to look into crimes committed by the White House. But when Cox and Judge Sirica demanded the tapes, Nixon ordered Attorney General Elliot Richardson to fire Cox. Richardson refused and was fired himself. The press called the twin firings on October 20, 1973 the "Saturday Night Massacre." Nixon went on TV to reassure the nation that, in his words, "I am not a crook."

New troubles emerged for the president the following year. It was discovered that the Nixon White House had spied on critics. In 1971, it had sent burglars to the office of Daniel Ellsberg's psychiatrist. Ellsberg had released a secret report on the Vietnam War to the nation's press. The Pentagon Papers showed how the government had lied about the war for years. Nixon hoped to find material to make Ellsberg look crazy. In addition, it was learned that Nixon had secretly, and illegally, ordered a bombing campaign against Cambodia and, in addition, had failed to pay the proper amount of income tax.

Nixon refused to release the tapes, offering transcripts, or written scripts, of them. But critics said the transcripts left out important parts. Then, Nixon released some of the tapes as well. One, however, had an important 18-minute gap. The White House claimed it was accidentally erased by a secretary, but few people believed that story.

Then the Supreme Court stepped in and ordered Nixon to release the tapes. The nation faced a constitutional crisis.

Would its highest official refuse to obey an order from the nation's highest court? On August 5, 1974, Nixon backed down and released the tapes. As many suspected, the tapes revealed that Nixon had ordered a cover-up.

Facing the possibility of impeachment and even prison, Nixon went on national television to say that he would leave office. In an emotional farewell, Nixon officially resigned at noon on August 9, the first and only president to resign from office in American history.

After being sworn into office, Gerald Ford tried to calm the nation by saying "our long national nightmare is over." But, a month later, he pardoned Nixon of all crimes committed during his presidency. This angered millions of Americans. They voted Ford out of office in 1976 and elected Democrat Jimmy Carter instead.

The Energy Crisis

World events, of course, did not stop because of Watergate. As the Nixon White House was falling apart, the nation faced a major crisis in the Middle East. In October 1973, the Arab nations attacked Israel. The Yom Kippur War, named after the Jewish holiday when it began, was the Arabs' revenge for their losses in the Six-Day War of 1967. During that earlier conflict, Israel had seized the West Bank, Gaza, and East Jerusalem from the Arabs.

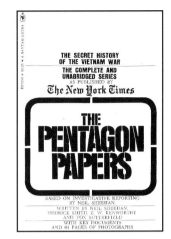

After an employee of the State Department named Daniel Ellsberg gave a copy of a secret government report on the Vietnam War called The Pentagon Papers to The New York Times, President Nixon ordered illegal wiretaps on journalists and government employees whom he suspected of leaks. The report was released to the public as a book, shown above.

Above: President Nixon waves good-bye as he boards a helicopter following his resignation from office.

Left: Gerald Ford was sworn in as president on August 9, 1974.

Above: In February 1979, the Three Mile Island nuclear power plant near Harrisburg, Pennsylvania, experienced a mechanical failure that triggered the worst radiation leak in the history of nuclear power.

America was Israel's main ally and the United States sent huge shipments of weapons to the Jewish state in the middle of the Yom Kippur War. This angered the Arabs. Using its huge oil reserves as a weapon, the Arab-controlled Organization of Petroleum Exporting Countries (OPEC) ordered a boycott of oil sales to the United States.

America, which imported nearly half its oil, faced an "energy crisis." As oil prices shot up over 400 percent, power plants had to cut back and homes and businesses went cold. Long lines formed at gas stations and violence broke out among frustrated motorists. The government asked people to cut back their energy use and ordered a 55-mile speed limit to save gas. Even Las Vegas turned off its neon spectacle during the crisis.

By mid-1974, however, warmer temperatures at home and calmer politics in the Middle East ended the immediate oil shortages and the Arab boycott. But the crisis had led to a new awareness of America's energy dependence. Environmentalists and the government told Americans that they needed to conserve energy.

The Environmental Movement

Although it wasn't until the energy crisis of 1974 that most Americans began to think about conservation and the dangers of environmental pollution, a number of writers and scientists had been studying the problem for many years. In 1962, writer Rachel Carson published

Silent Spring, about the effects of modern pesticides on wildlife. It was the first best-selling book on the subject of pollution.

By the late 1960s, a new environmental movement had joined the antiwar and civil rights movements. Politically, the environmental movement faced one of its first big challenges in Alaska. After oil was discovered on the North Slope, oil companies wanted to build a 1,000-mile-long pipeline to bring the crude oil to an ice-free port in southern Alaska. Environmental groups like the Sierra Club tried to stop them. While the pipeline was built, environmentalists forced the oil companies to put in many safety measures to protect Alaskan wildlife.

The environmental movement also led to the formation of the Environmental Protection Agency (EPA) of the federal government, the banning of DDT, a pesticide dangerous to wild birds, and the creation of Earth Day as an international holiday.

Following the energy crisis, Detroit plants started making more fuel-efficient cars, and people began insulating their homes and businesses better. Still, like most of the industrialized world, America was hooked on cheap energy. To prevent overdependence on Arab reserves, oil companies began opening new oil fields around the world. There was also talk of building more nuclear power plants.

Much of that talk was silenced in 1979. On March 30, alarm bells went off at the Three Mile Island nuclear power plant in Pennsylvania. Water pumps had failed to cool down the central core of radioactive material. For days, there was threat of a meltdown and the release of huge quantities of radioactive steam. Over 100,000 people had to be evacuated from the area. While a meltdown was avoided, the accident made many Americans think twice about nuclear energy as a substitute for oil.

The Iran Hostage Crisis

This need for new oil supplies was underlined by another Middle East crisis in the late 1970s. For years, America had been a major supporter of Shah Reza Pahlavi of Iran. The shah was anticommunist and supported U.S. interests in the oil-rich Persian Gulf that bordered on Iran. But the shah was also a brutal dictator. He imprisoned, tortured, and murdered thousands of Iranian citizens who disagreed with him.

By the late 1970s, the people of Iran were rising up against the shah's government. Led by their religious leader, the Ayatollah Khomeini, anti-shah Iranians blamed the United States for supporting a hated government. In February 1979, the shah was forced to leave the country.

In the fall, the shah was diagnosed with cancer. President Jimmy Carter invited him to receive treatment at a U.S. hospital. This angered people in Iran. On November 4, 1979, a group of Muslim students seized control of the U.S. embassy in the Iranian capital of Tehran and took 53 Americans hostage.

The violation of international law outraged Americans. It also stirred up a sense of frustration. Ever since America's withdrawal from Vietnam, it seemed to many that the nation had been pushed around on the international scene. Now, a group of students was holding American citizens hostage, burning the U.S. flag, and calling America the "Great Satan."

Every night, the evening newscasters would begin and end their broadcasts by announcing how many days the embassy officials had been held hostage. People began wearing yellow ribbons as a sign that they were thinking of the trapped Americans in Iran.

Yet, despite America's great strength, it seemed like there was nothing that could be done. The frustration was made worse after Carter ordered a rescue attempt in April, 1980. The attempt failed when helicopters collided in the Iranian desert. Scenes of Iranians dancing around the bodies of the fallen American soldiers angered the nation even more.

The Iranian revolution and hostage taking had also caused a replay of the earlier energy crisis. Once again, oil prices skyrocketed and people were forced to wait in long lines to fill their tanks.

By 1980, America was facing a long list of serious problems that had no easy

solutions. There was a continuing energy crisis, as well as the economic recession it caused. And it seemed like the hostage situation would never end. Many Americans blamed Jimmy Carter for the problems. He was not a strong enough leader, they felt, to handle the country's difficult domestic and international troubles.

With Watergate now six years behind them, the Republicans were ready for a comeback. But instead of turning to a moderate like George Bush or Bob Dole, Republican voters turned to the most conservative candidate running in the primaries.

Ronald Reagan, a former movie actor and governor of California, promised a tough new American foreign policy. He also promised to cut taxes and government spending on domestic programs, especially those that were aimed at helping the poor. Reagan liked to use examples of real, and sometimes made-up, people in his speeches. One of his favorites was the woman who drove a Cadillac to pick up her welfare check. The message was clear: The middle class was paying too much in taxes to help poor people who wouldn't help themselves.

Angry and frustrated American voters liked what Reagan had to say. In the 1980 election, they elected him president by a landslide. Reagan would begin his presidency with a fresh slate. As a final insult to Carter, the Iranian militants released the hostages on January 20, 1981, the day he left office.

On November 4, 1979, 500 Iranians broke into the U.S. embassy in Tehran and took more than 53 Americans hostage. Several of the captors are seen above parading one of their prisoners in front of the cameras.

AMERICAN TIMELINE

1946 In a capital ceremony attended by General MacArthur, President Harry S. Truman grants the Philippines its independence.

1947 Fearing a depression in war-ravaged Germany and the expansion of Communism, Secretary of State George Marshall proposes his plan to send monetary aid for the rebuilding of Europe.
■ Jackie Robinson signs a contract with the Brooklyn Dodgers, becoming the first African-American to play in the major leagues.

1948 In a landmark decision, the U.S. Supreme Court makes prayer illegal in public schools.
■ Maurice and Richard McDonald open the first fast-food burger restaurant, where everything is prepackaged, and nothing is made to order.

1950 Senator Joseph McCarthy begins a "witch hunt" for Communist spies in the U.S. government.
■ U.S. troops arrive in South Korea to fight off the invading North Korean and Chinese Communist forces.

1951 Race riots rock Chicago when an African-American family purchases a house in a white suburban neighborhood.
■ Marlon Brando and Vivian Leigh star in the film version of playwright Tennessee Williams's *A Streetcar Named Desire*.

1952 Former World War II General Dwight D. Eisenhower, affectionately known as "Ike," is elected president.

1953 Accused of selling government secrets to the Soviets, husband and wife Julius and Ethel Rosenberg are put to death.

1954 In a blow against segregation, the Supreme Court rules that a public school system divided along race lines is unconstitutional.
■ After four years of persecuting those he calls Communists, McCarthy is condemned by the U.S. Senate.

1955 President Eisenhower sends military advisors to South Vietnam in an attempt to help Vietnamese officials stem the tide of Communism.
■ Spurred by Rosa Parks's refusal to give up her seat to a white man, Rev. Martin Luther King Jr. leads the African-Americans of Montgomery,

WORLD TIMELINE

Above: The Nuremberg trials

1946 Nine former Nazi officials are executed after being found guilty of numerous war crimes, including the deaths of millions of innocent people.

1947 India and Pakistan become independent from Britain.
■ While tending his sheep, a Bedouin shepherd boy discovers the Dead Sea Scrolls in a cave.

Two thousand years old, these manuscripts outline almost the entire Old Testament.

1948 Jewish leaders declare Israel an independent Jewish state.
■ The Eastern European nations of Poland, Romania, Hungary, Bulgaria, and Czechoslovakia fall under Communist rule, and Europe is divided by an "Iron Curtain."
■ The Berlin airlift begins, as the Western powers begin airlifting supplies to Berliners blockaded into their city by the Soviets.

1949 Communist forces under Mao Zedong defeat the Nationalists and establish the People's Republic of China. They are immediately

Alabama, in a bus boycott. A year later, the Supreme Court rules that bus segregation is unconstitutional.

1956 Film star Marilyn Monroe stars in *Bus Stop*.

1957 Protected by the National Guard from a jeering, threatening mob, nine African-American teenagers begin attendance at the all-white Little Rock Central High School.

1958 The U.S. submarine *Nautilus* makes history's first voyage underneath the North Pole.

1959 The first Barbie doll appears on toy store shelves.
■ Alaska and Hawaii enter the Union.

Left: Marilyn Monroe

1960 African-Americans stage a series of sit-ins across the South to protest segregation of lunch counters and cafeterias.
■ A U.S. spy plane over the Soviet Union is shot down by the Russians, and its pilot is captured.

1961 John Fitzgerald Kennedy is elected president, just barely defeating his challenger, Richard Nixon.
■ Backed by the United States, anticommunist forces rebel against Cuban President Fidel Castro at the Bay of Pigs. The revolution is unsuccessful.
■ Rachel Carson publishes *Silent Spring*, which helps renew the environmental movement in the United States.

recognized by the Soviets, and by Britain a year later.
■ The Western nations sign the North Atlantic Treaty Organization (NATO), agreeing to ally themselves in war should an attack arise from the East.

1950 North Koreans invade South Korea and march on Seoul.

1953 Russian leader Joseph Stalin dies in Moscow.

1954 French forces fall to the Viet Minh at Dien Bien Phu. The United States warns that if Communist forces gain control of Vietnam, all of Southeast Asia will fall under the influence of the Soviets.

1955 The last of the foreign forces occupying Germany and Austria since the end of World War II withdraw.
■ The Warsaw Pact is signed by nations of the Eastern Bloc, unifying them militarily and effectively dividing the world into East and West.

1959 Cheered by crowds in the streets of Havana, the forces of Fidel Castro capture Cuba and take over the government.
■ Twelve nations sign a treaty making Antarctica neutral territory open to scientists from all nations and agreeing to preserve its natural state.

The poster at right, featuring Fidel Castro, celebrates the Cuban Revolution.

1960 The Congo becomes independent from Belgium, and Civil War breaks out as the wealthier region of Katanga secedes.

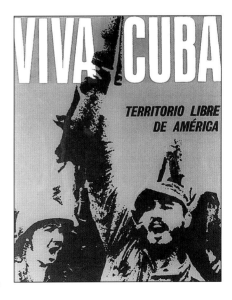

AMERICAN TIMELINE

1962 When American spy planes discover Soviet missile sites in Cuba, an angry President Kennedy demands the immediate withdrawal of all atomic weapons. The world breathes a sigh of relief when Soviet premier Nikita Khrushchev finally agrees.

1963 Martin Luther King delivers his famous "I Have a Dream" speech before a Washington, DC, crowd of 200,000.
■ President John F. Kennedy is assassinated in Dallas, Texas.

1964 President Lyndon Johnson signs the Civil Rights Act, prohibiting discrimination on the basis of race.

1965 Operation Rolling Thunder begins, with President Johnson

Above: Bob Dylan

ordering an increase of American troops in Vietnam and intensive bombing of North Vietnamese military targets.

1966 Folk rock singer Bob Dylan releases his record *Blonde on Blonde* to wide critical and popular acclaim.

1967 Antiwar protests sweep the nation as hundreds are arrested and as labor and civil leaders meet to form an opposition to the fighting in Vietnam.
■ Race riots break out in cities around the country, including Detroit, Michigan, and Newark, New Jersey.

1968 Martin Luther King Jr. is assassinated in Memphis as he stands on a motel balcony.
■ Senator Robert F. Kennedy, younger brother of the slain president John F. Kennedy, is shot and killed in Los Angeles,

WORLD TIMELINE

Above: The Beatles land in America.

1961 In an attempt to stop the steady stream of immigration to the West, the East Germans block all access to West Berlin by constructing the Berlin Wall.

1963 South Vietnamese president Ngo Dinh Diem is ousted in a military coup.

1964 The Beatles, a British rock group, arrive in the United States to begin their first concert tour of America.

1965 Ferdinand Marcos is elected president of the Philippines.

1967 To the embarrassment of Egyptian president Gamal Abdel Nasser, Israeli forces rout the surrounding Arabs and seize Jerusalem in a mere six days.
■ In Cape Town, South Africa, Louis Washkansky becomes the first recipient of a heart transplant.

1968 With the launching of the Tet Offensive, Viet Cong guerrillas attack over 100 cities in South

Above: Senator Robert F. Kennedy

moments after winning the California Democratic presidential primary.

■ The Democratic Party is split down the middle between those for and against continuing the Vietnam War, and violence erupts outside their convention in Chicago.

1969 Richard Nixon is inaugurated and begins withdrawing forces from Vietnam.
■ American astronauts Neil Armstrong and Edwin "Buzz" Aldrin land on the moon.

1970 Four college students are shot and killed at Kent State, as police officers fire on an antiwar demonstration that erupted in violence.

1971 Walt Disney World opens in Orlando, Florida.

1972 President Nixon arrives in Moscow to sign the Strategic Arms Limitation Treaty (SALT), becoming the first president to visit the Soviet Union since the beginning of the Cold War.

1973 In the landmark case *Roe* v. *Wade*, the Supreme Court declares that states do not have the right to restrict abortion during the first trimester of a woman's pregnancy.

1974 Charged with conspiring to obstruct justice in the Watergate scandal that rocked the White House, President Nixon resigns.

1975 The last of American troops are evacuated as the Communist Vietcong take over the South Vietnam capital of Saigon.

Vietnam in a massive assault.
■ Liberal leader Alexander Dubček takes power in Czechoslovakia, promising to relax restrictions on the press and to combine Marxism with personal liberty. In response, the Soviets invade, forcing him to repeal his democratic reforms.

1969 For five hours of heavy fighting, Irish Catholics and Protestants clash in the streets of Belfast.
■ Golda Meir, one of the signer's of Israel's Declaration of Independence in 1948, becomes prime minister at the age of 70.

1971 Pakistan is split in two, as easterners secede and form the new nation of Bangladesh.

Above: Israeli prime minister Golda Meir

1972 Arab terrorists attack Israeli athletes at the Munich Olympics,

killing 11. In retaliation, Israel launches air raids on Palestinian guerrilla bases in Syria and Lebanon.

1973 After 300 years of colonial rule, the Bahamas becomes independent from Britain.
■ In a protest against America's support of Israel, Arab nations halt all shipment of oil to the United States, causing prices to soar.

1974 While on tour in Toronto, Soviet ballet dancer Mikhail Baryshnikov defects.

1975 North and South Vietnam are united under the Communist Viet Cong, officially ending the Vietnam War.

X. TOWARD A NEW CENTURY

Above: Earth rises above the horizon of the Moon.

I N 1987, OUR CONSTITUTION became the oldest constitution still in use in the entire world. Since then, its strength has once again proven itself. For 70 years, the United States faced the Soviet Union as its chief rival. Today, the Soviet Union no longer exists, having crumbled not from enemy bombs, but from the weakness of its own form of government.

Although the United States now stands alone as the strongest nation on earth, recent history has taught that America cannot shape the world's destiny. Since the end of the Vietnam War, most U.S. military action has taken place as part of a larger UN-led force. And the fate of the U.S. economy has become more tightly tied to that of the entire world.

At home, the air and water is cleaner. Minorities face fewer legal hurdles on the road to equality than ever before. New technologies have created thousands of jobs for those with the skills to use them.

Challenges remain, however. Factory workers are still threatened by employers that abandon the United States to set up shop in foreign countries in order to use low-paid, nonunion, and sometimes underaged workers. Race relations in America remain strained. And the shadow of AIDS still clouds the health of Americans from all walks of life.

What is the government's role in solving these problems? Since 1980, Washington has taken a more conservative approach. The people seem to have mixed feelings. Voters say they want lower taxes and less government. They also want to keep all the programs that benefit them. Clearly the debate is far from settled.

New Frontiers in Space and Technology

"Houston, Tranquility Base here; the *Eagle* has landed." The announcement was simple, but it marked the beginning of a new era. For the first time, a human voice was speaking to Earth from the surface of the Moon.

The date was July 20, 1969. The *Eagle* was the landing craft of the *Apollo 11* spaceship. The men on the Moon were astronauts Neil Armstrong and Edwin "Buzz" Aldrin. With fellow astronaut Michael Collins, Armstrong and Aldrin had lifted off from Florida's Cape Kennedy Space Center several days earlier.

After a quarter-million-mile journey, they set their spacecraft down in the dust of the Moon's Sea of Tranquility, a region that had been named back when people thought the Moon had oceans.

Then, as more than a billion people around the world listened on the radio or watched on TV, Armstrong opened the door of the *Eagle* and climbed down the ladder. As he placed his foot on the surface of the Moon, he said, "That's one small step for man, one giant leap for mankind."

Above: **Gemini 2** *astronaut Ed White walks in space.*

Left: **Apollo 11** *astronaut Buzz Aldrin on the moon, after planting the American flag*

The U.S. Space Program

Unlike Christopher Columbus, who claimed the New World for Spain nearly 500 years earlier, Armstrong did not claim the Moon for the United States. Along with the Soviet Union and 80 other countries, the United States had signed a treaty saying the Moon belonged to all humankind and would never be used for military purposes.

Even so, when Armstrong planted an American flag on the surface of the Moon, he was sending a message to the people of the world. It was the democratic United States, not the Communist Soviet Union, that got there first. The Moon landing was the final goal in one of the most incredible, and expensive, "races" in human history.

In a way, the race to the Moon began over 50 years earlier. While science fiction writers like Jules Verne and H. G. Wells had talked of a journey to the Moon in the late 1800s, scientists in Germany made it a real possibility. Working for Nazi Germany in the 1930s and 1940s, Werner von Braun perfected the V-2 missile. The V-2 was used to shoot explosives across the English Channel into British cities.

After the Nazi surrender in 1945, American and Soviet officials captured German rocket scientists. Some went to work for the United States, others for the Soviets. The two countries each began building rockets, both for military and scientific purposes. But it was the Soviet Union that had the first big success.

On October 4, 1957, radio receivers around the world picked up a beeping sound coming from space. Americans quickly learned it was coming from *Sputnik*

THE *CHALLENGER* ACCIDENT

Despite the exciting success of the Apollo and Skylab programs, by the late-1970s NASA was in trouble. The growing national budget deficit had led to huge cuts in the space agency's annual spending. From 1975 to 1981, no Americans went into space.

Even with the cutbacks, NASA's technicians began to develop a new project called the space shuttle. The shuttle, which looked like a large airplane, would be launched on a rocket. Once in space, it would steer like a spaceship, and then land by itself like an airplane.

The first shuttle flight was launched in 1981, and proved a huge success. In 1983, astronaut Sally Ride became the first American woman in space when she served on board the shuttle *Challenger.*

The shuttle program was so successful that NASA decided that it would take civilians into space on future flights. The first was to be a teacher, so that, as President Reagan announced, "all of America will be reminded of the critical role teachers and education play in the life of our nation." In July 1985, Christa McAuliffe, a high school teacher from Concord, New Hampshire, was selected from over 10,000 applicants.

On the morning of January 28, 1986, the *Challenger* stood ready for launch. Seconds after takeoff, the shuttle rose ten miles from Earth. Then, as a horrified nation watched, the *Challenger* burst into flames and exploded. All seven members of the crew, including McAuliffe, were killed.

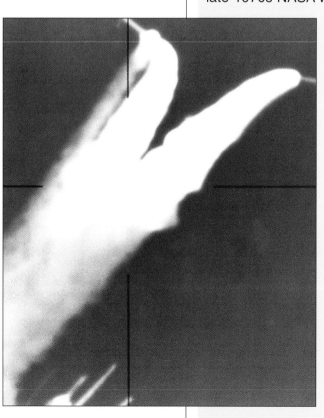

Above: A NASA photograph of the Challenger *explosion*

Left: The space shuttle Discovery *blasted off in 1988.*

Above: Skylab, *a space laboratory, was launched in 1974. Note Earth in the background.*

(Russian for "baby moon"), the first satellite ever launched into Earth's orbit.

Though it was less than a yard in diameter, and under 200 pounds in weight, *Sputnik* scared Americans. Could the Soviets use their rockets to launch nuclear bombs at the United States? *Sputnik* also shook the nation's self-confidence. If the United States was the greatest nation in the world, how did the Soviet Union beat it into space?

Sputnik spurred "rocket fever" in the United States. In 1958, Congress passed the National Defense and Education Act, offering nearly a billion dollars in college loans, in part to help improve science and math research. The United States also established the National Aeronautics and Space Administration (NASA) and began testing rockets. After early rocket tests kept failing, however, one journalist suggested they call the next one "kaput-nik."

In April 1961, the Soviets beat the Americans again. This time they put a man in space. Cosmonaut (the Russian word for astronaut) Yuri Gargarin circled the world for 108 hours. Three months later, on May 5, astronaut Alan Shepherd became the first American to be shot into space. Then, on February 2, 1962, John Glenn rode the *Mercury 7* space capsule into orbit.

President John Kennedy did not want the Soviet Union to beat America again. In a 1961 speech, he set the next great goal in space exploration. "This nation," he said, "should commit itself to achieving the goal, before this decade is out, of landing a man on the moon and returning him safely to the earth." The space race went into high gear.

By the mid-1960s, both the Soviet Union and the United States were sending rockets with two or three men into space. But it was America that soon pulled into the lead. In 1966, astronaut Scott Carpenter became the first man to walk in space from the *Gemini* spacecraft. And in 1968, three astronauts aboard *Apollo 8* became the first humans to leave the gravitational field of the Earth and travel to the Moon's. In early 1969, two more missions prepared the way for the Moon landing of *Apollo 11* on July 20, 1969.

There were to be seven more manned missions to the Moon before the Apollo program was abandoned in 1972. One of them, *Apollo 13*, nearly led to disaster when an oxygen tank aboard the spacecraft blew up halfway to the Moon. In a heroic rescue, astronauts and NASA engineers used the Moon's gravitational pull to slingshot the craft back to Earth.

Skylab, a space laboratory, and a

Fiber-optic technology has come to play a critical role in modern communications. Shown at right is optical diagnostic equipment that uses lasers to monitor the temperature of orbiting space shuttles.

Below: The Electronic Numerical Integrator and Computer (ENIAC) was the world's first digital computer. ENIAC's many consoles filled this entire laboratory.

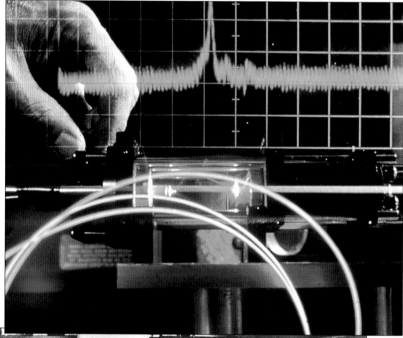

joint U.S.-Soviet mission rounded out the manned space program of the 1970s. Unmanned missions visited the other planets of the solar system. Two *Voyager* spacecrafts explored the outer planets, while the *Viking* landed on Mars in 1976, looking for evidence of life on the red planet.

For the first 20 or so years of space exploration, rockets and spacecraft were disposable, used for one mission only. In the early 1980s, NASA launched a reusable space shuttle to save money. In fact, the costs of the shuttle soared. Then, in January 1986, disaster struck when the shuttle *Challenger* blew up shortly after takeoff. Six astronauts and Christa McAuliffe, a schoolteacher from New Hampshire, were killed in the explosion.

The *Challenger* disaster only heightened concerns about the high cost of America's space program. All during the space program, many Americans questioned whether it was money well spent. Why should we go to the Moon, they asked, when there were still so many problems on Earth? Supporters said that there were many benefits from the space programs. These included weather and communication satellites. Products like microwave ovens and Velcro™ also came out of space research.

The Computer Age

The most important new technology of the late 20th century, the computer, was improved but not invented during the space race. The first one, the Electronic Numerical Integrator and Computer (ENIAC), dates back to World War II. Weighing more than 30 tons and using 18,000 vacuum tubes, ENIAC, said one scientist, sounded "like a roomful of ladies knitting." It could add about 5,000 ten-digit numbers a second.

But ENIAC had no memory and had to be reprogrammed by hand after every use. Next came the Universal Automatic Computer (UNIVAC), which predicted the results of the 1952 elections. The 1948 invention of the transistor and the 1959 development of the integrated circuit allowed small computers to run faster.

But it was the invention of the disk drive in the 1970s that made it possible for average people to use computers. In 1977, two California engineers named Steve Jobs and Steve Wozniak introduced the Apple computer. Within ten years, millions of people would be using computers at home and at work.

With the new technology came a new form of communication. In 1969, scientists at the University of California at Los Angeles became the first people to ever send a message directly from one computer to another. This communication network spread among research institutions and universities. In the early 1990s, the general public discovered the excitement of using the Internet. Soon after, millions were sending electronic mail and "surfing" the latest form of Internet communication, the World Wide Web.

Above: Steve Wozniak (left) and Steve Jobs (right), the founders of Apple Computer

"Government is not the solution to our problem. Government is the problem."

—RONALD REAGAN

Below: President Reagan and his wife, Nancy, wave to a crowd of supporters during the 1980 presidential campaign.

America in the 1980s

In 1986, a wealthy investor named Ivan Boesky came to speak to the business students at the University of California, Berkeley. Boesky had made hundreds of millions of dollars buying and selling stocks and bonds on Wall Street. "I think greed is healthy," he said. "You can be greedy and still feel good about yourself."

Like fellow financier Michael Milliken, Boesky specialized in arbitrage, a Wall Street word for borrowing huge sums of money to buy out companies. To save enough money to pay off the debt, the new owners often laid off thousands of employees.

"They locked the gates at 3:30 with no notice, no nothin'," said steelworker Frank Lumpkin. "That was seven years ago. Chase Manhattan [a major Wall Street bank], who was financing the checks, put a lock on the gate, 3,600 guys knocked out without notice."

Lumpkin eventually got a job in a soup kitchen, handing out donated food to his fellow unemployed workers, at a fraction of his former pay. Boesky and Milliken went to prison for violating

trading laws, but held onto their $100-million fortunes.

During the 1980s, America's wealthiest people saw their incomes go up faster than ever before. Many middle-class people also became wealthy, sometimes through the stock market, and sometimes by starting up their own businesses. Meanwhile, other middle-class workers struggled to keep pace. The number of families in which both parents had to work increased greatly, and many Americans were forced to work two jobs. Meanwhile, America's poor grew even poorer.

The Reagan Administration

Throughout most of the 1980s, the United States was led by President Ronald Reagan. Born to working-class parents in Illinois, Reagan moved to Hollywood in the 1930s. He had been a successful film actor, and later, a spokesperson for the General Electric Company.

Once a liberal supporter of Franklin Delano Roosevelt, Reagan drifted toward conservative politics during the 1950s. He ran for governor of California as a Republican in 1966, and won. Reagan

tried to win the Republican nomination for president in 1976, but lost to President Ford.

By 1980, the country was ready for Reagan. Following the embarrassments of Vietnam and the Iran hostage crisis, Americans looked for a leader who promised to make America strong and respected around the world once more. During his race against President Jimmy Carter, Reagan promised to rebuild America's military strength.

Reagan also promised to cut taxes and reduce the size of the federal government. Many Americans had come to feel that the federal government had grown too large, interfered in too many people's lives, and asked Americans to pay far too much in taxes in order to support hundreds of government programs that didn't work.

Ronald Reagan had something else that helped him win the presidency. Even more important than his campaign

promises or his political beliefs was his personality. Franklin Roosevelt had reassured Americans when he entered office that the United States would overcome the hardships brought by the Depression.

In the same way, Ronald Reagan reassured Americans that despite the setbacks of Vietnam, the Iran Hostage crisis, and the Watergate scandal, America could overcome these, too. And just as FDR had done, Ronald Reagan delivered his message in a friendly, confident style that people could relate to.

Reagan defeated Carter in a landslide victory, which helped his Republican Party take control of the Senate for the first time since the 1950s. After being shot in an assassination attempt in March 1981, his popularity soared even higher. His high approval ratings helped him pass a great number of programs through Congress early in his presidency.

At the center of Reagan's economic

Above: The New York Stock Exchange

Left: David Stockman, the director of the Office of Management and Budget, was one of the main architects of "Reaganomics."

program was a theory that the press nicknamed "Reaganomics." Reaganomics was based on a tax cutting idea called "supply side" economics. Supporters of the supply side theory argued that if businesses and rich individuals gave less of their money to the government in taxes, they could spend more money on other things, which would help the economy grow. A bigger economy would lead to more jobs for other Americans, who might then grow rich themselves. Reagan also promised to get rid of laws that he said were keeping businesses and industry from growing. His opponents called the "supply side" theory "trickle down" economics, since, they said, money was supposed to trickle down from the rich to everyone else.

In addition, Reagan also promised to lower the federal debt. According to his advisors, a larger economy would mean more tax money for the government. At the same time, they also called for cuts in government spending.

Reagan's tax cutting plan, known as the Economic Recovery Tax Act of 1981, passed Congress easily. The act provided for across-the-board tax cuts of 25 percent over three years. It also introduced tax bracketing, so that as people's wages increased, they wouldn't have to pay a higher percentage of their earnings in taxes. According to Reagan's critics, however, since the rich paid the most in taxes, it was the rich who gained the most by the new tax law.

Since Democrats in Congress were less willing to go along with Reagan's plans to do away with federal laws, the president appointed people who thought like he did to powerful positions. For example, Secretary of the Interior James Watt, helped timber companies cut

House the Homeless

During the 1980s, the cost of housing climbed rapidly and the number of homeless Americans increased to record levels. The button shown above promotes aid for the homeless.

Above: In 1948, Ronald Reagan starred in the movie Hellcats of the Navy. *His costar in the film was his future wife, Nancy Davis.*

RONALD REAGAN: THE EARLY YEARS

Nicknamed "The Great Communicator" by White House aides during his presidency, Ronald Reagan was considered a master of the presidential press conference. Through carefully orchestrated speeches, he conveyed enough good humor and enthusiastic patriotism to instill confidence and a renewed sense of pride in a discouraged nation.

Reagan had always possessed a remarkable ability to win over his audiences. After graduating from college in 1932, he landed a job as a radio sportscaster in Des Moines, Iowa. His all-American looks helped land him a job with Warner Brothers, and soon he was making movies. Yet Reagan wasn't satisfied with a Hollywood career. He was more interested in politics.

In 1964, Reagan delivered a well-received speech in support of Senator Barry Goldwater's presidential campaign, causing the Republican Party to sit up and take notice. Recognizing his talent as a political speaker, party members nominated him for California governor in the 1966 election. Reagan won the election by an unprecedented one million votes and served as California governor for eight years. When he ran for president in 1980, Reagan defeated the incumbent, Jimmy Carter, in a landslide. In the 1984 election, it became clear that his popularity had not waned. He was reelected, this time taking every state except Minnesota and registering the biggest victory in U.S. history. Despite the Iran-Contra scandal and other setbacks that rocked his second term, Reagan remained one of America's most popular presidents.

Left: President Reagan meets with his Council of Economic Advisors—the men responsible for guiding the administration's economic policy.

American industry has faced growing competition from overseas manufacturers who have flooded the U.S. market with inexpensive, high-quality products, including automobiles and television sets. Many labor leaders, concerned that these sales are costing Americans jobs, have called on the government to restrict the amount of imports sold in America. The poster below was produced by an American labor group.

more trees on federal land. Watt also refused to go after polluters who broke antipollution laws, and cut back on the number of government workers keeping track of industrial waste.

Although he was very popular during the early months of his presidency, Reagan's popularity began to drop by late 1981. Ever since the energy crisis of the 1970s, one of America's worst economic problems had been inflation, or rising prices. As the government organization in charge of the nation's money supply, the Federal Reserve Board had begun raising interest rates during the Carter Administration to keep prices down. Although this policy lowered the inflation rate from 12.4 percent in 1980 to four percent in 1982, it also helped push the country into its worst economic times since the Depression. At the height of the 1981–1982 recession, more than 10 percent of working-age Americans were jobless.

Reagan Cuts Aid to the Poor

For some, Reagan's cuts in federal programs, including those designed to help the unemployed and the poor, made things even worse. Some cuts were made by eliminating programs altogether, like the Comprehensive Employment and Training Act, which helped poorly educated young people find jobs. The administration made other cuts by simply refusing to spend the money Congress gave it to spend. One consequence of this strategy was that only 45 percent of those who lost their jobs in the 1981–1982 recession received unemployment compensation, compared to more than 75 percent during the sharp economic downturn of the mid-1970s.

Still, the three biggest expenses of the federal government—entitlement programs, defense, and interest payments on the federal debt—actually grew during the Reagan years. Entitlement programs include Medicare (medical care for the elderly) and Medicaid (medical care for the poor), two programs introduced by President Johnson in the 1960s. Another entitlement program, Social Security, dates back to FDR's New Deal program of the 1930s. It offers income to disabled and elderly Americans and their families.

Medicare, Medicaid, and Social Security are called entitlements because every American is entitled to receive the benefits they offer. All three grew in the 1980s because of the rapid rise in medical care costs and a growing population of elderly citizens.

More Money for Weapons

Defense spending grew even more dramatically in the 1980s. President Reagan's promise to build a stronger America cost a lot of money to fulfill. Over a five-year period, Reagan and Defense Secretary Caspar Weinberger spent over $1.7 trillion on defense.

Despite promises to cut the federal deficit (the gap between the amount of money the government spends and the amount it raises), the national debt tripled during the administrations of President Reagan and his successor in the White House, Vice President George Bush. The climbing debt caused interest rates to rise and forced the government to spend more and more money paying for what it had borrowed.

Life in the 1980s

Despite these problems, the American economy grew rapidly after the recession of 1981–1982 ended. Since that time, many Americans have made a lot of

RYAN WHITE AND THE FIGHT AGAINST AIDS

During the 1980s, a new, lethal virus called Acquired Immune Deficiency Syndrome (AIDS) appeared in America. At first, little was known about the disease and how it was spread. The television networks called it "a deadly, mysterious disease," "new and frightening," and "terrifying." *Newsweek* reported that AIDS was "breaking out," and "running rampant."

When the people of Kokomo, Indiana, learned that 13-year-old Ryan White had contracted AIDS from a contaminated blood transfusion, they were afraid. Rumors flew through the small community, and many thought that they would get AIDS merely by touching Ryan. Children ran away from him, angry men shot bullets through his window, and frightened parents demanded that he be forbidden to enter school grounds. Banned from school, Ryan went to court.

His case drew immediate national attention. Ryan appeared on all the major networks, and was chosen Peter Jennings's "Person of the Week" twice. "I've seen how people with HIV/AIDS are treated," Ryan said, "and I don't want others to be treated like I was." After several court battles, Ryan eventually won the right to return to school. But he remained an eloquent speaker for AIDS awareness until his death in 1990.

In his memory, Ryan's mother, Jeanne, and TV talk show host Phil Donahue established the Ryan White Foundation. RWF is a national organization that helps people deal with personal, family, and community issues related to HIV and AIDS. Through RWF, Jeanne hopes to continue the work against AIDS discrimination that Ryan had begun.

Above: Ryan White

Far left: Madonna, one of the top recording stars of the 1980s

Left: Actor Larry Hagman starred as the wealthy and ruthless oil tycoon, J. R. Ewing, on the television program, **Dallas**.

1980s were not shared by all. Many types of businesses faced severe crises. Car makers faced growing competition from less expensive imports from Japan. The steel industry was hurt as more and more manufacturers began making their products out of plastic. Even the rapidly growing computer industry experienced a bumpy ride after it overexpanded to meet demand.

During the recession of 1981–1982, so many manufacturing plants closed that large areas of the Midwest were called the "Rust Belt." Even after the nationwide

recession ended, many of the newly unemployed were forced to take jobs that paid far less than their old ones. For the first time since the 1960s, poverty rates began to climb in the 1980s, especially among Hispanics, blacks, and children. By the end of the decade, nearly 40 percent of America's poor were under 18 years old.

Despite these problems, the stock market continued to break new records nearly every month. Then, on October 19, 1987, it crashed. The Dow Jones average, a measure of the stock market's performance, fell by over 500 points, which soon led to the firing of some 15,000 Wall Street workers. For many, the "Crash of '87" marked the end of the 1980s boom.

Due to the many regulations and

money. Throughout the rest of the 1980s, the stock and real estate markets soared and those who knew how to profit from them grew rich overnight. Many of these newly rich Americans were young people. They were given the nickname "Yuppies," which was short for Young, Urban Professionals.

The Yuppies and other wealthy Americans of the '80s enjoyed spending their money even more than earning it. Sales of items such as fancy cars and yachts rose quickly. New, elegant restaurants and expensive boutiques brought new life to run-down neighborhoods, but sometimes forced poor inhabitants out in the process.

Many of the best-known figures of the decade were connected to money. Rock star Madonna became known as the "Material Girl" after releasing a song of the same name, while New York real estate tycoon Donald Trump published a best-selling book called *The Art of the Deal*. The most popular television shows of the 1980s were *Dallas* and *Dynasty*, one about oil millionaires in Texas and the other about a rich Colorado family.

As was the case during the economic boom of the 1920s, the good times of the

"For almost eight years, we've been led by those who view social good coming from private interests, who view public life as a means to increase private wealth. They have been prepared to sacrifice the common good of the many to satisfy the private interest and the wealth of the few. We believe in a government that's a tool of our democracy in service to the public, not an instrument of the aristocracy in search of private wealth . . ."

—JESSE JACKSON, *in a speech to the Democratic National Convention, 1988*

Above: President Bush and his wife, Barbara, at the Lincoln Memorial

Right: Looters carry stolen groceries out of a vandalized supermarket during the 1992 L.A. riot.

rules created during the New Deal, the crash did not lead to a new Great Depression. The economy slowly started to grow again.

The Bush Administration

In 1988, Reagan's vice president, George W. Bush, was elected president. Although President Bush generally followed the same policies that Reagan had, he was much less popular.

Among President Bush's problems was a crisis involving the country's savings and loan (S&L) banking industry. S&Ls were established in the 1930s to offer loans for small business people and homeowners. During the early Reagan years, regulations on the industry were eased. This allowed managers and owners of S&Ls to offer loans for very risky investments.

When depositors put money into an S&L savings accounts, the S&L then uses that money to make loans, at higher interest rates, to borrowers. But during the 1980s, many of the borrowers who had used their loans for risky investments were not able to pay back their loans. This caused a great deal of trouble, not just for the S&Ls, but for the federal government as well. The government, which insured savings accounts up to $100,000, was forced to bail out the S&Ls. At first, the government said the costs would not be high, then the estimates went up. By the early 1990s, the bill to taxpayers stood at over $500 billion, the largest financial scandal in American history.

Meanwhile, the economy had begun to worsen once again. As unemployment climbed once more, President Bush argued that the economy was doing just fine, and that any job losses would be temporary. More and more Americans began to feel that President Bush was simply out of touch with the lives of average citizens.

Another event also hurt President Bush's chances for reelection. On March 3, 1991, a speeding black motorist named Rodney King was pulled over by Los Angeles police. Dragged from his car, King was repeatedly beaten and kicked by the

Left: Bill Clinton and his running mate, Al Gore, work the crowd during their successful 1992 campaign.

arresting officers. Leaders of the Los Angeles black community said this was nothing new. What was different this time was the proof. A witness had videotaped the attack. It then was shown repeatedly on the evening news.

The police officers responsible were put on trial. Despite watching the video, the all-white jury acquitted the officers of any wrongdoing. Los Angeles's black community exploded in rage. Several days of looting and burning followed, leaving 60, mostly black, people dead.

The Clinton Administration

During the election of 1992, Bush faced the Democratic Party's candidate, Arkansas governor Bill Clinton. During the campaign, James Carville, Clinton's campaign manager, posted a sign at Clinton headquarters reminding campaign workers to focus on one issue. The sign read: "It's the economy, stupid." Throughout the campaign, Clinton again and again attacked Bush's failed economic programs.

Clinton won the election in a landslide, even though he won only 43 percent of the votes cast. In fact, he might not have won at all had President Bush had just one opponent to worry about.

Unfortunately for Bush, he faced two challengers. His second opponent was a wealthy Texas businessman named H. Ross Perot, who decided that he would run an independent campaign for president, paid for out of his fortune. Perot used his money to buy TV time attacking Bush for doing nothing about the rising national debt. He also attacked Washington politicians for being more interested in raising money for the next election than in solving the nation's problems. While Perot won no electoral votes, he

Above: Texas billionaire and presidential candidate H. Ross Perot

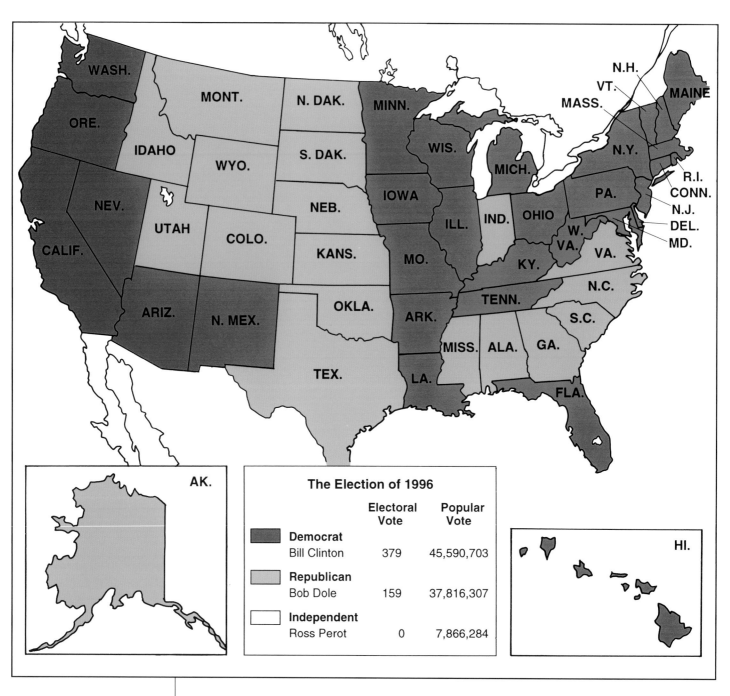

The Election of 1996

	Electoral Vote	Popular Vote
Democrat Bill Clinton	379	45,590,703
Republican Bob Dole	159	37,816,307
Independent Ross Perot	0	7,866,284

Above: Despite falling out of favor with the American public by 1994, President Clinton recovered his lost popularity and easily defeated Republican candidate Bob Dole in the election of 1996.

"The era of big government is over."

—BILL CLINTON, *in his 1995 State of the Union Address*

captured 20 percent of the popular vote, enough to tilt the election to Clinton.

Upon taking office, President Clinton followed in the Democratic tradition of President Franklin Roosevelt in his belief that the federal government should help make the lives of Americans better. One of his first efforts was to pass a law that guaranteed national health care to all Americans. Clinton set up a special committee to design the new law and put his wife, Hillary Rodham Clinton, in charge. The Clintons hoped that their health-care programs would do as much for the coun-

try as New Deal programs like Social Security had done. Clinton's opponents, particularly in the nation's health-care industry, spent millions to convince Americans that the president's plan would cost too much and intrude too much on people's lives. The plan was defeated.

A Republican Congress

Following the defeat of his health-care plan, President Clinton's popularity fell. In 1994, the Republican Party took control of both the House of Representatives and the Senate, something the party had not done since the early 1950s. Led by Georgia representative Newt Gingrich, the Republicans promised a "Contract with America" to, among other things, cut domestic spending, taxes, and regulations. When Clinton vetoed some of their legislation in 1995, the Republicans refused to pass the annual budget. Without a budget agreement, no money was available even to operate the government. The federal government shutdown lasted for weeks.

Both sides blamed each other for the shutdown, but the American people tended to blame the Republican Congress. Clinton's popularity rebounded, particularly after he began to promote traditionally Republican ideas like balancing the budget and cutting taxes for the middle class. During his State of the Union Address in 1995, Clinton declared, "The era of big government is over!" While he had begun his term by proposing a controversial government-led overhaul of the American health-care system, he had ended it by promoting a number of small but popular policies like preventing teenage smoking and encouraging school uniforms in public schools.

Not all of Clinton's newer policies were popular with everyone. In 1996, despite criticism from many of his liberal supporters, Clinton agreed with Republicans to end the long-standing Aid to Families with Dependent Children (AFDC) program. He also agreed to limit federal assistance to U.S. residents who had not become citizens.

While many liberals criticized Clinton's new, more conservative policies, he easily won election by defeating the Republican candidate, former Senate majority leader Bob Dole.

When Clinton agreed to limit assistance to noncitizens, he was addressing an issue that concerned many Americans. As the United States heads toward a new century, the old one is closing in much the same way it began: with a huge influx of new immigrants. Since quotas based

on national origin were eliminated in 1965, the country has seen wave after wave of new citizens coming from Latin America and Asia. Over seven million immigrants entered the country during the 1980s alone.

This time they did not come through Ellis Island, which was reopened during the late 1980s as a museum. Instead,

Above: Speaker of the House, Newt Gingrich, of Georgia

Left: Former Senator Bob Dole, Republican of Kansas

they came through airports like New York's JFK and Los Angeles's LAX. They also entered illegally along America's 2,000-mile border with Mexico. Altogether, immigration authorities estimated that about one-third of the people coming to the country were doing so illegally.

As in the 1920s, the massive flow of immigrants produced a negative reaction among many native-born Americans. In 1996, the voters of California approved Proposition 209, cutting off most social services to illegal immigrants, including nonemergency medical care and education. The new law, however, was put on hold as the courts declared it unconstitutional.

During the 1980s, many Americans protested against the Reagan Administration's nuclear weapons policy. The antinuclear movement began much earlier, however. The above antinuclear poster dates from the late 1940s.

Below: President Carter, the strain of office clearly visible on his face

The End of the Cold War

On Good Friday, 1986, a Chicago grandmother named Jean Gump entered the nuclear missile base at Holden, Missouri. She was not there as a tourist or to visit a grandson in the service. Gump was there to destroy the missiles, at least symbolically.

After hanging a banner on the base's fence that read "Swords into Plowshares: An Act of Healing," Gump and two other members of her church took out baby bottles filled with their own blood. They used it to paint a cross on the top of the silo, the concrete structure that held the nuclear missile.

Then, remembers Gump, "we sat down and waited in prayer. . . . About 40 minutes later, the soldiers arrived in an armored vehicle . . . They took things out of my pocket and put them on the ground. One of the items was a handkerchief."

But Gump had a cold. She picked up the handkerchief and blew her nose. The soldier told her to put the handkerchief back on the ground. "All right," Gump replied, "but if my nose should run again, I'll go over there and I will get my handkerchief and blow my nose.

"At this point," Gump recalled, "the poor soldier looked sort of crestfallen [embarrassed]. He was about the age of my youngest child." As Gump was carried away, she repeated the words she had spray-painted underneath the bloody cross: "Disarm and live."

The 1980s were a time of great hope and great fear for America and the world. The decade began with a new round of the Cold War and a new and very large build-up of nuclear arms. It closed with the collapse of Communism in the Soviet Union and throughout Eastern Europe, and the end of the 40-year-old Cold War. Two events in 1979 set the scene for U.S. foreign policy for the early 1980s.

U.S.-Soviet Relations

The Soviet Union, along with the United States, was threatened by the 1979 Islamic revolution in Iran. The country, which has tens of millions of its own Muslim citizens, shares a long border with Iran, and feared that the anticommunist revolution would spread. In Afghanistan, another Islamic country on the Soviet southern border, Muslim rebels rose against the Communist government there. To prevent the spread of an anticommunist revolution from Iran and Afghanistan, the Soviet Union set over 100,000 troops to defend Afghanistan's government against the rebels.

President Jimmy Carter reacted angrily. He ordered a U.S. boycott of the 1980 Olympic Games in Moscow and began sending arms to anti-Soviet Muslim guerrillas. For much of the 1980s, the Soviets found themselves in a war similar to America's in Vietnam. They tried to use their regular army to defeat a guerrilla army fighting with the support of its own people. And as had happened during the Vietnam War, the Afghanistan war grew more unpopular in the Soviet Union.

The Iran-Contra Crisis

The other major world event of 1979 occurred in America's own backyard. Ever since he was put in power by U.S. Marines in the 1930s,

Nicaraguan dictator Anastazio Somoza had ruled his country with an iron fist. After stealing much of the aid money given to his country after a 1972 earthquake, Somoza faced a nationwide rebellion, led by a guerrilla army called the Sandinistas. In 1979, the Sandinistas captured the capital and forced Somoza to flee to Miami.

The Sandinistas did not call themselves Communists. But some of their actions made U.S. leaders think that they were. The Sandinistas took over the plantations and ranches of wealthy Nicaraguans and foreigners and turned them into cooperatives run by the peasants. They also began to support rebels fighting against the U.S.-supported government in nearby El Salvador.

Not everyone in Nicaragua was happy about the overthrow of Somoza. Many Nicaraguans had their property taken from them, and they were determined to fight back. Some of them, known as "Contras," even took up arms. Many of their weapons, as well as military training and assistance, would come from the United States.

President Carter began the flow of money and arms to the Contras. But it was the Reagan administration that gave them enough to fight a full-scale war against the Sandinista government. In 1984, a Democratic Congress passed the Boland Amendment, banning further aid to the rebels. But this didn't stop certain members of the Reagan administration.

Beginning in the mid-1980s, National Security Advisor John Poindexter and his assistant, Oliver North, came up with a secret, illegal plan to raise money and deliver arms to the Contras. It was a complicated scheme that stretched halfway around the world and was connected to events in the Middle East.

In 1982, Israel invaded Lebanon, a multiethnic and multireligious country to its north. The invasion proved a disaster for Israel, and it soon pulled back its troops to near its own border. To keep the peace between Lebanon's Christian and Muslim populations, the United States sent in Marines.

As Israel's closest friend, the United States was hated by many of the Muslims fighting in Lebanon. In 1983, Muslim terrorists bombed both the U.S. embassy and the Marine compound, killing hundreds of Americans. The terrorists also began to kidnap Americans in Lebanon and hold them hostage. When U.S. troops left Lebanon later that year, they left these hostages behind.

To get them out, Poindexter and North agreed to secretly sell arms to Iran, the main foreign supporter of the terrorists. At the time, Iran was engaged in a long and bloody war with neighboring Iraq. It needed spare parts for the American planes and tanks purchased before the 1979 Islamic revolution. While the Reagan administration was publicly saying it would never make a deal with "terrorists," it was secretly trading arms for hostages.

Below: U.S. Marines look out over war-torn Beirut, Lebanon.

Right: Lieutenant Colonel Oliver North testifies in Congress.

Below: The findings of the congressional committees that looked into the Iran-Contra scandal were published in this book.

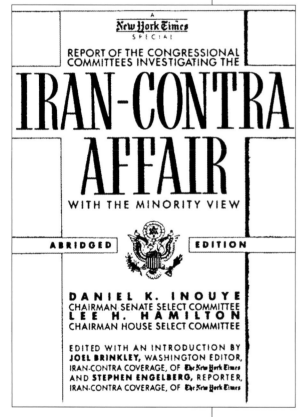

A
New York Times
SPECIAL

REPORT OF THE CONGRESSIONAL
COMMITTEES INVESTIGATING THE

IRAN-CONTRA
AFFAIR

WITH THE MINORITY VIEW

ABRIDGED   EDITION

D A N I E L   K.   I N O U Y E
CHAIRMAN SENATE SELECT COMMITTEE
L E E   H.   H A M I L T O N
CHAIRMAN HOUSE SELECT COMMITTEE

EDITED WITH AN INTRODUCTION BY
JOEL BRINKLEY, WASHINGTON EDITOR,
IRAN-CONTRA COVERAGE, OF **The New York Times**
AND **STEPHEN ENGELBERG,** REPORTER,
IRAN-CONTRA COVERAGE, OF **The New York Times**

When a Lebanese newspaper published the story in late 1986, it proved a major embarrassment for the Reagan administration. What made it illegal was the Nicaraguan connection. Poindexter and North were using the profits from the arms sales to buy weapons for the Contras, in violation of the Boland Amendment. Congressional investigations into the scandal, known as the Iran-Contra Affair, were televised across the country. Oliver North freely admitted that he had ignored the Boland Amendment, as well as the U.S. Constitution. Despite his admission, most Americans considered North a hero.

Support for the Contras was part of the Reagan administration's worldwide efforts not just to contain Communism, but to roll it back. In 1983, shortly after the bombing of the Marine compound in Lebanon, Reagan ordered an invasion of the tiny Caribbean island nation of Grenada. Several years earlier, Grenada had had a revolution leading to a Cuban-supported Communist government. Reagan's critics said the U.S. invasion was a way of turning the nation's attention away from the disaster in Lebanon.

Still, the main target of the Reagan administration's foreign policy efforts was the Soviet Union. After a Soviet fighter pilot shot down a Korean passenger plane that had strayed into Soviet airspace, Reagan called the Soviet Union "the focus of evil in the modern world."

In running for president, Reagan had promised to build up the U.S. military. Among the new defense projects was the Strategic Defense Initiative (SDI), popularly known as "Star Wars," after the movie. SDI was a multibillion-dollar project to use laser weapons to shoot down incoming nuclear missiles from space. Reagan said it would make nuclear war impossible. The majority of the nation's scientists, however, said it was technically impossible.

The End of the Cold War

While the Reagan administration was flexing the U.S. military muscle in the 1980s, the Soviet government, under its new leader Mikhail Gorbachev, was moving in the opposite direction. After taking office in 1985, Gorbachev embarked on two radical programs. Known by their Russian names "glasnost" (openness) and "perestroika," (restructuring), they were designed to allow more freedom and economic change.

Glasnost was a success. People in the Soviet Union became less afraid of the secret police and began to speak their minds. The nation's newspapers felt free to report more critically on the government. After the Chernobyl nuclear power plant in the Soviet republic of Ukraine blew up, killing thousands and spreading radioactive dust around the world, the Soviet press openly blamed the government.

Gorbachev had not been the first to push for reforms in the Communist world. Since the early 1980s, an illegal national trade union called "Solidarity," led by shipworker Lech Walesa, had been struggling against the Communist government in Poland.

By 1989, the winds of change were spreading across Soviet-controlled Eastern Europe. In Czechoslovakia, the peaceful "Velvet Revolution" led to the overthrow of the Communist government and to the presidency of Vaclav Havel, a playwright who had once been imprisoned for his anticommunist writings. In Romania, the Communist dictator Nicolai Ceaucescu was captured and killed by his own people.

But the most dramatic event of 1989 was the destruction of the Berlin Wall. Constructed in 1961 by East Germany to keep its citizens from fleeing to the West, the wall was a symbol of the Cold War and Communist dictatorship. As TV cameras beamed images around the world, East and West Germans smashed the wall with sledgehammers. Several years later, the two Germanys were reunited into one country again for the first time since the end of World War II.

But while Glasnost was a success in the Soviet Union, Perestroika was not. The Soviet-state-run economy, struggling throughout most of the 1980s, began to collapse. In August 1990, Communists in the military tried to overthrow the gov-

ernment. While they held Soviet leader Gorbachev hostage at his vacation home in the Crimea, president Boris Yeltsin stood up to the military and forced it to back down.

Although Gorbachev was blamed for the economic collapse, Yeltsin was held

Above: Happy Berlin residents climb the Berlin Wall that had kept them separated from loved ones for 30 years.

up as a hero. Within months of the failed coup, Yeltsin had replaced Gorbachev as the leader of Russia. At the same time, the Soviet Union, which had been founded over 70 years earlier following the Bolshevik Revolution, was broken up into 15 new nations. Led by Russia, the most populous and powerful republic, most of these nations would later form a loose new political system known as the Commonwealth of Independent States.

With the Soviet Union gone and the Cold War over, President Bush declared the beginning of a "new world order." Nobody knew exactly what this meant until events in late 1990 spelled it out.

The Persian Gulf War

On August 2 of that year, Iraqi dictator Saddam Hussein invaded the neighboring country of Kuwait. A tiny, oil-rich kingdom, Kuwait asked for help from the United States and the United Nations. By the end of the year, Bush had put together a coalition of 27 nations, including Russia, to force Hussein out of Kuwait.

While diplomats tried to solve the crisis peacefully, Bush and other coalition leaders sent over 500,000 troops to nearby Saudi Arabia. On January 16, 1991, they launched a counterattack, known as Operation Desert Storm. Within a few weeks, the Iraqi army was pushed out of Kuwait.

Many Americans wanted the coalition to march to the Iraqi capital of Baghdad and capture or kill Hussein. But the forces stopped in southern Iraq. When the Kurds, a badly treated people living in northern Iraq, rose up against Hussein, they were crushed by the Iraqi army.

Below: A commemorative pin from the Live Aid concert

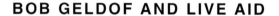

BOB GELDOF AND LIVE AID

On an October day in 1984, Irish rock star Bob Geldof turned on the television in his London apartment. He watched a documentary on the famine in Ethiopia. Moved by the suffering in the faces of the Ethiopian children, Geldof wrote the pop song "Do They Know It's Christmas?" Barely a month later, 40 of Britain's best known pop stars recorded Geldof's song together, donating the proceeds to famine relief efforts. The single was so successful that Geldof decided to organize a benefit concert that would take place in London and America at the same time. It would be called Live Aid.

American record producers, newscasters, and businesspeople were enthusiastic about the idea of a Live Aid concert. The question was, where could they have it? New York stadiums were booked for the summer season. Then, Philadelphia officials stepped forward. JFK stadium was available on July 13. The concert could be held there.

Musical acts such as U2, Sting, Paul McCartney, and Madonna were contacted and booked to perform. The stage was constructed, radio and TV technicians prepared to broadcast internationally, and publicists spread the word.

Then on July 13, for 16 hours, Geldof's Live Aid was broadcast via satellite to 110 countries worldwide. An estimated three billion people tuned in, and by the time the closing strains of the concert died away, over $127 million had been raised for hunger relief.

Over a million Kurds fled to neighboring Turkey and Iran. TV pictures of Kurds dying in the snowy mountains along Iraq's border forced the West into action. In Operation Provide Comfort and Operation Poised Hammer, coalition allies provided aid to the Kurds and set up a protected region for them in the north of Iraq.

The success of Desert Storm made Bush enormously popular at home in the months after the war. Millions of Americans lined New York's Broadway to welcome the troops home. Despite this burst of popularity, a weak economy soon turned voters against the president, and he was defeated in the election of 1992.

Clinton's Foreign Policy

Newly elected President Bill Clinton had not emphasized foreign affairs during his campaign, and as a former governor of the small state of Arkansas, had little experience in international affairs. Many men and women of the U.S. armed forces had little respect for Clinton. Their new commander in chief had not only avoided serving in the Vietnam War as a young man, but had actively protested against it. Critics also said his presidency lacked a clear and strong foreign policy. He refused to get America directly involved in the civil wars that were breaking out around the world in the 1990s, especially a long and bloody one in the former Yugoslavia.

Gradually, however, Clinton's foreign policy took shape. The new president emphasized the use of U.S. forces for humanitarian purposes. Troops were sent into Haiti to defend the democratically elected government of Jean Baptiste Aristide. In 1995, Clinton agreed to include U.S. troops as a part of a NATO plan to enforce a peace accord in Bosnia, once part of Yugoslavia.

Still, the biggest foreign policy event of the mid-1990s had little to do with Clinton. In 1993, Israel and its long-standing enemy, the Palestine Liberation Organization (PLO), negotiated the Oslo Accords (named after the Norwegian cap-

Left: Iraqi dictator Saddam Hussein

Below: President Bush visits American troops during Operation Desert Storm.

ital where the talks took place). The Oslo Accords began a peace process that was supposed to lead to Israeli withdrawal from the Palestinian territories it occupied since the 1967 Arab-Israeli war. In a dramatic ceremony on the White House lawn, Israeli prime minister Yitzhak Rabin and PLO leader Yasir Arafat signed the accords and symbolically shook hands.

But the nearly 50-year-old conflict would not go away. After withdrawing from most of the urban areas of the occupied territories, Israel was struck by violence. In November 1995, a religious, anti-peace-accord Jew assassinated Rabin. In early 1996, the Islamic group Hamas set off a series of terrorist bombs around Israel, killing dozens of civilians.

Both religious Jews and Muslims wanted to destroy the peace process. The former said it violated Jewish law by giving away Jewish land. The latter said the

peace process was just another way for Israel to keep control of the territories.

In May 1996, a nervous Israeli public voted out Shimon Peres, Rabin's replacement, and elected conservative Benjamin Netanyahu, who promised "peace with security." Netanyahu's refusal to continue Israeli withdrawal led to renewed violence in the Occupied Territories. Many people in Israel and around the world worried that the peace process was dead.

Overall, the international scene in the 1990s was a confusing one. With the Soviet Union gone and the Cold War over, economic interests dominated American foreign policy thinking. New technologies allowed corporations to invest in countries around the world.

Many in the business community said this was a good and necessary thing. It

Above: The strategy behind Operation Desert Storm came primarily from General Colin Powell (left), the Chairman of the Joint Chiefs of Staff under President Bush, and General Norman Schwarzkopf (right), the commander of the U.S.-led allied forces.

Right: President Clinton stands by as Israeli prime minister Yitzhak Rabin (left) shakes hands with long time foe Yasir Arafat (right) of the Palestine Liberation Organization, in 1994.

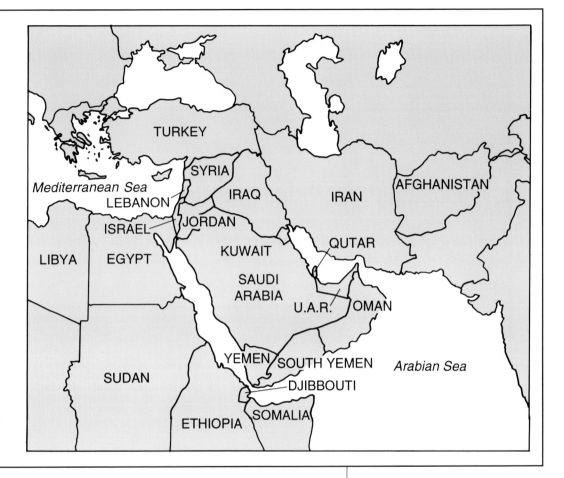

The U.S. and the Middle East: 1978-Today

1978: With assistance from U.S. President Jimmy Carter, Israel and Egypt sign the Camp David Peace Accords.

1979-1981: Iran storms the U.S. embassy and takes 53 Americans hostage.

1983: Terrorists bomb U.S. Marine headquarters in Lebanon, killing 260 American soldiers.

1986: In an effort to free U.S. hostages held in Lebanon, the Reagan administration sells missiles to the government of Iran.

1986: U.S. planes bomb Libya, including the home of leader Muamar Khaddafi as punishment for Libya's support for terrorists, 1986.

1991: American troops lead a UN force against Iraq after that country invades neighboring Kuwait; at the end of the four-day war, UN troops remain in northern Iraq to protect the country's Kurdish people.

1992: UN forces, led by American marines, arrive in Somalia to allow for food deliveries to that famine-stricken country, the troops remain until March, 1995, in a failed attempt to restore peace to the country as well.

1994: Israel and the Palestine Liberation Organization announce agreement to negotiate peace.

1995: Prime Minister Yitzhak Rabin of Israel is assassinated by an anti-Arab soldier in the Israeli army.

made America more competitive. Clinton agreed. In 1993, he signed the North American Free Trade Agreement (NAFTA) to allow freer trade between Canada, the United States, and Mexico. Many Americans were opposed to NAFTA. They worried that American corporations would move their jobs to low-wage Mexico.

One thing, however, has become clear in the late 1990s. Despite the end of the Cold War, America can never go back to its old isolation. The rise of the European and Japanese economies in the 1960s and 1970s has challenged America's economic power. The newly industrializing countries of the developing world have become new competitors for American business and labor. At the same time, international communications has made it possible for Americans to be in personal touch with people all over the world.

As the 21st century dawns, the United States finds itself the only remaining military superpower. People around the globe look to America for leadership in solving political and military conflicts. In addition, the United States still maintains the world's richest and most powerful economy.

Despite the nation's strength, the American people will continue to face new challenges, both at home and overseas. At home, relations between the races remain strained, and in a land of plenty, many still go hungry. Overseas, the threat of terrorism has surpassed the threat of Communism. Despite a cleaner environment at home, worldwide pollution has gotten worse.

America's history has often been the story of challenges met and challenges conquered. In the years to come, more and more solutions will come from the United States working peacefully with the other nations of the world. While many pressing problems remain to be solved, Americans will continue to strive for the perfect balance between the sometimes competing ideals of "life, liberty, and the pursuit of happiness."

The map above indicates some of the most significant events involving the United States in the recent history of the Middle East.

AMERICAN TIMELINE

Above: Fireworks over New York harbor during the Bicentennial celebration in 1976

1976 America celebrates its 200th anniversary on the Fourth of July.
■ Jimmy Carter is elected president, narrowly defeating the incumbent Gerald Ford.

1977 President Carter issues a presidential pardon to most of the nation's Vietnam draft resisters.

1978 President Carter urges a summit between Egyptian and Israeli rulers, where they map out the Camp David Accords, bringing peace to their countries after 31 years of war.

1979 In the worst nuclear accident in American history, radiation leaks from the Three Mile Island power plant in Harrisburg, Pennsylvania.
■ The shah of Iran arrives in New York for medical treatment. A few days later, a mob in Iran seizes the U.S. embassy and captures 53 American hostages, demanding the return of their hated shah.
■ Fundamentalist minister Jerry Falwell founds Moral Majority, Inc., a political action group that registers thousands of conservative voters who will later help elect Ronald Reagan president.

WORLD TIMELINE

1976 Argentinian president Isabel Martinez de Peron is arrested on charges of corruption and is replaced by Lieutenant General Jorge Rafael Videla.

1977 Fossils of single-celled organisms that are 3.4 billion years old are found in Africa. Scientists call these the earliest Earth life forms.
■ In a historic speech, Egyptian President Anwar el-Sadat officially recognizes Israel and calls for peace. He adds, however, that Israel must withdraw its troops from occupied Arab lands and recognize Palestinian rights.

1978 Former Italian prime minister Aldo Moro is kidnapped by Communist terrorists demanding the release of their comrades in prison. The Italian government refuses to meet their demands, and Moro is killed.
■ Pope John Paul I dies and is succeeded by Polish-born Pope John Paul II.

1979 In Great Britain's general election, Margaret Thatcher becomes the first woman elected prime minister of that country.
■ President Somoza of Nicaragua is overthrown by Sandinista rebels.
■ After 15 years of exile, Ayatollah Khomeini returns to Iran, where he leads an Islamic Revolution.

Above: Ayatollah Khomeini

1980 An attempt to rescue the hostages in Iran has disastrous results, with eight Americans dead and the hostages still in Iranian hands.
■ Ronald Reagan defeats Jimmy Carter in a landslide victory.

1981 IBM, or International Business Machines, introduces its personal computer, declaring that the new machine will change the workplace forever.
■ American and French doctors identify a new and deadly virus. They call it Acquired Immune Deficiency Syndrome, or AIDS.
■ Iran releases the American hostages, who return to a joyous welcome in the United States.

1982 The Vietnam Veterans Memorial is dedicated in Washington, D.C. Designed by Maya Lin, a

Above: A close-up of the Vietnam War Memorial

22-year-old architecture student, the memorial quickly becomes the most visited in Washington.

1983 A militant terrorist group, the Islamic Jihad, bombs the U.S. embassy in Beirut. Six months later, U.S. Marine barracks are also bombed. President Reagan announces that the United States will not be intimidated, and will not be forced into leaving Lebanon.
■ President Reagan declares Martin Luther King Jr.'s birthday a national holiday.

1984 Michael Jackson's *Thriller* becomes the best-selling record album in history.
■ The Democratic challenger for the presidency, Walter F. Mondale, chooses Geraldine Ferraro as his running mate. She is the first woman in American history to become a major party's nominee for the vice presidency.

1980 Britain's colony of Rhodesia is granted independence at midnight on April 18th and becomes the nation of Zimbabwe.

1981 Prince Charles of Great Britain and Lady Diana Spencer are married at St. Paul's Cathedral. They divorce in 1996.
■ Arab terrorists attack a Viennese synagogue in protest against the Israeli occupation of Palestinian lands.

1982 Argentinian forces invade the British-governed Falkland Islands, causing Britain to mobilize troops and launch a counterattack. The British win the short war easily.

■ Beirut, Lebanon, erupts in warfare as Israeli troops attempt to forcibly evict PLO (Palestinian Liberation Organization) members from the area.

1983 A Korean jetliner is shot down by Soviet planes off the coast of Siberia. The Soviets claim the jetliner was a U.S. spyplane flying in restricted airspace.

1984 In the first presidential elections since 1977, El Salvadorans fight through gunfire from antigovernment rebel troops in an attempt to cast their ballots.
■ Bishop Desmond Tutu of South Africa is awarded the Nobel Peace Prize for his nonviolent campaign to end apartheid.

1985 After the death of Soviet leader Konstantin Chernenko, Mikhail Gorbachev comes to power. He calls for immediate arms reduction and economic reform.

Above: Mikhail Gorbachev and Ronald Reagan

AMERICAN TIMELINE

1985 After 16 years of searching, diver Mel Fisher and his crew discover the shipwreck of the Spanish galleon *Nuestra Señora de Atocha,* which sank off the coast of Florida in 1622.

1986 Seventy-three seconds after a perfect takeoff, the space shuttle *Challenger* explodes in midair, to the shock of NASA officials and the nation.

■ In retaliation for the role of Libyan terrorists in the bombing of a Berlin disco, U.S. warplanes bomb Libya. To avoid further attacks, President Reagan warns Libya "to end its pursuit of terror for political goals."

■ The U.S. airplane *Voyager* makes the first nonstop trip around the world without refueling. The flight takes nine days.

1987 Colonel Oliver North testifies in Congress on his role in selling U.S. arms to Iran, which violates federal and international law. The White House remains silent on the issue, despite the investigating committees' final conclusion that the fault in the Iran-Contra affair lies with the president.

1988 Reagan's vice president, George Bush, is elected president.

1989 U.S. forces enter Panama and capture President Manuel Noriega, who is brought to the United States on drug-trafficking charges.

1990 In response to Iraqi President Saddam Hussein's invasion of Kuwait, President Bush helps to organize UN forces against Iraq. Hussein is quickly driven from Kuwait.

Above: President George Bush

1991 The Senate Judiciary Committee confirms Supreme Court nominee Clarence Thomas, despite charges of sexual harrassment brought by law professor Anita Hill.

1992 Riots erupt in Los Angeles after the acquittal of four police

WORLD TIMELINE

Above: President Corazon Aquino

1986 Corazon Aquino, widow of Benigno Aquino, is elected president of the Philippines, defeating Ferdinand Marcos, who many believe was responsible for the assassination of her husband and other Marcos political opponents.

1987 Ronald Reagan and Mikhail Gorbachev sign the Intermediate Nuclear Forces (or INF) Treaty, beginning nuclear arms reduction.

1988 In a speech at the United Nations, Russian leader Gorbachev declares an end to 40 years of the Cold War.

1989 Communist rule slowly crumbles in the Eastern European

countries and the Berlin Wall comes down.

1990 Military revolutionaries launch an unsuccessful attempt to overthrow Gorbachev. The Soviet Union crumbles into factions following the attack.

1991 An outbreak of cholera devastates the population of Peru and quickly spreads to Ecuador and Colombia.

1992 A militia from the Yugoslav republic of Serbia launches a military campaign to seize Bosnia-Herzegovina. In a series of "ethnic cleansings," they wipe out entire villages of Muslims and Croats.

officers in the beating of African-American Rodney King.

■ Democrat Bill Clinton defeats President Bush and independent candidate H. Ross Perot to become the first Democrat to hold the office since 1980.

Above: Senator Ben Nighthorse-Campbell

■ Ben Nighthorse-Campbell of Colorado is elected to the U.S. Senate. He is the first Native American elected to that body.

1993 Islamic militants bomb New York's World Trade Center. Although the building suffers severe damage to its underground parking garage, it remains standing.
■ A heavily armed religious cult's compound in Waco, Texas, is stormed by FBI agents. Cult leader David Koresh and 80 of his followers die when federal agents rush the compound, leading Koresh and his followers to burn the compound to the ground rather than surrender.
■ The North American Free Trade Agreement (NAFTA) is signed. It eliminates all trade barriers and tariffs between the United States, Mexico, and Canada over a 15-year period.

1994 Astronomers find proof of the existence of planets outside Earth's solar system

1995 A federal government building in Oklahoma City is bombed, killing over 160 innocent men, women, and children. A former soldier with a hatred for the federal government is arrested. He is convicted of the crime two years later.

1996 An unexplained explosion destroys TWA Flight 800 over Long Island, New York, killing all aboard.
■ Bill Clinton is elected to a second term as president, defeating longtime senator Bob Dole.

1997 President Clinton signs a bill that begins a major overhaul of the federal welfare system.

1993 Czechoslovakia splits into two, with the urban Czech Republic in the west and the rural Republic of Slovakia in the east.
■ Queen Elizabeth II celebrates her 40th year on the throne of England.

1994 Nelson Mandela, imprisoned by the white South African government for over 30 years, comes to power in the first South African election open to all races.
■ The completion of a tunnel that runs underneath the English Channel allows trains to travel from France to England in a mere 35 minutes.

Above: Queen Elizabeth II of England

■ Despite the protective presence of UN forces, Bosnian Serbs attack the Muslim-occupied Bihać and slaughter many civilians.

1996 In the second democratic elections in Russia, President Boris Yeltsin is reelected.

1997 The NATO alliance expands to include the former Soviet-bloc nations of Poland, the Czech Republic, and Hungary.
■ Diana, Princess of Wales, and former wife of Prince Charles, Prince of Wales and heir to the British throne, is killed in an automobile accident.

THE FIFTY STATES

Listed below is information on each of the fifty states, in order of the state's admission to the Union.

Delaware

Date of Admission: 1787
Capital: Dover
Population (1995): 717,197
Source of the Name: Named after Sir Thomas West, Lord de la Warr, the Virginia Company's first governor.

Pennsylvania

Date of Admission: 1787
Capital: Harrisburg
Population (1995): 12,071,842
Source of the Name: King Charles II named the land after William Penn, (*sylvania* is Latin for woods, and thus Pennsylvania means "Penn's woods.")

New Jersey

Date of Admission: 1787
Capital: Trenton
Population (1995): 7,945,298
Source of the Name: Named by Sir John Berkeley and Sir George Carteret after England's Isle of Jersey.

Georgia

Date of Admission: 1788
Capital: Atlanta
Population (1995): 7,200,882
Source of the Name: James Oglethorpe named the state after King George II of England.

Connecticut

Date of Admission: 1788
Capital: Hartford
Population (1995): 3,274,662
Source of the Name: The name is derived from the Algonquin word *quinnehtukqut*, which means "long river place."

Massachusetts

Date of Admission: 1788
Capital: Boston
Population (1995): 6,073,550
Source of the Name: The state is named after the Massachusetts Indian tribe; the tribe's name means "large hill place."

Maryland

Date of Admission: 1788
Capital: Annapolis
Population (1995): 5,042,438
Source of the Name: Named after Queen Henrietta Maria, the wife of Charles I of England.

South Carolina

Date of Admission: 1788
Capital: Columbia
Population (1995): 3,673,287
Source of the Name: The Carolinas were originally named the Province of Carolana by King Charles I of England; *Carolus* is the Latin name for Charles.

New Hampshire

Date of Admission: 1788
Capital: Concord
Population (1995): 1,148,253
Source of the Name: Captain John Mason named the area after the central English county of Hampshire, a place he spent much of his youth.

Virginia

Date of Admission: 1788
Capital: Richmond
Population (1995): 6,618,358
Source of the Name: Named by Sir Walter Raleigh in honor of Queen Elizabeth, the Virgin Queen of England.

New York

Date of Admission: 1788
Capital: Albany
Population (1995): 18,136,081
Source of the Name: Named after England's Duke of York and Albany, the brother of King Charles II.

North Carolina

Date of Admission: 1789
Capital: Raleigh
Population (1995): 7,195,138
Source of the Name: The Carolinas were originally named the Province of Carolana by King Charles I of England; *Carolus* is the Latin name for Charles.

Rhode Island

Date of Admission: 1790
Capital: Providence
Population (1995): 989,794
Source of the Name: Dutch explorer Adrian Block named the state "Roodt Eylandt" in his native tongue, which means "red island." Under English rule the name was anglicized to Rhode Island.

Vermont

Date of Admission: 1791
Capital: Montpelier
Population (1995): 584,771
Source of the Name: Named from the French words *vert,* which means green, and *mont,* which means mountain, by Samuel de Champlain.

Kentucky

Date of Admission: 1792
Capital: Frankfort
Population (1995): 3,860,219
Source of the Name: The state's name is a Wyandot word meaning "plains."

Tennessee

Date of Admission: 1796
Capital: Nashville
Population (1995): 5,256,051
Source of the Name: Tanasi was the name of Cherokee villages on the Little Tennessee River.

Ohio

Date of Admission: 1803
Capital: Columbus
Population (1995): 11,150,506
Source of the Name: The Iroquois word for "fine or good river."

Louisiana

Date of Admission: 1812
Capital: Baton Rouge
Population (1995): 4,342,334
Source of the Name: Named after King Louis XIV of France by the explorer Sieur de La Salle.

Indiana

Date of Admission: 1816
Capital: Indianapolis
Population (1995): 5,803,471
Source of the Name: The name means "land of the Indians."

Mississippi

Date of Admission: 1817
Capital: Jackson
Population (1995): 2,697,243
Source of the Name: Probably derived from the Chippewa words *mici zibi,* which means "great river."

Illinois

Date of Admission: 1818
Capital: Springfield
Population (1995): 11,829,940
Source of the Name: The name is French for *Illini,* an Algonquin word meaning "men" or "warriors."

Alabama

Date of Admission: 1819
Capital: Montgomery
Population (1995): 4,252,982
Source of the Name: The state received its name from the river, which in turn was named after the Indian tribe that settled on its banks.

Maine

Date of Admission: 1820
Capital: Augusta
Population (1995): 1,241,382
Source of the Name: The origin of this state's name comes either from the French province of Mayne or from the common term among early explorers to describe a mainland (distinct from the many coastal islands).

Missouri

Date of Admission: 1821
Capital: Jefferson City
Population (1995): 2,697,243
Source of the Name: The name is an Algonquin Indian word meaning "river of the big canoes."

Arkansas

Date of Admission: 1836
Capital: Little Rock
Population (1995): 2,483,769
Source of the Name: Arkansas is the French name for Quapaw (a Sioux people), which means "downstream people."

Michigan

Date of Admission: 1837
Capital: Lansing
Population (1995): 9,549,353
Source of the Name: European explorers named Lake Michigan after the Chippewa word *majigan,* which means "clearing"; the state, in turn, was named after the lake.

THE FIFTY STATES

Florida

Date of Admission: 1845
Capital: Tallahassee
Population (1995): 14,165,570
Source of the Name: Ponce de Leon named the state on Easter Sunday in 1513, in honor of Pascua Florida, the Spanish Feast of the Flowers at Eastertime.

Texas

Date of Admission: 1845
Capital: Austin
Population (1995): 18,723,991
Source of the Name: The Spanish used the Caddo word *teysha,* which means "friends" or "allies," to refer to the friendly tribes throughout Louisiana, Oklahoma, and Texas. The tribes of the Caddo Confederacy in eastern Texas and Louisiana came to be called "the kingdom of Texas."

Iowa

Date of Admission: 1846
Capital: Des Moines
Population (1995): 2,841,764
Source of the Name: The state was named after the Iowa River, which in turn was named after the Iowa Indians. The tribal name "Ayuxwa" means "one who puts to sleep."

Wisconsin

Date of Admission: 1848
Capital: Madison
Population (1995): 5,122,871
Source of the Name: The state name is derived from the Chippewa term *Ouisconsin,* which means "grassy place."

California

Date of Admission: 1850
Capital: Sacramento
Population (1995): 31,589,153
Source of the Name: Named by Spanish conquistadors after an imaginary island in a Spanish romance novel, *Las Sergas de Esplandian,* written by Garcia Ordonez de Montalvo in 1510.

Minnesota

Date of Admission: 1858
Capital: St. Paul
Population (1995): 4,609,548
Source of the Name: The word "Minnesota" was derived from the Dakota word *mnishota,* which means "cloudy water"; the state was named after the Minnesota River.

Oregon

Date of Admission: 1859
Capital: Salem
Population (1995): 3,140,585
Source of the Name: The origin of the name "Oregon" is unclear. One possibility is that it may have come from the French Canadian word *ouragan,* which means "storm" or "hurricane." It may have also come from the Spanish word *orégano,* or wild sage, which grows abundantly in eastern Oregon.

Kansas

Date of Admission: 1861
Capital: Topeka
Population (1995): 2,565,328
Source of the Name: The name means "south wind people" in the Sioux language.

West Virginia

Date of Admission: 1863
Capital: Charleston
Population (1995): 1,828,140
Source of the Name: The state became known as West Virginia in 1863 when western counties of Virginia refused to secede from the United States.

Nevada

Date of Admission: 1864
Capital: Carson City
Population (1995): 1,530,108
Source of the Name: Nevada is a Spanish word meaning "snow-clad." Early sailors saw mountains in California from the sea and named them Sierra Nevada, or "snowy range." The state's name is a shortened version of Sierra Nevada.

Nebraska

Date of Admission: 1867
Capital: Lincoln
Population (1995): 1,637,112
Source of the Name: Nebraska is named after the Platte River, which was called *Nibôápka,* or "broad river," by the Omaha Indians.

Colorado

Date of Admission: 1876
Capital: Denver
Population (1995): 3,746,585
Source of the Name: Colorado is the Spanish word for red, which was first applied to the color of the Colorado River.

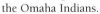

North Dakota

Date of Admission: 1889
Capital: Bismarck
Population (1995): 641,367
Source of the Name: Dakota is a Sioux word meaning "friends" or "allies." North and South Dakota were separated in 1889.

South Dakota

Date of Admission: 1889
Capital: Pierre
Population (1995): 729,034
Source of the Name: Dakota is a Sioux word meaning "friends" or "allies." North and South Dakota were separated in 1889.

Montana

Date of Admission: 1889
Capital: Helena
Population (1995): 870,281
Source of the Name: Derived from the Latin word *montanus*, which means "mountainous."

Washington

Date of Admission: 1889
Capital: Olympia
Population (1995): 5,430,940
Source of the Name:
Named in honor of George Washington.

Idaho

Date of Admission: 1890
Capital: Boise
Population (1995): 1,163,261
Source of the Name: "Idaho" is said to be a coined term meaning "gem of the mountains." Another theory says that the name is the Kiowa Apache term for the Comanche tribe.

Wyoming

Date of Admission: 1890
Capital: Cheyenne
Population (1995): 480,184
Source of the Name: Derived from an Algonquin word *mecheweamiing*, meaning "at the big flats."

Utah

Date of Admission: 1896
Capital: Salt Lake City
Population (1995): 1,951,408
Source of the Name: The White Mountain Apache referred to the Navajo as *Yuttahih*, or "one that is

higher up." Europeans thought that they were referring to the Utes, who lived farther up the mountains. The land of the Utes became Utah.

Oklahoma

Date of Admission: 1907
Capital: Oklahoma City
Population (1995): 3,277,687
Source of the Name: A combination of two Choctaw words, *ukla*, or person, and *humá*, or red, the name Oklahoma means "red person."

New Mexico

Date of Admission: 1912
Capital: Santa Fe
Population (1995): 1,685,401
Source of the Name: The land north and west of the Rio Grande was called "Nuevo Mexico" by Fray Jacinto de San Francisco in 1561 in the hopes that this area would be as treasure-rich as Mexico.

Arizona

Date of Admission: 1912
Capital: Phoenix
Population (1995): 2,483,769
Source of the Name: The name is probably derived from *Aleh-zon*, which means "little spring" in the Pima language. Another theory is that the name sprang from the Aztec word *arizuma*, meaning "silver-bearing."

Alaska

Date of Admission: 1959
Capital: Juneau
Population (1995): 603,617
Source of the Name: The name is taken directly from the Aleut word *aláxsxaq*, meaning "the object toward which the action of the sea is directed."

Hawaii

Date of Admission: 1959
Capital: Honolulu
Population (1995): 1,186,815
Source of the Name: There are two theories on the origin of the name Hawaii: The first suggests that the state was named after the traditional discoverer of the islands, Hawaii Loa; the second, that Hawaii comes from the words *hawa*, meaning traditional homeland, and *-ii*, which means both small and raging (which may refer to Hawaii's volcanoes).

PRESIDENTS OF THE UNITED STATES

George Washington

Birthplace: Virginia
Term: 1789–97
Highlights: Washington was unanimously elected the country's first president in 1789 on the strength of his heroic leadership of the Continental Army during the Revolutionary War. In 1791, he signed a bill creating the first Bank of the United States. He was easily reelected in 1792. In 1794, he led 15,000 troops in putting down the Whiskey Rebellion, an uprising of Pennsylvania grain farmers who refused the pay the federal tax on the manufacture of whiskey. Although offered a chance to run for a third term as president, he declined and retired to his Mount Vernon, Virginia, in 1797.
Interesting Facts: Contrary to popular myth, George Washington did not have wooden teeth, but rather a set of poorly fitting silver teeth. In 1799, during a ride around his estate in the snow and rain, Washington contracted laryngitis. In an effort to cure him, doctors bled him, a common treatment at the time; as a result, he died on December 14, 1799, of what had begun as a minor illness.

John Adams

Birthplace: Massachusetts
Term: 1797–1801
Highlights: Vice president during the Washington administration, John Adams became president in 1797, defeating Thomas Jefferson by three electoral votes. The next year, Adams exposed what came to be known as the XYZ Affair, in which France tried to make the United States pay $10 million to conduct diplomatic negotiations. However, Adams became very unpopular in 1798 for supporting the Alien and Sedition Acts, which restricted the rights of citizens to criticize the government. He was defeated by Jefferson in the 1800 election.
Interesting Fact: John Adams and Thomas Jefferson, political rivals and close friends in their old age, both died on July 4, 1826, the 50th anniversary of the signing of the Declaration of Independence.

Thomas Jefferson

Birthplace: Virginia
Term: 1801–09
Highlights: Thomas Jefferson, author of the Declaration of Independence, became president in 1801. Although Jefferson and Aaron Burr tied in the 1800 presidential election, the House of Representatives ultimately elected Jefferson president and Burr vice president. In 1803, Jefferson purchased the 800,000-square-mile Louisiana Territory from France for $14.5 million, doubling the size of the United States. A year later, he ordered Meriwether Lewis and William Clark to explore the newly acquired land. Jefferson was reelected for a second term in 1804. Although he was a slave owner himself, he asked Congress to ban the African slave trade in 1806. Congress agreed the next year, but the illegal slave trade continued. In response to British and French attacks on American merchant ships, Jefferson also asked Congress to pass the Embargo and Non-Importation Acts in 1807, which forbade all foreign trade in or out of U.S. ports. As a result, the country fell into an economic depression. At Jefferson's urging, Congress passed the Non-Intercourse Act in 1809, which permitted U.S. ships to trade with all countries except England and France.
Interesting Facts: Jefferson was a skillful architect, violinist, inven-

tor, philosopher, and an expert on agriculture. He was also the founder of the University of Virginia and designed its original buildings. Following Thomas Jefferson's first inauguration, a minister from Massachusetts presented to Jefferson a 1,600-pound piece of cheese.

James Madison

Birthplace: Virginia
Term: 1809–17
Highlights: Author of much of the U.S. Constitution, James Madison was inaugurated as president in 1809. The next year, he bought from Spain part of western Florida, which later became Alabama and Mississippi. In 1812, Madison asked Congress to declare war on Britain. Inaugurated for a second term in 1813, Madison was forced to flee Washington, D.C., that same year when the British set fire to the city. In 1814, he signed the Treaty of Ghent that ended the War of 1812.
Interesting Fact: James Madison helped found the University of Virginia, of which he became rector in 1826.

James Monroe

Birthplace: Virginia
Term: 1817–25
Highlights: James Monroe was elected president in 1816, ushering in what one newspaper man called the "Era of Good Feelings." In 1819 Monroe negotiated the Adams-Onis Treaty with Spain, which gave Florida to the United States. Monroe was inaugurated for a second term in 1821. He supported the anti-slavery position that led to the Missouri Compromise of 1820. His biggest achievement as president came in 1823 with the presentation of the Monroe Doctrine to Congress, which stated that countries in the Western Hemisphere would no longer be "considered as subjects for future colonization by any European powers."
Interesting Facts: The capital of the African country of Liberia, established as a homeland for African-Americans by whites in the 1830s, was named Monrovia after Monroe. In 1794, Monroe rescued statesman Thomas Paine from a French prison. At the end of his life, financial problems forced Monroe to move to New York City to live with his daughter.

John Quincy Adams

Birthplace: Massachusetts
Term: 1825–29
Highlights: John Quincy Adams was elected president in 1824 by the House of Representatives when none of the candidates won a majority vote. As president, he favored a more active role for the federal government; as a result Adams was an unpopular president and lost his bid for reelection in 1828.
Interesting Facts: John Quincy Adams was the only son of a president to also become president. He spoke seven languages and helped establish the Smithsonian Institution in Washington, D.C.

Andrew Jackson

Birthplace: Tennessee
Term: 1829–37
Highlights: In 1830, Jackson signed the Indian Removal Act, which called for the relocation of Native Americans from the Southeastern states to land in Oklahoma. He was reelected in 1832. In 1833, he removed all government funds from the Bank of the United States, and placed them in state, or "pet," banks around the country. Jackson also authorized federal troops to enforce the "Tariff of Abominations," which put high taxes on goods manufactured overseas. In 1835, Richard Lawrence attempted to assassinate the president but Jackson was unharmed. In one of his last presidential acts, Jackson recognized the Republic of Texas as an independent nation in 1837.
Interesting Facts: Jackson was nicknamed "Old Hickory" because his toughness reminded many of a hickory tree's hard wood. A virtual riot broke out during a celebration in the White House after Jackson's first inauguration. He also suffered from tuberculosis and carried three bullets—from three different fights—in his body for much of his life.

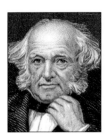

Martin Van Buren

Birthplace: New York
Term: 1837–41
Highlights: The Panic of 1837, caused by over-investment in public works projects, began an economic depression at the start of Van Buren's presidency that caused his popularity to quickly fall. His major accomplishment was to remove government funds from state banks and to redeposit them in federal banks. He was defeated in his bid for reelection.
Interesting Fact: After his defeat in the 1840 election, Van Buren tried to win the Democratic presidential nominations again in both 1844 and 1848; he was defeated both times.

William Henry Harrison

Birthplace: Virginia
Term: 1841
Highlights: A military hero during the War of 1812, Harrison died from pneumonia after only a month in office. Despite cold weather in Washington on the day of his inauguration, Harrison refused to wear a coat. He became sick afterward, and never recovered.
Interesting Fact: Harrison still holds the record for the longest inaugural address: 8,500 words and two hours long.

John Tyler

Birthplace: Virginia
Term: 1841–45
Highlights: Vice president under Harrison, Tyler became president in 1841 after Harrison's death. Soon after, Tyler vetoed a bank bill, and all but one member of his cabinet resigned. In 1842, Tyler signed the Webster-Ashburton Treaty, which established the boundary between northern Maine and Canada. Although Tyler supported a treaty of annexation with Texas, antislavery senators feared Texas would be admitted as a slave state.
Interesting Facts: Because he was never elected president himself, John Tyler's critics called him "His Accidency." Tyler had fifteen children, more than any other president in history.

James Knox Polk

Birthplace: North Carolina
Term: 1845–49
Highlights: With Polk's support, Congress declared war on Mexico in 1846. The war ended in 1848 with the signing of the Treaty of Guadeloupe Hidalgo, which gave the United States California and much of the Southwest. Polk also signed a treaty with Great Britain in 1846 settling the boundary of the Oregon Country at the 49th parallel.
Interesting Fact: Polk died only a few weeks after leaving office.

Zachary Taylor

Birthplace: Virginia
Term: 1849–50
Highlights: Although he was a slave owner, Taylor worked to admit California as a free state. He also worked to resume the spoils system, by which government jobs were given out to supporters and friends. Sixteen months after taking office, he fell ill and died.
Interesting Facts: Before becoming president, Taylor had been a military hero, serving in the War of 1812, Black Hawk's War, and the Mexican War. Although he was elected the nation's 12th president, Taylor had no political experience and had never even voted before.

Millard Fillmore

Birthplace: New York
Term: 1850–53
Highlights: Following Taylor's death, Vice President Millard Fillmore became president. His first act as president was to sign the Compromise of 1850, which admitted California as a free state, and New Mexico and Utah as states where the slavery issue was undecided. In addition, the compromise also outlawed the slave trade in Washington, D.C., and strengthened the Fugitive Slave Law. These policies angered both expansionists and slaveholders, and he was unsuccessful in his bid for reelection.
Interesting Fact: Fillmore helped to found both the University of Buffalo and the Buffalo Historical Society in Buffalo, New York.

Franklin Pierce

Birthplace: New Hampshire
Term: 1853–57
Highlights: Nine months after taking office, Pierce approved the "Gadsden Purchase," the acquisition of 30,000 square miles of land (the present-day southern borders of New Mexico and Arizona) from Mexico. Although against slavery, Pierce supported the Kansas-Nebraska Act in 1854, which allowed settlers in these territories to decide the slavery issue. This support made him wildly unpopular in the North. He was not renominated by the Democratic Party for the next presidential election.
Interesting Fact: Pierce and Nathaniel Hawthorne, the author of *The Scarlet Letter,* were classmates at Bowdoin College in Brunswick, Maine. They became close friends and Hawthorne wrote Pierce's campaign biography.

James Buchanan

Birthplace: Pennsylvania
Term: 1857–61
Highlights: Buchanan was inaugurated during a time when the slavery issue was tearing the nation apart. The 1857 *Dred Scott* Supreme Court decision, which protected slavery throughout the country, as well as violence between pro- and anti-slavery groups in Kansas, caused Buchanan to lose support from the North. He did not seek reelection for a second term.
Interesting Fact: Buchanan was the first and only bachelor president in the White House.

Abraham Lincoln

Birthplace: Illinois
Term: 1861–65
Highlights: When Lincoln was inaugurated in 1861, seven states had already seceded from the Union and four others soon followed. Together they formed the Confederate States of America. When the Confederates began shelling Fort Sumter in April 1861, the Civil War began. Late in 1862, Lincoln issued the Emancipation Proclamation, which freed the slaves in the Confederacy. It became law on January 1, 1863. In November of that year, Lincoln gave his famous Gettysburg Address. He was inaugurated for a second term in March 1865, and on April 9 the Confederate Army surrendered, ending the Civil War. Five days later, Lincoln was assassinated.
Interesting Fact: Lincoln considered the Gettysburg Address a "flat failure."

Andrew Johnson

Birthplace: North Carolina
Term: 1865–69
Highlights: Soon after Johnson's inauguration, he outlined his Reconstruction plan. He pardoned all Confederates who agreed to pledge loyalty to the United States. In April 1866, Johnson vetoed the Civil Rights Act of 1866, which guaranteed U.S. citizenship to African-Americans. Leaders in Congress, who were hostile toward the South, overrode his veto. The next year, Congress passed the two Reconstruction Acts, which placed the former Confederacy under military rule and made strict rules for the reentrance of ex-Confederate states back into the Union. Congress also passed the Tenure of Office Act, which prohibited the president from firing a cabinet member without Senate approval. In August 1867, Johnson ignored this law and fired Secretary of War Edwin Stanton. The House of Representatives voted to impeach him, but he was acquitted by one vote. He was not renominated for the 1868 election.
Interesting Facts: Beginning when he was twelve years old, Johnson served as an apprentice to a tailor in exchange for room and board. His wife taught him to read and write.

Ulysses Simpson Grant

Birthplace: Ohio
Term: 1869–77
Highlights: Although Grant's first term began with the financial disaster nicknamed "Black Friday," he went on to establish the Civil Service Commission, passed the Ku Klux Klan Acts, which led to the arrest of hundreds of Klan members, and oversaw the signing of the Treaty of Washington, which led to a $15 million payment by Britain to the United States for shipping losses caused by British-built Confederate ships. Grant's second term, however, was marred by repeated scandals including the 1872 Crédit Mobilier scandal, the "Whiskey Ring" scandal in 1875, and corruption in both the Treasury Department and the Indian Service. Although Grant was not directly involved in these scandals, he was not nominated for a third presidential term.
Interesting Facts: Grant graduated near the bottom of his class at West Point. He was also tone-deaf and had difficulty keeping step when his company at West Point marched to music.

Rutherford Birchard Hayes

Birthplace: Ohio
Term: 1877–81
Highlights: Although more people voted for Hayes's opponent Samuel J. Tilden, a dispute in the Electoral College results led to an election compromise following the 1876 election. Hayes was given the presidency in exchange for the removal of federal troops from the South. In 1877, Hayes used federal force to stop a nationwide railroad strike, and he vetoed a bill meant to limit Chinese immigration in 1879. He also advocated the repeal of the Tenure of Office Act and proposed civil service reforms. He did not run for reelection.
Interesting Fact: Hayes was the first president to use a telephone in the White House.

James Abram Garfield

Birthplace: Ohio
Term: 1881
Highlights: Soon after he was inaugurated in 1881, Garfield ordered the secretary of the treasury to pay off all money owed by the government in the form of U.S. bonds in order to lower the national debt. In July 1881, Garfield was seriously wounded in an assassination attempt and died eighty days later.
Interesting Fact: Garfield eventually died not of his gunshot wound, but rather from blood poisoning brought on by unsterile instruments used to treat the wound.

Chester Alan Arthur

Birthplace: New York
Term: 1881–85
Highlights: Following Garfield's assassination, Arthur became president. He began his term by authorizing the construction of four new armor-plated warships. Although Arthur vetoed an 1882 act that would have forbidden Chinese laborers from entering the United States for twenty years, Congress passed the Chinese Exclusion Act, which prohibited entrance for ten years. In 1883 Arthur signed the Pendleton Civil Service Act, which distributed civil service jobs on the basis of ability rather than as political favors. This was not popular with Democratic party leaders, and he was defeated for renomination in 1884.

Interesting Facts: When Arthur became president he had twenty-four wagonloads of items removed from the White House, including a pair of Lincoln's pants, one of John Quincy Adams's hats, and an old suitcase belonging to Abigail Adams. Arthur prided himself on dressing well. He owned eighty pairs of pants.

Grover Cleveland

Birthplace: New Jersey
Terms: 1885–89; 1893–97
Highlights: During his first term, Cleveland established a special committee to oversee labor disputes. He supported the Presidential Succession Act, which said that the secretary of state would become president if the president and vice president died in office. He lowered tariffs on imported goods and expanded the civil service. He was defeated by Benjamin Harrison in the 1888 election, but was reelected again in 1892. Cleveland's second term was hurt by an economic depression. In 1893, five major railroads went bankrupt. In 1894 he sent federal troops to the Midwest to disband the Pullman strike.
Interesting Fact: Cleveland was the only president elected to two nonconsecutive terms.

Benjamin Harrison

Birthplace: Ohio
Term: 1889–93
Highlights: Although Grover Cleveland won the popular vote in the 1888 election, he lost to Benjamin Harrison in the Electoral College. In 1890, Harrison urged Congress to pass the Dependent and Disability Act, which provided pensions to veterans, regardless of the cause of their disability. Two years later, he opened 3 million acres of Native American land in Oklahoma to white settlers.
Interesting Facts: Harrison was the only grandson of a president (William Henry Harrison) to also become president. He was also the first president to use electric light in the White House.

William McKinley

Birthplace: Ohio
Term: 1897–1901
Highlights: McKinley won the 1896 election by more than a million popular votes. In 1898, on McKinley's recommendation, Congress annexed Hawaii. That same year, the Spanish-American War began. The Treaty of Paris ended the conflict in 1899. Spain surrendered to the United States the Philippines, Puerto Rico, and Guam. McKinley was elected for a second term in 1900, but was shot and killed in Buffalo, New York, in 1901.
Interesting Facts: During the Civil War, McKinley served under future U.S. President Rutherford B. Hayes. McKinley also always wore a red carnation in his lapel for good luck.

Theodore Roosevelt

Birthplace: New York
Term: 1901–09
Highlights: Vice President Roosevelt became president after William McKinley's assassination in 1901. He spent his first term fighting business trusts and political corruption. In 1902, he sided with striking miners and ordered coal mine owners to negotiate a deal.

He easily won reelection in 1904. That year, he announced the Roosevelt Corollary, an extension of the Monroe Doctrine, which stated that the United States had the right to interfere in Latin American affairs to maintain peace in the region. In 1906, he helped pass the Pure Food and Drug Act and was awarded the Nobel Peace Prize for helping end a war between Russia and Japan. He also authorized the military occupation of Cuba and went to Panama to oversee the construction of the Panama Canal. He decided not to run again in 1908, but did run as a leader of the Progressive Party in 1912.
Interesting Facts: Roosevelt was the first president to travel abroad while in office. He loved the outdoors and helped enlarge the national park system. The "Teddy Bear" was named in his honor.

William Howard Taft

Birthplace: Ohio
Term: 1909–13
Highlights: During his presidency, Taft tried to carry on Roosevelt's antitrust policies and established the Department of Labor. In 1909 he was criticized for his support of the Payne-Aldrich Tariff Act, which set high taxes on imported goods and primarily helped big business. In 1913, under the Taft administration, Congress passed both the Sixteenth and Seventeenth Amendments, which made income tax constitutional and put the power of electing senators in the hands of the people, respectively. He was defeated in a four-way presidential race in 1912.
Interesting Facts: Taft was the heaviest president in history, weighing in at 330 pounds; he had to have a special bathtub installed in the White House before he moved in. In addition, he was the only ex-president to serve on the Supreme Court.

Woodrow Wilson

Birthplace: Virginia
Term: 1913–21
Highlights: During Wilson's first year in office, Congress passed the Federal Reserve Act, which established a new banking system in the United States. In addition, Wilson went before Congress to propose lowering the tariff on imports. In 1915, he sent troops to Haiti to restore peace and the following year, to Mexico to protect U.S. interests during the Mexican Revolution. Although Wilson had declared neutrality in World War I in 1914, America was forced to join the conflict in 1917. In 1918, Wilson presented his Fourteen Points peace plan to Congress, a summary of conditions for keeping world order. One of them was the establishment of the League of Nations. Although he suffered a stroke in 1919, Wilson remained in office until the end of his second term. He was awarded the Nobel Peace Prize for his peace efforts during World War I.
Interesting Fact: Wilson served as president of Princeton University from 1902 through 1910, when he was elected governor of New Jersey.

Warren Gamaliel Harding

Birthplace: Ohio
Term: 1921–23
Highlights: Harding was elected president in 1920, advocating a "return to normalcy." During his administration, he gave former president Taft a seat on the Supreme Court. He worked to reduce taxes, and signed the Immigration Restriction Act of 1921, which

established the first quotas on U.S. immigration. Harding suffered a stroke in 1923 and died in office. Following his death, numerous scandals, including the Teapot Dome Scandal, became public.
Interesting Fact: Harding was the first president to speak over the radio.

Calvin Coolidge

Birthplace: Vermont
Term: 1923–29
Highlights: During his administration, Coolidge helped pass numerous tax laws favorable to business and the wealthy, and also managed to reduce the national debt. In 1926, Congress passed the Air Commerce Act, which placed commercial aviation under the control of the federal government. He vetoed the McNaury-Haugen bill twice, which would have provided needed relief to American farmers. Coolidge decided not to run for reelection.
Interesting Fact: Coolidge generally slept eleven hours a night and took a two- to four-hour nap in the afternoons.

Herbert Clark Hoover

Birthplace: Iowa
Term: 1929–33
Highlights: Only months after being inaugurated as president, Hoover faced his first major crisis: the 1929 stock market crash. Following the crash, the country plunged into the Great Depression. In 1930, Hoover signed the Smoot-Hawley Tariff, which raised the cost of imports and caused the depression to worsen. Throughout his term, Hoover withheld government aid to the unemployed and homeless, although he did create the Reconstruction Finance Corporation in 1932, which loaned money to banks and businesses. Hoover lost to Roosevelt in the 1932 election.
Interesting Fact: When Hoover was twenty-two years old, he was acclaimed as the highest paid man of his age in the world, making $83,000 per year as a mining engineer in China.

Franklin Delano Roosevelt

Birthplace: New York
Term: 1933–45
Highlights: Following FDR's inauguration in 1933, Congress put his "New Deal" program into effect, establishing numerous agencies such as the Works Progress Administration and the National Recovery Administration. In August 1935, Congress passed the Social Security Act, which guarantees benefits to senior citizens, the unemployed, and mothers with children. During Roosevelt's second term, war broke out across Europe. Although Roosevelt initially vowed neutrality for the United States, he signed the Lend-Lease Act, which promised the Allies money and arms to fight the Germans. In 1940, Roosevelt won a third term. On December 7, 1941, the Japanese bombed Pearl Harbor and Roosevelt declared war on Japan. In response, Germany and Italy declared war on the United States. Roosevelt won an unprecedented fourth term in 1944, but died of a brain hemorrhage on April 12, 1945, before the war was over.
Interesting Facts: Roosevelt was the first president to appoint a woman to his cabinet, and the only man to win election four times. He was also the first to appear on television.

Harry S. Truman

Birthplace: Missouri
Term: 1945–53
Highlights: Less than four months after taking office, Truman dropped the atom bomb on Hiroshima, Japan; three days later, he dropped another on Nagasaki. The Japanese surrendered a week later, marking the end of World War II. In 1947, Truman presented the Truman Doctrine to Congress, which committed U.S. help to any nation struggling against Communism. That same year, Truman also signed the National Security Act, which created the National Security Council and the Central Intelligence Agency. He was also a supporter of both the Marshall Plan and NATO. On the home front, he proposed the "Fair Deal," a continuation of Roosevelt's New Deal, and a guarantee of civil rights for African-Americans. In 1950, the United States entered the Korean War, and Truman's popularity fell. The Twenty-second Amendment was adopted in 1951, barring presidents from seeking a third term in office.
Interesting Facts: Truman was an accomplished pianist and owned a hat store before entering politics. The "S" in his middle initial does not stand for anything.

Dwight David Eisenhower

Birthplace: Texas
Term: 1953–61
Highlights: In 1953, Eisenhower became the first Republican president in twenty-four years. During his two terms in office, he focused on foreign policy: He brought an end to the Korean War, cut the defense budget by $10 billion, even while building up America's nuclear weapons to defend against the Soviet Union, and endorsed treaties with Taiwan and Southeast Asian countries. At home, Eisenhower allocated money to build a 42,000-mile highway system across the country. In 1957, he sent troops to Little Rock, Arkansas, to enforce school desegregation.
Interesting Fact: When Eisenhower's name was mentioned as a possible presidential candidate in 1948, it was revealed that he had never in his life voted; he felt as though it was a soldier's duty to remain above politics.

John Fitzgerald Kennedy

Birthplace: Massachusetts
Term: 1961–63
Highlights: Following Kennedy's inauguration in 1961, he suffered numerous foreign policy disasters: the Bay of Pigs invasion, a plan to topple the Cuban Communist regime; a near-nuclear war with the Soviet Union; and the growth of America's involvement in Vietnam. Nevertheless, he also successfully demanded that the Soviet Union dismantle missile bases in Cuba, showed strong but slow support for civil rights, and greatly expanded medical care for the middle aged. In addition, Kennedy funded a $5 billion space program in an effort to get a man on the Moon by the end of the decade. On November 22, 1963, he was assassinated in Dallas.
Interesting Facts: During World War II, a torpedo boat Kennedy commanded was rammed by a Japanese destroyer. Kennedy seized the life jacket of a wounded crew member between his teeth and tugged him to an island three miles away. He won the Navy and Marine Corps Medal for saving his crew. Kennedy was the youngest man ever elected to the presidency.

Lyndon Baines Johnson

Birthplace: Texas

Term: 1963–69

Highlights: Inaugurated in 1963 following Kennedy's assassination, Johnson quickly waged "war on poverty." He was best known for allocating $1 billion to ten antipoverty programs, including the Job Corps and the Head Start program. He pushed the Civil Rights Act of 1964 and the Voting Rights Act of 1965 through Congress. Reelected in 1964, Johnson set up the Medicare and Medicaid programs and worked to pass environmental and consumer laws. He is often criticized for drawing the United States deeper into the Vietnam War. He decided not to run for reelection in 1968.

Interesting Facts: Johnson worked his way through college as a garbage collector and spent one year teaching before entering politics.

Richard Milhous Nixon

Birthplace: California

Term: 1969–74

Highlights: Following election in 1968, Nixon began to slowly remove troops from Vietnam. In 1972, Nixon became the first U.S. president to visit Communist China; he also traveled to Moscow to sign the Strategic Arms Limitation Treaty (SALT), which reduced tensions between the United States and the Soviet Union. Reelected in 1972 by a large margin, Nixon soon lost support when his role in the Watergate break-in and cover-up was revealed. Faced with impeachment, Nixon resigned the presidency on August 9, 1974.

Interesting Fact: Nixon is the only president to resign from office.

Gerald Rudolph Ford

Birthplace: Michigan

Term: 1974–77

Highlights: Ford was appointed vice president after his predecessor, Spiro Agnew, was forced to resign. He became president when President Nixon also resigned. He began his presidency by granting Nixon a full pardon for any crimes committed during his administration. Ford survived two assassination attempts in one month in 1975. During his term, the country suffered its worst inflation and unemployment rates since the Depression. An oil embargo caused gasoline prices to jump 70 percent. He was not reelected in 1976.

Interesting Facts: Ford was the only president who was never elected to either the presidency or the vice presidency. As a young man, Ford once worked as a male model.

James Earl Carter

Birthplace: Georgia

Term: 1977–81

Highlights: A weak economy, inherited from the Ford administration, hurt Jimmy Carter's popularity. Despite serving as president with a Democratic-controlled Congress, Carter had a poor relationship with party leaders. He tried to start energy conservation programs but was only able to get one minor law passed. He was an invaluable participant in the peace talks between Israel and Egypt that led to the Camp David Accords in September 1978. Following a Soviet invasion of Afghanistan, Carter broke off talks with Soviet leader Leonid Brezhnev, imposed a grain embargo on the Soviets, and ordered the U.S. Olympic team to boycott the 1980 summer Olympics in Moscow. The Iranian hostage crisis in November 1979, during which Carter was unable to secure the release of 53 American prisoners, caused his public image to suffer badly. He was defeated in the 1980 election.

Interesting Facts: Carter was a nuclear physicist and spent some time running his family's peanut farm before entering politics.

Ronald Wilson Reagan

Birthplace: California

Term: 1981–89

Highlights: On his inauguration day, the Iranian hostages were freed. Two months later, John Hinckle Jr. attempted to assassinate Reagan; he was wounded, but quickly recovered. During his first term, he signed the largest tax cut in history in an effort to jump-start the economy, although things did not begin to improve until 1982. Reagan also increased defense spending dramatically, authorized the invasion of Grenada, and gave aid to rebels trying to topple Nicaragua's leftist government. He was reelected in 1984. His administration's reputation was hurt by the Iran-Contra scandal, in which members of his administration secretly sold arms to Iran to gain the release of American hostages. In 1987, Reagan signed a treaty with the Soviet Union in which both countries agreed to destroy nuclear weapons.

Interesting Facts: Reagan was the oldest president ever elected. In addition, he was the only movie actor to become president, and the only president to have been divorced.

George Herbert Walker Bush

Birthplace: Massachusetts

Term: 1989–93

Highlights: During his one term in office, Bush focused primarily on foreign policy. In 1989, he sent troops to Panama to arrest president Manuel Noriega for drug trafficking. The following year, after Iraq invaded neighboring Kuwait, Bush rounded up support and military assistance from a number of other nations, and launched the U.S.-led Operation Desert Storm. The short military action won Bush the highest popularity rating of his term. An economic recession hurt Bush's chances for reelection.

Interesting Facts: Bush earned his pilot's wings at the age of nineteen, making him the youngest pilot in the navy. He won a Distinguished Flying Cross for completing a 1944 World War II mission in an aircraft disabled by enemy fire.

William Jefferson Clinton

Birthplace: Arkansas

Term: 1993–

Highlights: Clinton won a victory over Bush and Perot in 1992. During his first term, he proposed sweeping health-care reforms, which were rejected and helped turn the public against him. He also strongly backed the North American Free Trade Agreement. Although he has concentrated on domestic politics, he has struggled to bring peace between Arabs and Israelis. After his Democratic Party lost control of Congress in 1994, Republicans tried to force Clinton to sign a federal budget that would have slashed spending by forcing a shutdown of the government. When he refused to give in, his popularity rebounded. Since then, he has moved to cooperate with Republicans. In 1996, he signed a bill aimed at reforming the federal welfare system. He also succeeded in passing an anticrime bill, and increased the minimum wage. Having weathered many personal and political scandals, his popularity remains high.

Interesting Fact: In 1963, as a teenager on an American Legion trip from Arkansas to Washington, D.C., Clinton was given an opportunity to shake the hand of then-president Kennedy.

Note: Page numbers in italic refer to illustrations.

A

- Abernathy, Ralph, 227
- abolitionists, 75-76, 77-79, 99
- abortion, 231
- Adams, Abigail, 43, 50
- Adams, John, 39, 43, 51, 53-54, 80, 278
- Adams, John Quincy, 68, 278
- Adams, Sam, 38, 39, 40
- Adams, Samuel Hopkins, 142, 143
- Addams, Jane, 126, 139
- advertising, 122, 161
- Afghanistan, Soviet Union in, 262
- African-Americans
  - abolitionists, 75-76, 78
  - in armed forces, *84*, 93-94, *98*, 116, 197-198, 226
  - in Black Power movement, 230
  - of Harlem Renaissance, 166
  - in labor force, 102, 194
  - in music, 130, 164, 181
  - in Nation of Islam, 226, 229-230
  - and New Deal, 177, 182, *183*
  - northern migration of, 106, 150
  - organizations of, 142, 143, 199-200, 224, 227-228
  - and police brutality, 230, 258-259
  - in politics, 105-106, *107*
  - in race riots, 93, 152, 154, 230, *258*, 259
  - during Reconstruction, 99, 102, 103, 105-106, 107
  - in science, 50
  - segregation of, 107, 198, 224-225
  - separatism, 166-167
  - in sports, *190*
  - violence against, 93, 154, 166
  - voting rights of, 104, 136, 138
  - women, 76, 78, 181, 182
  - writers, 166, 177
  - *See also* civil rights movement, slavery
- Agent Orange, 235
- Agnew, Spiro, 239, 283
- Agricultural Adjustment Act (AAA), 173
- agriculture. *See* farmers and farming
- Agriculture Department, 143
- Aguinaldo, Emilio, 131
- Aid to Families with Dependent Children (AFDC), 261
- Alabama, 87, 104, 275
  - civil rights movement in, 224, 228, *229*, 229
- Alaska, 128, 240, 277
- Aldrin, Edwin "Buzz," *247*
- Alexander II, czar of Russia, 108, 132
- Alexander VI, Pope, 30
- Algonquian, 9, 10
- Ali, Mohammed, 80
- Alien and Sedition Acts, 54, 278
- Allen, Ethan, 40
- Alliance for Progress, 233
- amendments, constitutional, 97, 103, 104, 137, 138, 144, 155, 281, 282
- American Civil Liberties Union (ACLU), 162
- American Federation of Labor (AFL), 123, 145, 177
- American Indian Movement (AIM), 230-231
- American Revolution. *See* Revolutionary War
- Americas
  - discovery of, 8, 10, 13-14
  - migration to, 9
  - Spanish conquest of, 14-15
  - *See also* colonies
- Anasazi, 10-11, *11*
- Anderson, Marian, *181*
- Anderson, Robert, 88, 108
- Anthony, Susan B., 83, 132, *138*
- Anti-Federalists, 51, 53
- Anti-Saloon League, 155
- antitrust laws, 141-142
- antiwar movement, *216*, 236-237
- Apache, 9
- *Apollo* space program, 247, 250
- appeasement policy, 192, *194*
- Aquino, Benigno, 272
- Aquino, Corazon, 272
- Arafat, Yassir, 267, *268*
- Arapaho, 115
- arbitrage, 252
- Aristide, Jean Baptiste, 267
- Arizona, 114, 116, 277, 279
- Arkansas, 87, 104, 227, 275, 283
- armed forces
  - African-Americans in, *84*, 93-94, *98*, 116, 197-198, 226
  - camel corps in, *114*
  - in Civil War, 85, 89-93
  - desegregation of, 226
  - draft, 93, 150
  - in Indian wars, 56-57, 68-69, 116, 117
  - -McCarthy hearings, 222
  - in Mexican War, 72-73, *73*
  - in Operation Desert Storm, *267*, *268*
  - recruitment, *152*, 197
  - in Revolutionary War, 44-47
  - in Spanish-American War, *129*, 131
  - spending on, 256, 282
  - in Vietnam War, 232, *235*, 235-236
  - women in, 197
  - in World War I, 146, *151*, 151, *152*
  - in World War II, *188*, 202-203, 205-209, *209*
  - *See also* navy
- Armstrong, Neil, 247, 248
- Arnold, Benedict, 40
- Arthur, Chester A., 112, 280-281
- Articles of Confederation, 48
- arts
  - beatniks, 223
  - Harlem Renaissance, 166
  - lost generation, 166
  - and WPA, 176-177
- Atahualpa, 15
- atomic bomb, 203, 209, *210*, 211, 219, 222, 282
- Attucks, Crispus, 39
- Austria, 147, 148, 192
- automobile, social impact of, 162-163
- automobile industry, 171, *175*, 177, 257
- Aztecs, 11, 14

B

- Bach, Johann Sebastian, 35
- Bacon, Nathaniel, 21
- Bal, Suleiman, 60
- Baltimore, Lord, 20
- banks and banking
  - consumer borrowing, 162
  - failure of, 169
  - foreclosures, 170
  - and New Deal, 173
  - regulation of, 144
  - savings and loan (S&L) crisis in, 258
  - state, 279
- Bank of the United States, 68, 278, 279
- Bannecker, Benjamin, *50*
- Bao Dai, 233
- Barnum, P. T., *102*
- Bartholdi, Frédéric-Auguste, 126
- Barton, Clara, *90*
- Baruch, Bernard, 150, 174
- baseball, 164, *224*, 225
- Bataan Death March, 202, *209*
- battles
  - Alamo, 71
  - Antietam, 90, *91*
  - Appomattox, 96, 97
  - Bad Axe, 69
  - Belleau Wood, *152*
  - Brandywine Creek, 45
  - Britain, 192-193
  - Buena Vista, 73
  - Bull Run, *88-89*, 89, 90
  - Bunker Hill, 41
  - Concord and Lexington, 39
  - Coral Sea, *203*, 208
  - Dien Bien Phu, 233
  - El Alamein, 204, 205
  - Falling Timbers, 56
  - Front Royal, 94
  - Gettysburg, 85, 92-93, *93*
  - Horseshoe Bend, 68
  - Iwo Jima, 208
  - Lake Erie, 57
  - Leyte Gulf, 208
  - Little Big Horn, 116
  - Long Island, 44
  - Marne, 148, 151
  - Midway, 208
  - Monmouth, *46*
  - Moore's Creek, 41
  - New Orleans, *56-57*, 58-59, 92
  - Okinawa, 208
  - Palo Alto, *73*
  - Peleliu, 208
  - San Jacinto, 71
  - San Juan Hill, *129*, 131
  - Saratoga, 45
  - Seven Days, 90
  - Shiloh, 91
  - Somme, *147*, 149
  - Stalingrad, 205
  - Thames, 58
  - Tippecanoe, 56-57
  - Verdun, 149
  - Vicksburg, 92
  - Wounded Knee, 117, 231
  - Yorktown, *47*
  - *See also* forts
- Bay of Pigs attack, 234
- Bear Flag Republic, *71*, 72
- beatniks, 223
- Beauregard, P. G.T., 88, 94
- Beethoven, Ludwig van, 80
- Bell, Alexander Graham, 111, 120
- Benton, Thomas Hart, *160*
- Benz, Karl, 133
- Berlin Airlift, *220*, 221
- Berlin Wall, *265*
- Bernhardt, Sarah, 134
- Bernstein, Carl, 238
- Bessemer, Henry, 119
- Bethune, Mary McLeod, *182*
- Bienville, Sieur de, 35
- Bill of Rights, 51, 54
- "Billy the Kid," *115*, 116
- Bismarck, Otto von, 109, 134, *146*, 147
- Black Codes, 102
- Black Hawk's War, 68-69
- Black Kettle, 115
- blacklisting, 217
- Black Muslims. *See* Nation of Islam
- Black Panthers, 230
- Blacks. See African-Americans; slavery
- *blitzkrieg*, 192
- Bloomer, Amelia, 138
- Boesky, Ivan, 252
- Boland Amendment, 264
- Bolivar, Simon, 63
- Bolsheviks, 151, 217
- *Bonhomme Richard*, 46
- Bonney, William H. "Billy the Kid", *115*, 116
- Bonnie and Clyde, 187
- Bonus Army, 171
- Boone, Daniel, 60
- Booth, John Wilkes, 100, 101
- Borglum, Gutzon, 213
- Bosnia, 147, 267
- Boston, 22, 76, 126
  - Massacre, 39, *40*
  - police strike in, 154
  - Tea Party, *37*, 39
- Bowie, Jim, 71
- boxing, 164
- Boyd, Belle, *94*
- Boylston, Zabdiel, 22
- Brando, Marlon, 242
- Britain, 210
  - appeasement policy of, 192, *194*
  - empire of, 129, 146
  - explorers of, 15
  - and Greek civil war, 220
  - industrialization of, 65
  - Lend-Lease to, 194
  - U.S. relations, 53, 57, 72, 89, 130, 194-195, 279, 280
  - in War of 1812, *57*, 57-59
  - wars with France, 28, *28*, 29, 37
  - in World War I, 147, 148, 149, 151, 152
  - in World War II, 192-193, 204, 205, 206, 218
  - *See also* colonies; Revolutionary War
- Brown, Henry, *76*
- Brown, John, *74*, 83, 97
- Brown, Moses, 65
- Bryan, William Jennings, 123, 162
- Buchanan, James, 280
- buffalo, *113*, 116
- Bulge, The, 206
- Bull Moose Party, 143-144
- bully pulpit, 141
- Burke, Edmund, 38
- Burnside, Ambrose, 109
- Burr, Aaron, *54*, 62, 273-273
- Bush, George, 256, *258*, 258, 259, 266, 267, 283
- business. *See* industry
- Butler, Andrew, 79
- Butterfield, Alexander, 238

C

- Cabot, John, 15
- Cahan, Abraham, 124-125
- Cahokia, 11
- Calhoun, John C., 76, 77
- California, 115, 199, 222, 252, 254, 276, 279
  - Bear Flag Republic, *71*, 72
  - farmworkers union in, 231
  - gold rush in, 70-71
  - illegal immigrants in, 261
  - under Mexico, 71
  - statehood, 77, 87
  - *See also* Los Angeles; San Francisco
- Calley, William, 236
- camels, *114*
- Camp David Accords, 283
- Canada, 116, 221, 269, 279
  - English capture of, 28, 29
  - under France, 17, 28
  - and Revolutionary War, 41
  - in War of 1812, 57, 58
- canals, 66, 118
- Capone, Al, 185
- Carmichael, Stokely, 230
- Carnegie, Andrew, 119, 122
- Carolinas. *See* North Carolina; South Carolina
- Carpenter, Scott, 250
- carpetbaggers, 104
- Carson, Kit, 114
- Carson, Rachel, 240
- Carter, Jimmy, 239, 241, 253, 255, 262, 270, 271, 283
- Carteret, John, 22
- Cartier, Jacques, 15, 31
- Carville, James, 259
- Catherine II, 35, 60
- Catholic Church, 16, 17, 18, 20, 190
- cattle, 113
- Cayuga, 9
- Ceaucescu, Nicolai, 265
- Centennial Exhibition, 118
- Central Intelligence Agency (CIA), 238, 282
- *Challenger* explosion, 248, 251
- Chamberlain, Neville, 192, *194*
- Champlain, Samuel de, 17, 32
- Chaney, James, *229*
- Chapman, John (Johnny Appleseed), 62
- Charles, Prince, of Great Britain, 271
- Charles I, King of England, 19, 23, 33, 274
- Chase, Salmon P., 107
- Chavez, Cesar, *231*
- Checkers speech, 222-223
- checks and balances, 51
- Chernenko, Konstantin, 271
- Cherokee, 68, 69, 117
- Chesnut, Mary, 88
- Cheyenne, 114, 115
- Chiang Kai-shek, 184
- Chicago, 120, 165
  - Democratic Convention (1968) in, 237
  - Hull House, 126, 139
  - meatpacking industry in, 142
  - race riots in, 154
  - strikes in, 121, 122
- Chicanos. *See* Mexican Americans
- Chickasaw, 69
- China, 12, 129, 191, 192, 210, 221-222, 283
- Chinese Exclusion Act, 280
- Chivington, John M., 114, 115
- Choctaw, 69
- Church of England, 18, 19
- Churchill, Winston, 194-195, *205*, 205, 207, 218, 215, 219
- circus, 102, 117
- cities
  - colonial, 23, *24-25*, 24, 26-27, *27*
  - growth of, 120-121
  - immigrants in, 124, 126-127, *127*
  - political corruption in, 140
- civil disobedience, 73
- Civilian Conservation Corps (CCC), 174
- Civil Rights Acts, 228, 280
- civil rights movement
  - and changing attitudes, 225-226
  - events of, *225*
  - freedom rides, 228
  - March on Washington, 228
  - Montgomery bus boycott, 224
  - nonviolent resistance in, 226, 229-230
  - school desegregation, 226-227, 282
  - Selma March, 229
  - sit-in protests, *227*
  - voting rights campaign, 228, 229
- civil service reform, 139, 280
- Civil War
  - African-American troops, *84*, 93-94, *98*
  - blockade of Confederacy 91
  - casualties in, 85, 91, 97
  - draft riots during, 93-94
  - Emancipation Declaration, 92
  - events leading to, 74-79
  - military campaigns of, 85, 89-93, 94-96
  - outbreak of, 88-89
  - secession of Confederate states, 87, 89
  - surrender of Confederacy, 94-95, *95*
  - weapons and supplies for, *88-89*, 91, 119
- Clancey gang, 116
- Clark, William, 55, 62, 278
- Clarke, Kenneth, 227
- Clay, Henry, 63, 68, 77, *78*, *82*
- Cleveland, Grover, 112, 130, 133, 281
- Clinton, Bill, 283
  - economic policy of, 261, 269, 274
  - election of, *259*, 259-260, 273-274
  - foreign policy of, 267-269, *268*
  - health care plan of, 260
- Clinton, Dewitt, 66
- Clinton, Hillary Rodham, 260
- Cody, William "Buffalo Bill," *117*
- Cold War
  - and Communist scare, 217, 222
  - domestic impact of, 226
  - end of, 264-266
  - foreign policy of, 218-221
  - Iron Curtain speech, 219
  - Korean War, 221-222
  - nuclear weapons in, 218, *219*, 222
  - space race in, 248-250
- colleges and universities
  - civil rights movement in, 227-228
  - colonial, 19, *25*
  - Communist scare in, 222
  - Vietnam War protests in, *216*, 236, 237
- Collins, Michael, 247
- Colombia, 131
- colonies
  - Carolinas, 17, 23, 27
  - cities and towns in, 23, 24, *25*, 26-27, *27*
  - daily life in, 24-27
  - under Dutch, 17, *21*, 21-22
  - farming in, 18, 20-21, 23, 26
  - under French, 17, *20*, 28, 29, 55
  - Georgia, 23
  - Indian warfare in, 28-29, 37
  - Maryland, 20
  - medicine in, 22
  - New England, 18-20, 22, 25, 28-29
  - New York, *21*, 22, 24, 26, 29
  - Pennsylvania, 22-23, 24, 25, 26
  - religion in, 19, 20, 24, 25, 27
  - science in, 25, 50
  - Spanish, 17, *20*
  - taxation of, 27, 38-39
  - trade with, 22, 24, 39
  - *See also* Massachusetts colony; Revolutionary War; Virginia colony
- Colorado, 114, 276
- Columbus, Christopher, 8, *13*, 13-14, *14*, 30
- *Common Sense*, 41
- Commonwealth of Independent States, 266
- communications
  - Internet, 251
  - Pony Express, 113-114
  - radio, 163-164, 180
  - telephone, 120, 121
  - television, 222-223, 257
- Communism, fear of, 154-155, 217, 222
- Comprehensive Employment and Training Act, 255
- Compromise of 1850, 77, 279
- computers, *250*, 251
- Comstock Lode, 73
- concentration camps, 207
- Confederacy
  - blockade of, 91
  - formation of, 87
  - surrender of, 94-95, *95*
  - *See also* Civil War
- Confiscation Act, 92
- Congress, 115, 131, 201, 249, 278
  - African-Americans in, 105, *107*
  - checks and balances, 51
  - Communist scare in, *217*, 217, 222
  - declaration of war, 150, 195
  - and foreign policy, 152, 193, 195, 220
  - and Indian policy, 69, 116, 117
  - Iran-Contra investigation by, 264
  - isolationists in, 193, 220
  - and New Deal programs, 172, 173, 181
  - and progressive reform, 138-139, 141, 143
  - during Reconstruction, 102-103, 104, 280
  - representation in, 50, 75, 144
  - Republican majority in, 102, 103, 253, 260-261, 283
  - and slavery issue, 77, *78*, 79, 87, 97

and Vietnam War, 234-235
Watergate investigation of, 238
women in, 150
Congress of Industrial Organizations (CIO), 177
Congress of Racial Equality (CORE), 200, 228
Connecticut, 19, 58, 274
Connor, Eugene "Bull," 228
conquistadors, 14-15
Constitutional Convention, 49-51, 75
constitutions, state, 48
Constitution, U.S., 36, 107
amendments to, 97, 103, 104, 137, 138, 144, 155, 281
Articles of Confederation, 48
and congressional representation, 50, 144
division of powers, 50-51
ratification of, 51
and slavery, 50, 59, 74-75
and voting rights, 46, 48, 104, 144
consumer spending, 161, 162, 257
containment doctrine, 219
Continental Congress, 39, 40, 41, 48, 74-75
Continental Divide, 55
Contract with America, 261
Contras, in Nicaragua, 263, 264
Cook, James, 60
Coolidge, Calvin, 154, 167, 184, 282
Cooper, Peter, 67
Copland, Aaron, 177
CORE. See Congress of Racial Equality
Cornwallis, Lord, 47, 61
Coronado, Francisco, 14-15, 15, 31
Cortéz, Hernando, 14
cotton gin, 65
cotton production, 65, 89
Coughlin, Charles, 175, 176
courts
checks and balances, 51
Scopes trial in, 162
Zenger case in, 37
See also Supreme Court
Cox, Archibald, 239
Crazy Horse, 116
creation story, 9
Creek, 59, 68, 69
crime
gunslingers, 115, 116
during Prohibition, 155, 165
Sacco and Vanzetti case, 155
Crisis, The, 142, 143
Crittendon, John, 87
Crockett, Davy, 63, 65, 71
Crusades, 12
Cuba
under Castro, 234
in Spanish-American War, 128, 130-131
Cuban missile crisis, 234
Cumberland Gap, 66
Custer, George Armstrong, 110, 111, 116
Cuzco, 11, 15
Czechoslovakia, 192, 265

D

Daguerre, Louis, 80
Daily Forward, 124-125
Daley, Richard, 237
Dalton gang, 116
Dare, Virginia, 32
Darrow, Clarence, 162
Darwin, Charles, 162
Dasch, George, 205
Daughters of the American Revolution (DAR), 181
Davis, Jefferson, 87, 88, 99, 110, 114
Davis, John, 184
Dawes Act, 117
D-Day, 206
DDT, 240
Dean, John, 238

Debs, Eugene V., 145. 158
Declaration of Independence, 26, 41, 42-43, 42-43, 44
Declaration of Rights and Grievances, 39
"Deep Throat," 238
De Gama, Vasco, 30
Deganawida, 31
De las Casas, Bartolomeo, 16
Delaware, 23, 24, 87, 274
democracy
Jacksonian, 68
Jefferson on, 52
Democratic Party
1968 Convention of, 237
in South, 106, 107
and Watergate burglary, 238
See also Presidential elections
Democratic-Republicans, 53, 54, 57, 59, 68
Dempsey, Jack, 164
depression and recession, 118, 141, 255, 257, 281
See also Great Depression
De Sepulveda, Juan Gines de, 16
de Soto, Hernando, 14, 31
Dessalines, Jean-Jacques, 63
Dewey, George, 131
Diana, Princess of Wales, 271
Diaz, Porfirio, 111
Diem, Ngo Dinh, 233, 234
Dillinger, John, 186
DiMaggio, Joe, 213
disease
AIDS epidemic, 256
in colonial period, 18, 22
division of powers, 50-51
Dix, Dorothea, 81
Dixon, Jeremiah, 35
Dole, Bob, 261
Doolittle, Jimmy 214
Dorantes, Estevan, 14
doughboys, 151
Douglas, Stephen, 79
Douglass, Frederick, 75, 75-76, 81
draft
riots, 93
in World War I, 150
Drake, Edwin, 120
Drake, Francis, 15, 31
drug industry, regulation of, 142
Dubois, W. E. B., 142, 142, 143
Dumas, Alexandre, 83
Durocher, Leo, 225
Dust Bowl, 170, 172, 173, 174
Dylan, Bob, 244

E

Earhart, Amelia, 187
Earp, Wyatt, 116
Eastern Europe, 218, 219, 221, 265
East Germany, 221
Eastman, George, 120
economic policy
under Bush, 258
under Clinton, 261, 269
under Coolidge, 167
under Hoover, 171
under Reagan, 253-255
under Roosevelt (Franklin). See New Deal
under Roosevelt (Theodore), 141-143
See also taxation; trade
Economic Recovery Tax Act, 254
Ederle, Gertrude, 185
Edison, Thomas Alva, 120, 121, 132
Edward VIII, King of England, 187
Edwards, Jonathan, 27
Ehrlichman, John, 238
Eichmann, Adolf, 207
Eiffel, Gustave, 134
Einstein, Albert, 212
Eisenhower, Dwight, 214, 222, 223, 227, 242, 282
elections. See Presidential elections
Electoral College, 51, 59, 107, 280, 281

electricity, 120, 121, 179
Electronic Numerical Integrator and Computer (ENIAC), 250, 251
Elizabeth I, Queen of England, 15, 274
Elizabeth II, Queen of England, 273
Ellis Island, 124-125, 261
Ellsberg, Daniel, 239
Emancipation Proclamation, 92, 280
Embargo and Non-Intercourse Acts, 54, 278
encomienda system, 16-17
energy crisis, 240
England. See Britain
ENIAC, 250, 251
Enola Gay, 211
entitlement programs, 255-256, 261
environment
Native Americans and, 10
pollution of, 240, 255
Reagan's policy on, 254-255
Roosevelt's (Theodore) policy on, 140
environmental movement, 140, 240
Environmental Protection Agency (EPA), 240
Era of Good Feelings, 59, 278
Ericsson, Leif, 30
Erie Canal, 66
Ervin, Sam, 238
explorers, 8, 12-15

F

Fair Employment Practices Committee, 194
fallout shelters, 218, 219
Falwell, Jerry, 240
farmers and farming
Dust Bowl, 170, 172, 173, 174
Jefferson on, 52
Native American, 9
New Deal programs for, 173
plantation system, 18, 20-21, 23, 27, 65
Populists, 123
sharecroppers, 105-106, 107, 123, 173
in Shay's Rebellion, 49, 51
tenants, 26
union, 231
yeomanry, 21
Farragut, David, 92, 109
fascism, rise of, 190-192
Federal Communications Commission (FCC), 170
Federal Deposit Insurance Corporation (FDIC), 173
Federal Emergency Relief Administration (FERA), 174
Federalist Papers, 51
Federalists, 51, 53, 54, 58, 59
Federal One project, 176-177
Federal Reserve system, 144, 255, 281
Federal Theater Project (FTP), 177
Federal Trade Commission, 144
Feminine Mystique, The (Friedan), 231
Ferdinand, Archduke of Austria, 146, 148, 158
Ferdinand, King of Spain, 13, 30
Ferraro, Geraldine, 271
feudal system, 12
54-40 or Fight, 72
Fillmore, Millard, 279
fireside chats, 172, 194
Fisher, Mel, 272
fishing, Native American, 16
Fitch, John, 61
Fitzgerald, F. Scott, 166
flagpole sitting, 166
Fleming, Alexander, 185
Florida, 14, 17, 57, 87, 104, 107, 247, 276, 278
race riot in, 154
Seminole War, 69

Floyd, "Pretty Boy," 186
Flynn, Elizabeth Gurley, 145
Folsom, Fanny, 133
Food and Drug Administration, 143
Ford, Gerald, 239, 239, 253, 270, 283
Ford, Henry, 135, 162, 163
Ford Motor Company, 171, 175
foreign policy
Britain, 53, 57, 72, 89, 130, 194-195, 279, 280
containment doctrine, 219
Cuba, 234, 282
France, 52-54, 278
Germany, 149-150, 218
Grenada invasion, 264, 283
Haiti, 267, 281
Iran-Contra scandal, 254, 262-264
Iran hostage crisis, 240-241
isolationism, 193, 220
Israel, 239-240, 263, 267-268, 283
Latin America, 129-131, 233-234, 262-263, 281, 283
and League of Nations, 152
Marshall Plan, 220
Monroe Doctrine, 129-130, 281
NATO alliance in, 221
neutrality, 149
Soviet Union, 218-222, 234, 262, 264, 283
Truman Doctrine, 220
West Germany, 218, 221
and World War I, 150-151
and World War II, 193-195
See also treaties; Vietnam War
Forrest, Nathan Bedford, 106
forts
Defiance, 114
Duquesne, 29
McHenry, 58
Sumter, 88
Ticonderoga, 40, 45
Forty-Niners, 70
49th parallel, 72
Fourteen Points, 152, 281
France, 210
appeasement policy of, 192
colonies of, 17, 20, 28, 129
explorers of, 15
Louisiana Purchase from, 55, 278
in Revolutionary War, 45
Revolution in, 52-53
in Vietnam, 233
wars with England, 28, 29, 37
in World War I, 147, 148, 149, 151, 152
in World War II, 192, 195, 206, 206
and XYZ Affair, 53-54, 278
Franco, Francisco, 187
Franklin, Benjamin, 10, 25, 26, 36, 40, 51, 60
Freedmen's Bureau, 101, 103
Frederick II, 34, 35
freedom rides, 228
freedom summer, 228
Fremont, James, 72
French and Indian War, 28, 28, 29, 37
French Revolution, 52-53
Frick, Henry, 122
Friedan, Betty, 231
Fugitive Slave Act, 77, 279
Fulton, Robert, 67

G

Gable, Clark, 180
Gadsden Purchase, 279
Gallaudet, Thomas Hopkins, 63
Galle, J. G., 82
Gandhi, Mahatma, 184
Garibaldi, Guiseppe, 108
Garfield, James, 132, 138, 280
Gargarin, Yuri, 249
Garner, John Nance, 169, 181
Garrett, Pat, 116

Garrison, William Lloyd, 75, 76
Garvey, Marcus, 167
Geldof, Bob, 266
Gemini space program, 247, 250
Genet, Edmund, 52-53
George III, King of England, 38, 39, 41, 47, 60, 63
Georgia, 11, 23, 46, 69, 87, 94-95, 274
German Americans, 154
Germany
division of, 220-221
and Naziism, 188, 190, 191-193, 192, 193, 207
Nuremberg trials in, 207
reunification of, 265
rocket science in, 248
war reparations debt of, 152, 189-190
in World War I, 146, 147, 148, 149-150, 151
in World War II, 188, 202, 204, 205-207
Geronimo, 133
Gestapo, 191
Gettysburg Address, 92, 93, 280
Ghost Dance, 117
Giffard, Henri, 83
Gilded Age, 120
Gingrich, Newt, 261
Ginsburg, Alan, 223
Gladstone, William, 133
glasnost, 265
Glass-Steagall Act, 173
Glenn, John, 249
gold rush, 70-71, 114, 116
Goldwater, Barry, 254
Gompers, Samuel, 123
Goodman, Andrew, 229
Gorbachev, Mikhail, 264-265, 271, 272
Gore, Al, 259
Goswold, Bartholomew, 32
Grant, Ulysses S.
in Civil War, 91, 94, 95, 96-97, 97, 109, 110
in Mexican War, 72
presidency of, 104, 104, 105, 118, 280
Great Awakening, 27
Great Compromise, 50
Great Depression, 160
Bonus Army in, 171
Dust Bowl in, 170, 172, 173, 174
economic decline in, 169-170
in Germany, 191
Hoover's policies for, 171
movies of, 180
Roosevelt's policies for. See New Deal
and stock market crash, 167, 168-169
Greece, 219-220
Greene, Nathaniel, 46-47
Grenada, invasion of, 264
Grenville, George, 38
Grenville, Richard, 32
Guiteau, Charles, 132
Gulf of Tonkin Resolution, 234-235
gunslingers, 115, 116
Guthrie, Woody, 174

H

Hagman, Larry, 257
Haiti, 267, 281
Hakluyt, Richard and Richard, Jr., 17
Haldeman, H. R., 238
Hamilton, Alexander, 51, 52, 53, 54, 62
Hancock, John, 37, 39, 43
Harding, Warren, 166, 167, 184, 281-282
Harlem Renaissance, 166
Harpers Ferry, raid on, 74
Harrison, Benjamin,134, 281
Harrison, Caroline, 134
Harrison, William Henry, 56-57, 62, 81, 279
Hartford Convention, 58
Harvard College, 19
Hauptmann, Bruno, 186

Havel, Vaclav, 265
Hawaii, 131, 277, 281
Hayes, Mary "Molly Pitcher," 46
Hayes, Rutherford B., 107, 112, 280
Haywood, William ("Big Bill"), 145
health care plan, 260
Hearst, William Randolph, 130
Held, John, Jr., 165
Hemingway, Ernest, 166
Henry, Prince of Portugal, 13
Henry, Patrick, 38, 39, 41
Henry VIII, King of England, 18
Hewes, George, 37, 39
Hiawatha, 31
Hidalgo y Castilla, Miguel, 71
Hill, Anita, 272
Hinckley, John, Jr., 283
Hirohito, Emperor of Japan, 211
Hiroshima, bombing of, 211, 219
Hitler, Adolf, 184, 186, 187, 188, 190, 191, 191, 192, 206, 212, 214, 215, 218
Ho Chi Minh, 233
Holland. See Netherlands
Holocaust, 207
Homestead Act, 116
Homestead strike, 122-123
Hooker, Thomas, 19
Hoover, Herbert, 160, 167, 168, 171, 185, 186, 282
Hoovervilles, 169, 171
Hopkins, Harry, 174
House of Burgesses, 18, 21
House of Representatives, 50, 75, 87, 150, 217
See also Congress
House Un-American Affairs Committee (HUAC), 217
Houston, Sam, 71, 81
Howard, O. O., 103
Howe, William, 44, 45
Hudson, Henry, 8, 15, 31
Huerta, Victoriano, 158
Hull House, 126, 139
Humphrey, Hubert, 237
Hungary, 147, 148, 219
hunting, buffalo, 113, 116
Hurston, Zora Neale, 166, 177, 177
Hussein, Saddam, 266, 267, 272
Hutchinson, Anne, 20
Hutchinson, Thomas, 38
hydrogen bomb, 222

I

Ice Age, 9
Idaho, 277
Illinois, 56, 68, 76, 101, 275, 280
See also Chicago
immigrants
Chinese exclusion, 280
in draft riots, 93
illegal, 261
in labor force, 65, 115, 124
living conditions of, 124-125, 126-127, 127
negative reaction to, 127, 154, 155, 166, 261
passage and arrival of, 124-125, 126, 261
quotas for, 127, 261
reasons for immigration, 125-126
Immigration Restriction Act, 281-282
Incas, 11, 15
indentured servants, 21, 26
Indiana, 56, 275
Indian Removal Act, 69, 279
Indians. See Native Americans; names of tribes
indigo, 24
Industrial Workers of the World (IWW), 145
industry
anti-trust policy, 141-142, 143, 281
buy outs, 252

growth of, 66, 118, *119*, 119
Hamilton-Jefferson debate
over, 52
New Deal programs for,
173-174
plant closings, 257
regulation of, 139, 142-
143, 144, 255, 258
and stock market crash,
169, 257
sweatshops, 124, 143
Teapot Dome scandal, 167
technology, 118, 119-121
textile mills, 65, 145
war factories, 150, 152,
154, 194, 196, 197, *199*
See also labor; labor unions;
specific industry
inflation, 154, 255
Internet, 251
Interstate Commerce
Commission, 139
Intolerable Acts, 39
inventions. *See* technology
Iowa, 276, 282
Iran
-Contra scandal, 254, 262-
264, 283
hostage crisis, 240-241, *241*
Islamic revolution in, 241,
262
Iraq, in Persian Gulf War,
266-267, 283
Irish immigrants, 65
ironclads, 91
Iron Curtain, 219
Iroquois Confederation, 9-
10, 29
irrigation, 9
Isabella, Queen of Spain, *13*,
13, 14, 30
isolationism, 193, 220
Israel, 239-240, 263, 267-
268, 283
Italy
fascism in, 190, 191-192
in World War II, 202, 206
Ivan IV, czar of Russia, 31

J

Jackson, Andrew, *68*, 279
and Indian wars, 68-69
in presidential elections,
68
in War of 1812, *56-57*, 59,
64
Jackson, Jesse, 257
Jackson, Michael, 271
Jackson, Thomas
"Stonewall," 90, 94, 109
James I, King of England, 17,
32
James, Jesse and Frank, 116
Jamestown settlement, 17-18
Japan
atomic bombing of, 211, 219
in China, 191, 192
fascism in, 190-191
Pearl Harbor attack by,
150, 188, *189*, 189, 195
U.S. trade with, 129, 195,
257
in Vietnam, 233
in World War II, 202-203,
203, 207-211
Japanese Americans, internment of, 200-201, *201*
Jay, John, 51, 53
Jazz, 130, 161, 164, *165*
Jazz Age, 161-162
Jefferson, Thomas, *42*, 48,
50, 61, 80, 279
and Anti-Federalists, 53, 54
and Declaration of
Independence, 41, 42-43
on democracy, 52
on Hamilton, 53
on Missouri Compromise,
59
and slavery, 42, 43, 84
trade embargo of, 54
and westward expansion,
55
Jenner, Edward, 62
Jews, 20, 203
in Holocaust, 207
immigrants, 124-125
in Nazi Germany, 191

Jim Crow, 198
jingoism, 130
Jobs, Steve, *251*
Joffre, Joseph, 150
John Paul I, Pope, 270
John Paul II, Pope, 270
Johnson, Andrew, 101-102,
103, 104, 109, 239, 280
Johnson, Lyndon, *234*, 283
and civil rights, 228, 229, 244
and Vietnam War, 234-235,
236-237, 244
Johnson, William, 29
Jones, John Paul, 46
Joplin, Scott, *130*
Joseph, Chief, 116
journalists, muckrakers, 139-
140, 142
Juarez, Benito, 198
judicial review, 54
Jungle, The (Sinclair), 142

K

Kamehameha, 63
kamikaze attacks, 209
Kang-hsi, 34
Kansas, 74, 79, 226-227, 276
Kansas-Nebraska Act of
1854, 79, 279
Kearny, Stephen, 73
Kelley, Florence, 139
Kellogg Will Keith, 122
Kelly, Alvin ("Shipwreck"),
166
Kennan, George, 219
Kennedy, John F., 228, 282
assassination of, 228, 234
and civil rights, 228
foreign policy of, 233-
234, 244
-Nixon debates, *232*
and space program, 249-
250
Kennedy, Robert, 228, 237,
244
Kent State University, 237
Kentucky, 52, 66, 87, 89,
275
Kerensky, Alexander, 150,
151
Key, Francis Scott, 58
Khomeini, Ayatollah, 241, 270
Khrushchev, Nikita, *234*, 244
King, John, 108
King, Martin Luther, Jr., 224,
226, 226, 228, 229, 230,
242, 244, 271
King George's War, 29
King, Rodney, 258-259
King William's War, 29
Kissinger, Henry, 237
Knights of Labor, 122
Korean War, 221-222, 282
Koresh, David, 273
Kristallnacht, 191
Ku Klux Klan, 106-107, *107*,
166, 228, 280
Kurds, in Iraq, 266-267
Kuwait, 266, 283

L

labor
African-American, 102, 194
child, *144*
conditions of, 143, 144
Federal programs for, 255-
256
in Great Depression, 169-
170, 171
immigrant, 65, 115, 124
indentured servants, 21,
26
industrialization impact
on, 121
New Deal programs for,
174, 176-177
during World War II, 194,
196, 198
women, 65, 143, 145, 150,
182, 196, 199
See also slavery; unem-
ployment
labor unions, 144-145
farmworkers, 231
in nineteenth century, 121-
123
radical, 145
red scare and, 154-155

Roosevelt (Theodore) and,
140-141
during World War II, 198-
199
See also strikes
land
Homestead Act, 116
Indian, 37-38, 56, 58, 68,
69, 117, 281
Lange, Dorothea, *172*
Larcom, Lucy, 65
La Salle, Rene de, 17, 34
La Follete, Robert, 184
Latin America
early civilizations of, 11
U.S. policy in, 129-131,
233-234, 281
Laudonniére, René de, 31
Lavoisier, Antoine Laurent, 61
Lawrence of Arabia, 159
Lawrence, Richard, 279
Lawson, John Howard, 217
Lazarus, Emma, 126
League of Nations, 152, 191,
192, 281
Lebanon, and Iran-Contra
scandal, 263-264
Le Duc Tho, 237
Lee, Richard Henry, 41, 96
Lee, Robert E., 90, 93, 96-
97, *97*, 108, 110
Leigh, Vivian, 242
Lend-Lease, 194, 282
L'Enfant, Pierre, 50
Lenin, Vladimir, 150, 151, 159
Lewis, Robert, 215
Lewis, John L., 177, *200*
Lewis, Meriwether, 55, 62, 278
Liliuokalani, Queen of Hawaii,
134
Lincoln, Abraham, *86*, 280
assassination of, *100*, 100-
101, 110
election of, 79, 83, 87
Emancipation
Proclamation, 92, 280
family of, 86
Gettysburg Address, 92,
93, 280
military leadership of, 88,
89, 90, 94
Reconstruction plan of,
99-100
on slavery, 74, 79
Lindbergh,Charles, 185, 186
Little Turtle, 56
Live Aid, 266
Long, Huey, 175-176, *179*
Long Walk, The, 114
Lopez, Francisco, 110
Los Angeles
riots in, *200*, 230, *258*, 259
Rodney King case in, 258-
259
lost generation, 166
Louis XVI, King of France, 62
Louis Napoleon, King of
France, 82
Louisiana, 87, 104, 107, 275
Purchase, 55, 278
See also New Orleans
Lovejoy, Elijah, 76
Lowell, Francis Cabot, 65
Lowell, Josephine Shaw, 139
Lowell Mills, 65
Lusitania, sinking of, *148*,
149
Luther, Martin, *16*, 30
lynchings, 154, 166

M

MacArthur, Douglas, 186,
208, 211, 215, *221*, 221-
222, 242
Mackenzie, William Lyon, 80
McAuliffe, Christa, 248, 251
McCarthy, Eugene, 236-237
McCarthy, Joseph, *217*, 222,
242
McClellan, George, *89*, 90, 108
McDonald, Maurice and
Richard, 242
McDowell, Edwin, 108
McKinley, William, 123, 128,
130-131, *131*, 135, 140,
156, 281
Madero, Francisco, 158
Madison, Dolley, *56*, 63

Madison, James, *48*, 51, 57,
278
Madonna, *257*
Magellan, Ferdinand, 30
Magoon, Charles, 157
Mahan, Alfred, 128
mail delivery, 26, 113-114
Maine, 59, 75, 275, 279
Maine, 128, 130
Malcolm X, *226*, 226, 229-230
Mandela, Nelson, 273
Manhattan Project, 203, 209,
211
manifest destiny, 73
Mao Zedong, 221
March on Washington, 228
Marsh, Reginald, *178-179*
Marshall, George, 220, 242
Marshall, James W., 70
Marshall, John, 54, 69, 81
Marshall, Thurgood, 226-
227, *227*
Marshall Plan, 220, 282
Marx, Groucho, *180*
Marx, Karl, 82
Mary, Queen, 31
Maryland, 20, 66, 87, 89,
239, 274
Mason, Charles, 35
Massachusetts, 274, 278,
282, 283
Shay's Rebellion in, 49, *51*
textile mills in, 65, 145
See also Boston
Massachusetts colony
Boston Massacre, 39, *40*
Boston Tea Party, *37*, 39
Pilgrims in, 18-19
Puritans in, 19, 20, 24, 25
Revolutionary War in, 39,
41
Salem witch trials in, 25
Sons of Liberty in, *37*, 38,
39
Mather, Cotton, 22, 24, 25
Maximilian, Archduke of
Mexico, 109
Mayans, 11
Mayflower Compact, 18
Meat Inspection Act, 143
meatpacking industry, regu-
lation of, 142-143
Medicare/Medicaid, 255, 256
medicine
in Civil War, 90
in colonial period, 22
national health care plan,
260
Meiji, Emperor of Japan, 111
Mein Kampf (Hitler), 191, 193
Menéndez, Pedro de, 31
Merrimack, 91
Metacom (King Philip), 28-
29, 34
Mexican Americans, 200, 231
Mexico
early civilizations of, 11
under Spain, 14, 16-17, 71
war of Texas indepen-
dence, 71
war with U.S., 72-73, *73*,
279
Michigan, 56, 122, 137, 275,
283
Miller, Arthur, *177*
Milliken, Michael, 252
mining
coal, 119
gold, 70-71, 114, 116
labor unions, 140-141, 199
silver, 73
Minnesota, 120, 230, 276
Minuet, Peter, 17
Minutemen, 39
Mississippi, 11, 87, 92, 105,
228, 229, 275
Mississippi River, 14, 17, 55,
90, 91-92
Missouri, 59, 79, 87, 89,
275, 282
Missouri Compromise, 59,
75, 79, *79*, 84, 87, 278
Mitchell, John, 140, 238
Mitchell, Margaret, 187
Mitchell, Maria, 82
Mitchell, William, 165
Mohawk, 28
"Molly Pitcher," 46

Molotov, V. M., 219
Moltke, Helmuth von, 148
Mondale, Walter, 271
Monitor, 91
Monroe, James, *59*, 63, 129
Monroe Doctrine, 129-130,
278, 281
Montana, 150, 277
Montcalm, Marquis de, 28
Montezuma, 14
Montgomery, Bernard, *205*
Montgomery bus boycott,
224
moon landing, *247*, 247, 248
Moors, 13
Moro, Aldo, 270
Mott, Lucretia, 138
mound builders, *10*, 11
movie industry, blacklisting
in, 217
movies, 164, 180, 199
muckrakers, 139-140, 142
Mudd, Samuel, 101
Muhal, Mumtaz, 33
Muir, John, 140
music, 130, 161, 164, 165,
174, 223, 266
musket, grooved barrel, 91
Muslims, 12, 13
Mussolini, Benito, 159, 186,
188, *191*, 192, 206, 212
mustard gas, 146
My Lai massacre, 236

N

NAACP. *See* National
Association for the
Advancement of
Colored People
NAFTA. *See* North American
Free Trade Agreement
Nagasaki, bombing of, 211,
219
Naismith, James, 134
napalm, 236
Napoleon, 55, 62
Napoleon III, 83, 110
Narragansett, 20, 28
NASA. *See* National
Aeronautics and Space
Administration
Nation, Carrie, 118
National Aeronautics and
Space Administration
(NASA), 248, 249, 250,
251
National Association for the
Advancement of
Colored People
(NAACP), 142, 143,
198, 199-200, 226-227
National Council of Negro
Women, 182
National Defense and
Education Act, 249
National Labor Relations
Act, *175*, 176-177
National Labor Relations
Board (NLRB), 176
National Organization of
Women (NOW), 231
National Park System, 140
National Recovery
Administration (NRA),
171, 173-174, 176, 282
National Road, 66
National Security Act, 282
National Women's Caucus,
231
Nation of Islam, 226, 229-230
Native Americans
American Indian
Movement (AIM), 230-
231
attacks on settlers, 28-29,
37, 64, 116
buffalo hunting of, 113,
116
and constitution, 48
early societies, 9-11
farming of, 9
fishing of, *16*
Five Civilized Tribes, 69,
113
land of, 37-38, 56, 58, 68,
69, 117, 281
in Lewis and Clark expedition, 55

migration from Asia, 9
mound builders, *10*, 11
relations with settlers, 18,
19, 21, 23, 26, 114
religion of, 9, 10, 16, 117
removal of, 69, 113, 114-
115, 279
and Revolutionary War, 40
Sand Creek massacre of,
114, 115
in slavery, 14, 16-17, 19
Spanish conquest of, 14, 16
trade with, 8, 10
treaties with, 29, 37-38,
114, 115
in War of 1812, 58
wars with U.S. army, 56-
57, 68-69, 116, 117
in Wild West Show, 117
See also names of tribes
NATO. *See* North Atlantic
Treaty Organization
Navajo, 114
Navigation Act, 22
navy
in Civil War, 90-91, 92
expansion of, 128-129
Pearl Harbor attack on,
188, *189*, 189, 195
in Revolutionary War, 46
in Spanish-American war,
131
in War of 1812, 57
in World War II, 208
Nazis, 190, 191-193, *192*,
193, 207
Nebraska, 79, 115, 276
Nelson, "Baby Face," 186
Netherlands
colonies of, 17, *21*, 21-22
in Revolutionary War, 46
Neutrality Act of 1935, 193
Nevada, 73, 276
New Amsterdam, 17, 22
New Deal, 160, 282
first hundred days, 172-
174
second, 174-179, 181-182
success of, 183
and Supreme Court, 176,
181
New Hampshire, 48, 274,
279
New Jersey, 24, 54, 120, 274,
281
New Mexico, 17, 277, 279
New Netherlands, 17, *21*, 22
New Orleans, 17, 126, 164
Civil War in, 92
War of 1812 in, *56-57*, 58-
59
Newport, Christopher, 32
Newton, Huey, 230
New York (City)
colonial, 17, 22, 27
draft riots in, 93-94
growth of, 120-121
immigrants in, *124-125*,
126, *127*
Triangle Shirtwaist fire in,
143
Washington's inauguration
in, 51, 52
New York (State), 137, 274,
279, 280, 281, 282
constitutional ratification
by, 51
Emancipation Act of, 78
Erie Canal, 66
New York colony, 24
under Dutch, 17, *21*, 21-22
Iroquois Confederation in,
29
Stamp Act Congress in, 38
tenant farmers in, 26
Zenger case in, 37
New York Consumers
League, 139
New York Stock Exchange,
167, *253*
Nez Perce, 116
Nicaragua, 262-263, 264, 283
Nicholas, of Russia, 80
Nighthorse-Campbell, Ben, 273
Nipmuck, 28
Nixon, Richard
Checkers speech, 222-223
foreign policy of, 283

-Kennedy debates, 232
resignation of, 239, 239, 282
and Vietnam War, 237
and Watergate scandal,
238-239
nomads, 9
nonviolence, 226
Noriega, Manuel, 272, 283
North, Oliver, 263, 264, 272
North American Free Trade
Agreement (NAFTA),
269, 283
North Atlantic Treaty
Organization (NATO),
221, 267, 282
North Carolina, 87, 104,
274, 279, 280
civil rights movement in,
227
colonial, 23, 27
in Revolutionary War, 41,
47
North Dakota, 277
North Star, The, 76
Northwest Ordinance of
1787, 48
Norton, Joshua Abraham, 72
Nostradamus, 31
NOW. See National
Organization of Women
nuclear power, 240
nuclear weapons
atomic bomb, 203, 209,
210, 211, 219, 222, 282
disarmament treaty, 283
fear of, 218, 219, 249
hydrogen bomb, 222
Nuremberg trials, 207
Nye, Gerald, 193

O
Oakley, Annie, 117
Obregon, Alvaro, 185
Office of Price
Administration and
Civilian Supply (OPA),
197
Oglethorpe, James, 23, 23,
35, 274
Ohio, 11, 56, 275, 280, 281
oil industry, 120, 140, 141-
142, 240
Oklahoma, 69, 113, 117,
174, 277
Olmecs, 10, 10
Olympic games
in Nazi Germany, 190
U.S. boycott of, 262, 283
Oneida, 9
Onondaga, 9
OPEC. See Organization of
Petroleum Exporting
Countries
Operation Desert Storm,
266-267, 268, 283
Oppenheimer, Robert, 203,
211
Oregon, 72, 116, 276, 279
Oregon Trail, 70, 72
Organization of Petroleum
Exporting Countries
(OPEC), 240
Osceola, 69
Oslo Accords, 267
O'Sullivan, John, 73
Oswald, Lee Harvey, 234
Ottawa, 29
Ottoman Empire, 147
Owens, Jesse, 187, 190

P
Pahlavi, Shah Reza, 240-241,
270
Paine, Thomas, 41, 41
Palmer, A. Mitchell, 155
Palmer raids, 155
Panama, 283
Panama Canal, 131, 281
Papineau, Joseph, 80
Parker, Alton B., 156
Parks, Rosa, 224, 242
patroons, 22
Payne-Aldrich Tariff Act, 281
Peace Corps, 233
Pearl Harbor, attack on, 150,
188, 189, 189
Peary, Robert, 257
Pedro II, King of Brazil, 134

Pendleton Act, 138-139
Penn, William, 22-23, 23, 34,
274
Pennsylvania, 45, 48, 120,
274, 280
Civil War in, 92-93
colonial, 22-23, 24-25, 24,
26
Three Mile Island incident
in, 240
See also Philadelphia
Pentagon Papers, 239
Pepperell, William, 29
Pequot, 19
Peres, Shimon, 268
perestroika, 269
Perignon, Dom Pierre, 34
Peron, Isabel Martinez de, 270
Perot, H. Ross, 259, 259-260,
273
Perry, Matthew, 129
Perry, William, 57
Pershing, John J., 150
Persian Gulf War, 266-267,
268, 283
Philadelphia
Centennial Exhibition
in, 118
colonial, 23, 24-25, 26
fugitive slave in, 76
in Revolutionary era, 39,
41, 50
Philippines, 131, 202, 208
Pickett, George, 85, 93
Pierce, Franklin, 279
Pike, Zebulon, 55
Pilgrims, 18-19
Pingree, Hazen, 140
Pinkerton, Allan, 122
pirates, 15, 54
Pitt, William, 28
Pizarro, Francisco, 15
Plymouth colony, 18-19
Pocahontas, 17, 17, 19
Poindexter, John, 263, 264
Poland, 192, 206, 207, 219,
265
Polk, James, 72, 73, 81, 82,
279
pollution, 240, 255
Polo, Marco, 12, 12, 13, 30
Pontiac's rebellion, 29, 37
Poniatowski, Stanislaus, 60
Pony Express, 113-114
Populist Party, 123, 139
Portugal, explorers of, 13
potato famine, 65
Potawatomi, 56
Potsdam Conference, 219
Pottawatomie Creek
Massacre, 74
poverty, 169, 169-170, 171,
174, 257
Powell, Colin, 268
Powhatan, 17, 19, 32
presidential elections
of 1796, 53
of 1800, 54
of 1820, 59
of 1824, 68
of 1828, 68
of 1832, 68
of 1860, 79
of 1876, 107
of 1896, 123
of 1904, 141
of 1908, 143
of 1912, 144, 145
of 1928, 167
of 1932, 160, 170, 171-172
of 1936, 181
of 1952, 222
of 1960, 232
of 1964, 254
of 1968, 236-237
of 1972, 238
of 1976, 253
of 1980, 241, 252, 253,
254
of 1984, 254
of 1992, 259-260, 266
of 1996, 261
See also Electoral College
Presidential Succession Act,
281
Presley, Elvis, 223, 223
Proclamation of 1763, 29,
37-38

Proclamation of Neutrality of
1793, 52, 53
Progressive Era, 137-138
muckrakers in, 139-140, 142
Populism in, 123, 139
Roosevelt administration
reforms, 140-143
and spoils system, 138-
139, 140
Taft administration
reforms, 143, 144
Wilson administration
reforms, 144-145
Prohibition, 144, 155, 165
Protestant Reformation, 16, 17
Public Works Administration
(PWA), 174
Pueblo, 9, 15, 114
Puerto Rico, 131
Pullman, George, 123
Pure Food and Drug Act,
143, 281
Puritans, 19, 20, 24, 25

Q
Quakers, 20, 23, 26
Quebec, 17, 28, 29
Queen Anne's War, 29

R
Rabin, Yitzhak, 267, 268
race riots, 93, 154, 230, 258,
259
radio, 163-164, 180, 223
railroads
in Civil War, 91
elevated, 121
first, 67
regulation of, 139
routes, 115, 118
strikes, 122, 280
transcontinental, 113, 115-
116
Raleigh, Walter, 17, 31
Randolph, A. Philip, 194, 200
Rankin, Jeannette, 150
rationing, wartime, 197, 198
Raza Unida, La, 231
Reagan, Ronald
defense spending of, 256
economic policy of, 253-
255, 255, 283
election of, 241, 252, 252-
253, 254, 270-273
and entitlement programs,
255-256
foreign policy of, 264, 283
and Iran-Contra scandal,
254, 262-264
recession, 255, 257
Reconstruction, 98-107, 280
Red Cloud, 116
red scare, 154-155, 217, 222
regulators, 27
religion
Crusades and, 12
freedom of, 20, 23
Great Awakening, 27
Islamic revolution, 241, 262
Native American, 9, 10,
16, 117
Protestant Reformation,
16, 17, 18
Puritan, 19, 20, 24, 25
radio preachers, 166, 175
in Scopes trial, 162
Remington, Frederic, 130
Remsen, Ira, 132
Republican Party
in Congressional majority,
102, 103, 253, 260-261,
283
Lincoln and, 79
Radical, 102, 103, 104, 105
and Watergate scandal, 238
See also Presidential elections
Revere, Paul, 60
Revolutionary War, 278
Continental Congress and,
39, 40, 48
Declaration of
Independence, 26, 41,
42-43, 42-43, 74
divisions over, 40
events leading to, 37-39
military campaigns of, 41,
44, 44-47, 46
Scott, Winfield, 73

outbreak of, 39
radical ideas in, 41
surrender at Yorktown, 47
taxation during, 48-49
trade boycott in, 41
women in, 46, 48
Rhode Island, 20, 51, 65, 274
Rhodes, Elisha Hunt, 85
Richardson, Elliot, 239
Richmond, Virginia, Civil
War in, 89-90, 96
Ride, Sally, 248
roads, 66
Roanoke settlement, 17
Robinson, Jackie, 224, 225, 242
Roca, Julio Argentino, 132
Rockefeller, John D., 120, 140
Roggeveen, Jacob, 34
Rolfe, John, 18, 32
Romania, 265
Rommel, Erwin, 204, 214
Roosevelt, Eleanor, 171, 181,
182, 182
Roosevelt, Franklin Delano,
168, 169, 170, 175, 186,
187, 212, 213, 215, 253,
282
background of, 170, 171
critics of, 175-176, 181
death of, 207
disability of, 170, 171, 172
election of 1932, 160, 170,
171-172
fireside chats of, 172, 194
foreign policy of, 193, 194-
195
and Supreme Court, 181
wartime leadership of, 195,
197, 203
at Yalta Conference, 205, 218
See also New Deal
Roosevelt, Theodore, 156,
171, 281
Bull Moose Party of, 143-
144
foreign policy of, 131, 136
progressive reforms of,
140-143
in Spanish-American War,
128, 129, 131
Roosevelt Corollary, 281
Rosenberg, Julius and Ethel,
222, 242
Rosewood race riot, 154
Rough Riders, 129, 131
Ruby, Jack, 234
Rural Electrification
Administration, 179
Russia
Bolshevik Revolution in,
151, 217
in World War I, 147, 148,
150-151
See also Soviet Union
Ruth, Babe, 164

S
Sacajawea, 55
Sacco, Nicola, 155, 184
Sadat, Anwar el-, 270
St. Augustine, 17
Salem witch trials, 25
Sand Creek massacre, 114,
115
Sandinistas, 263
San Francisco, 70, 71, 72
Santa Anna, Antonio Lopez
de, 71, 81
Santa Fe, 17
Santos, Juan, 35
Sassoon, Siegfried, 149
Saturday Night Massacre,
239
Sauk and Fox, 68-69
scabs, 121
scalawags, 104
school desegregation, 226-
227, 282
Schwarzkopf, Norman, 268
Schwerner, Michael, 229
science, 25, 50, 203, 248, 249
SCLC. See Southern
Christian Leadership
Conference
Scopes, John, 162
Scott, Dred, 83
Scott, Winfield, 73

Seale, Bobby, 230
segregation, racial, 107, 198,
224-225
Selassie, Haile, 186
Selective Service Act, 150
Selma March, 229
Seminole War, 69
Senate, 50, 53, 77, 78, 87,
104, 144, 222, 238, 253
See also Congress
Seneca, 9
separate but equal, 225
Sequoyah, 63, 68, 69, 69
Serbia, in World War I, 148
settlement houses, 126
Seven Cities of Gold, 15
Seward, William, 100, 128
Shabbona, 56
Shahn, Ben, 172
sharecropping, 105-106, 107,
123, 173
Shawnee, 56, 58
Shays' Rebellion, 49, 51
Shelley, Mary Wollstoncraft, 63
Shepherd, Alan, 249
Sheridan, Philip, 95, 95-96
Sherman, William Tecumseh,
94, 110
Sherman Anti-Trust Act, 141
Shinnecock, 10
shipping, 59, 66, 115
Shuckburgh, Richard, 35
Shuja al-Mulk, 81
Silent Spring (Carson), 240
Silk Road, 12
Sinatra, Frank, 215
Sinclair, Upton, 142, 143
Singleton, Benjamin "Pap,"
106
Sioux, 116, 117, 231
Sirica, John, 238, 239
sit-ins, 227
Sitting Bull, 116, 116, 117
Slater, Samuel, 65
slavery
abolition in North, 85-86
conditions of, 79
and Constitution, 50, 59,
74-75
Emancipation
Proclamation, 92, 280
and Jefferson, 42, 43, 74, 84
Lincoln on, 74, 79
Native American, 14, 16-
17, 19
opposition to, 74, 75-79
plantation labor, 23, 24,
27, 65, 86
population in, 86
rebellions, 59, 76-77
and Revolutionary War,
40, 45, 46
runaways from, 76
trade, 17, 21, 24, 31, 278,
279
See also African-Americans
slavery, extension of
Compromise of 1850, 77
Kansas-Nebraska Act, 79,
279
in Mexican territories, 71,
73, 77
Missouri Compromise, 59,
75, 79, 84, 87, 278
proslavery position on, 86-
87
Wilmot Proviso, 77
smallpox, 22
Smith, Bessie, 165
Smith, Jebediah, 80
Smith, John, 17, 32
Smith, Jonathan, 49-50
SNCC. See Student Non-
Violent Coordinating
Committee
Socialist Party, 145
Social Security, 173, 179,
255-256, 282
Somoza, Anastazio, 262-263
Sons of Liberty, 37, 38, 39
Souls of Black Folk, The
(Dubois), 142
South Carolina, 67, 274
in Civil War, 87, 95
colonial, 23, 27
constitution of, 48
Reconstruction in, 104,
105, 107

in Revolutionary War, 41, 46
slave revolt in, 59
slavery issue in, 76
South Dakota, 116, 117, 231,
277
Southern Christian
Leadership Conference
(SCLC), 227
Soviet Union, 210
in Afghanistan, 262
civil war in, 151, 218
collapse of, 265-266
and Cuban missile crisis,
234
in Eastern Europe, 218,
219, 221
Gobachev's reforms in,
264-265
government repression in,
217-218
-Nazi pact, 192, 193
nuclear weapons of, 222
space program of, 248-
249, 251
U.S. relations, 218-222,
234, 262, 264, 283
in World War II, 193, 204,
205, 206
and Yalta agreements, 218
space program, 247-251
space shuttle, 248, 249, 251
Spain
colonial empire of, 17, 20,
71, 131
conquest of Americas,
14-15
discovery of America, 13-14
fascism in, 192
in Revolutionary War, 46
and slavery, 16-17
Spanish-American War, 128,
129, 130-131, 181
Spanish Armada, 15
speakeasies, 165
Spock, Benjamin, 215
spoils system, 138-139, 140,
279
sports, 164, 190, 225
Sputnik, 248-249
Squanto, 19
Stalin, Joseph, 185, 192, 205,
205, 215, 218
Stamp Act, 38
Standard Oil, 120, 140, 141-
142, 143
Stanford, Leland, 115-116
Stanton, Edwin, 100, 104, 280
Stanton, Elizabeth Cady, 132,
138
"Star Spangled Banner," 58
states, 274-277
See also names of states
Statue of Liberty, 126
steamboats, 67
steam engine, 66, 118
steel industry, 119, 177, 178,
257
Steffens, Lincoln, 139, 140
Steinbeck, John, 170
Stevens, Alexander, 101
Stevens, Thaddeus, 103
Stockman, David, 253
stock market, 167, 253
crash, 168-169, 257
trading violations, 252
Stone, Lucy, 137, 138
Stowe, Harriet Beecher, 77,
79, 82
Strategic Defense Initiative
(SDI), 264
strikes
automobile, 175, 177
minute, 198-199
in 1919, 154
in 19th century, 121-123,
280, 281
sit-down, 177
steel, 122, 177, 178
of Wobblies, 145
Stuart, Gilbert, 63
Student Non-Violent
Coordinating Committee
(SNCC), 227-228
Stuyvesant, Peter, 34
submarines, 149
suburbs, 163
Sucre, Antonio de, 80
suffrage movement, 137,
139, 150

- Sugar Act, 38
- Sulayman I, 30
- Sumner, Charles, 79
- Sunday, Billy, 166
- supply side economics, 254
- Supreme Court
  - and civil rights, 225, 226-227
  - constitutional provisions for, 51
  - and Indian removal, 69
  - judicial review in, 54
  - and New Deal programs, 176, 181
  - and Nixon tapes, 239
  - and progressive reforms, 141, 143
  - Roosevelt's plan for, 181
  - and slavery issue, 79, 87, 280
- Supreme Court decisions
  - *Brown v. Board of Education*, 226-227
  - *Dred Scott*, 79, 280
  - *Marbury v. Madison*, 54
  - *Muller v. Oregon*, 143
  - *Plessy v. Ferguson*, 225
  - *Roe v. Wade*, 231
- Surrat, Mary, 101
- Sutter, John, 70

T

- Taft, William Howard, 143, 144, 157, 281
- Taino, 14
- Taiwan, 221
- Taney, Roger, 79
- Tarbell, Ida, 139, 140
- tar and feathers, *39*
- taxation, 281
  - of colonies, 27, 38-39
  - cuts in, 241, 253, 261
  - and New Deal, 179, 181
  - during Reconstruction, 105
  - Whiskey Rebellion against, 52, 278
  - in World War II, 196
- Taylor, Zachary, 69, 73, 279
- Teapot Dome scandal, 167
- technology
  - computer, *250*, 251
  - in nineteenth century, 118, 119-121
- Tecumseh, 56, 57, 58, 62
- television, 222-223, 257
- temperance movement, 118, 155
- Temple, Shirley, *180*
- tenements, 124, 126, *127*
- Tennessee, 87, 162, 279
- Tennessee Valley Authority, 179
- Tenochtitlán, 11, 14
- Tenskwatawa, 56, 58
- Tenure of Office Act, 280
- Teotihuacán, 11
- Tet Offensive, *236*
- Texas, 71-72, 72, 87, 276, 279, 282, 283
- textile mills, 65
- Thanksgiving, 19
- Thatcher, Margaret, 270
- Thomas, Clarence, 272
- Thoreau, Henry David, 73, 82
- Three Mile Island incident, *240*
- Thurmond, Strom, 226
- Tilden, Samuel, 107, 280
- tobacco plantations, 18, 20-21, 24
- Todd, William, 71
- Tojo, Hideki, 195
- Tom Thumb (dwarf), *102*
- Tom Thumb (locomotive), 67
- Torres, Luis Vaez, 33
- Townshend, Charles, 39
- Townshend, Francis, 175, 176
- Townshend Acts, 39
- Tracy, Benjamin, 129
- trade
  - China, 12, 129
  - colonial, 22, 24, 39
  - growth of, 128
  - import restriction, 255
  - with Japan, 129, 195, 257
  - Jefferson's embargo on, 54, 278
  - NAFTA agreement, 269, 283
  - open door policy, 129
  - slave, 17, 21, 24, *31*, 278, 279
  - tariffs, 279, 281
- Trail of Tears, 69, 113
- transportation
  - automobile, 162-163
  - canals, 66, 118
  - in Civil War, *88-89*, 91
  - roads, 66
  - steamboats, 67, 118
  - westward trails, *64*, *70*
  - *See also* railroads
- treaties
  - Adams-Onis, 278
  - of Ghent, 58
  - of Greenville, 56
  - of Guadeloupe Hidalgo, 73, 279
  - Jay's, 53
  - of Paris (1763), 29
  - of Paris (1783), 47, 49
  - Strategic Arms Limitation (SALT), 283
  - Versailles, 152, 189, 190, 192
  - Washington, 280
  - Webster-Ashburton, 279
- Triangle Shirtwaist fire, 143
- Truman, Harry S., 210, 215, 282
  - atomic bomb decision of, 211, 219
  - and civil rights, 226
  - and MacArthur, *221*, 221-222
- Truman Doctrine, 220
- Trump, Donald, 257
- Truth, Sojourner, *78*
- Tubman, Harriet, *76*
- Tunney, Gene, 164
- Turner, Nat, 77, 80
- Tuskegee Airmen, 197
- Tuskegee Institute, 142
- Tutu, Desmond, 271
- Twain, Mark, 120-121
- Tyler, John, 279

U

- *Uncle Tom's Cabin* (Stowe), *77*, *79*
- underground railroad, 76, 77
- unemployment, 118
  - in Great Depression, 169, 174, *178-179*, 183
  - in 1980s, 252, 255, 257, 258
- unemployment compensation, 255
- United Mine Workers, 140, 177
- United Nations, 210, 219, 221, 266
- United Negro Improvement Association, 166-167
- UNIVAC, 251
- Universal Automatic Computer (UNIVAC), 251
- universities. *See* colleges and universities
- Utah, 115, 277

V

- Van Buren, Martin, 71-72, 279
- Vandenburg, Arthur, 220
- Vann, John Paul, 232-233, *233*
- Vanzetti, Bartolomeo, *155*
- Vermont, 275, 282
- Verrazano, Giovanni de, 31
- Vesey, Denmark, 59
- Vespucci, Amerigo, 14
- Victoria, Queen of England, 135, 156
- Videla, Jorge Rafael, 270
- Viet Cong, 232, 233, 236, 237
- Viet Minh, 233
- Vietnam War
  - antiwar movement, *216*, 236-237
  - and Diem regime, 233, 234
  - escalation of, 232, 234-236
  - France in, 233
  - My Lai massacre, 236
  - Pentagon Papers on, 239
  - U.S. advisors in, 232-233, 234
  - U.S. withdrawal from, 237
- Villa, Pancho, 159
- Virginia, 74, 274, 278, 279, 281
  - Civil War in, 87, 89-90, 91, 95-97, *96*, *97*
  - at Constitutional Convention, 50
  - slave rebellion in, 77
- Virginia colony, 20-21, *25*
  - House of Burgesses, 18, 21
  - Jamestown settlement, 17-18
  - in Revolutionary War, 41, 47
  - Stamp Act protest in, 38
  - tobacco plantations in, 20-21
- von Hindenburg, Paul, 186
- voting rights
  - African-American, 104, 136, 138
  - in civil rights movement, 228, 229
  - and property rules, 48, 67
  - for women, 136, 137, 138, *139*, 150
- Voting Rights Act, 229

W

- Wade-Davis Bill, 102
- Wagner Act. See National Labor Relations Act
- wagon trains, *64*, *112*
- Waldseemuller, Marin, 30
- Walesa, Lech, 265
- Wallace, George, 229
- Walton, J. C., 184
- Wampanoag, 28
- wampum, 10
- War of 1812, *56-57*, 57-59, 64, 279
- war bonds, 196
- war hawks, 57
- War Industries Board, 150, 197
- War Powers Act, 197
- Warren, Earl, 234
- Warren Commission, 234
- Warsaw Pact, 221
- Washington, Booker T., 132, *142*
- Washington, George, *36*, *38*, 39, 59, 61, 278
  - character of, 38
  - in French and Indian War, 29
  - presidency of, *36*, 51-53, *52*
  - in Revolutionary War, 40, *44*, 44-45, 46
- Washington (D.C.), 50, 58, 90, 100
  - March on, 228
- Washington (State), 277
- *Washington Post*, 238
- Watergate scandal, 238-239
- Watt, James, 254-255
- Watts riots, 230
- Wayne, "Mad Anthony," 56, 62
- weapons, 91, 119, 146, 197, 206, 236
  - *See also* nuclear weapons
- Weaver, Buck, 184
- Webster, Daniel, 77
- Weems, Mason Locke, 38
- Weinberger, Caspar, 256
- Welch, Joseph, 222
- welfare policy
  - under Clinton, 261, 283
  - under Reagan, 255-256
- Welles, Orson, 177, 180
- Welty, Eudora, *177*
- West Germany, 221
- Westinghouse, George, 121
- West Virginia, 89, 276
- Wheatley, Phyllis, 61
- Whigs, 59
- Whiskey Rebellion in, 52, 278
- White, Ed, *247*
- White, John, 32
- White, Ryan, *256*
- Whitfield, George, 27
- Whitney, Eli, 62, *65*
- Williams, Eugene, 154
- Williams, Roger, 20
- Williams, Tennessee, 215
- Wilmot, David, 77
- Wilson, Woodrow, 137, *144*, 158, 159, 281
  - Fourteen Points of, 152, 159, 281
  - progressive reforms of, 144-145
  - and World War I, 148, 149, 150
- Winthrop, John, *19*, 19, 20
- Wisconsin, 276
- witch trials, 25
- Wobblies, 145
- Wolfe, James, *28*
- women
  - abolitionists, 76, 78, 79
  - African-American, 76, 78, 181, 182
  - in armed forces, 197
  - in civil rights movement, 224
  - in Civil War, 90, 94
  - consumer spending by, 161
  - housewives, 163, 231
  - liberation movement, 231
  - Native American, *17*, 17, *19*, 55
  - in politics, 150, 231
  - progressive reformers, 126, 139
  - Puritan, 20, 25
  - in Revolutionary War, 46, 48
  - in space, 248
  - voting rights for, 136, 137, 138, *139*, 144, 150
  - workers, 65, 143, 145, 150, 182, *196*, 196, *199*
- Women's Christian Temperance Union, 155
- Women's Political Council (WPC), 224
- Woodward, Bob, 238
- workers. *See* labor; labor unions
- Work Projects Administration (WPA), 176-177, 282
- World War I
  - boundaries after, *153*
  - events leading to, *146*, 146-149
  - peace treaty, 152
  - and Russian Revolution, 151
  - U.S. entry into, 150-151
  - U.S. neutrality in, 149-150
- World War II
  - casualties in, 211
  - in Europe, 192-193, *202*, 202, 203-207, *206*, *207*
  - events leading to, 189-192
  - and Holocaust, 207
  - homefront during, 196-200
  - Japanese internment during, 200-201, *201*
  - in North Africa, *204*
  - outbreak of, 192
  - in Pacific, 202-203, 207-211, *208*, *209*
  - sabotage attempt in U.S., 204
  - U.S. entry into, 188, 189, 195
  - U.S. preparations for, 193-195
- World Wide Web, 251
- Wovoka, 117
- Wozniak, Steve, *251*
- Wright, Orville and Wilbur, 156
- Wyoming, 137, 167, 277

X

- XYZ Affair, 53-54, 278

Y

- Yalta Conference, *205*, *218*, 218
- Yeltsin, Boris, 265-266, 273
- yeomanry, 21
- Yom Kippur War, 239
- York, Alvin, 151
- Yuppies, 257

Z

- Zedong, Mao, 242
- Zenger, John Peter, 37
- Zimmerman telegram, 150
- zoot suit riots, *200*

CREDITS

AAIAL American Academy and Institute of Arts and Letters; **AC** Apple Computer, Inc.; **AP** AP/Wide World Photos; **AVNET** Avnet, Inc.; **BB** Bantam Books; **BN** Birmingham News; **BNC** Office of Sen. Ben Nighthorse-Campbell; **CG92** Clinton-Gore '92; **CNB** Custer National Battlefield; **CP** Culver Pictures; **DOD** Department of Defense; **DP** Dover Publications; **ELA** Collection, Equitable Life Assurance Society of the U.S.; **FCC** Federal Communications Commission; **FDR** Franklin Delano Roosevelt Library; **FFACT** Fiber, Fabric & Apparel Coalition for Trade; **FMC** Ford Motor Company; **GRF** Gerald R. Ford Library; **HG** Hulton Getty Picture Collection; **HI** Hoover Institution, German Pictorial Collection; **HS** Honolulu Star; **HSTL** Harry S Truman Library; **JCL** Jimmy Carter Library; **JFK** John F. Kennedy Library; **LC** Library of Congress; **LIN** London Illustrated News; **LSM** Louisiana State Museum; **McC** McClung Museum, University of Tennessee; **MPI** Media Projects Archive; **MSN** Movie Star News; **NAACP** National Organization for the Advancement of Colored People; **NGC** National Gallery of Canada; **NP** The New Press; **NPS** National Park Service; **NYCVP** New York Convention and Visitors Bureau; **NYPL** New York Public Library Picture Collection; **NYT** New York Times; **OE** Otis Elevator Co.; **ORD** Office of Robert Dole; **OWI** Office of War Information; **P96** Perot '96; **PC** Private Collection; **P/E** Protzmann/Eckert, Verlag "Visuell"; **RA** Remington Arms Company; **RRL** Ronald Reagan Library; **RWF** Ryan White Foundation; **SHSC** State Historical Society of Colorado; **SI/NPG** Smithsonian Institution/National Portrait Gallery; **UN** United Nations; **UPA** University of Pennsylvania Archives; **USAF** US Air Force Art Collection; **USCOS** United States Congress, Office of the Speaker; **USDI** U.S. Department of the Interior; **USIA** U.S. Information Agency; **USN** U.S. Navy; **WF** Wells Fargo; **WH** White House; **WP/DCPL** Washington Post Collection/DC Public Library; **WPMC** West Point Museum Collection.

Read from top to bottom of page, left to right:
5 (all) LC; **6** (top to bottom) CP, ELA, USN, LC, NASA; **8** LC; **9** McC; **10** (both) MPI; **11** NPS; **12** LC; **13** (both) MPI; **14** MPI; **15** LC, DP; **16** MPI, LC; **17** LC; **18** LC; **19** (both) LC; **20** MPI, LC; **21** (both) LC; **22** LC; **23** LC, MPI; **24-25** (both) LC; **26** (both) LC; **27** (both) LC; **28** MPI, NGC; **29** MPI; **30** LC, MPI; **31** MPI; **32** MPI; **33** (both) LC; **34** LC; **35** MPI; **36** LC; **37** LC; **38** LC; **39** LC; **40** LC; **41** (all) LC; **42** LC; **42-43** LC; **44** LC; **45** MPI; **46** LC; **47** LC; **48** LC; **49** LC; **50** LC; **51** LC; **52** LC; **53** LC; **54** (all) LC; **55** MPI; **56** LC; **56-57** LC; **58** LC; **59** LC; **60** LC; **61** MPI; **62** MPI; **63** LC (top, middle), MPI (bottom); **64** LC; **65** LC; **66** LC; **66-67**, LC; **68** MPI; **69** (both) LC; **70** LC; **71** (both) LC; **72** WF; **73** LC; **74** LC; **75** MPI, LC; **76** LC (both); **77** LC; **78** (both) LC; **79** LC; **80** LC; **81**; HG; **82** LC, HG; **83** SHSC, HG. **84** LC; **85** MPI; **86** LC; **87** LC; **88** LC; **88-89** LC; **89** WPMC; **90** (both) LC; **91** (both) LC; **92** (both) LC; **93** (both) LC; **94** LC; **95** MPI, LC; **96** LC; **97** LC; **98** (both) LC; **99** LC, PC; **100** (both) LC; **101** LC; **102** LC, SI/NPG; **103** (both) LC; **104** LC; **105** LC; **106** NYPL, PC;**107** (both) LC; **108** LC, MPI; **109** HG; **110** LC; **111** LC, MPI; **112** LC; **113**; (both) LC; **114** DP; **115** (both) LC; **116** WPMC, CNB; **117** (both) LC; **118** PC; **119** RA; **120** LC; **121** OE; **122**; NYPL; **123** MPI, LC; **124-125** NPS; **126** LC; **127** LC; **128** LC; **129** LC; **130** LC; **131** LC; **132** LC, HG; **133** USDI, HG; **134** LC; PC; **135** PC, HG; **136** CP; **137** MPI; **138** SI/NPG; **139** LC; **140** LC; **141** LC; **142** (top and center) LC, (bottom) SI/NPG; **143** NAACP; **144** NA, LC; **145** LC, NA; **146** PC, LIN; **147** LIN; **148-149** NYT; **149** LC; **150** LC; **151**(both) LC; **152** NA, USMC; **153** MPI, PC; **154** MPI; **155** LC; **156** LC, NA; **157** LC, HG; **158** LC, NA; **159** LC; **160** ELA; **161** FMC; **162** (both) PC; **163** LC; **164**, LC; **165** (both) LC; **166** LC; **167** LC; **168** LC; **169** (both) LC; **170** FCC; FDR; **171** LC; **172** (both) LC; **173** LC, MPI; **174** SI/NPG; **175** LC, FDR; **176** LC (top, center), NP; **177** AAIAL, LC, MPI; **178** LC; **178-179** LC; **179** LSM; **180** (all) MSN; **181** SI/NPG; **182**; SI/NPG, LC; **183** (both) LC; **184** LC, HG; **185** SI/NPG, (bottom, both) MPI; **186** LC, HG; **187** (top, both) LC, (bottom) NA; **188** USN; **189** HS, USN; **190-191** NA; **191** LC (both); **192** LC; **193** OWI; **194** (both) HG; **195** LC, OWI; **196** (both) NA; **197** NA, LC; **198** NA; **199** (both) NA; **200** LC; AP; **201** (both) NA; **202** MPI; **203** USAF, NA; **204** (top) NA, (bottom) FBI; **205** NA, LC; **206** NA; **207** USIA; **208** MPI; **209** (both) NA; **210** (both) UN; **211** LC; **212** (top, both) LC, (bottom) HG; **213** NPS, MSN, USN; **214** (both) NA; **215** MSN, NA; **216** LC; **217** LC; **218** UN; **219** NA, MPI; **220** HG, HI; **221** HSTL; **222** LC, PC; **223** MSN, AAIAL; **224** WP/DCPL, LC; **225** MPI; **226** (both) LC; **227** WP/DCPL, NYPL; **228** LC, **229** FBI, BN; **230** NYPL; **231** LC, BF; **232** LC; **233** DOD; **234** (both) LC; **235** (both) DOD; **236** DOD; **237** NA; **238** PC; **239** BB, AP, GRF; **240** LC; **241** NA; **242** LC; **243** MSN, LC; **244** MSN, HG; **245** LC, SI/NPG; **246** NASA; **247** (both) NASA; **248** NASA; **249** (both) NASA; **250** AVNET, UPA; **251** AC; **252** RRL; **253** WH, MPI; **254** PC, MSN, **255** WH, FFACT; **256** RWF; **257** (both) MSN; **258** AP (both); **259** CG'92, P'96; **260** MPI; **261** ORD, USCOS; **262** LC, JCL; **263** DOD; **264** AP, BB; **265** P/E; **266** PC; **267** HG, DOD; **268** DOD, WH, **269** MPI; **270** NYCVB, HG; **271** NPS, WH; **272** (both) WH; **273** BNC, PC; **274** (all) LC; **275** (all) LC; **276** (all) LC; **277** (all) LC; **278** (all) LC; **279** (all) LC; **280** (all) LC; **281** all LC, except Harrison and Taft (SI/NPG); **282** (all) LC, except Kennedy (JFK); **283** LBJ, RRL, LC, WH, GRF, WH, JCL, CG'92